←ice!

Oy Alkoholiliike

Vodka

Scotch
Guinness Beer
Cider Gin Continental beers
Cognac wines and spirits
Tokay
Port Retsina Georgian
Ouzo Wine
Sherry Arrack etc.
Madeira Boukha Sabra
Tafia Pachwai

Whisky
Bourbon
BERMUDA
Rum VIRGIN ISL. CANARIES
Tia Maria BARBADOS
Curacao
Cabaña PalmWine

Pisco Waragi

MAURITIUS

Chilean Wine
URUGUAY South African
Argentinian Wine
Wines CAPE TOWN PAARL

The World of Drinks and Drinking

an international distillation by John Doxat

The World of Drinks and Drinking

Drake Publishers Inc New York

© John Doxat 1971

Published in 1972 by
Drake Publishers Inc
381 Park Avenue South
New York, N.Y. 10016

ISBN 0-87749-254-9

LCCCN 72-1340

All Rights Reserved. No part of this publication may be reproduced, stored in a retrieval system, or transmitted, in any form or by any means, electronic, mechanical, photocopying, recording or otherwise, without the prior permission of the Copyright owner.

Printed in Great Britain

INTRODUCTION

I am conscious that I may be considered presumptuous in entering the periphery of a constellation where shine such stars as the late André Simon and Alexis Lichine, Harold J. Grossman, Oscar A. Mendelsohn, David A. Embury, L. W. Marrison, Hugh Johnson, Pamela Vandyke Price, Cyril Ray . . . to name but a few authors who have given me pleasure and instruction and to whom, together with others mentioned at the end of this volume, I acknowledge my indebtedness.

Yet it was such writers who in part inspired this book, for, in looking through my vinous and spirituous library, I noticed that in fields so apparently copiously covered there were obvious lacunae. For instance, drinking is a social matter, but most authors ignore this. Actual producers of great beverages rarely obtain their due, despite the interest inherent in the stories of many of them. There are specialized books galore dealing in the greatest detail with virtually every important drink in the world—in some cases a great many books on a single subject. Perhaps only gin has not obtained the attention it merits. Soft drinks have received meagre notice.

There are dictionaries; composite volumes by invited experts; anthologies; at least one notable encyclopedia. Recipe books abound. There are dull books, which oppress the lay readers by their sheer expertize. There are amusing books, illumined by anecdote, reminiscence, and the author's opinions. There are books for the trade; books for beginners; books for Masters of Wine. Wine, in fact, dominates the great majority of drink books (so I have confined my cursory treatment of wine to the basic or to the less travelled paths).

Reviewing a fraction of this vast literary output about potables, the notion started to germinate in my mind (would ferment be a better word?) that there was a place for a single guide to drinks and drinking that would really break new ground. Thus I feel I must explain my intentions in order that this volume may be understood as to scope and form—and limitations. What I have endeavoured to produce is a reference volume that should also be worth dipping into at random for entertainment. I intend to appeal to the intelligent amateur: to the seeker, if you like, of that engaging thing that has been dubbed "useless information", rather than to the highly informed. I believe I do give new facts and sidelights. I have endeavoured to be factual and reasonably comprehensive, while avoiding undue pedantry or excessive erudition. (The latter I do not, in any event, possess). I know I am occasionally, and deliberately, provocative and digressive, but I trust will not be found unduly flippant. I have aimed at impartiality without fear of expressing my own views and even airing my prejudices, for, to be worth the paper on which it is printed, a volume such as this must be highly personal.

Introduction

As is immediately apparent, entries, both as to subject and treatment, are wholly of my own choosing. They reflect my own tastes and interests, which I believe to be reasonably representative.

I am aware I set myself a considerable problem which I have had to resolve in a sensible number of pages, to be published, within terms of modern book production, at a price most truly interested persons can afford; designed not to moulder on shelves nor temporarily to grace the coffee table, but to be perused by the many who are intrigued by, and involved in, a broad and fascinating facet of civilized human activity that has existed, in various forms, since the dawn of history. I have had arbitrarily to define the limit of how much of this activity can be covered.

British in origin, this book is international in outlook. I realize that some readers may find it difficult to understand why certain well-known brands, companies and products receive scant attention, or none, and why some entire countries are absent. These gaps are due to various causes: my own admitted ignorance, the difficulty of obtaining sound information, the inhibitions of space, personal selectivity, simple oversight, and in some instances the presumably justifiable reluctance of those concerned to show regard for being included. Omission should not be regarded as implying any criticism. At the same time, I would like to thank the many firms, agents, specialized representatives, embassies, trade associations, and kindred organizations who did co-operate with me: if I have in their estimation done less than justice to their interests, I tender my unrepentant regrets. I cannot hope to please everyone. While great effort has been made to ensure accuracy, because of actual changes in circumstances since compilation, or through sheer human error, some unwitting factual mistakes may mar these pages: I hope not, but apologize in advance for any that may have crept in.

I sincerely thank my friend, A. E. (Bob) Cox, the well-known export director of Booth's Distilleries Ltd., London, for his valuable help in expanding the international scope of this work. This was due to the good offices of his managing director, William Forrest, who kindly wrote the foreword. I would also express my indirect thanks to Michael B. Henderson, my erstwhile boss, now managing director of Haig's, who encouraged me to write this book at a time when it was designed to take a somewhat different form; also to my current managing director, Derek J. Hayman. In the matter of references, I am in especial debt to Prof. R. J. S. McDowell whose *Whiskies of Scotland* gave me much confirmatory information on details of a complex and very important subject.

My unbounded gratitude goes to Mary Wallis, who devoted much of her precious free time to typing my appalling drafts, and whose constant reminders ("you'll never finish it") overcame my sanguine temperament ("I've lots of time"). Without her encouragement I honestly believe I would never have completed my happy task: and I trust I am not immodest when I use the word "task" in connection with compiling this book over six months in the spare time from an exacting and felicitous job. I considerably over-wrote: the equivalent of a short book has been excised from my original typescript by the publishers at *their* discretion!

Any peculiarities in the use or non-use of capital letters, quotation marks and punctuation, are not necessarily my own but occur as a result of the publisher's policy or whim.

I would further express my appreciation of the interest, indeed enthusiasm, shown by my publisher's editor at Ward Lock, Ken Smith, who had added some interesting information on his own initiative but with my entire approval; and it would be ungracious not to mention here Ted Marshall, who, when we were having trouble deciding between a variety of pro-

Introduction

jected titles, cut the Gordian knot by saying, "Well, if it's about drinks and drinking, why not just call it that?"

Entries are strictly in alphabetical order. Where it has been deemed necessary to insert cross-references within the body of the text, either the word or words referring to the main heading are in capitals, or a phrase is used, such as "see Bordeaux", indicating under what heading further information may be found. There are also extra explanatory notes at the foot of some sections. I believe readers will find this a simple system, avoiding the eternal *q.v.* of some books, and I hope they will quickly find their way around. To these readers I now commit the fruits of my omni-bibulous labours.

John Doxat

Kensington,
London, 1971

In the bottle, Discontent seeks for Comfort, Cowardice for Courage, and Bashfulness for Confidence.

Dr. Samuel Johnson

ILLUSTRATIONS

The publishers and author are grateful for the very considerable help given by the many individuals and organizations in supplying or submitting the photographs for this book. In particular we would like to thank Mr. Michael Friend, of Planned Public Relations Ltd., for his unstinting help in connection with the following pictures: Château Loudenne (Plate 6), Heidsieck champagne cellars (Plate 8), Hennessy wine press (Plate 9), Hennessy cognac still (Plate 10), view of Oporto (Plate 11), wine press at Beaune (Plate 14), Hennessy cognac cooper's tools (Plate 15), Justerini and Brooks premises (Plate 22), "Bols Tavern" (Plate 23), River Douro (Plate 24), Croft's port vineyard (Plate 25), and the cellarman at Piat Père et Fils (Plate 31).

Further help was given by J. Allan Cash (who took the picture of Château Loudenne); Group Public Relations, International Distillers and Vintners Ltd.; The Bourbon Institute and William J. Dugan, public relations manager (sampling bourbon, Plate 1); Hiram Walker & Sons Ltd. (Peoria distillery dedication, Plate 32); Charrington & Co. Ltd. and Hugo Marden-Ranger, public relations officer (Anchor Brewery, Plate 2); Australian News and Information Bureau, Australia House (Barossa Valley wine festival, Plate 3, and grape harvesting, Plate 33); National Association of Cider Makers and Eric Buston and Associates Ltd. (cider making, Plate 5); Comité Interprofessionel Du Vin De Champagne and Maurice J. Buckmaster (rémuage, Plate 7); The Bordeaux, Burgundy and Rhone Wine Association and G. Bligny (Hospice de Beaune, Plate 13); the German Embassy and Presse und Imformationsamt der Bundesregierung (River Mosel, Plate 16, and Munich beer festival, Plate 17); Allied Breweries (UK) Limited and David White, press officer ("The Australian", Plate 18, and "The Old Bull and Bush", Plate 26); British Tourist Authority (two public house scenes, Plates 19 and 27); Guinness Information Office (O'Neill harp, Plate 20); Buchanan Booth's Agencies Ltd. (Dry Martini drinking, Plate 12); Booth's Distilleries Ltd. (gin distillery, Plate 4, and sampling gin, Plate 30); Shannon Free Airport (making Irish coffee, Plate 21); The Scotch Whisky Association (Speyside distillery, Plate 28, and blending, Plate 29).

Endpapers and maps by Constance and Brian Dear Ltd.

A

ABBOCCATO
Generic Italian term to describe sweet wine.

ABRICOTINE
A liqueur made from fresh apricots, a well-known proprietary brand being *Apry*. There are sticky apricot *crèmes* which are not at all the same thing.

ABSINTHE
This aniseed and wormwood-based spirit, with other herbs, was invented in Switzerland, and the recipe was acquired by M. Pernod at the end of the Eighteenth Century. It became the drink notably of the artists and writers leading *la vie de Bohème* in Paris and hastened some of them to an untimely, but possibly happy, demise. Although wormwood has been noted for years as a medicine, absinthe gained so notorious a reputation as a source of chronic insobriety, that it was banned in France and many other countries.

Its place was taken by Pernod and other *pastis* (RICARD is another big name) which are very similar in flavour to true absinthe but of generally lower strength than the original spirit and without the wormwood. Spain allows absinthe, and it used to be smuggled into France, and may still be for all I know. In my young days in Paris a glass of absinthe was called a *piano* though its effects were to make one decidedly *forte*!

ABSOLUTE ALCOHOL
Usually defined as 175.25° PROOF (British), 100° GAY LUSSAC, or 200° PROOF (American); clinically pure alcohol. In fact there will always be minute traces of water.

ADEGA
Portuguese equivalent of Spanish BODEGA.

ADVOCAAT
Sweetened egg yolks blended with brandy and other ingredients, this liqueur originated in the Netherlands, where the best is made, but why it is there called "lawyer" does not appear clear. The usual explanation is that its effect is to make one "talk like a lawyer". Its "advocates" in Britain have given sales a great fillip, mainly among the younger age group, through a craze for drinking it with fizzy lemonade: a *Snowball*. An *Egg Flip* is not unlike advocaat in taste though the base is somewhat different and the strength lower.

AGAVE
An attractive cactus-like Mexican plant, from the sap of which is fermented the national alcoholic drink, PULQUE.

AGE
Undue reverence is sometimes paid to age. Over-aged wines can "go over the top". On the other hand, aged claret or port may be extremely palatable (see Maturing). Wines which have outlived the life of their corks may, in certain circumstances, be rebottled and further improve.

Wine will age differently in different containers. A particular wine may be past its best in a bottle and not yet at its best in a magnum.

AGUARDIENTE
Literally "fire-water", and probably the origin of that description for poor whiskey in the U.S.A. It is a generic term for cane spirit and similar distillations in Spain, Portugal and Latin America, and covers TEQUILA.

ALCOHOL
This is to be found in natural form in many sources. Human blood, even of a lifelong abstainer, contains about 0.003% alcohol. In potable form alcohol was presumably a coincidental and accidental discovery in many

Alcohol

lands in remote times—the fortuitous fermentation of some vegetable matter, a timid sampling of this natural brew, the realization that it produced a pleasing effect. Thus began early experimentation—and the invention of wine and beer-like brews.

WINE has existed since the dawn of civilization in those countries blessed with the vine; it was its alcoholic content that certainly formed its earliest attraction. There is evidence that until comparatively modern times, most wine required additives to make it truly palatable.

However, despite its application to the other alcoholic beverages, the word alcohol tends to denote something highly intoxicant—spirits, the products of DISTILLING. The word itself implies this. We owe it to a cosmetic, the Arabic *Al-koh'l* (kohl), the fine metallic powder—antimony or a similar mineral—used to stain eyelids. The term came to be applied to anything very highly refined and hence to distillates.

It is thought that though Islamic chemists may in medicinal research have produced fairly pure alcohols, the first complete separation of alcohol from water took place in France—*alcool vini*—say, some 800 years ago. But before that *uisge beatha* was being drunk by Irish warrior chieftains; and the pattern for the joys, the virtues, the problems of strong alcohol was already being established.

There are two basic types of alcohol. With one we need hardly concern ourselves for it is a virulent poison, methyl alcohol (methanol), known as wood alcohol. Now mainly produced synthetically, it has a very wide range of industrial uses, including rocket fuels. To consume it is to court paralysis, blindness and death. The beneficent alcohol with which we are dealing in one way or another almost throughout this book is ethyl alcohol.

Alcohol and Alcoholism Alcohol remains in the bloodstream some 18 hours after drinking. It is a "depressive", clinically, in that it depresses centres of anxiety: thus it is, in a popular sense, stimulating. It can be addictive, but only a tiny percentage of regular, or even heavy, drinkers become addicted. Tolerance to alcohol is of two types, inherent and acquired. Some people have an inherent *lack* of tolerance for alcohol, either in the form of a physical allergy—it makes them ill—or that they become unduly quickly inebriated (colloquially, they "have a weak head").

Experiments in Stockholm have shown that a dose of vitamins before drinking spirits can make moderate drinkers feel substantially less intoxicated than after the same amount of alcohol without that preliminary. After taking vitamins before drinking, the human guinea-pigs' performance in aptitude tests was better than when they were entirely sober.

Alcoholism is now widely accepted as a disease and treated as such. There is a great difference between a regular or heavy drinker and an alcoholic (the words "drunkard" and "dipsomaniac" are little used today). A man may drink a bottle of spirits a day for years, live to a healthy and ripe old age, and never come within striking distance of being an alcoholic. An alcoholic has a craving for alcohol, for physical or psychological reasons, and yet it is a poison to *him*.

As Alcoholics Anonymous, the organization for helping alcoholics, admits: a man does not stop being an alcoholic because he has stopped drinking. He is simply a non-drinking alcoholic; that is, one who has both recognized and controlled his congenital dependence on alcohol. He knows that the moment he relapses, that dependence may again become total. An alcoholic cannot control his drinking; he can only cease it. The normal, regular, or heavy drinker has control of his drinking; only when he loses that control has he become an alcoholic.

Alcoholism is a problem in many countries,

an acute one in some; France has an official organization concerned with the matter. Alcoholism is often extremely hard to detect; a man or woman may be able for years to hide their alcoholism under a social cloak, the addiction coming into the open only at a time of no return when mental and bodily collapse is past redemption. Alcoholism can be cured only under the essential proviso that the patient wishes to be cured. Alcoholics Anonymous pioneered the work of self-redemption of alcoholics by mutual support. It now has some 6,000 sections throughout the world, and despite a recent tendency to inject a certain religiosity into its activities, has been of untold benefit to tens of thousands.

Undoubtedly a great deal can be done through education, in the broadest sense, to stamp out alcoholism, and of even greater significance, to prevent it. It certainly cannot be done by repressive laws—nothing is as conducive to mass inebriation as prohibition. The young may be taught by good example, and it has been proved that in alcoholism environment plays a much greater role than heredity. Children of alcoholics brought up by moderate-drinking foster parents have shown no disposition to excessive drinking, while the spouse of an alcoholic is quite likely to succumb to that condition. Alcoholism knows no social barriers. There is the methylated spirit drinker on "skid row" and the millionaire boozer: both can share the same disease. See Great Britain; Scotland; France.

Merits of alcohol While it is entirely right that I should mention candidly the problems of alcohol, the vast majority of people have little likelihood of ever meeting a victim of alcoholism.

The employment of narcotics, be they alcohol or "drugs", is as old as civilization. Virtually all the peoples of the world, from stone-age Papuan to New York socialite, use, enjoy, and benefit from, some form of alcohol. Alone the Eskimo seems to have been omitted from nature's bounty: surrounded by enough ice to refrigerate drinks on a global scale, his environment is so lacking in vegetable matter that he once lived exclusively on meat and lacked materials to produce fermented beverages. Only with the advent of explorers did alcohol reach the Eskimo, while in tropical lands pioneers from Europe found sundry local spiritous drinks.

Alcohol, in wine, is approved or ritually employed by several faiths. Conversely, on religious grounds some countries are, indeed, "dry". This mainly applies only to the very devout or the very poor, since bootlegging is inevitably active and the wealthy can relax in less fanatical neighbouring states. In some countries officially eschewing alcohol, the use of hashish or harder drugs is endemic, and these are certainly much more insidious, addictive and debilitating than sensible use of wines and spirits. The international "hard drugs" menace makes any threat from conventional intoxicants look mild indeed.

There is no acceptable medical evidence that alcohol in itself has any deleterious effect on a *healthy* human body. Its virtues as a medicine have often and widely been acclaimed. Dr. Maurice E. Chafetz, of Harvard Medical School, in *Liquor—the Servant of Man*, says it is very important to remember that 95 per cent of the people who drink have absolutely no alcohol problem. "Good liquor and good drinking experience are the best possible tonics. It relaxes you, it heightens pleasure, and makes you feel good . . ." Dr. Chafetz heads the alcohol clinic at Massachusetts General Hospital in Boston. He opines that while alcoholism can be a problem, liquor is not one. A man of exceptional knowledge, he is on the side of regular and moderate use of liquor.

No one has ever tried to coerce people into drinking alcohol: elsewhere I quote a few of the numerous examples of the deplorable

Alcoholism

effects of trying to prevent people from drinking by law. Advocacy of TEMPERANCE is right in a *free* society; so is sensible promotion of stimulants. Harsh, repressive or impractical legislation in this field has never succeeded, and never will. Education, knowledge (including self-knowledge), and legislative sanity, mutual toleration between drinkers and abstainers form the basis for a healthy national and personal attitude to drinking.

Alcohol exists for man's enjoyment. It is for those who appreciate this, who accept alcohol as a gay partner, who use it not as a crutch but as an adjunct to the good life, that I have compiled this tome.

He occasionally takes an alcoholiday.
                                                    Oscar Wilde

ALCOHOLISM See Alcohol.

ALE See Beer.

ALEXANDER
A form of cocktail consisting of a measure of cognac, crème de cacao and fresh cream. Shake thoroughly with ice and strain into an adequately stemmed glass.

ALGERIA
Like MOROCCO Algeria has a Moslem population which shows little interest in alcoholic liquors.

Wine The wine from Algeria enjoys a worse reputation than it deserves. As a result, in countries where its name has suffered one does not always see Algerian wine labelled as such. The large quantities of Algerian wine exported for blending are by no means all inferior, and the country has an old-established and large wine industry and is quite capable of producing excellent wine, particularly reds.

ALLIED BREWERIES
One of the giants of the British brewing industry, owning about 10,000 public houses, ten breweries and two specially notable brands, *Double Diamond* beer and *Skol* lager, plus an excellent canned or draught beer, *Long Life*, which reciprocal trading arrangements also make available in very many other brewers' houses. Of course, there are other beers as well. Through their Grants of St. James's subsidiary (which runs an exemplary training school for the licensed trade) the group is very active in the wine business, and has the agency, among others, for POMMERY champagne, COURVOISIER cognac, ANGOSTURA bitters and COINTREAU. The combine is based on an amalgamation of Ind Coope, Tetley, Walker and Ansells.

Ind Coope's name is synonymous with Burton-upon-Trent, largely because of the company's fame as brewers of *Double Diamond* brewed only at Burton. But the company had its beginnings in Romford, Essex, where they are vastly extending their huge brewery and bottling hall which can turn out 80,000 bottles an hour.

The man who started it all was Mr. Edward Ind. In 1799, the *Star Inn* at Romford, which brewed its own ale and also sold it to pubs in the neighbourhood, was bought by Mr. Ind and a partner. When his partner left him after 17 years, Mr. Ind was joined in 1845 by a Mr. O. E. Coope and the company then became known as Ind Coope and Company. Mr. Ind died three years later and his two sons succeeded him.

In 1845 came the turning point in the company's early history. Business had been so successful that Ind Coope decided to brew in Burton-upon-Trent as well as Romford. And it was at this point that Allsopps, a well-known brewing firm in Burton, entered the picture, for Ind Coope decided to build their brewery next to Allsopps. Only a wall divided the two enterprises and it was almost inevitable that they should have become

Allied Breweries

linked, but they were not to merge until 80 years later.

Burton's fame as a brewing town dates back 1,000 years when a community of monks discovered the waters were perfect for brewing ale and decided to settle there. Burton beer became famous and in the 1700s Benjamin Wilson started brewing there. His business grew and his daughter married James Allsopp, whose son Samuel Allsopp gave his name to that company.

Samuel Allsopp and Company prospered with their beer being exported throughout Europe, including Russia and the Balkans. In fact, by the early 1800s their trade was so dependent on exports that in one blow they nearly lost all they had gained. Napoleon, then in control of much of Europe, closed Continental ports to British trade, thus severing Allsopp's export connections.

Having depended so much on exports during the past 100 years, a new beer was needed urgently for the home market. The new beer was to be a bitter with a strong mixture of best quality hops. The idea then was revolutionary, especially for a brewery which depended for its livelihood on the sale of strong, dark Burton ale.

A development in 1822 really put the company back on its feet—the brewing of the first *India Pale Ale (I.P.A.)*. Allsopps had been advised to try for the Indian beer market. Quite by chance, Samuel Allsopp was given a bottle of beer to taste which had acquired a unique flavour having been to India and back. He was told that if he could copy its flavour, he would make his fortune. After weeks of trial and error, the company's veteran maltster Job Goodhead brewed the first *I.P.A.* in a tea pot. In four years, its success was complete and the beer originally intended for export became as popular in England as it did in India. Today, that same beer goes by the name of *Double Diamond*, Britain's largest-selling pale ale.

Both companies had been so keen to expand their free trade that they did not bother about building up their own estate of pubs through which to sell their products. To remedy this, they expanded at a reckless rate, furiously buying up properties. In 1910 both companies were near to financial disaster, having overreached their financial resources. Receivers were appointed and the finances were sorted out satisfactorily.

The First World War and the boom that followed it stimulated the beer trade. But with the slump of the 1920s "rationalization" was the cry and breweries began to amalgamate.

The wall separating the Ind Coope and the Allsopp brewery in Burton was demolished in 1934 and the two companies merged to become Ind Coope and Allsopp Limited. It was a sensible move. New areas were opened up to each company. For example, Ind Coope had only one house in Birmingham, where Allsopps were strongly represented. Allsopps had very few houses in south-eastern England where Ind Coope had its stronghold. The united company was further strengthened by the purchasing of public houses in Liverpool and Croydon.

By 1939, most of the inevitable problems following the merger had been solved. Following the war, expansion continued and other breweries were acquired.

A major amalgamation took place in 1957. This was the purchase of Benskin's Watford Brewery with 800 public houses in the Greater London area, Buckinghamshire and Hertfordshire.

Three years later, Ind Coope (the Allsopp part of the name had been discontinued) acquired Taylor Walker Limited for £7 million with three breweries and 1,360 pubs and off-licences in London, Essex and Kent. This important acquisition boosted still further Ind Coope's interests in the South.

In April, 1961, the most far-reaching de-

Almaden

velopment in the company's history was announced, the merger between Ind Coope, Tetley Walker of Leeds and Warrington, and Ansells of Birmingham. At the time, the line-up was conceived as a "commonwealth" of the brewing industry, by which each company continued to operate under its own management.

Two years later, Ind Coope acquired Friary Meux Limited with 710 pubs, 176 off-licences and a brewery at Guildford. This was an important asset in Ind Coope's development of tied trade in southern England. Early in 1964, Thomas Ramsden and Sons' brewery in Sheffield with 200 properties was acquired. Since that time, the company has grown within the Allied Breweries group.

Its chain of 53 hotels ranges in size from the five-star 260-bedroom Hotel Piccadilly, Manchester, to the small but historic Hopcrofts Holt Hotel at Steeple Aston, near Oxford, which has eight comfortable bedrooms. The group also operates the big Victoria Wine/Tyler's off-licence chain.

ALMADEN
A big name in American wines. Hugh Johnson has praised this firm's champagne-style wine, produced on a system which seems analogous, though not necessarily technically similar, to that employed by KRITER.

ALSACE
That greatest of experts on Rhine wines, Fritz Hallgarten, has pointed out that only in very recent times has this region become a major producer of fine wines. Always highly productive, the wine industry of Alsace has suffered through annexation by Germany and restitution to France, and from the resultant ambivalance of attitudes to production by its vine-growers. The wine area of Alsace is extensive: from Strasbourg southwards almost to the Swiss frontier.

A peculiarity of Alsatian wines is that they are the only still wines of France where *appellation contrôlée* laws are applied by grape types and not by topology. From the time of the French Revolution the wine industry of Alsace has been very fragmented; there are a mass of small-holders, good wine being produced alongside indifferent. A great deal of *vin ordinaire* is produced; rarely bottled and not worth exporting, it is excellent as a local carafe wine. Amongst the greatest pleasures a wine-lover can enjoy is to quaff a young and unpretentious Alsatian wine in the lovely old town of Riquewihr.

The Alsatian wines in general commerce will carry the names of the grape varieties RIESLING, SYLVANER and TRAMINER. Allied to the imprint of a reputable shipper these are comparable to their German equivalents, but nothing approaching a truly great hock comes from Alsace. In France you may encounter *Tokay d'Alsace*, a long-established misnomer for it bears no relation to TOKAY other than that it is a wine with much more body than other Alsatian wines. The region produces a huge variety of wines, red as well as white.

AMARONE
Indicates the best VALPOLICELLA.

AMERICAN DISTILLING CO. INC.
See Light Whiskey.

AMERICANO
This is made with 2 measures of sweet vermouth, 1 measure of CAMPARI. Pour over ice cubes in wine goblet. Fill with soda-water and add slice of orange.

AMERICAN WHISKEY (bourbon)
The United States has made many contributions to the world of drinks but more in the fields of usage and customs than in actual products—always excepting *Coke*! Yet there is one "distinctive produce of the United States", to quote an Act of Congress of 1964, that very much demands attention—bourbon whiskey.

Plate 1. Tasters sample American bourbon whiskey for flavour and bouquet.

Plate 2. An old print of Charrington's Anchor Brewery, built 1757, at Mile End, London (see Bass Charrington Ltd.).

American Whiskey

The Act decreed that the name bourbon be spelled with a capital B, but in keeping with the general style of this book it is spelled in our pages with a small initial letter.

Bourbon is therefore a protected name, though in the United States it may be used colloquially, if inaccurately, for any domestic whiskey. It must be distilled at not above 160° proof but in practice is distilled at a considerably lower strength. (No American whiskey may be distilled at above 190° proof, but see Light whiskey for an important development concerning this).

Bourbon's origins were, strangely, ecclesiastical, and it has a history exactly coincident with that of the U.S.A. as an independent country. In 1789, the year George Washington became first president, the Rev. Elijah Craig, a Baptist minister whose outlook must have been surprisingly liberal, started distilling at Georgetown, Bourbon County, Virginia (later Kentucky). This was not the first distillation in the country, for the Dutch were distilling something referred to later as whiskey in New Amsterdam (New York) as early as 1640, though it is my belief that it would have been genever.

The infant sovereign state was, typically, not slow to impose taxes on distillates, and this led to the "whiskey rebellion" of 1794, which had the effect of spreading the taste for whiskey both by introducing it to troops sent to quell the uprising, and by forcing some distillers to seek new pastures in the wilderness where they would not be easily subject to taxes.

The best bourbon is "straight"—that is to say it is the product of a single distillery during a given year and is unblended with other distillations. That labelled "bottled in bond" is sometimes considered the best of all and the title may only be applied to straight whiskies. These will have been aged in new, charred-oak casks for a minimum of four years and will be bottled at 100° proof (U.S.).

Bourbon must be made from a mash of at least 51 per cent maize (corn).

"Blended straight" bourbon is another form, being the product of several distillations, the equivalent of the Scotch vatted malts. Because of the comparatively low strength at which the best bourbons are normally distilled, they are highly flavoured and gain extra taste from the new wood. This may be one reason why the taste for bourbon has not caught on around the world in the same way as Scotch, though it is nonetheless a major product and a fine spirit. Unfortunately, the bad reputation of some blended American "whiskies" which may legally contain as little as 20 per cent whiskey and matured only two years—the rest being neutral spirit—rubs off on bourbon; which is unjust but undeniable. The true home of bourbon is still Kentucky, but it is also distilled in California, Georgia, Illinois, Indiana, Ohio and Pennsylvania.

Rye The other best known American whiskey is rye, the regulations being similar to those for bourbon but with rye substituted for corn. "Straight rye" and "blended straight" rye are made, but on the whole rye tends to be a blend. The taste tends to be sharp, and quality varies enormously.

Corn This is a whiskey made from at least 80 per cent corn base. Unlike bourbon it may be aged in any barrels, new or old, for two years.

Blended whiskey As stated, this may contain only 20 per cent of matured whiskey, the rest being unmatured neutral spirit. This mixture is legally "blended whiskey". However, some top-selling brands are carefully made with a larger amount of matured whiskey, further matured after marrying with neutral spirit.

American whiskies are drunk straight, with or without a "chaser", as a HIGHBALL, SOUR, COLLINS, or in certain well-known cocktails and mixed drinks such as BOURBON FOG, MANHATTAN, MINT

American Wine

JULEP (the great classic drink of the Deep South), OLD FASHIONED and SAZERAC.

AMERICAN WINE See U.S.A. (Wine).

AMER PICON
A famous sharp-tasting French aperitif.

AMONTILLADO See Sherry.

AMOROSO See Sherry.

ANGOSTURA
The registered trademark of the famous Angostura bitters, the aromatic and alcoholic herbal compound that is essential to many mixed drinks. Originally evolved by Dr. J. G. B. Siegert, founder of the firm still bearing his name, in 1824 in the town of Angostura, Venezuela. The town was renamed Cuidad Bolivar in 1846, and subsequently production of the celebrated flavouring was moved to Port-of-Spain, Trinidad. There are two Siegerts on the board of the company.

In Britain the price of Angostura was halved under the Finance Act of 1970, the bitters being reclassified as a food flavouring despite the high alcohol content. This was good news for PINK GIN drinkers.

ANIS
Generic term for a wide variety of PASTIS.

ANJOU See France (Wine).

ANTIGUA (West Indies)
My informants claim that locally produced non-alcoholic drinks are the most popular beverages. Rum is, as one expects in the West Indies, the principal local spirituous product, and wine, gin, vodka and whisky are made. The main imports are Scotch whisky, beer and, surprisingly for the tropics, stout. Gin with *Coke* and a slice of cucumber is a favoured mixture and *Coke* is also used with whisky, as is ginger ale.

APERITIF
Stimulant, appetizer; a term employed both in connection with proprietary French "aperitifs" and as a general word covering pre-prandial potions from a glass of sherry to an elaborate cocktail.

APHRODISIAC
I need hardly quote Shakespeare's dictum on alcohol's effects on desire as against performance. No wine or spirit can be an active aphrodisiac, despite legends about champagne. The only amatory effect of alcohol is to lessen inhibitions and thus, by liberating passion otherwise stifled by habit or social usage, its effects may appear aphrodisiacal. Therefore it may be an aid to seduction where either parties suffer from timidity. It is also a fact that a woman may look twice as attractive as she is, when viewed through eyes dilated by six Dry Martinis.

APPELLATION CONTROLEE
I do not wish to get unnecessarily involved in this complex business, but I will try to explain its practical application in simple terms, for it does affect drinkers and producers alike. The complicated laws of *appellation contrôlée* were enacted in order to protect the good name of French wines of specific origin (beaujolais, bordeaux, etc.), to give consumer protection in a commerce notoriously careless, or worse, in trade descriptions, and to insure the honest grower against misuse of his rights to a name.

At one end of the business you had château and domaine-bottled wines providing an absolute guarantee, and at the other extreme bulk *vin rouge*, *blanc* or *ordinaire*, which left no room for doubt about just what to expect, and there were well-established blends with famous brand names, with whose merits or defects consumers were wholly familiar. But there was a wide middle strata in which adulteration and misrepresentation were rife. It was reported that the Beaujolais area, for instance, exported alone more than its considerable actual annual production, and there were stories (possibly exaggerated but not much so) of trainloads of containers filled with Algerian "plonk" spending a night in a siding in, say Dijon, and proceeding on their way in the morning as authentic product of the region.

In effect, the *appellation contrôlée* laws have stamped out many abuses in France and if you see those words on a bottle the contents will certainly be what the label indicates. Much the same applies to good wine exported in bottle. As far as bulk exports are concerned, the law has been less successful since it is not recognized, for example, in Britain. Rapacity is a fault not uncommon in French wine-growing circles (and not in France alone) since much of it is still a peasant industry at its grass roots, and there are traditions of adulteration and evasion that have become virtually hallowed by antiquity. Nor can one exonerate certain importers of French wines, in collusion with exporters, though in Britain in *The Sunday Times* Mr. Nicholas Tomalin's celebrated exposés in 1966 of abuses must have deterred some from perpetrating malpractices similar to those he ably probed. The deliberate mislabelling of wine has now declined.

At the time of writing, the Consumer Council was pressing for application of the French laws in Britain, though the important Wine and Spirit Association sees practical objections, one being that the French themselves wish to iron out certain irrationalities in their own laws. The possible terms of the entry of Britain into the Common Market also bear upon the question. Further, the association opines that the Trades Description Act provides excellent protection against false labelling and misrepresentation.

Of course, one does see *appellation contrôlée* used in Britain: the well-known André Simon range springs to mind, or the famous (French-bottled) *Piat Beaujolais*. If these words appear in conjunction with a shipper and bottler of repute, they may provide an extra source of reassurance for the purchaser. However, primarily it will always be the shipper's reputation and experience that are the principal guarantee for the consumer that he is getting what he thinks he is getting. As I have said before, "know your shipper, find a merchant you trust, discover the brands that suit you and your pocket". Knowledge will provide you with more protection than any laws can.

Sometimes the lack of wine law in Britain can work to the advantage of the U.K. consumer and then probably the United States drinker is being deceived.

Most of the wine trade is honest and because U.K. wine buyers have a great knowledge of the wine and the public, the U.K. enjoys better wine than most.

The appellation laws refer a great deal to the quantity of wine a vineyard will produce. Modern techniques have improved the size of crop per acre. This means, for example, a grower will produce 60 casks of wine, but only 45 casks can carry a certificate.

The U.K. skipper is offered two deals: one at a higher price for the 45 with certificates, or all 60 casks without certificates. The U.K. skipper buys all the casks and labels the wine *appellation contrôlée* because it is that quality. The grower is then left with 45 certificates for *appellation contrôlée* wines and these he can attach to casks of no great merit, but can command *appellation contrôlée* prices, say on the U.S.A. market, because the casks carry the necessary certificate.

APPLEJACK
The American equivalent of CALVADOS.

APPLE JUICE
BULMER'S have introduced their own brand of pure apple juice; excellent for both soft or alcoholic drinks or on its own. See also Shloer.

APPLE RUM PUNCH

Stick 6 fresh oranges with a dozen cloves each, and bake in oven slowly until well browned. Place them in a warm punch bowl. Add one bottle of well-flavoured rum; half-bottle brandy and 4 tablespoons of brown sugar. Stir well and ignite warm mixture. Extinguish the flames with 3 bottles of fresh apple juice. Sprinkle with ground cinnamon and grated nutmeg. Serve warm in punch glasses or suitable mugs. (This, like other recipes in this field, lends itself to adaptation to individual taste).

APPLETON

Appleton Estate is claimed to be the most popular rum in Jamaica; their white rum has been introduced to Britain with some success by Grants of St. James's.

AQUAVIT

With various spellings akavit, etc. this covers plain or flavoured colourless Scandinavian and other spirits. In practice it means much the same as "schnapps". It is derived from the Latin *aqua vitae*, the ancient general term for distilled alcohol, whence are also derived the Scottish *usquebaugh* and Irish Gaelic *Uisge beatha* or *whisk(e)y* and EAU-DE-VIE.

Digression Following a Swedish gastronomic seminar in England, a friend of mine gave me a "do-it-yourself" aquavit kit from the Aurora Restaurant, Stockholm. It consists of a traditional Swedish *gumma* (old lady), a rather attractive minute decanter, in which aquavit used to be served in restaurants. It is part-filled with botanical ingredients and the idea is to top it with gin or vodka and leave them to steep. One then adds this spirit, more or less highly flavoured according to the time factor, to flavour tots of spirit (or a bottle of it). I cannot say how this works out: I still have the *gumma* all "gumma'd" up and awaiting full fruition.

ARGENTINA

Wine, *aperitifs* and beer are much drunk, and, up country, cane spirit or locally produced gin. Imports of Scotch and American whiskies would probably be higher but for fluctuating trading regulations and exchange problems. Wines are exported to Latin America. Labels of brands must be approved by the authorities and products are subject to official analysis for purity. There are sundry taxes on alcohol.

The Argentinian likes particularly to drink *aperitifs* not only before meals but at any hour, with a modern tendency to substitute whisky for the traditional vermouths and similar drinks. Wine is mainly reserved in cities for the evening meal. Beer, especially popular in summer, recently went into sharp decline owing both to its generally poor quality and also to a strong vogue for *Colas*, *Seven-Up*, *Fanta* and other fizzy drinks, but it is now being noticed that the young are returning to beer. Champagne (of which types are made in the country) and cider are considered festival-time drinks. The fashionable like gin cocktails, and London quality dry gin is produced by Booth's (*High & Dry* brand). Martini dry vermouth with dry gin is a smart drink; in hot weather effervescent fruit-flavoured waters are taken with gin or vodka. There are no restrictive regulations on the promotion or sale of alcohol.

Wine By far the largest producer of wine in South America and fourth largest producer in the world. Nearly all the wine made in Argentina is consumed there, for it has very much a wine-drinking populace. Except for a small production of quality wine, as one would expect, by far the highest proportion of production is ordinary table wine. Vermouth manufacture is on a very large scale. "Champagne" is made and can occasionally be found abroad though I have never seen it listed in Britain.

Argentine table wines have lately entered the very competitive British market through arrangements made with a subsidiary of Matthew Clark & Sons.

ARMAGNAC
Well south of Cognac to the west of Toulouse lies the Armagnac country where the grape brandy is produced that some connoisseurs prize, at its best, above that of the better-known district. It is the product of a single distillation and is normally aged longer than Cognac so that 20 year olds are commonplace and much older ones less rare than for cognacs.

Armagnac production is about a quarter that of cognac and a higher proportion of this production is drunk in France than for the former. Armagnac is usually sold in flat flask-shaped bottles. Lesser distillations go for the making of liqueurs requiring a sound brandy base, and this is an important aspect of the trade. Vintage armagnacs are rare, like cognacs, but they can be superb. I find it impossible to describe tastes, but, to compare armagnac with its only worthy rival, I would say it is usually darker, and stronger on the palate, without being any less smooth.

ARRACK
Arak, raki, etc. Almost invariably a raw spirit, made in many forms from the Levant to the distant Orient. Frequently, and some say in its best form (if there be one), it is distilled from TODDY, the fermented sap of palm trees; but it is also made from dates, grape juice, rice, and sugar cane or milk. The Arabic from which variants on the widely used name come originally meant "sweat", not a bad general description.

ASBACH
Apart from Dujardin this is virtually the only German brandy sold in Britain.

ASTI
Italian sparkling wine of which there are many varieties and qualities. The supreme is probably RICCADONNA PRESIDENT *brut* which is of limited production and is almost wholly exported to the U.S.A. See Vin Mousseux.

ATHOLL BROSE
1 A Scotch "cocktail": 2 measures of Scotch whisky; 1 each measure of pure cream and honey. Mix in warm glass; allow to cool. Or do not use cream, and top with hot milk. 2 More traditionally, Scotch, finely ground oatmeal, honey and (optionally) cream, well shaken and left to stand for a few days. Proportions to personal taste.

AUSLESE
GERMAN wine made from selected bunches of grapes, containing none not entirely ripe; unsweetened by blending.

AUSTRALIA
By far the most popular beverage is beer, but wine is coming up which is sensible, for the country is a producer of excellent table wines. Spirits imported are, of course, headed by Scotch whisky which is very popular. Gin and vodka are produced locally.

The infamous 6 p.m. (18.00 hours) closure ("the 6 o'clock swill") having been abolished, licensing is in the hands of individual states, and opening is generally from 10.00 to 22.00 hours, with midnight extension where food is served. There are exceptions but licensed premises are mainly closed on Sunday: it is for local magistrates to decide.

Private clubs are popular. The pub follows a vaguely English pattern with public bars, saloon and lounge, plus beer gardens, since Australians lead an outdoor life. A pub should have accommodation and meals for travellers even if in a suburban site. In "hotels" women are not allowed in public or saloon bars, but sometimes have their own rooms. It is a democratic country and even smart hotels have public bars. There are also

Australia

wine saloons, selling only wine, and "wine cellars" can be smart places for luncheon. The *Australian Encyclopedia* says "consumption of liquor in Australia is high . . ." The Australian Capital Territory (Canberra) had prohibition until 1928 but is now on a similar basis to the individual states.

Wine Wine of all the basic types (including fortified wines, sparkling wines and also brandy) is produced in Australia in commercial quantities; local appreciation of them is growing, and while the table wines in particular are of excellent quality (notably the reds), sheer distance from the most likely markets does have a mildly inhibiting effect on export. Australian wines have been shipped in bulk for some time but I think the increased use of bulk containers might bring more wine from the prolific Australian vineyards to Britain competitively, if not to other countries.

Equable climatic conditions, less subject than European vineyards to wild variations in sunshine, mean that Australian wines tend to be of consistent quality from year to year; in fact, until lately "vintages" were almost unknown in Australia. However, vintage Australian wines are now quite usual, as the Australian palate has become more educated to the merits of the country's own production. Wine is made in New South Wales, Queensland, Victoria, Western Australia and South Australia, site of the famous Barossa Valley where the notable annual wine festival is held.

The vine is not indigenous to Australia. The first vines, from South Africa and Brazil, were planted in New South Wales by that colony's first governor, Captain Arthur Phillip, in 1788. The land was badly chosen. On a better choice of ground three years later, Captain Phillip planted 3 acres of fresh vines in 1791. These prospered, and a request to England for expert assistance resulted in the two French war prisoners being sent out as "experts". This was a mistake. Doubtless the Frenchmen were delighted to exchange indefinite sojourn on Dartmoor, or a prison hulk, for the sunshine and comparative freedom of an Australian penal colony, but someone had assumed any French citizens must know about wine. These two did not, and the experiment failed.

But in 1816, in the same district (Parramatta), the explorer Gregory Blaxland, persisted with vine-growing, so successfully that only six years later he shipped 30 gallons of his wine to England, which enterprise gained him a silver medal from the organization that is now the Royal Society. Proprietors of estates made small quantities of wine for their own use, but the first commercial production, 20,000 gallons, came in 1827. This was made by John Macarthur, founder of the Australian sheep industry. Indirectly, his effort was due to the celebrated Captain Bligh with whom, when Bligh was governor of New South Wales, Macarthur had quarrelled. As a result he was exiled to Europe and made a long tour of vineyards whence he returned to his home in the Antipodes with the information, and cuttings, that were in effect to establish Australia as a major wine producer.

Macarthur's pioneering efforts were followed by those of James Busby, from Scotland, a noted viticulturist, who came to Australia to take charge of an orphan's home. In addition to his annual salary of £100, he received one-third of the product of a vineyard established for educational purposes, for which, of course, the orphans formed the nucleus of a labour force. Busby left for New Zealand before his efforts bore full fruit, but he had laid sound foundations for an important industry.

Wine came to Victoria when, four years after the state (then a colony) was founded, in 1833 William Ryrie planted vines at

"Yering" in the Lilydale district north of Melbourne. Largely owing to two Swiss experts, who eventually bought the estate, this area produced the first truly great Australian wines, a red known as *Lilydale Yering* gaining international fame. These vineyards have now gone, owing to a change in local farming patterns and the encroachment of the state capital's suburbs.

South Australia now holds premier position in the industry with a production of 25 milliom gallons out of the 35 million gallons produced nationally. Queensland's production is negligible, and Western Australia's only about 4 per cent of the total. Total export is running at around 2 million gallons, principally to Britain—but in 1927 Britain took nearer 4 million gallons (figures due to an export subsidy, imperial preference and much less active British import of European table wines). Canada is the principal importer of Australian brandy.

Australia is endowed by nature with every attribute for a successful wine industry. Fortunately she also has an exploding, increasingly prosperous and well-educated population to benefit from this bounty.

AUSTRIA

Despite comparatively low prices, demand for imported potables is relatively small, the Austrians at all social levels being very loyal to local productions. Spirits are controlled by a state monopoly, and laws covering descriptions of drinks are rigorous. Wine, principally white, is highly esteemed, not only for drinking with food but after meals. White wine is exported to Germany, and the principal imports are vermouth, whisky, brandy and wines from Italy, Spain, Hungary, Yugoslavia and France. Rum, vermouth, slivovitz, brandy, dessert wines, as well as table wines, are produced and these are the most popular drinks, spirits being mainly taken with soda-water or drunk straight. The Austrians do not down the vast quantities of beer associated with their Teutonic neighbours.

Wine Nearly all wine production is white; some quite distinguished but not well enough known abroad, though they have been available in Britain for some time. Most is sound "hock" type. I feel the customs associated with wine-drinking in the country are more interesting than the actual wines.

Austrian wines are drunk very young, often in January following the previous autumn harvest. This fresh wine is served, especially around Vienna, on the premises of wine-growers. These are the famous *Heurigen* establishments. Ancient laws lay down precisely when each producer may sell his own wine from his own place. When the time comes, he puts out above his door a pole with a pine branch on the end. The *Heurigen* is not only an ancient institution but a highly democratic one, all sitting together on benches at long tables without social distinction. There is often music and people do not sit in their own groups, but mingle with and talk to strangers. The great Viennese composers, Beethoven, Schubert, Strauss, loved these places and many a melody, whether coming to fruition or not, has been jotted on the back of a bill.

AVERYS OF BRISTOL
Great name in the Bristol wine trade.

B

BABYCHAM
The immensely successful sparkling perry that made the fortunes of SHOWERINGS.

BACARDI
This is truly one of the great names of the world of drinks and drinking. Though *Bacardi* is a rum, it is virtually a product on its own. It has been found necessary to seek —and it has gained—legal protection in Britain, the U.S.A. and elsewhere. The widespread fashion for "white" rum stems largely from *Bacardi's* great success and prestige.

Ironically, the founding family played a major role in Cuba's struggle for independence from Spain; after Cuba went through another revolution (to gain independence from Batista in order to find herself under Castro) the Bacardi company was expropriated. Yet since that happened, in 1960, *Bacardi* has further grown enormously in international stature.

The original company was founded in 1862 with a capital of $3,500. It was started on Don Facundo Bacardi's conception of a new type of rum that should be totally different to the dark pungent spirits then in normal commerce. This would be an altogether more civilized drink, light, bland, smooth, pure. Don Facundo was supported by a worthy son in Emilio Bacardi y Moreau who, for his revolutionary activities, was lucky to escape with only two spells of exile. He returned from his first forced sojourn abroad to find that *Bacardi* had won a prize in the Philadelphia International Exposition of 1876, only 14 years after the product saw light.

As early as 1885 it was necessary for the firm of Bacardi to bring actions to prevent imitation of its trademark and misuse of its name. In 1892, the heir to the Spanish throne (Alfonso XIII) was very ill. He was administered *Bacardi* rum, and it sounds almost too good to be true, but his fever abated and the royal physicians wrote to Cuba to say that *Bacardi* had saved the future king's life. Despite their demonstrated republicanism, the Bacardis were not averse to using the Spanish royal arms on their labels: perhaps it was considered a good insurance. It did not pay off, however, for when trouble again broke out with Spain, Don Emilio once more found himself exiled. After the American-Spanish war, Cuba was independent (though a form of American dollar colonialism was to come) and Don Emilio returned in triumph (joined by his son, Emilio Bacardi y Lay, who had fought a good war) and attained many public offices, as Mayor of Santiago doing much for the city.

Barcardi's first true expansion started in 1908; in 1910 the first overseas plant, in Barcelona, was established. Momentum has increased ever since. During Prohibition, and in the "Cocktail Age" (see Cocktails), *Bacardi* became an internationally famous drink in smart circles, if only through the *Bacardi* (DAIQUIRI) cocktail (which, in the U.S.A. may today only legally be made with *Bacardi* rum if ordered specifically as a *Bacardi Cocktail*). American tourists poured into Havana and took home a taste for CUBA LIBRE, almost inevitably made with *Bacardi*.

Today *Bacardi* is a giant of the spirit commerce. Its headquarters are in Nassau; its main distillery is that in Puerto Rico, which being American, means that no import levies are payable on *Bacardi* coming thence into the U.S.A. Apart from Spain, other distilleries are in Mexico and Brazil. There are two *Bacardi* rums in normal trade, *Carta*

Oro, slightly more coloured and flavoured than the *Carta Blanca*, a very refined, colourless, light-bodied spirit. The drink continues to be produced in Cuba. *Bacardi* is made by continuous (PATENT) distillation under the most up-to-date technical conditions: the blending is said to be the main secret of its pre-eminence, plus a special strain of yeast used in the fermentation of the molasses. The end product would certainly not be faulted by Don Facundo who started it all.

BACCIO PUNCH
One bottle of dry gin, 1 bottle of pure grapefruit juice, 1 bottle of champagne, siphon soda-water, half bottle of anisette. Other than champagne, mix ingredients in large bowl with a lump of ice or numerous ice cubes, plus seasonable fruit. At last minute add iced non-vintage dry champagne.

BAHAMAS
Naturally these elegant and urbane islands, full of millionaires and self-indulgent visitors, are considerable consumers of fine potables. In order of volume, these are lager beer, rum, whiskies, stout, wines and gin. *Bacardi* rum is produced, and exported principally to the U.K. and Commonwealth. The four principal imports are rum, whiskies, gin and cognac, in order of importance.

The remarkable *Nassau Royale* liqueur—invented by Mr. Len Rosen, who has a long experience in the liquor industry—is not only particularly popular but is becoming an export item, from his Nassau factory, of growing importance.

To retain the islands' charm, no billboards may exhort one to order a particular brand; liquor advertisements may not assail one on the radio, and signs on vehicles are much curtailed. Cinema advertizing has lately been permitted. Drinking patterns are markedly American, though a popular local mixture is whisky and milk (fresh or canned).

A speciality of the famous Coral Harbour Club is a *Windjammer*, designed to be shared from a single glass by honeymooners: ¾-oz. *Myer's* rum; ¾-oz. crème de cacao; ¾-oz. Trinidad rum; 6-oz. pineapple juice. This is blended in an electric mixer, served in a 28-oz. goblet and topped with two ounces of cream, sprinkled with grated nutmeg. As good a beginning to a marriage as any, I suppose.

GEORGE BALLANTINE & SONS
This well-known Dumbarton Scotch company (HIRAM WALKER) has been particularly successful with its *Ballantine's* whisky in a number of overseas markets.

BANTU BEER
Also known as "Kaffir" beer; brewed from corn, millet and other grain. It is classed as a type of liquor in a special lower tax category under the fairly sensible licensing regulations of SOUTH AFRICA.

BAR
In the sense that has relevance for this book, this word appears under the 28th of many definitive entries for it in the Oxford English Dictionary. It derives from middle English *barre*; was first in our sense printed in 1592, was employed by Shakespeare, and is defined with splendid precision as a "barrier or counter over which drink (or food) is served out to customers in an inn, hotel or tavern, and hence in a coffee-house, at a railway station, etc.; also the space behind this barrier and sometimes the whole apartment containing it".

The British, whose social customs are well laced with social snobbery, cling to divisions in their PUBLIC HOUSES. Although the one-bar pub is increasingly the thing, the majority have at least a "saloon bar" and a "public bar", the amenities usually, and the price of beer always, being lower in the latter. Additionally a "lounge" (sometimes providing waiter service) is common. Disappearing are further departmentalizations, such as the "private bar", "snug", "jug and bottle", "smoke room", "ladies bar", but choice examples may be found. Unfortunate additions to my mind, are such things as "games room" and "children's room". Billiards (snooker) rooms are increasingly rare.

The first "American bar" in London was said to be the *Criterion*, opened around 1910. American bars were prolific in the "Cocktail Age" but simply "cocktail bar" is more usual a description nowadays, indicating that draught beer is not sold, and that there is a degree, which varies much, of professionalism in the service.

Bar equipment Apart from a COCKTAIL SHAKER, you can set up as amateur bartender with minimal equipment, though there are many attractive accessories once you are bitten by the bug. You do need a good-sized, strong, plain mixing jug, and long bar spoon for doing the mixing. A *Hawthorn* strainer, the kind with the springy wire edge, is another must. A bottle opener, a fruit knife, and corkscrew are the only other prime essentials.

BARBADOS
One of the earliest, if not the earliest, commercial centres for the production of rum; this product of Barbados is renowned for its high quality and is widely exported. It is generally light in colour and body, and of distinctive delicate flavour. Some Barbados rum is long aged in wood and experts treat it with respect and drink it without additives.

Beer is also produced locally and a little gin and vodka. Scotch and American whiskies, London gin, and vodka, are imported. It is easy to obtain licences to sell liquor which is sold through every sort of outlet including department stores. This paradisiacal island is extremely sociable and cocktail parties in homes or public resorts are a feature of local life, where Scotch and soda, gin-and-tonic and rum and ginger ale are the most popular combinations.

BAROSSA VALLEY
The principal wine-growing district of AUSTRALIA, noted for its wine festival.

BARRELS
Traditional barrels are disappearing in the BEER trade, more modern containers replacing them. The "reputed" sizes of British beer barrels, and they will not contain less, are shown below. See Casks.

Butt	108 gallons
Puncheon	72 ,,
Hogshead	54 ,,
Barrel	36 ,,
Kilderkin	18 gallons
Firkin	9 ,,
Pin	$4\frac{1}{2}$,,

BARSAC
District contiguous to Sauternes in the BORDEAUX district and producing sweet wines mainly, of which a few are excellent, though the name is associated with rather sickly products. Before the war, on one of those wine lists which pretend to describe each wine, I saw barsac listed somewhat ambiguously as "a nice lady's wine".

Digression Speaking about ladies, and though the anecdote should perhaps appear under Pubs, there used to be a tavern in London, on the fringes of Soho, a district noted both for the excellence of its restaurants and the easy virtue of many of its denizens, which had a large and unpunctuated notice running prominently along the top of the bar: "Ladies unaccompanied by gentlemen are requested not to sit in the bar and oblige".

BARTENDER
Not to be confused with a barman simple. A bartender should have a fair knowledge of mixed drinks, of brands and their qualities,

of the nature of the most used spirits and other adjuncts of his profession. He is an expert, quick, polite, his bar spotless, and a diplomat, confidant, and fine judge of human frailties. He need not be, but in Britain may be, a member of the United Kingdom Bartenders Guild.

BASS CHARRINGTON LTD

This biggest of British brewery combines was formed on 1st October, 1967 as a result of a merger of Charrington United Breweries and Bass, Mitchells & Butlers. The new group, the largest brewing business in Europe, has over 15 breweries and operates 11,100 pubs, hotels and off-licences. Its main national brands of beer, such as *Bass*, *Worthington*, *Carling Black Label* lager and, in Scotland, *Tennent's* lager, are also sold extensively in the free trade.

Bass Charrington is also strongly represented in wines and spirits through Bass Charrington Vintners which either owns or has the agency for nationally and internationally known brands such as BACARDI rum, MOUTON CADET claret, *Emva Cream* Cyprus sherries, Ruffino chianti, Old BUSHMILLS Irish whiskey and VAT 69 Scotch whisky.

The group has an important interest in soft drinks through a subsidiary, Canada Dry (U.K.), which holds the United Kingdom franchise for the Canada Dry range of products.

The group's export interests are operated by Bass International, which exports 30 per cent of all beer exported from Britain. It also owns a subsidiary, Bass Import Bottlers S.A. in Belgium and has pubs in Sweden, Switzerland and the Bahamas.

Charrington United Breweries and Bass, Mitchells & Butlers were both the result of a series of mergers. Charrington's history goes back to the Eighteenth Century when the company first began to brew at Mile End, London. Under successive Charringtons the business expanded and in 1833 the company acquired the Stratford, London, brewery of Steward and Head, the first of a series of subsequent acquisitions.

A hundred years later Charringtons were still growing. In that year it doubled in size by acquiring Hoare & Co., and with it the now famous *Toby* trade mark.

In 1962 Charrington & Co., strongly represented in London and the South of England with over 2,500 houses, merged with United Breweries of York to form Charrington United Breweries with over 5,000 outlets and becoming at that time the third largest brewing group in the country.

Expansion continued for the next five years. J. & R. Tennent of Glasgow, Offilers of Derby, Masseys Burnley Brewery and other smaller concerns all joined the Charrington United Group making it, at the time of the merger with Bass, Mitchells & Butlers, a company with great strength in Scotland and the North and in London and the South East.

Bass, Mitchells & Butlers was the result of the merger in 1961 of Bass, Ratcliff & Gretton of Burton and Mitchells & Butlers of Birmingham. Bass, Ratcliff & Gretton was the successor of Bass & Co., founded by William Bass in 1777, and Worthington & Co., started in Burton by William Worthington in 1744. Bass and Worthington merged in 1926.

Bass and Worthington both built their fortunes on the export trade, at first to the Baltic until that trade was crippled by the introduction of prohibitive tariffs in 1822. The two Burton brewers then began to sell to the Far East where the large British military and civil service establishments provided a ready market. This was the origin of India Pale Ale which still appears on some labels.

It was only by accident that *Bass* came to

Basserau

be sold on a wide scale in Britain. A ship bound for the Far East was wrecked in the Irish Sea. Underwriters sold the salvaged cargo which included casks of *Bass*. The beer made such an impression on local palates that people wanted more. So Bass became a brewer for Britain as well as the export trade.

While Bass and Worthington were expanding two other Midlands brewers, Henry Mitchell and William Butler, were making names for themselves in Birmingham. They amalgamated in 1898 and steadily expanded, increasing their trade and owned outlets in Birmingham and the surrounding Midlands. The company also acquired other breweries including Atkinson's of Aston and W. Butler of Wolverhampton.

In 1960 Mitchells & Butlers merged with Bass, Ratcliff & Gretton. At that time the company had a large nationwide free trade, particularly with its *Bass* and *Worthington* beers, and a stronghold of outlets in the Midlands.

So when the Bass Charrington merger took place in 1967 the new company had at one stroke gained complete national coverage in its owned properties, added the big selling *Carling* lager to the *Bass* and *Worthington* national brands and provided for future economies in production and distribution.

Bass *Red Triangle* and Worthington *White Shield* deserve special mention as they are, I am told, the only remaining major British beers which are not pasteurized; that is, they are matured in bottle. These are widely relished by connoisseurs and need careful storing and handling, though there are some devotees who like them "all in", with any sediment that has been thrown. The Bass *Red Triangle* was the first trade mark registered in Britain.

BASSERAU

A brand of sparkling BURGUNDY. This type of wine is popular in the U.S.A.

BEAUJOLAIS

To the possible annoyance of some pedants, I have treated of this wine under Burgundy, for geographical reasons. At least in Britain, it is possibly a vinous term more abused even than that of burgundy. While one can indeed get admirable beaujolais from reputable wine merchants, and there is in the mass market the APPELLATION CONTROLLEE André Simon brand and the excellent French-bottled *Piat* beaujolais, there is far too much "beaujolais" drunk in the U.K. for it all to have come from the district—or even from France.

Under the Trades Description Act, it would be possible to prosecute the seller of "beaujolais" that was not in fact true beaujolais, but there is a certain amount of documentational skullduggery in the French wine business and a prosecution might largely have to rest on expert witnesses, of whom the courts are notoriously, and often justifiably, suspicious.

Beaujolais should normally not be drunk over 5 years old: it is a light wine, in truth much different from the burgundy-style blend often offered as cheap "beaujolais". In France beaujolais is drunk on the chilled side.

Recently there has been increased British interest in beaujolais *nouveau* (new). I tasted CALVET's wine of this type, shipped by Williams & Humbert (*q.v.*) from the 1970 vintage. We sampled it on the first of December, delicious, fruity, full-flavoured, a wine not for sipping but for quaffing. From year to year we shall hear more of such wine, long popular in France and several adjacent countries, but it is unlikely they will reach the mass market since they are past their prime by around March the following year. Beaujolais *de l'année* (this year's) is not dissimilar but is made to last somewhat longer, officially existing until the next vintage is marketed.

BEAUNE
The *Hospices de Beaune* is an ancient charity which still looks after the indigent poor for whose relief it was founded in the Fifteenth Century. It also owns extensive vineyards, and its annual wine auctions are the thermometer by which the whole BURGUNDY wine trade judges commercial prospects.

BEBE (BABY)
A very small optic measure used in France, which did a lot to introduce the French to the virtues of Scotch whisky: notably *un bébé Johnnie (Walker)*.

BEEFEATER GIN See Burrough; Kobrand Corporation.

BEER
Beer has a history at least as old as wine. It is made, with raw materials ranging from milk to rice, the world over; even the most primitive peoples have something which broadly qualifies as beer, if beer be fermented matter other than from grapes. The Belgians, not the Germans, are the biggest beer drinkers, knocking back around 30 gallons annually per head. Possibly the only time this has been exceeded is by the British who achieved 34 gallons for every man, woman and child in 1876: consumption is much less impressive today.

Beer as a word derives from the Continent, coming in with the introduction of hops to England in the Fifteenth Century. Previously the English drank ale (*ealu* in old English). Subsequently beer referred to a hop-flavoured brew and ale to one without hops. These definitions have paled lately, and beer can be taken to include ale, bitter, stout, porter, lager, etc.

Until comparatively recently, though beer was served in taverns of all sorts, it was also part of a housewife's duties to prepare beer for domestic use; indeed country mansions might produce a considerable quantity for the establishment, and farmhouse kitchens were the forerunners of the village inn. The commercial production of beer in Britain may be dated from the grant of a charter by Henry IV to the BREWERS' Livery Company of the City of London. Breweries proliferated with the growth of towns during the Industrial Revolution, and in the last century vast fortunes were founded on beer with the consequent elevation of many brewers to the House of Lords.

The recent trend has been for the big breweries of Britain to merge into enormous combines, controlling many breweries, tens of thousands of public houses, hotels, catering subsidiaries, off-licences, agencies for imported lines, brands of wine, and almost any ancillary activity. Inter-trading arrangements have increased the range of beers available for customers, though choice in other potables tends to be restricted through concentration on brewers' own or consortium brands.

Beer was first taxed in Britain in 1660. The "ale conners'" instrument for deciding whether the beer was "strong" or "small" was their trousers! These were of leather. They would sit in a pool of beer: on the extent to which they stuck to the bench depended the rate of duty. Today beer is taxed on its SPECIFIC GRAVITY, a system introduced in 1880 though the tax is, of course, astronomically higher than then. It is, however, effectively lower than on spirits which are taxed on actual alcoholic content.

A return to the past may be noted. Thousands of Britons now make beer at home, with varying success.

Production of Beer Beer is basically very simple, though today normally produced on such an enormous scale that highly sophisticated equipment is used. Barley is the basic ingredient. This is allowed to germinate, and

Beer

is then dried, to a pale hue for light beer and a darker colour for dark beers. The malted barley is then crushed. It is mixed with hot water (liquor) and the resultant wort is drawn off, leaving behind the solid matter. These solids are further mixed with liquor to obtain any residual extract. Sugar is then added to the wort, and hops are boiled into the wort if required. Cooled and transferred to fermenting vessels, the yeast is added, which converts the sugar into alcohol. The system, which is here described in the simplest way, is analogous to preparing a wash from which whisky is made.

Hops, while giving bitter beer its character, play a less important role than formerly. Today other cereals as well as barley are used, unmalted, to produce lighter beers with a more pronounced "head".

Types of Beer Bitter beer is a traditionally English type. It is today mainly served under pressure and arrives ready for drinking in bulk containers, whence it is pumped into vessels in the pub cellar. Keg beers are increasingly popular, with the brewers anyway. The keg is a handy self-contained unit, having its own built-in pressure and needing no more than connection to a serving tap. My complaint is that too much of the gas in practice finds its way into the beer. Another form of draught beer is the big "party" can, but these do not have a very long store life and must be sold quickly.

Light ale is self-descriptive.

Mild ale is a disappearing drink at the top end of the trade and especially in southern England. A sweetish, low gravity dark beer, it has a "public bar" image.

Burton, a strong dark beer is not brewed by all brewers, but some make it for the winter trade. It is especially good for cooking and for "mulled ale".

Barley wine is staging something of a comeback: it is the most powerful of bottled beers, usually coming in "nips" (three bottles to the pint). WHITBREAD's *Treble Gold* is a prime example.

Bottled beer is said to have been discovered by the Dean of St. Paul's, Alexander Nowell, in 1563, when, during a fishing expedition, he left á bottle of ale by a river and, on recovering it later found that it had matured in bottle, was fizzy and excellent.

Bottled bitter comes in a considerable range. Another strong bottled beer is *Yorkshire Stingo*, and probably the strongest of all British beers is COURAGE BARCLAY's *Imperial Russian Stout*, a "vintage" beer. *Coronation*, *Audit* and other special ales, usually brewed for a special occasion such as a royal visit to a brewery, are very strong and are collector's pieces.

Stout virtually means GUINNESS. A big brewery tried to bring in a rival: the public did not want to know. The only other considerable one on the English market is Mackeson's. Draught Guinness is increasingly available.

Lager has come tremendously to the fore in the U.K. of recent years. I do not think the domestic variety, which is much drunk by the young with lime juice cordial to destroy the beer taste, is in the same class as Continental lager. However, *Skol* and *Harp* sell in great quantities, both draught and bottled. Carling's *Black Label* is another considerable seller. Of many imported lagers, CARLSBERG has a particularly wide hold on the market but there are many others of note; for my money *Löwenbrau* and *Holsten* are specially good, but I give first prize to PILSNER URQUELL.

English beer is flowing very freely in parts of Europe, especially in Belgium and in France where *les pubs* sell it at prices which make even a tax-inured Briton squirm. French (*bock*) beer may now be obtained in Britain. It is akin to American beers. See also Barrels.

BEERENAUSLESE
German wine made from individually picked grapes.

BEGG LTD., JOHN
I have seen it stated that this company's *Royal Lochnagar* sherry-cask matured malt is the costliest whisky in Scotland: the public cannot buy it, but it goes into some famous blends. The Lochnagar distillery was built as a result of the 1823 Act referred to in the Scotch entry. Queen Victoria and Prince Albert took up residence in Balmoral, thus helping to popularize the Highlands and, incidentally, Scotch whisky. The royal family visited John Begg's new-built establishment —hence its royal prefix. Begg's *Blue Cap* and *Gold Cap* (de luxe) are their marketed brands.

BELGIUM
The Belgians are great drinkers, and producers, of beer; their other favoured potables being aperitifs, port, champagne, sherry, Scotch whisky and wine. The Belgians are noted connoisseurs of the heavier French red wines, and are France's greatest export market for burgundies. Mineral waters are also much drunk. Scotch, wine, cognac, aperitifs, champagne and some French liqueurs are the main imports. Exports are negligible. Beer, Geneva gin and liqueurs are produced in the country in quantity. Scotch and soda-water is the up-and-coming drink; fruit juices are favoured with imported London dry gin or with vodka. Despite an active bartenders' union, cocktails are little used outside very cosmopolitan circles.

Licensed shops may make "off" sales in minimum quantities of 2 litres, and there is no legal consumption of alcohol in public. That may seem strange to those acquainted with the country, but it is the *law*, as passed in 1919. In *fact*, it simply is not enforced; sales are made in any quantities the purchaser requires and wines and spirits are freely available in the normal Continental way in bars and restaurants. Alcoholic drinks are widely advertised. As I write, I understand measures are being prepared to bring legislative sanity into line with *de facto* practice.

BELL'S OF PERTH
The company of Arthur Bell & Sons Ltd., is one of the largest independent houses in the Scotch whisky business. In recent years the brand has penetrated England forcefully. The business was founded in 1825.

They have three Highland malt distilleries. Much of the firm's modern success has been due to the energy of Mr. W. G. Farquharson, who joined the company in 1925 and became chairman and managing director during the war. Bell's is no longer a family company and Mr. Farquharson became responsible for administering the large trust funds set up by the late Mr. A. K. Bell for the people of Perth. The company's Blair Atholl Distillery, in the tourist centre of Pitlochry, is one of the most visited and visually attractive aspects of the industry.

BENEDICTINE
The great French liqueur of closely guarded formula, made since 1510 in the monastery at Fécamp, is based on fine cognac. The initials *D.O.M.* which are virtually its trade mark stand for *Deo Optimo Maximo* (To God, Most Good, Most Great). Bénédictine is often taken half-and-half with cognac by those who find it too sweet; the proprietary *B & B*, already expertly blended, is then best. I rate Bénédictine highly as a delicious digestive.

BERMUDA
"A great deal all the time," was the reply I received to an enquiry about local Bermudan social drinking customs. Every type of alcohol is imported, with rum and Scotch predominating, but gin and vodka recently increasing their share. Ginger ale and tonic-water are the popular additives. No liquor is produced. Taxes are negligible. Licensing laws are said to be on the lines of Great Britain.

BERRY BROS. & RUDD

Anyone who has ever strolled up St. James's Street, London, which is the only sensible way of appreciating this beautiful street, will have noticed the spendid façade of this comparatively ancient firm of wine merchants, "a bottle's heave" from St. James's Palace. In 1803, George Berry, of Exeter, came to this building to take control of his grandfather's business. The Rudd element did not arrive until 1920, with Hugh Rudd, who had, through his own family's wine business in Norwich, an excellent knowledge of the trade.

It assumed its present title and became a limited liability company as late as 1940, reflecting the leisurely nature of the British wine trade—which is positively cut-throat today under a still-pleasing veneer of gentility! It was the habit of persons of quality to drop into Berry Bros. and take a glass of wine with one of the partners, perhaps even going so far as to place an order. It was an amusing quirk of the establishment to record the weight of distinguished visitors, if they would condescend to mount the scales, which most did, including the Duke of Wellington.

But something like a gale, and it certainly was *not* an ill wind, was to blow through this quiet and highly esteemed business when a couple of Americans, one a former Prohibition "G-man," decided that Berry's *Cutty Sark* brand, practically unknown, was just what the U.S. public wanted after years of bootleg booze, much of it "cut" with God knows what alcohol. Getting the agency for *Cutty Sark*, they set up the Buckingham Corporation, later controlled by SCHENLEY, and the rest is history. *Cutty Sark* soared to the position of single biggest-selling Scotch in the United States. Charles Guttman, one of the founders of Buckingham, subsequently started Paddington Corporation and repeated his success with *J. & B. Rare*—but that is another story.

BETTY JAMES

The well-known writer Betty James (her guides to London, in particular, are hilarious as well as instructive) always puts me in her books. I reciprocate. The cocktail named after her is: 1 measure dry gin; half-measure each of lemon juice and maraschino; dash Angostura. Shake with ice and strain into cocktail glass.

BHANG

Indian intoxicant brewed mainly from hemp.

BIANCO

Italian for "white," specially associated with pale sweet VERMOUTH.

BISHOP

There are many versions of this old-established drink. *English Bishop* is worth the making as a winter warmer. Stick a dozen cloves in an orange and bake it in a moderate oven until browned. Quarter and put into a saucepan. Pour on a bottle of heated port and over very low heat (it must not boil) mix in allspice, grated nutmeg, rum and brandy to taste, and adjust sweetness with sugar if required. Serve in mugs or insulated glasses if you have sold your silver punch goblets.

And in contrast, *Bishop* (an old American recipe) is made by dissolving in a tall glass a tablespoon of powdered sugar; a teaspoon of lemon juice; the juice of half an orange; a wine-glass of soda-water. Put in plenty of ice and top with burgundy. Stir and top with Jamaica rum; adding fruit in season.

The extreme diversity of these two recipes —though each is a *Bishop*—is an outstanding example of the difficulty faced by people like the author when asked for "a recipe for *Bishop*, please." I think it is most readily thought of as a mulled wine mixture, and some authorities associate it essentially with claret, which has also tended to enjoy an episcopal reputation.

Plate 3. A 70-year-old wine cask is used as a coach at the Barossa Valley wine festival, S. Australia.

Plate 4. Modern gin-rectifying distillery equipment: in the background are three flavouring stills. To the left are rectifying stills, and to the right are condensers through which alcoholic vapours pass to be converted into liquid.

BISQUIT Dubouché
A very fine brand of Cognac.

BLACK & WHITE (Scotch Whisky) See Buchanan, James.

BLACK CURRANT
The syrup made from this fruit is known in France, and indeed more widely, as CASSIS. The French use it greatly as an additive to vermouth and it is the basis of KIR. (*Ribena*, in Britain, is a splendid substitute for cassis). If rather sweet for some palates, used with discretion this healthful syrup, widely available, is a tasteful as well as colourful addition to mixed drinks and blends very well with citrus flavours and gin. In alcoholic form the cordial, crème de cassis, is much favoured in the Burgundy district.

BLACK RUSSIAN
A measure each of vodka and KAHLUA over ice cubes in a small tumbler. Stir.

BLACK VELVET
Excellent invigorator composed of half-and-half Guinness and chilled champagne. Do not put ice in it. Best served in a silver tankard. A traditional accompaniment of oysters in Britain.

BLANC DE BLANCS
Meaning wine, notably champagne, produced exclusively from white grapes, and frequently, but not always, indicative of high quality.

BLANC DE NOIRS
White wines from black grapes.

BLANDY
A famous name in Madeira, going back to the original John Blandy, a Berkshireman, who came to Madeira in 1807. A member of the British forces, garrisoning the island against Napoleon, he returned there later to set up business in the wine trade. The firm was founded in 1811. His son, Charles Blandy, made a business coup by buying up stocks of old wine unaffected by a disease which struck the grape vines in 1852. Blandy's continued to expand and is now represented on a world-wide scale in the wine trade, and has other important banking and shipping interests.

BLEND, BLENDING
Also known as "marrying". Virtually all the inexpensive table wines of commerce are a blend, as distinct from the costlier single wines of a given year from one vineyard. Properly carried out, this blending of wine is both an expert and necessary operation, epitomized on the grand scale by the standard brand-name wines of the huge Nicholas concern in France, now available in Britain. By this means, wines of unvarying character can be produced. The process of blending is obviously subject to misuse, and is widely abused by diluting expensive wines with inferior ones in order to market them under misleading labels. However, that impinges on malpractices elsewhere considered.

Blending is a vital aspect of Scotch whisky production. The world-famous brands of normal commerce are blends of anything up to 60 separate whiskies; the skill needed to maintain continuity of flavour verges on the miraculous. "Single" malts are, by definition, not blends though some pure malts are (Vatted malts). American whiskey, at the cheaper end of the market, can be a blend containing not only whiskey but a very high proportion of neutral spirit. Almost all cognac is a blend to maintain brand consistency. The same, in relation to their methods of production, applies to sherry and port. The best London dry gin is blended in the sense that the products of different days' rectifications are "married" to ensure complete uniformity of taste. Blending, to different degrees of art and technique, is a universal practice to which we owe the essential character and the quality of very many of the world's finest potables.

BLOOD & SAND
A half-measure each of Scotch, cherry brandy, orange juice and sweet vermouth. Shake with ice and strain into cocktail glass.

BLOODY MARY
Vodka and tomato juice was probably the only vodka-based mixed drink at all drunk before World War II. As the *Bloody Mary*, though I think the name did exist before, it came into its own when vodka started its epic struggle in the U.S.A. in the late 'forties. It did as much as the MOSCOW MULE and SCREWDRIVER in establishing vodka. It is a pleasant drink, not necessarily associated with a HANG-OVER by any means, and is capable of infinite variation. Basic recipe: double measure of vodka; bottle of tomato juice; dash of celery salt; teaspoon of *Worcester* sauce. Stir together with ice and strain into adequate goblet. Tabasco and cayenne pepper are optional extras; sometimes Angostura is used.

Cajoling me to rejoin the human race on a morning when I was suffering one of my rare bouts of E.P.L. (*q.v.*), my invaluable secretary, Mary, produced a mammoth and remarkable *Bloody Mary* which had an extra zing, the provenance of which I do not think I would have perceived, even had my tongue not temporarily been carpeted with what seemed like heavy felt. I ingested the potion with relish. It turned out that the new ingredient was a good measure of CRABBIE's *Green Ginger Wine*. I tested this mixture again under different conditions; really excellent for those who like something just that bit different. In Mary's honour it is christened the "Bloody Wal". Other writers please copy.

BOAT, PUSHING OUT THE
The phrase "pushing out the boat" (e.g., "it's your turn to . . ." buy a round of drinks) probably had a PORT wine origin. In the Eighteenth Century when the port circulated after dinner, and the ladies had left, it was often in decanters placed on wheeled coasters taking the form of a ship, in recognition of Britain's sea power. Precisely why port is ceremoniously always circulated from right to left is obscure. It is said that it enabled a man at a banquet to serve himself and his guest, but why should the guest have sat on his host's left?

A better theory may be that as most people are right-handed this directional method is demonstrably the more convenient. Normally each person present helps himself, always passing it on to the man on *his* left, never leaving the decanter standing in front of himself. See Slang.

BOBBY BURNS
Two measures of Scotch whisky; 1 measure of sweet vermouth; teaspoon of Bénédictine. Shake well with ice and strain into cocktail glass; squeeze twist of lemon rind over drink.

BODEGA
1 See SHERRY. 2 Sometimes used to describe a bar specializing in wine.

BOLLA
A name to look for when you are in an Italian restaurant, especially in connection with SOAVE or VALPOLICELLA, wines distinctly above the run-of-the-mill in their field.

BOLLINGER
One of the pleasures of compiling a book like this is that its personal nature gives opportunity to air one's own views and prejudices. If it came to naming my ultimate choice in champagne, regardless of price or availability I would probably name a *Krug 1949* in magnums, but, more realistically, if I were asked what is the *best* all-round champagne that one may reasonably afford, that is utterly consistent from year to year, and widely available, I would unhesitatingly name *Bollinger* non-vintage.

The great reputation of Bollinger, handled in London from the offices of Mentzendorff & Co. in the charming oasis of Pickering Place, off St. James's Street, rests on solid foundations. First, they are one of the few remaining companies to use small casks for the primary fermentation of their wine, in place of the giant vats more usually employed. This is the superior and traditional method. In champagne, grapes are classified by quality from 75 per cent to 100 per cent: grapes employed by Bollinger have the very high average rating of 97 per cent. Bollinger employ cellar corks during the REMUAGE, for all their wine. Most makers today use a type of "crown cork" closure for non-vintage wine and some use the same for all their production. These stoppers do not, in Bollinger's opinion, produce such good results as a cork, though infinitely cheaper, for the wine cannot breathe. *Bollinger* is *brut*, very dry, but without any touch of acidity; it is lively but I have never experienced a bottle with the excessive effervescence which I find displeasing.

Bollinger is a family business, headed by the widow of the founder's grandson. Jacques Bollinger, who married a de Villermont, owners of vineyards in the Ay region of Champagne, started the firm in 1821 to market what had hitherto been a small production of champagne for household use and hospitality. Bollinger's strength today lies much in the company's 270 acres of vineyards.

There is another Bollinger champagne which I should mention, though it is costly and in limited supply; this is their *R. D. (récemment degorgé)*, recently disgorged, a wine matured longer than usual and disgorged only a few weeks before shipment.

BOLS

Oldest of Dutch distillers and thus the oldest gin house in the world—presumably the world's oldest commercial distillers—Bols was founded in 1575, at Schiedam, now over-run by Rotterdam. At one time Schiedam had 300 distilleries! Now there are only four, of which Bols own three. Apart from their *Zeer Oude Genever* gin in the famous stoneware flagon, Bols make a "London dry" style of gin, and cordials.

Digression The international Bols Woodcock Club was founded by Erven Lucas Bols of Amsterdam in 1949. Those sportsmen who achieve a right and left at shooting woodcock (i.e., using both barrels of a double-barrelled gun) may become members. To qualify, a brief statement should be sent giving the date and location of the event together with a short description signed by two witnesses. The woodcock must be shot during the autumn/winter season, not during the spring migration period, as woodcock shooting is not permitted in Holland during that period. Some 1,700 members from 18 different countries are registered. Prominent members include H. R. H. Prince Bernhard of the Netherlands and F. W. W. Baron van Tuyll van Serooskerken who, since enrolment, has shot 16 rights and lefts! The club sends its newly registered members a silver hat-badge and a bottle of Bols apricot brandy.

BOND

Premises under the control of customs officers where dutiable wines and spirits may be stored, the duty only being paid on withdrawal of stocks, thus saving unnecessary outgoings of large sums. Wine such as port is often aged in bond.

BONNIE PRINCE CHARLIE

One measure of brandy, half-measure of Drambuie, 1 measure of lemon juice. Shake with ice and strain.

BOORD & SON LTD., LONDON

It is often difficult to date precisely the origin of an ancient company. Boord & Son, now claiming 1726 as their foundation, gave 1850 as the date of their establishment in a publi-

Booth's Distilleries

cation they put out in 1894, one of a series, *Miscellany of Curious & Amusing Facts*, of which a complete collection would make a rare collector's item. These were described as export leaflets, and the copy I have contains a fascinating engraving of *Adoration of Boord's Gin in a Tibetan monastery*! This old, and in many parts of the world, well-known, firm no longer possesses its own distillery, but it is very much alive as a subsidiary of D.C.L., working from Booth's headquarters in London. It is principally celebrated for its OLD TOM gin, under the *Cat & Barrel* insignia, though its dry gin has a place in several markets abroad. (It does not sell under its own label in the U.K.). The *Cat & Barrel* was one of the earliest celebrated trade marks in London gin and Boord's had to fight a series of actions for infringement in Britain and elsewhere. In 1898 Boord's obtained in California alone 22 injunctions (with costs) against infringers.

The Boord family is of great antiquity; probably the first written record of them concerned the will of John Bord (or Borde, it was a long time before people spelt their names consistently). The will was proved in Bristol in 1385. It is assumed he was an ancestor of Samuel Boord, a maltster in the same city, born 1722 and thus of Joseph Boord, born 1804, distiller, of London. The famous *Cat & Barrel* mark was designed by him in 1849. The company's apogee was reached at the turn of the century. Under sundry titular changes, it went from strength to strength, particularly in the Far East, in India, and not inconsiderably in the U.S.A. It then dealt in also whisky, brandy, wines and cordials; the market house side of the firm gradually ran down with changing conditions, and today its sole business is in bulk and bottled gin.

BOOTH'S DISTILLERIES LTD.

This is the senior firm of London gin distillers. The Booth family came to London from the North East in the Seventeenth Century, entered the brewing and wine commerce, and were established as distillers by 1740. At this time the spirit trade was settling down after the more disastrous Gin Acts, though another decade would pass before something like sanity prevailed. By 1778, the Booth's were sited in Cow Cross (now Turnmill) Street, Clerkenwell, a couple of hundred yards from their present Red Lion Distillery.

In 1780, foreseeing the outbreak of violence which subsequently become known as the Gordon Riots, Philip Booth armed his staff with muskets, some of which the curious may see today in the company's offices.

Around 1815, two of Philip's sons, John and Felix, reorganized the business, the latter soon taking over. Felix Booth became England's greatest distiller, established a second distillery at Brentford (near Booth's present bonded warehouse and bottling plant on the Great West Road), a brewery, an hotel and other interests.

He personally financed the second expedition (1829-33) of Captain John Ross to find the legendary North West Passage, the explorers being armed with the muskets which had earlier saved the family business. As a consequence a large portion of Arctic Canada is marked on the map as Boothia.

As a result of this and his long-standing friendship with William IV, he became Sir Felix Booth, baronet. He died in 1850, a bachelor. The male Booth line became extinct in 1896, when the firm was reconstituted as a limited liability company.

Booth's were pioneer exporters of gin in bond from London: recently the company received part of an ancient bottle bearing their seal from the site of a former convict settlement in Tasmania. This settlement was founded in 1830, and while the bottle cannot be that old, it is further proof of the company's long-standing overseas connections.

Expansion continued rapidly, Booth's continuing to engage (until quite recently) in the wine trade. In 1937, the company joined D.C.L. In World War II, their distillery was badly hit and invaluable records lost from the office block. In 1959, the present Red Lion Distillery was opened: it contains one still from the original premises, made in 1828. The U.K. sales and promotion of Booth's products (but not exports) were taken on in 1969 by BUCHANAN BOOTH'S AGENCIES LTD.

Booth's Gin is characterized by its very pale golden colour. This originated when, a long time ago, some Booth's gin was stored in sherry casks and by accident left there a long time. Dismay at its appearance turned to delight when it was tasted, and for many years afterwards Booth's was matured in cask for at least three years. Today this is neither practicable nor necessary, but *Booth's Gin* retains its unique "cask-mellowed" characteristics. Other principal Booth's products are HOUSE OF LORDS gin and crystal clear HIGH & DRY gin (home, export, and overseas production). Booth's Red Lion Distillery also produce BOORD'S gins and COSSACK vodka.

Retaining, of course, their Red Lion Distillery, in 1970, just 230 years after their establishment, Booth's moved from Clerkenwell and set up a new international headquarters at 93 Park Lane, a splendid mansion, at one time the London home of Benjamin Disraeli, Lord Beaconsfield.

Note It is so common for people to ask whether there be any connection between the Booths of gin fame and those of Salvation Army renown, that it is worth recording there neither is nor has been any in a familial sense. However, the Booth family home at Stanstead Abbotts, Hertfordshire, was eventually willed to the Salvation Army. It is known as the Felix Booth Eventide Memorial Home, and a bust of Sir Felix greets the residents each time they pass through the entrance hall. So in one respect the spirituous and the spiritual Booths ultimately did join forces.

BOOTH'S PARTY PUNCH
One bottle of *Booth's Gin*, 2 wine-glasses of Cointreau, 1 wine-glass of brandy, juice of 6 lemons, heaped tablespoon of powdered sugar (or more to taste). Mix in large bowl with plenty of ice, add flagon of fizzy lemonade and decorate with rounds of cucumber.

BOOZE
This semi-affectionate name for (mainly hard) drink or the action of ingurgitating it, may come from the Old English "bousen" (to drink deep) or possibly for "bowse", an ancient falconry term, describing the dipping and rising of a bird's head as it drinks. See Slang.

BORDEAUX
This is the premier wine district of France and thus of the world, producing awe-inspiring vintages from the great châteaux and a mass of indifferent blended wines containing not a little wine that has crossed the Mediterranean. Ancient Bordeaux throbs at the region's heart; to the north of the city lie Médoc and Haut Médoc; to the east are Pomerol, St. Emilion and Entre-Deux-Mers; and to the south, Graves and Sauternes, to give the broadest of topological distinctions and the most widely known regional names of this vast and complex area where the laws of APPELLATION CONTROLEE are rigidly applied. These concern themselves with quantity as well as the provenance of wines, only a certain amount of a given type being allowed to go out under the title in question; this gives rise to complications which I leave to such as Alexis Lichine to evaluate.

In speaking of that great expert, one must mention the vexed question of the classification of Bordeaux wines. The classi-

Bordeaux

fication in actual force is that made for an exhibition in Paris in 1855; it dealt only with médoc and sauternes and thus left out a number of outstanding châteaux, and, while it is tolerably accurate, it contains such glaring faults as listing Mouton-Rothschild as a Second Growth *(2eme cru)*. No classification of such a date can now be wholly reliable in any event, owing to inevitable changes. There are divided opinions as to the relative values of the various classifications. The 1855 classification, in spite of subsequent changes, is still considered by some to be pretty reliable, and not every expert agrees with Alexis Lichine. A fresh classification was made in 1961 but has never been officially adopted. It is generally conceded that it should not be. Many consider that the unoffical 1966 Lichine classification of the red wines of Bordeaux is the best. Here it is in part (from *Encyclopaedia of Wines & Spirits*).

Outstanding growths (crus hors classe)

Châteaux (Médoc) Lafite-Rothschild, Latour, Margaux, Haut-Brion, Mouton-Rothschild. (St. Emilion) Cheval Blanc, Ausone. (Pomerol) Petrus.

Exceptional growths (crus exceptionnels)

Châteaux (Médoc) Beychevelle, Brane-Cantenac, Calon-Ségur, Cantemerle, Cos d'Estournel, Ducru-Beaucaillou, Gruaud-Larose, Lascombes, Léoville-Barton, Léoville-Las-Cases, Léoville-Poyferré, Lynch-Bages, Montrose, Palmer, Pichon-Longueville, Pichon (Comtesse de Longueville), Rausan-Ségla. (St. Emilion) Belair, Canon, Figeac, La Gaffeliere. (Pomerol) La Conseillante, L'Evangile, Vieux-Château-Certan. (Graves) Domaine de Chevalier, La Mission-Haut-Brion.

A long list of great, superior and good growths follows, which is too detailed for this entry, which does nonetheless provide one with many names of fine wines that will be unfamiliar to most ordinary wine-drinkers: one may thus discover a wine that is as good as, but less sought after and less costly than, its more famous neighbours. Except for the outstanding growths, the list is alphabetical; I have not included the subdivisions of areas (St. Julien, Paulliac, etc.) and again refer those who wish further information to M. Lichine's great work itself.

In Britain Bordeaux wines are mainly associated with the red wines of Médoc, Pomerol and St. Emilion in the quality field, plus in white wines the top sauternes, and "Graves" are relegated to a class of unimportant sweet white wines: with some justification on the evidence of mass exports. But Graves does produce good dry whites and excellent reds as indicated above. As to Entre-deux-Mers, this considerable area produces a lot of the wine simply labelled *Bordeaux*, without more information being given. The wines named as Entre-deux-Mers rarely have any distinction and are normally light and sweetish, suitable as carafe wines.

BOTHAN
Illegal drinking club, prevalent in Scotland in local "dry" areas, and a further indication of how prohibition always leads to evasion.

BOTTLES
Such natural containers as gourds and skins are still used for wine containers. From the wine-skin of ancient times evolved the Spanish *porrón;* Greek vases show wine being drunk as from a *porrón,* by squirting it directly into the mouth. Earthenware is still also widely used. Glass bottles were treasured in the eastern Mediterranean, the cradle of civilization three-and-a-half millenia ago, but the satisfactory mass-production of glass bottles is an invention of the present century.

Until the use of cork for stopping came into general commerce, bottles were more a way of bringing wine to table than for storage.

Gradually, bottles for different types of wine took on agreed shapes and standard contents, and proprietary brands of all drinks were given distinctive containers. It is reckoned that around 150 million gross of new bottles are required by the world each year; a high proportion being returned and filled several times. Metal cans have lately become increasingly used for beer and mineral waters, and even for wine, providing a massive addition to household rubbish. The non-returnable bottle for tonic-water and the like is popular. Large catering establishments require machines to grind thousands of used bottles which otherwise would present a manacing disposal problem.

Experiments continue with plastic on the grounds of lightness and strength.

Glass research is producing tougher and lighter glass, which in itself is a very inexpensive material. Dark and fortified wines are customarily in dark bottles, also champagne; while white wines are in clear or faintly tinted bottles—but there are exceptions. Champagne bottles, which need to be specially strong, have a heavy concave indentation at the base, and this is used in some other wine bottles, the original intention being to help catch the sediment. This is known as the "punt", or "kick", sometimes the *voleur* (thief).

BOTTLE SIZES

A "bottle of wine" is approximately the same the world over, averaging about 0.75 litres, or around 26⅔ fluid ounces (1⅓ pints, also known in Britain as a "reputed quart"), the same as a standard bottle of British spirits. Half-bottles and quarter-bottles contain those proportions of the standard bottle. A few top brands of champagne make, for the British market, an imperial (that is, a true) pint, more than half but less than the whole bottle; admirable for one person. Standard American spirit bottles are either the "fifth" (5th of the U.S. gallon, or the same as a British standard spirit bottle) or a quart (quarter of a U.S. gallon), which is 33.3 British fluid ounces.

The 40 ozs. spirit bottle is fairly common in British bars, which is an imperial quart, as opposed to a "reputed quart" (26⅔ fl. ozs.). I take no blame for any confusion here: the sooner we decimalize in this regard, preferably using pints and fractions of a pint (with which measure the British public are long familiar) the simpler things will be. The French, and people in lots of other countries, do things more logically, marking bottles (and even glasses in public places) by their capacity in centi-litres. One litre equals 0.22 British gallons. Vermouths and some liqueurs are available in both bottle and full litre sizes. Litre (usually "returnable") bottles are widely used on the Continent for table wines; sometimes in Britain.

The only other wine bottle size in general commerce is the magnum (two bottles), though the double magnum (Jeroboam) is sometimes encountered. Larger sizes exist but are very rare or only blown for display purposes. The origin of their Biblical names is forgotten, nor are sizes precise, but the rest of the list, with approximate bottle contents in brackets, is Rehoboam (6); Methuselah (8); Salamanazer (12); Balthazar (16); and Nebuchadnezzer (20).

Spirit bottles in Britain come in a very considerable range, down to the miniature (no more than one tot in effect), the actual cost to the purchaser obviously increasing in inverse ratio to the size.

BOUKHA
Eau-de-vie distilled in Tunisia.

BOURBON See American whiskey.

BOURBON FOG
One quart each of chilled very strong black coffee; bourbon whiskey; vanilla ice cream. Blend together in punch-bowl.

BRAND
A brand denotes an actual make of a product, sometimes unique (e.g. PIMM'S), sometimes a distinctive make of something manufactured for universal sale (e.g., *Booth's Gin*). Brand names are extremely important from a consumer's viewpoint: through experience they can tell him of certain tastes that he prefers and may be indicative of higher or lesser quality, greater or smaller price.

In the matter of drinking, the British tend to be singularly non-brand-minded when buying by the tot; that is, when they are paying maximum prices for drinks. A large majority of regular drinkers simply order "whisky", "sherry", etc., without further specification. However, when buying by the bottle (at a much smaller actual price than when ordering by the tot) they are usually fully brand-minded and know whose products they want. This does not make good sense. Brand-awareness is the purchaser's best protection: he should exercise his freedom of choice at *all* times, both as an indication of his discrimination and knowledge and in order to indulge his preferences. This applies as much to soft drinks and wines as to expensive spirits.

BRANDY
The most probable origin of this word is the Dutch *brandewijn* (burned wine), "burning" being at one time synonymous with distilling and the Netherlands being the birthplace of European commercial spirit production. In Sixteenth-century England "brandewine" (brandywine) was a generic word for spirits. Brandy is normally thought of as any of the sundry vinous distillations from the finest COGNAC or ARMAGNAC to the rankest MARC. Yet it also embraces slivovitz (see Yugoslavia), also known as *quetsch*, made from plums; apricot brandy; KIRSCH; CALVADOS (applejack); and possibly ARRACK. The definitive boundaries between brandy on the one hand and schnapps and aquavit on the other are vague.

The following are well-known brandy-based cocktails: ALEXANDER, BONNIE PRINCE CHARLIE, SIDECAR and YANKEE INVIGORATOR.

Note I need hardly say that brandy is distilled in all wine-producing countries, so to list the varieties would be impossible. In my estimation the nearest to cognac is the best South African brandy. In Madrid I have tasted very old Spanish brandy (coñac) from the wood that was marvellous, but those brandies in normal commerce are blander and seemingly sweeter than the French; the same applies to Greek brandies, and both Greek and Spanish are best drunk in their own countries. There are admirers of German brandy, and of Italian brandy, which are sold in Britain, but they do not measure up to cognac in my estimation, and I am not being snobbish. Cyprus brandy is perfectly adequate for some mixed drinks requiring brandy fortification.

The Russians produce a great deal of brandy, and it is an interesting sidelight on the global position that California distils more brandy than France, the country which is supremely associated with the word.

BREATH
It may sometimes be politic to disguise the tell-tale aroma that alcohol gives the breath and which is easily detectable by one who has not been inbibing. Peppermint is fairly effective and so is parsley, apart from proprietary pastilles designed for the purpose. One trouble is that a wife, say, noticing an unusual bouquet will jump to the conclusion one hoped to avoid.

BREATHALYZER

A device employed to determine the level of alcohol in a person's system and thus to establish his or her ability to drive a vehicle. I do not myself drive, but am informed that a measure of evasion may be achieved by use of the proprietary preparation called *Expel*. There are other specifics. See Driving.

BREATHE

It is desirable that wine should be allowed to "breathe" before being drunk, that is to say, rested with the cork removed. Red wines need a longer period than white, the latter being specially prone to pick up extraneous odours, so the breathing should take place in a room uncontaminated by cooking or other smells. Two hours is sufficient, though some savants prefer a longer period.

BREWERIES

I give separately the stories of the following "big six" British brewery combines. The extent of their activities is indicated by the following table taken from *The Times*.

	On-licences	Off-licences	Hotels etc.	Total
Allied	8,147	1,582	56	9,785
Bass Charrington	9,357	1,419	280	11,056
Courage (without Smith's—q.v.)	4,381	502	67	4,950
Scottish & Newcastle	1,700	70	130	1,900
Watney	6,398	1,242	40	7,680
Whitbread	8,350	1,071	45	9,466

GUINNESS, another true giant, have a single on-licence and are not concerned with direct retail.

Note Apart from the above, a number of other breweries have their own entries: they far from fully cover the field. Despite constant amalgamations and take-overs, there are still many independent, or autonomous, breweries in Britain. The figures given above for Whitbread do not include those for BRICKWOODS BREWERY.

BREWERS' LIVERY COMPANY

Incorporated by Henry VI in 1437 this City of London guild was then known as the "Mistery of Free Brewers". While in earlier times, households normally made their own beer, and a farmhouse might well be a "brewery" (and ale-house), supplying local thirst, at the latest by 1414, the "bruer" as a trader was recognized. See Beer.

BREWING See Beer; Breweries.

BRICKWOODS BREWERY

This famous Portsmouth concern is unique for having, in effect, been founded by a woman. In 1848, Henry Brickwood, a licensee in the city suggested to his sister-in-law, Fanny, that she leave London and enter the liquor trade in Portsmouth. She agreed and, changing the course of the career of her son, Harry, sent him on a week's brewing course, which indeed seems short training on which to establish a business. Two years later Fanny bought a small brewery and coal business, these two commerces being in the past often associated. Neither Fanny, nor Harry, long survived but Harry's sons were apprenticed to brewers, thus enjoying rather more protracted training than their father.

It was they who got Brickwoods on the road to great expansion and prosperity, the company eventually absorbing 40 other breweries. In 1971, terms were announced for merging Brickwoods, valued at nearly £20 million, with WHITBREAD.

BRISTOL CREAM

The celebrated HARVEYS sherry. They alone have the right to use this name, as opposed to BRISTOL MILK. It is said that the name originates from the occasion when a lady was visiting the firm's cellars in Bristol. She was offered a *Bristol Milk* to taste, and

Bristol Milk

she exclaimed that it was so good that it deserved to be called "cream" rather than "milk". Subsequently the firm registered the words—much to their profit. *Bristol Cream* is a sweet *Oloroso* style sherry and enjoys tremendous prestige and popularity in Britain, and is widely exported, the U.S.A. being a major market.

Digression Some years ago, when I had a professional association with Harveys, I remember the then export director telling me of one of his promotional trips to the U.S.A. He was particularly interested in how people drank their sherry, Harveys being pioneers in pushing the idea of chilled sherry (I think I organized the first exclusively chilled sherry reception given in London) or sherry on the rocks. At a party, one lady expressed her devotion to *Bristol Cream*, whereupon my friend asked whether she liked it chilled. No, she answered, she always started the day with a glass of it with an egg in it.

BRISTOL MILK
This is a name of great antiquity and occurs in the Fourteenth Century. Anyone may label a sherry as *Bristol Milk*, and there are a large number of brands, as opposed to *Bristol Cream*. *Bristol Milk* is usually decidedly sweeter than most sherry, and the word, in conjunction with a famous brand-owner, denotes quality.

BRITVIC
In my opinion the best of bottled fresh fruit juices in Britain. Only bottled in small sizes, since they *are* fresh and are for using upon opening.

BRIZARD, MARIE
Well-known Bordeaux liqueur firm; also makers of a French, London-style, dry gin.

BROLIO
Probably the best chianti, of which the highest quality is dignified by being in bottles instead of the popular straw-covered flasks.

BRONTE
This is Yorkshire's own liqueur and a must for visitors to England's largest county.

BRONX
Half-measure of dry gin; quarter measure each of sweet and dry vermouth; juice of quarter-orange. Shake with ice and strain into cocktail glass.

BROWN-FORMAN DISTILLERS CORPORATION
This is a fairly rare type of American family liquor company business (a fourth generation Brown heads it) in that it is a century old. It was started in 1870 on "Whiskey Row", an area off Main Street, Louisville, Kentucky, by George Brown. He was the first to give a personal written guarantee of the quality of his whiskey, and it still appears as Brown-Forman's well-known *Old Forester Bottled in Bond Straight Bourbon*. Though now spelt with a single "r", the name is thought to come from that of the Confederate General Nathan B. Forrest. The firm holds a number of big-name importing agencies, such as USHER'S Scotch Whisky, and is associated with JACK DANIELS Whiskey.

BROWN & PANK LTD.
This was the wine and spirit free trade subsidiary of WATNEY'S, but is now controlled by I.D.V.

BRUT
A term indicating extreme dryness in champagne or other quality sparkling wines. (It has been most successfully applied to a range of masculine toiletries).

BUCHANAN BOOTH'S AGENCIES Ltd.
A comparatively new D.C.L. subsidiary currently handling in the U.K. market the interests of *Black & White* Scotch whisky, *Buchanan's De Luxe* Scotch whisky, *Booth's Gin*, *High & Dry* gin, *House of Lords* gin,

Cossack vodka and *Cabaña* rums; also bulk gin and vodka; and HINE cognac.

BUCHANAN & Co. Ltd., JAMES

Most large enterprises have small beginnings, and the story of James Buchanan's *Black & White* Scotch is no exception. James Buchanan was one of the pioneers in introducing and marketing blended Scotch whisky as we know it now.

In the early days, the demand for Scotch whisky in Britain was met by blending together heavy malt whiskies produced in the distilleries in the North of Scotland. These, however, were considered too heavy by the average consumer of whisky, and during the latter half of the last century the idea was conceived of blending these malts with the lighter grain whiskies, produced in the south of Scotland. The introduction of this blending technique vastly increased the size and scope of the market for Scotch whisky at a time when, in Britain, gin, brandy and Irish whiskey were the popular spirit drinks of the day. Within a short space of time, Scotch whisky had easily superseded these in popularity.

In 1879, James Buchanan had established himself in London as agent for a Scottish firm in the whisky trade. He arrived at a fortunate time and, with the growing popularity of Scotch whisky in London, he determined to set about creating his own blend sufficiently light and old to satisfy the majority of tastes. He called it the *Buchanan Blend*. His outstanding personality, charm and vigour assured its success in the busy world of London. His first office was in the City, in the shadow of the Bank of England, and one of his early successes with the *Buchanan Blend* was to obtain, in the face of keen competition, an order for the supply of his whisky to the bars of the House of Commons.

Black & White Scotch, as a brand, was first registered in 1904. It is interesting to record that it was the public who first gave the brand its name. The *Buchanan Blend* came in a black bottle with a neat white label and, when the brand was liked and appreciated, the public started calling for "that black and white whisky". The name stuck, and has proved a winning combination ever since.

James Buchanan was a great lover of animals and always featured in the advertisements various breeds of dogs and horses which were black and white in colour. Out of these came the combination of a black Aberdeen terrier and a white West Highland terrier, known everywhere as the *Black & White* scotties. These are the registered trademark today.

Horses played a big part in James Buchanan's life, and his successes in racing included two of his horses winning the Derby at Epsom, "Captain Cuttle" and "Coronach", both bred by him.

It was in 1922 that James Buchanan, who had started in his small way, was raised to the peerage and become Lord Woolavington.

In his earlier days, his salesmanship was of a modern complexion. One anecdote about him says that in his efforts to break into the West End of London, he ordered a big dinner for a dozen people at a famous hotel. When his party arrived he ordered his whisky. None was available, so, expressing concern for the establishment's amenities, the party upped and left. Another story shows he was master of the "soft sell". He took to dining regularly in an hotel, until he got to know the owner. On hearing that Mr. Buchanan was in the whisky business, the proprietor expressed surprise he had not approached him for an order. James Buchanan replied that he had not liked to bother so important a man until he knew him better. You can bet he got a whacking order!

Within the company, part of D.C.L., the family connection still remains: a recent chairman was Major Sir Reginald Macdonald-Buchanan, K.C.V.O., James Buchanan's son-in-law; and his son, James Macdonald-Buchanan, grandson of the founder is also in the business and a director of the company. In 1969, the company opened a £5 million headquarters at Stepps, Glasgow. See also Buchanan's Scotch Whisky; Strathconon.

BUCHANAN'S SCOTCH WHISKY
The "de-luxe" brand distilled by James Buchanan & Co. Ltd., as distinct from their famous blend, *Black & White*. It is relished by the discriminating in many countries and is now increasingly available in the British market through top class bars and merchants. Retailing only slightly above other brands in the U.K., it offers remarkable value for true whisky connoisseurs and may be described as outstanding in this respect in the "premium" Scotch field in Britain.

Note Since such pictures are necessarily taken way in advance of publication, unfortunately the bottle of Buchanan's in the foreground of our jacket illustration is not the recently redesigned one, though instantly recognizable to cognoscenti.

BULGARIA
Naturally the manufacture and sale of drinks are a state monopoly, but there is a measure of independence on the part of co-operative farmers, who regulate their own production of wines and brandies. The most popular drinks are grape brandy (pliska) and plum brandy (slivova) and the excellent red and white wines of the country, both dry and sweet. I have drunk the robust reds with contentment. For the growing tourist trade London gin, Scotch whisky, vodka and German and Polish beers are imported. I gather that licensing laws are reasonably permissive regarding consumption.

Wine A substantial wine industry suffered badly after World War II, but rather over 20 years ago a complete rationalization took place with the entire production coming under a state monopoly, Vinprom. This has considerably improved quality and quantity. About three-quarters of the entire wine production is exported, but only token amounts have reached Western Europe. Reds slightly predominate. Types are similar to those of adjacent Romania.

BULLSHOT
This splendidly restorative vodka drink is made to individual tastes, but this recipe provides guidelines. Per two persons: a can of *Campbell's* condensed consommé; 2 ounces of *Cossack* vodka; teaspoon of Worcester sauce; juice of half a lemon; dash of cayenne, celery salt and *Tabasco*. Mix vigorously with plenty of ice and strain into tumblers.

A variation, apparently favoured in Canada, and served in the *Magdala Tavern*, Hampstead, London, consists of a slug of vodka, an *Oxo* cube and hot water.

BULMER LTD., H. P.
The company was founded in 1887 by Mr. H. P. Bulmer, younger son of the Rev. C. H. Bulmer, rector of Credenhill, near Hereford. In that year he made CIDER from apples grown in the rectory orchard, and his efforts were so successful that he engaged in cider-making on a larger scale in the following year and took an acre of land in Ryelands Street, Hereford, where the company's head office is still situated. In 1889 his brother, Mr. E. F. Bulmer, came down from Cambridge, joined the business and took over marketing.

The firm grew steadily and by 1891 the rest of the Ryelands Street site, 9 acres in all, was purchased. In 1936 this site, too, proved inadequate and extra land was purchased and the Moorfields factory established a few hundred yards from the old site. Today the factory covers more than 80 acres and is the largest cider-making plant in the world.

In the early days of the firm, Bulmer's cider was held in casks of less than 100 gallons capacity. Today the company has a total storage capacity in excess of 12 million gallons and containers include eight steel tanks, seven of which hold more than 500,000 gallons; the eighth is the largest container for alcoholic drink in the world, holding 1,100,000 gallons.

The company's, and the world's, best-selling cider is *Woodpecker*, sold in flagons, half-pint bottles and 4-paks. In addition to the sparkling *Woodpecker*, a still variety is sold in 2-gallon polyjars, 1-gallon jars and ½-gallon flasks. The bottled cider is slightly sweeter than the still and is popular among the 18–25 year olds (especially women).

Strongbow, on the other hand, is generally regarded as a man's drink. Drier in taste than *Woodpecker*, it, too, is sold in sparkling or still form in similar containers to the latter. Keg *Strongbow*, chilled and with a light sparkle, is fast proving a success among those who prefer a draught cider and has gained a rapid foothold in pubs and clubs throughout selected areas in Britain.

Bulmer's also make Britain's only champagne cider—*Pomagne*—with a sparkle that results from a natural secondary fermentation. Produced in sweet or dry form, *Pomagne* is made from specially-selected cider apples.

Bulmer's ciders are made from certain varieties of apples grown for the purpose, and the cultivation of these is therefore of special importance. Since the establishment of the Bulmer nurseries in 1927, more than 270,000 cider apple trees have been planted for the company by Herefordshire growers. Herefordshire, with more than 8,000 acres, is the leading county in the production of genuine bitter-sweet cider apples. A large-scale orcharding programme to ensure the future supply of cider apples is operated by the company. In addition to fundamental research, an advisory service is available to all local growers, and new cider apple trees are planted for growers at cost price. Growers undertaking semi-intensive or intensive cider apple production are assured of a guaranteed market for 15 years.

In addition to buying fruit from local growers, the company also own and run their own large orchards. Since 1967 Bulmer's have been engaged in a programme to ensure that 4,000 acres of new intensively productive orchards are established by 1977. This is to supplement the production from new and existing privately owned orchards to meet a forecast need for 50 per cent more cider apples within 15 years. Bulmer's use some 50,000 tons of fruit a year.

The national cider sales figures in volume are difficult to assess with accuracy, but are known to be in excess of 25 million gallons. Bulmer's share of the total market is over 60 per cent, and, in the case of bottled and bottling ciders, more than 68 per cent.

Digression In the likelihood that there are drinkers who are also railway enthusiasts, it is worth mentioning that Bulmer's saved the famous "King George V", first of the great class in steam locomotives that ran on the old Great Western Railway, father of the world's major railroads, engineered by Brunel. It was rusting in Swindon till Bulmer's acquired and totally restored it. It can be seen at the Hereford factory, where it sometimes runs, pulling the unique Bulmer's exhibition train, converted from five of the glorious old Pullman coaches. Unlike other British locomotives, the "King George V" carries a big brass bell. In 1927 the locomotive went to the U.S.A. for the Baltimore & Ohio Railroad centenary exhibition.

BURGUNDY (Bourgogne)

The many wines of this large area are not classified in the Bordeaux fashion. Though there are analogies between the two great

Burgundy

districts and such obvious governmental regulations as APPELLATION CONTROLEE are common to both, the regulation of the Burgundy wine commerce is highly complicated, if only due to the growing habit of tagging village names on to those of prestigious *domaines* (estates) in order to give some wines a *cachet* that will not mislead the highly educated, but may well deceive the more modestly informed drinker.

All burgundy wines are dry and about one quarter are white. Not many are domaine bottled, but the finest are. However, itinerant bottlers may bottle some quite unimportant wines at their place of production (these becoming *domaine* bottled) again for the deception of the ignorant. I prefer my burgundies to be French bottled, though burgundies bearing such names as Geisweiler and Sichel, if bottled in Britain, will be of high quality since the shippers will not tolerate adulteration of their wines. (One cannot stress too strongly the importance of wine-drinkers finding shippers and bottlers whom they can implicitly trust).

Premier, or *Grand*, *Cru* on burgundy labels tend not to mean a great deal.

Red Burgundies I suppose *Chambertin* is the best known in this category. I do not propose to analyze any wines in depth, but for the guidance of the general drinker, the word *Chambertin* by itself, and especially if not allied to the name of a noted shipper, will probably indicate little more than a heavy burgundy; if from a reputable source, this word will indicate a robust, well-rounded wine that is particularly admirable with steaks and game. The most notable of the variants, and normally finer than simple *Chambertin*, are *Gevrey-Chambertin* and *Charmes-Chambertin*.

Other great names in red burgundies are: *Musigny*, and particularly *Chambolle Musigny*, distinctly lighter than *Chambertin*; *Clos de Vougeot*, notably dry; *Grands Echezeaux*, usually costly; *Vosne-Romanée*, *Romanée Conti*, *Chassagne Montrachet*, *Romanée St. Vivent*. Wines preceded by the definite article enjoy a special prestige, such as *La Romanée*, *La Tache*, *Le Richebourg*, *Le Aloxe-Corton*. Of less renown *Beaune*, *Corton*, *Pommard*, *Volnay*, *Mâcon Rouge*, and, especially, *Nuits St. Georges*, are produced under many labels and my proviso about shippers firmly applies here.

It is sometimes the habit to list BEAUJOLAIS wines as something quite distinct from burgundy, but the Beaujolais area is a southern continuation of Burgundy, offering no special geographical separation, and it is logical here to mention these wines, though I have separately penned certain strictures about them. At their best these attractive light red wines will probably be found under *Moulin-a-Vent*, *Julienas*, *Fleurie*, *Morgon*, *Beaujolais Villages*, and *Brouilly*, my favourite. *Beaujolais Supérieur* has a geographical not a quality connotation.

Unlike robust true burgundies which may have a considerable bottle life, beaujolais wines should rarely be over five years old and I think reach their best at three.

Again often listed separately are the wines of that other continuation of Burgundy, the *Côte du Rhône*. The most famous of these is the very robust *Châteauneuf du Pape*, on the earthly side but which I consider a real "man's wine" for quaffing with, say, a well-hung grouse. It needs more than normal maturing or it will be distinctly rough. Other good names are *Hermitage* and *Côte Rôtie*.

In dealing with red burgundies very broadly, I have purposely left to the conclusion what I think is a vinous abomination, sparkling red burgundy, though I may be treading on some American toes, for this type enjoys some vogue in the U.S. Excellent white sparkling wines are indeed made from Aligoté grapes grown through the Burgundy district, using that term liberally, but these wines do not advertise a Burgundian origin.

White Burgundies The greatest dry white wines of France are from Burgundy. Generically chablis is the type most generally known, and it is enormously copied and abused. It is strong and very dry and is much appreciated by connoisseurs of oysters. Undistinguished chablis, bearing no known provenance, is often simply acid instead of dry. *Petit Chablis* is more seen in France than abroad. *Mâcon Blanc* is another pretty vague term, but, when reliable, is like a less expensive, duller chablis. True chablis is an excellent wine.

There is some overlapping from the reds with the whites in burgundy, as will be seen from comparison of lists of the most famous names. These include *Corton Charlemagne*, *Meurseult*, and *Montrachet*, the last-named being in its costlier form allied with *Bâtard-*, *Puligny-*, and *Chassagne*.

Beaujolais produces virtually only one white, *Beaujolais Blanc*, which in normal commerce is frankly indistinguishable from *Mâcon Blanc*, except by experts who are, in any event, unlikely to be amused by either.

Pouilly Fuissé is a widely esteemed mâconnais, and can be excellent, subject to my customary warning. It is often mispronounced. Pundits tend to prefer *Pouilly Fumé*, somewhat more delicate, but this is a LOIRE wine, not a burgundy.

Virtually no ROSE wine is made in Burgundy, except *Tavel* from the Rhône, but a beaujolais rosé, called *Marsannay*, is mentioned by Hugh Johnson as enjoying some popularity in the U.S.A.

Sparkling white burgundies at least lack the vinous contradiction of the aforementioned sparkling red, but outside France herself they receive scant attention.

BURNETT'S WHITE SATIN GIN

The firm of Sir Robert Burnett was sold by D.C.L. to SEAGRAM'S nearly a decade ago. *White Satin* was well-known for a long time in Britain to a number of people who appreciated its distinctive flavour, rather stronger than most, and, to my mind, reminiscent of OLD TOM gin. Seagram's redesigned the bottle and label very attractively, and considerably reduced the botanical content while retaining the basic *White Satin* characteristic. Recently the pack in the U.K. has been brought into line with that used overseas and, if I am right, the gin formula has been made "drier".

BURROUGH & Co., JAMES

In the middle of the last century after apprenticeship to a pharmaceutical chemist in Exeter, James Burrough spent six years in America, and on returning to England bought a Chelsea firm of gin and liqueur distillers. He was well established in the gin trade by the time he died in 1897. In 1908 the family moved the business to Hutton Road, Lambeth.

The international fame of the company started its phenomenal growth shortly after World War II with the introduction into the U.S.A. of Burrough's *Beefeater* gin, the success of which was largely due to the energy of the late Eric Burrough. It is now the largest-selling *imported* gin in the United States, not the largest-selling gin. It became particularly associated with the ultra-dry Dry Martini cocktail.

In 1958 it became necessary to increase production beyond the scope of the existing distillery: two years later a new *Beefeater* distillery was opened in 1960 in Kennington near the famous Oval cricket ground.

Note A symbol is a valuable commercial asset and Burrough's have majored on their *Beefeater* image and its strongly London connotation. Beefeaters is the colloquial name for the Yeomen of The Tower, the picturesque *corps d'élite* selected from retired armed

Bushmills

services' non-commissioned officers who are the official guardians of the Tower of London, as distinct from its garrison, and act as guides to its precincts in their Tudor uniforms. They were established as a bodyguard by Henry VII, and the name is probably derived from *buffetiers*, waiters upon the French king's table, or perhaps those entitled to share some of his repasts as part of their emolument. Or they may have been called beefeaters because they once ate handsomely at the sovereign's expense.

BUSHMILLS
The spot in Co. Antrim, on the northern coast of Northern Ireland, that has given its name to Ireland's only Irish malt whiskey—*Old Bushmills*—a spirit of marked characteristics, and delicate flavour that is unique. For long famous in its country of origin, *Old Bushmills* was exported to America and the West Indies as early as 1784, and is today better known overseas than on the mainland of Britain, where of late the demand has been almost wholly for Scotch whisky.

For connoisseurs of IRISH WHISKEY, the long-aged liqueur *Old Bushmills* needs no sacriligeous additives: it is worthy of drinking on its own. *Uisge Beatha*, the Irish spirit that evolved into whiskey, was made at Bushmills in the Thirteenth Century, a then landlord of the district allowing his warriors a long draught of it before battle. The process of malting was not used until 1590, when it may be surmised the Bushmill distillation took on something approaching its modern taste.

BUTT See Barrels.

BYRRH
The famous French aperitif (unfortunately pronounced "beer", so English-speaking drinkers had better say "aperitif *Byrrh*"), said to have been invented by Simon Violet who died in the early Nineteenth Century near Thuir, where it is still made. Unlike other aperitifs, it apparently improves with bottle storage.

C

CABANA
A brand name for fine Demerara rums from Guyana of exceptional purity, distilled by Caribbean Distillers Ltd. *Cabaña Blanca* is the white variety, a light rum of great delicacy, owing much to special yeasts isolated and cultured at Diamond, Guyana, on the River Demerara. *Cabaña* dark rum has equal distinction in its own field.

CABERNET
One of the finest of Bordeaux grapes, varieties of which are used in the better wines of some other districts and overseas countries.

CABINET (KABINETT)
Indicative of a high quality German wine, originally meaning that it was reserved for the growers' own use.

CALIFORNIAN WINE
See U.S.A. (Wine).

CALORIES
According to the British public analyst, the normal $\frac{1}{6}$ of a gill measure of whisky or gin in Britain provides about 55 calories. The figures for the number of calories per glass given below are approximate since one is simply referring to a "normal".

Plate 5. An old picture of farmhouse cider manufacture shows a typical scene a hundred years ago in the West Country of Britain. Apples were brought in from the orchard in wicker baskets to be pulped in the cider mill (centre background), and then pressed between layers of straw in the press (left). The juice ran into a tube and was then taken to the vats.

Plate 6. Château Loudenne is surrounded by vineyards adjoining the banks of the River Gironde in the Médoc region of Bordeaux. Built in the Eighteenth Century, it has belonged to Gilbeys since 1875. It is one of the very few properties in France where the Union Jack flies at vintage time. *Château* literally means a castle—the more humble buildings for producing or storing the wine are called the *chais*.

Champagne	73
Sparkling hock or similar wines	72
Dry bordeaux wine	74
Dry white wine	80

CALVADOS
The taste for this brandy distilled from cider in Normandy has not spread much abroad, possibly because the best of it is principally retained for local use. It requires very long ageing, or it will be little better than cider MARC. It is well worth trying a long-matured one should you be in Normandy or in a restaurant priding itself on its calvados.

CALVERT
Celebrated U.S. distillers and blenders; also producers of bottled cocktails.

CALVET
J. Calvet et Cie., of Bordeaux, is one of those truly great names to which I refer in general under Wine as giving a guarantee of excellence; look for their eagle insignia. The company was founded in 1818 by the great-grandfather of the present managing director. They are said to be the largest shippers in Bordeaux and are almost equally important in Burgundy.

CAMPARI
The highly distinctive *Campari* bitters is one of the world's greatest proprietary drinks, exported the world over from the firm's mighty headquarters and factory in Milan and produced in 16 overseas countries. Insofar as it has an affinity with vermouth, it is essentially Italian, but it is not a vermouth. It is a drink in a class all of its own and, because of its strength, 45° proof (British), it is classed as a spirit by the British customs and excise, as many an unwary traveller has discovered when trying to sneak a bottle in under his wine "allowance"!

I have visited the vast and magnificent factory but shall not try to describe the process of manufacture. It is the end product with which I am concerned. It is magnificent as an aperitif or cooling drink simply with soda; the NEGRONI is my second choice of cocktail, and the less powerful AMERICANO has much to recommend it. (If citrus fruit be added to *Campari*, I think it should always be a slice of orange, not lemon). In Milan they turn out millions of bottles of *Campari*-soda, single servings, and I hope we shall see these in Britain: they ensure a correct mix. It is pointless to describe *Campari;* the firm has done so in its consistently entertaining and instructive advertising. It does have a cryptically bitter-sweet taste; it does owe its special charm to having sundry herbs macerated in the basic fortified wine. It is an attractive colour; its aroma is pleasing. It is unique.

This "empire" started in 1842 when Gaspare Campari left home at the age of 14 to find his fortune in Turin. Though it was not in the home city of Vermouth that he did find it, he was there apprenticed to the well-known liqueur shop, Bass (a startingly English name but certainly unconnected with the celebrated brewers!). Having mastered the art of liqueur-making, Gaspare moved away to a smaller town to start on his own, eventually settling in Milan and establishing the recipe for *Campari* bitters that his son Davide was to make world-famous. Originally the firm produced a mass of liqueurs, including *Cordial Campari,* for which strong medical claims were made in accordance with the practice of the day. It is only comparatively recently that such drinks are allowed to stand on their own merits simply as pleasing drinks; it was formerly thought correct to ascribe other virtues to them.

The Gaspare Campari formula is known to a handful of people only; as one chemist retires he hands the secret on to his successor. It is a devotedly loyal firm, and though no direct descendant of Gaspare Campari survives, there is evident to any visitor a sense of family tradition that even the complexities of multi-million pound modern commerce will not in the foreseeable future eradicate.

CANADA

I do not think I would wish to be in the wholesale or retail liqueur trade in the Dominion of Canada, nor concerned with brand advertising there. A singular confusion of laws and differing provincial or local regulations has grown up. One aspect of this is typified by sheets purporting to give a simple outline of liquor advertising and promotion regulations (in those provinces where they are permitted at all). It is certainly not the fault of *Marketing Magazine,* which produced the list, that it has had to be heavily annotated. According to one annotation in New Brunswick liquor advertising is permitted by law, with liquor control board approval—but the provincial board has never given any such authorizations and has no plans to do so!

In general most provinces, and the Yukon territory, permit newspaper and magazine advertising of liquor, but the law is hedged by detailed local rules concerning size and content. Until recently, only British Columbia and Newfoundland allowed bottles to be shown in advertisements. Thus in the important Quebec market, the agents for *Cincinnatti* beer, whose celebrated trademark is a waiter carrying a bottle of the beer on a tray, had to depict this trademark—by itself the brand's usual advertisement—with an empty tray. This brought ridicule on the regulation! Quebec now permits depiction of bottles, and Manitoba is said to be following suit.

There are moves towards a more liberal approach, but as things stand such elementary trade aids as price lists are everywhere prohibited, as are exterior signs except on actual manufacturing premises. Other normal promotion activities are either totally banned or technically permitted in one province and not in an adjoining one.

These trade difficulties stem mainly from the existence of the provincial liquor control boards, which tend to be very autocratic. They reflect an excessive decentralization and provincial independence, and stem from a puritanical revolt against the wide-open frontier spirit of less settled times. For example, until quite lately the Prince Edward Island control board was called the Prince Edward Island *Temperance* Commission, and though a change of title should have indicated a new social approach, the commission continues to forbid the public consumption of alcohol in any form: no bars, no licensed restaurants. The visitor may not any longer need to pay a doctor for a prescription to buy a bottle, but he must convince the liquor store salesman that he will take it immediately and unopened to his hotel room. Such draconian laws naturally cause evasion and bootlegging.

Outside the Province of Quebec, whose French stock would hardly tolerate vicious anti-drinking regulations, some very odd powers lie with control boards and I am indebted to the influential *Maclean's Magazine* for some amusing or lugubrious examples of their whims.

In Nova Scotia a policeman at his own discretion can at any time enter any building and seize any liquor there, it being the owner's concern to prove he had a legal right to the seized goods. In Saskatchewan, public drinking is illegal and a private dwelling may be declared a "public place", thus prohibiting the householder from drinking in his own home. At the same time, if convicted he is not allowed to drink anywhere in the province for five years.

In Toronto, it was long believed that a drinker could only have a single glass in front of him in a bar. In fact, there is no such law, but because the control board likes the nonexistent law to be observed, observed it is.

Even in Quebec you may drink on Sunday only if you live in a town with 50,000 inhabitants. If you happen to reside in one with only 49,999, you must not drink on Sunday.

In British Columbia there exist wide powers to confiscate the cars of people concerned directly or indirectly in liquor offences. One man, though cleared of a "bootlegging" charge, could not repossess his vehicle. Discovering that it was technically being "held at the Queen's pleasure" he put through a call to Buckingham Palace in London. He gained the ear of a sympathetic official, and within 24 hours the provincial lieutenant-governor had ordered the car to be returned.

Canada's premier manufactured liquor is CANADIAN WHISKY. Dry gin, vodka and other sophisticated spirits are also produced, and there are considerable imports, notably Scotch whisky, American whiskey and such items as cognac and European wines and liqueurs.

Wine The wine industry is considerable, with a production of around 9 million gallons. Nearly all of this comes from the Niagara area, contiguous with the main vineyards of New York State. A small amount of wine is produced in British Columbia. Most Canadian wine is blended sweet dessert wine, but the demand for dry table wines seems to be growing. Viticulture conditions are excellent in Ontario, where the department of agriculture has an active wine research section keenly aiding development of local wines and extension of variety and quality.

CANADA DRY
Brand specially noted for ginger ale, though, of course, producing other mixers.

CANADIAN CLUB
Universally famous blended Canadian whisky by Hiram Walker; second only to Seagram's *V.O.* in the U.S.A., and third largest-selling spirit there.

CANADIAN WHISKY
Though a long way behind it, Canadian whisky has gone forth from its native land in a tide second only to that of Scotch. At least two brands are internationally famous: CANADIAN CLUB and SEAGRAM's *V.O.* The great popularity of Canadian whisky in parts of the U.S.A. is referred to in my U.S.A. entry. There are five principal distillers with a century's experience and about 15 others of more recent foundation.

Since lightness of flavour and body are distinctive aspects of Canadian whisky, it is attuned to today's tastes: to my mind it is smoother, though less flavoursome, than straight BOURBON, is much superior to ordinary American blended whiskey, but lacks the special character inherent in a fine SCOTCH; and I am endeavouring to be descriptive and not pejorative when I say it is a "compromise" spirit.

Corn is the main grain used, together with rye and some wheat plus malted barley. Continuous, rather than pot-still, distillation is customary and the most rigorous government supervision attends production right down to the time the whisky is bottled. The legal minimum maturing age is two years but the best blends will contain whiskies of much greater cask-age. Both charred and uncharred barrels are used. For the Canadian market the usual strength is the same as in Britain, 70° proof (Sykes), but export strengths vary widely according to local preferences.

Canadian whisky has similar applications for mixed drinks to those listed for Scotch or American whiskey.

CANARY ISLANDS
These Atlantic islands produce rum and wine, but not for export. They import whisky, gin, vermouth and some table wines. Prices are extremely attractive. The better-off inhabitants have shown lately a strong

Cane Spirit

liking for whisky and gin; adequate additives in the form of tonic-water, soda-water and ginger ale are produced locally. Liquor may be sold 24 hours a day, seven days a week; as a result, intemperance is almost non-existent.

CANE SPIRIT
Alcohol distilled from a residual product of sugar production, molasses. At its best it is a very dry and excellent spirit and is the basis of some of the finest gins and vodkas, etc. For no good reason today, it does not enjoy the prestige of GRAIN spirit, though some cane spirits in parts of the world hardly achieve the stands of quality that apply in Britain.

CANNON BREWERY, THE
So named in 1751, these premises in CLERKENWELL had probably been used for brewing much earlier. It went through many changes and amalgamations, was badly hit in the blitz, and is now the headquarters of the London division of the IND COOPE section of the huge ALLIED BREWERIES LTD.

CAPITAL WINE AGENCIES LTD.
The agents for STOLICHNAYA and other Russian vodkas and wines, and a number of unusual wines from Eastern Europe, as well as more conventional items.

CAPRINO
An old Jamaican liqueur, coffee-flavoured, the pride of a small Kingston company, and drier and less tacky than some similar products.

CAPTAIN MORGAN RUM
Well-known brand being heavily pushed on the British market.

CARAFE
Container used in France for bringing a restaurant's "house wines" from cask to table. Elsewhere "carafe wine" has come to mean also a "house wine" though it is often poured from bottles into carafes. Few carafes hold a bottle, and these wines should be correspondingly less expensive, and sometimes are. Many small restaurants and some big groups have excellent wines in carafe, but you should know your establishment or have a reliable recommendation before committing yourself to carafe wine. Carafes can vary widely in size and cost.

CARAFINO
Brand name for a range of sound, blended wines in the popular price range; available in economy-size jars that are splendid for parties.

CARAMEL
Tasteless burnt sugar used to put colour into, or adjust the colour of, whisky, brandy, etc. It has no effect on flavour.

CARBOHYDRATES See Diabetic.

CARBONATED
Artificial, as opposed to natural, infusion of sparkle into drinks by use of carbon dioxide; used in cheap *vin mousseux* for the French market.

CARBON DIOXIDE (CO_2)
The gas produced during FERMENTATION; it is this that puts the fizz into sparkling wines or into effervescent soft drinks.

CARDHU
A fine 12-year-old single malt Scotch whisky by Johnnie Walker from their Cardow Distillery, Morayshire. (When a bottle of blended or vatted Scotch states an age, it is the cask age of the youngest whisky in it. In the instance of a single unblended whisky, such as *Cardhu Highland* malt, it is the actual age of the whisky in the bottle).

CARLISLE
During World War I, the British government sequestered the breweries and pubs of

Carlisle and surrounding district including some over the border in Scotland. This was intended to control temporarily the sale of alcohol to immigrant munition workers from across the Irish Sea, though some saw it as an experimental thin end of a nationalization wedge. Despite local wishes, when war ended the regional industry was not returned to private enterprise, and it is generally considered that Carlisle provides an awful example of the standards of product and service one can expect from state control of a commerce inherently unsuited to such conditions. As I write there are indications the Government will end the monopoly and auction off the 173 state-run pubs in the Carlisle district.

CARLSBERG
This celebrated beer was started in Copenhagen in 1845 by J. C. Jacobson and was exported to Britain as early as 1870: it is still very highly esteemed in the U.K. A £12 million brewery to produce Carlsberg is projected for the Midlands of England.

CARONI
A white rum of exceptional lightness produced by continuous distilling in Trinidad.

CARPANO See Vermouth; Punt e mes.

CASE
Twelve bottles, or equivalent in volume, of wines or spirits.

CASKS
Wooden casks are used in great quantities in all aspects of the wine, and in much of the spirit, trades. Actual contents may vary considerably, but the following is a general guide in broad terms to casks most commonly in use. See also Barrels.

Scotch whisky
　Butt　　　　108 gallons (U.K.)
Rum
　Puncheon　　100　　,,
　Hogshead　　56　　,,

American and Canadian Whisk(e)y
　Barrel　　　40 gallons (48 U.S.)
Port
　Pipe.　　　115 gallons (U.K.)
Sherry
　Butt　　　　108　　,,
　Hogshead　　54　　,,
Brandy
　Puncheon　　120　　,,

France uses many casks with regional names and varying capacities. The best-known is the Bordeaux *barrique* of about 50 gallons (U.K.), a similar cask being known as a *pièce* in Burgundy. In Germany a fairly standard cask is the *doppleohm* of 65 gallons. Australian and South African hogsheads contain about 10 gallons more than the British.

CASSIS See Black currant.

C. & C.
Cantrell & Cochrane; brand covering most mineral waters, jointly owned by two breweries and Schweppes.

CHABLIS See Burgundy.

CHAMBERTIN
A noble BURGUNDY.

CHAMBÉRY
The distinctive VERMOUTH from the Savoy department of France, and a name protected by law. There are four producers, the oldest being Dolin which was founded in 1821. There are several types of *Chambéry*; the classic dry vermouth of the district is distinctively fresh and clean-tasting. The red is full-flavoured, and there is a bitter-sweet *Americano*, but the real winner to my mind is the unique *Chambéryzette*, a dry vermouth delicately but decidedly flavoured with the juice of wild strawberries. Chilled, by itself it makes a delightful and different aperitif. Gin combines well with it, if you want more zest.

CHAMBRE
See Room temperature (Chambré).

CHAMPAGNE
The very word champagne is evocative of the luxurious, the costly, a thing of quality, and rightly so. Here is a wine of unique distinction that delights the palate, pleases the eye, and elates one's whole being: it is a reward and a tonic.

The semi-legendary father of champagne (in the effervescent form with which we associate it) was Dom Perignon, by repute blind, wine-master of the great Abbey of Hautevillers for some 50 years from 1668. He certainly was a pioneer in the blending of the wines of the Champagne district (which had been producing wine since Roman times) and he is credited with introducing cork stoppers in place of the wooden or rag bungs of earlier times: without this innovation champagne could not exist.

The basic process *(methode champagnoise)* has often been described, but I will outline it. The wine is made in the normal way, from a mixture of black Pinot Noir and white Chardonnay grapes, or from one or the other. Some houses own their own vineyards but others may buy wholly or partly from independent proprietors. Wines are blended in large vats (or casks in the instance of the finest brands). The following spring the wine is bottled and fitted with a cellar cork, though increasingly, less expensive non-porous metal closures are being used; in the case of non-vintage wines this is the general rule except, I believe, for BOLLINGER and KRUG alone.

The bottles are placed neck down in long racks, (the cellars are often miles in length) and the secondary fermentation begins. The bottles are turned (the *remuage*) to ensure that the sediment falls constantly into the neck: the process is attributed to the VEUVE CLICQUOT. Meanwhile the carbon dioxide gas produced by fermentation dissolves in the wine to give it its special character. After a time the neck of the bottle is plunged into a freezing mixture, and, on removal of the cellar cork or other temporary closure, *(dégorgement)*, the natural gas in the wine forces out the solidified sediment. The bottle then receives the *dosage*. This is sugar, more or less according to the type of champagne required. Even *brut* (very dry) champagne normally receives a minute amount of sugar, plus a tiny quantity of grape brandy and possibly a little wine to top up. The wine then receives its final cork, wired on. (The custom of using wire originated because rats often gnawed through the string formerly used).

The wine will then continue to improve according to its quality. Over the years some effervescence is lost, and it is a matter of taste whether one finds this attractive: personally I much prefer vintage champagnes that have exceeded what is popularly considered their normal age. The vast majority of champagne made is non-vintage. (Cheaper champagne may be made by the CUVE CLOSE method).

There exist a great number of brands apart from buyer's own brands (b.o.b.): wines made for a specific shipper under his own label (only experience will tell you which are good value). The great brands which collectively account for getting on for three-quarters of champagne sales are *Ayala*, BOLLINGER, VEUVE CLICQUOT-PONSARDIN, *Deutz & Geldermann*, HEIDSIECK *Monopole*, Charles HEIDSIECK, *Irroy*, KRUG, LANSON, MERCIER, MOET et CHANDON, MUMM, PERRIER-JOUET, Piper HEIDSIECK, POL ROGER, POMMERY & *Greno*, ROEDERER, RUINART, TAITTINGER (my own list). Some make champagne other than under their own labels for b.o.b. purposes, and several produce costly vintage wines that are comparative rarities: others concentrate solely on straight vintage and fine non-vintage wines.

Most champagne sold on the British market

Champagne

is extra dry or *brut* (indicating a very dry one), sometimes emphasized as *Brut de Brut*. American tastes run to slightly less dry champagne and the French tend to like positively sweet champagne for the general market. Champagne is, of course, a highly protected word; and under French law may only come from a carefully designated area around Rheims, Epernay and Ay. The word champagne is sufficient in itself, and alone of French *appellation contrôlée* wines need not carry that actual description. Following a celebrated law suit, only champagne as recognized by French law may be so described in Britain, but this does not apply in many other countries (e.g., the U.S.A.), which have been making "champagne" for a long time.

Drinking Champagne A great deal of champagne is drunk by people who do not really care for it, because it has become traditional at weddings and other festive occasions. It is sometimes drunk for no more than snobbish reasons. It is ideally an aperitif wine though it may, if one wishes, be used during, or at the conclusion of, a luxurious meal. However, its delicacy really makes it unsuitable with well-sauced dishes. It is frequently drunk much too cold. The universal rule is that the better the wine the less it should be refrigerated. To air a personal opinion, a fine champagne is best taken at the temperature it would have if brought directly from a deep cellar.

The business of opening a bottle of champagne worries some people. Corks do stick, though you will very rarely encounter this with the best brands, and pliers (special ones may be bought) are then used. The cork should be eased very gently from the bottle, not allowed to blow out with an ostentatious detonation. (I am indebted to Jack de Manio on the B.B.C.'s splendid "Today" radio programme for the glorious piece of "useless information" that the average speed of ejection of a champagne cork is 42 feet per second, and that there has been noted a growing incidence of eye damage from this cause among British restaurant personnel. This indicates carelessness).

As for glasses, I loathe the SAUCER glass. The correct champagne glass is a FLUTE, but a TULIP or a simple stemmed wine glass will suffice: anything but a "saucer".

CHAMPAGNE (Drinks)

Champagne à L'Orange is a mixture of half-and-half of champagne and chilled fresh orange juice, with or without a measure of cognac. An excellent morning drink, often known in London as *Buck's Fizz* from its use at Buck's Club. *Champagne Cocktail* A rather smart abomination which ruins the wine. In a wine glass (and if you must have this drink, do not add bad taste to injury by employing a beastly saucer-glass) a lump of sugar, on which has been shaken some Angostura: a measure of brandy; topped with very cold champagne. Serve with round of orange. *Champagne Punch* Two bottles non-vintage champagne, 4 measures of brandy, 4 measures of Cointreau, 3 measures of maraschino, siphon soda-water. Mix the liquors, add very cold champagne and soda-water, decorate bowl with fruit; do not add ice.

Champagne may be used to make a slightly unconventional KIR.

Digression The medicinal, restorative, properties of champagne have long been appreciated, both as personal therapy and by doctor's order. The late Dr. Gregorio Marañon y Posadillo, the noted Spanish doctor, whose researches led him to conclude that wine, and spirits in moderation, never caused any disease in themselves and were indeed beneficial, reported an interesting case. He came across an American banker, aged 76, who rejoiced in a regular daily diet of two bottles of champagne, in addition to other incidental wines and spirits. It was estimated that he had consumed, since the age of 30, at least 13,000 bottles of champagne alone! For the past 15 years the man had suffered from gout and his physician naturally attributed this to his above-average intake of alcohol. Consequently he went into a sanatorium and had no drink for a month, which must have been sheer murder for him.

His gout was just as bad, if not worse. Dr. Marañon was consulted and suggested that the patient instantly leave hospital, cut his food intake by a third and submit to imbibing only one bottle of champagne a day. Two years later the banker, now a robust 78 years' old wrote to thank Dr. Marañon; his gout had virtually disappeared and he had followed the advice—except that he was again drinking his two bottles of champagne daily! See Gout.

CHAMPAGNE ROSE
This type of *vin rosé* is little more than a fad, which enjoyed an ephemeral vogue after World War II. It is not taken seriously by most champagne-lovers, though it is made by several distinguished houses, as well as lesser ones, to supply a small regular demand.

CHANNEL ISLANDS
These autonomous British island dependencies enjoy low taxes compared with the mainland, making them an alcoholic paradise for fiscally thwarted mainland topers, who not only celebrate during their holidays to delightful Jersey, Guernsey and Alderney not to mention tiny, feudal Sark but bring back a sea of spirits under the watchful but fairly benevolent eyes of British Customs officers. In Jersey, licensed premises open from 09.00–22.00 hours in winter and an hour longer in summer; Guernsey's open an hour later; restaurants have an extra evening hour but residents in hotels suffer no restrictions whatsoever on their thirst. There is a Sunday midday period of official abstinence, though I have not found this always seriously observed. Alderney, notable for the small proportion of inhabitants to pubs, *officially* follows Guernsey's regulations. In a decade, sale of whisky in Jersey has considerably more than doubled and is now around the 78,000 proof gallon mark (the island measures about 10 miles by 5).

CHARRING
The slight burning of the inside of new or remade casks in which whisky is to be stored, and an integral part of the process of maturing the spirit.

CHARRINGTON See Bass Charrington Ltd.

CHARTREUSE
Of this famous liqueur it is the *green* that is the stronger; the *yellow* is of lower proof and sweeter. It was invented in the Seventeenth Century, but not commercialized until the middle Nineteenth Century. The Carthusian Order suffered many vicissitudes in France, including total expulsion in 1903, but at all times the monks preserved the secret of their liqueur, and eventually brought it back to its homeland in the Grenoble area. It is distilled today on the original basis involving some 130 herbs. Apart from the two internationally known types there is *Elixir Végétal* (probably the nearest thing to the first medicinal production), which at 136° proof (British) is a trifle powerful for universal commercial distribution. The monks control distillation, but do not drink their own ambrosia which is bottled and distributed on a royalty basis by a secular company.

CHASSAGNE-MONTRACHET
Outstanding BURGUNDY white wine.

CHATEAU
Literally a castle, but in practice a wine estate of the Bordeaux area of which the residence

may be splendid, modest or non-existent. Chateau-bottled wines, meaning that they have been bottled on the spot and not sold to a shipper, give a special guarantee of quality, are generally vintage wines, and are correspondingly costly. Château Margaux bottles its own non-vintage production, this is done when the wine is not considered good enough to have the vintage year added. The greatest châteaux are listed in the classification of the red wines of BORDEAUX.

CHERRY BRANDY

This is not usually a true brandy, for though it may once have been a distillate from cherry juice it is now usually a liqueur, flavoured both with cherries and cherry stones, the latter adding a touch of attractive bitterness to the very sweet cherry flavour. It may be based on grape brandy (or on neutral rectified spirit in which case in Britain it may not be described as a brandy) and is in any event of considerably lower strength than a brandy. The best known brand, which is specially popular in the U.S.A., is the Danish *Cherry Heering*. *De Kuyper's Cherry Brandy* is another outstanding brand. *Cherry Rocher* (strange how they use the English word) is the leading name in France. Grant's *Morella* is the principal brand made in England.

Digression If you happen to be a sherry addict and are in France, if you ask for a "sherry" you will almost certainly get a *Cherry Rocher*; you should order a *vin de Jerez*.

CHEVAL BLANC

A château producing a notable claret, and a trap for the unwary who think that from its name it must be a white wine.

CHIANTI

The popularly best known of Italian red wines, tending to be robust and well attuned to washing down *pasta* dishes. Possibly many people are attracted by the straw-covered *fiascos* in which it is sold as by the wine. It is the best of the rather aggressive Tuscany wines.

CHILE

Most popular drinks are PISCO, vermouth, gin and whisky, all of which except the last, are produced locally. Scotch or other blends may only be imported for diplomatic use, but vatted malts are brought in for making Chilean "whisky". With import duties running at 85 per cent of value, this makes local whisky about $8 U.S. a bottle. Drinking laws themselves are liberal and advertising free from restrictions, but outlets for strong drinks are rigorously controlled. Upper-class Chileans follow American drinking habits.

Wine There is a very large wine production. I myself respect Chilean burgundy-style wines as excellent table wine.

According to which set of figures you consult, Chile is placed from around ninth to fifteenth in the global wine production tables. She is generally considered to produce the best wines in South America, particularly the reds which dominate production. Chilean wines are, when you find them, usually very good value.

CHILLING

In the new ice age in which we live, fine wines that need little more than the mildest refrigeration are chilled so that the taste buds they should enthrall are numbed, and the wine does not show to its best advantage. The better the wine, the less the refrigeration; only cheap sweet wines deserve, and may have their limitations masked by, excessive cooling. Ice should not be put into any but the least important of beverage wines to turn them into a thirst-quencher.

Beer, too, is often over-chilled. British bitter which used contemptuously to be referred to by ice-conscious Americans as "warm beer" does its best when no more than cool, and fine imported lagers come best as if from a cool cellar. Light beers and lagers may justifiably be chilled to extinction. ICE should not be put into decent beer.

CHIVAS REGAL
A fine premium 12-year-old blend of Scotch whisky enjoying a high reputation in many countries, and considering its price doing well in the British market. Owned by SEAGRAM'S.

CHRISTIAN BROTHERS, THE
The largest vineyard owners (1,100 acres) in the CALIFORNIAN wine industry, this is a religious Catholic teaching order, at Napa, Cal., whose products are marketed by Fromm Sichel Inc., on a world-wide scale. In Britain, the comparatively new London Wine Company (Shippers) Ltd. are agents: this firm deals extensively with fine wines for the American market. Notable Christian Brothers' wines are their very dry claret-style *Cabernet Sauvignon* and a delectable *Chenin Blanc* made from grapes transplanted from the LOIRE.

CHRISTOPHER'S
During the reign of Charles II (1660–85), Christopher's were established as wine merchants in the City of London, but the Great Fire of 1666 forced them west, first to Bloomsbury, then to Pall Mall, and today they are elegantly situated in Jermyn Street. The whole trend of the wine and spirit trade is towards bigger and bigger units, even if some firms thus absorbed into combines retain, at least temporarily, something of their own identity. Christopher's, though still not unique, are a splendidly independent survival from a more gracious past, typical of the best in traditional but progressive London wine business. I hope those are right who assure me they are secure from joining conglomerates.

Not that the firm is concerned only with fine clarets for laying down in deep cellars and rare vintage ports: you may be quite at ease in stepping into No. 94 and ordering a single bottle of sound burgundy to aid your dinner. Though they have been sending their own blend of Scotch to the U.S.A. for 60 years on a distinctively exclusive basis, they have recently built up stocks with a view to expanding the sale of *Christopher's Choice*, though it is still limited to the prestige market.

CIDER
At least one excellent independent English maker calls this "apple wine", which is not a bad description. It is widely drunk in Britain, and principally produced in Herefordshire and the West Country, in Normandy and in north-eastern U.S.A., apart from some other countries. It is made today mainly on the scale of a modern industry. The washed apples are reduced to a pulp, POMACE. This is spread in layers on coarse cloth and pressed. The juice settles in vats and is then pumped into vessels where fermentation is immediately started by the natural yeasts present in the apple skins. Cultivated yeasts are sometimes added. For dry cider, fermentation will be completed; for sweeter varieties it will be stopped at an appropriate stage. "Champagne" cider is made by natural production of carbon dioxide through secondary fermentation in bottle (notably *Pomagne* by BULMER) but cheaper sparkling ciders are artificially carbonated. In Britain, apart from *Bulmer*, there are numerous brands of cider, but the bulk of other ciders are produced by Coates, Gaymers and Whiteways which, through SHOWERINGS, come under ALLIED BREWERIES. See also Merrydown.

Cider can play a useful part in mixed drinks; it is fine in PUNCH, where it may often be a substitute for wine (see Booth's Party Punch). It goes well with gin, but with peculiarly lethal effects. CIDER CUP is an excellent cooler. Ciders vary enormously in strength, character (still or fizzy) and degree of sweetness. People visiting the West Country of England should certainly taste Somerset or Devon "scrumpy", remembering that it has a notorious reputation for enfeebling the legs.

Historical note When Julius Caesar landed in Britain in 55 B.C. cider was already a popular drink. Its history is hidden even further back in the mists of Celtic mythology, when the apple was sacred and an apple god is known to have been worshipped. Primitive cider was made from the bitter apples growing wild in the forests. It is from the descendants of these trees that today's cider apples are gathered.

Cider has continued to give pleasure in every age. In the early Middle Ages, for example, there are many references to cider in monastic writings, a drink apparently much enjoyed by the monks. It appears at one time to have referred to any strong drink.

Eleanor de Montfort, wife of Simon de Montfort (1208?–65), recorded that it was a less fashionable drink among the members of the baronial class of her time. It was clearly popular in the Fourteenth Century. William of Shoreham reflected the church's concern for the niceties of sacramental rites by stating that young children were not to be baptized with cider. Cider became a welcome substitute for French wine during the Hundred Years' War (1337–1453), when supplies from the Continent were reduced, though its popularity was by no means always universal.

William Langland refers to cider in his poem *Piers Plowman*, a religious work describing much of the life of the Middle Ages in England. Shakespeare mentions it in *A Midsummer Night's Dream*. Sir Francis Bacon, the Elizabethan philosofer and statesman, praised cider. Daniel Defoe, the novelist, observed that Hereford people "boaft the richeft cider in all Britain," and Samuel Pepys noted in his diary that on May 1st, 1666, he "drank a cup of Syder". Around about the Seventeenth Century much verse was written on the subject of cider. It was praised in poems of varying literary merit, both as an aid to good cheer and a homely cure for almost every ailment known to man.

Cider making in those days was essentially a craft of cottage and farm. Today making cider has become a large modern industry producing well-known brands of bottled and draught cider for distribution throughout Britain. There is a small export from Hereford, mainly to the Commonwealth.

CIDER CUP

A flagon of still, dry cider; half-pint of orange squash or fresh juice; juice of a lemon; small wine-glass of Cointreau. Chill the cider, mix with ingredients in punch-bowl. Before serving add siphon soda-water, ice cubes, and slices of orange and lemon. Decorate glasses with cocktail cherries. You can play around with this recipe; for instance, substitute *Pomagne* for still cider (using 2 bottles) and omit soda-water. Spike with gin if you want to stir things up.

CINZANO

The Cinzano family were living in the Turin area in the Sixteenth Century, in the village of Pecetto, which was established in 1224. They were certainly producers of wine but it was in 1757 that the name Cinzano appeared in the roles of the Confectioners' and Distillers' Guild of Turin, and on this basis Cinzano claims to be the oldest-established VERMOUTH house, for it seems likely that it was the guild that did much to establish Turin's pre-eminence in the burgeoning vermouth industry. As early as 1707 a Cinzano received authority to distil brandy and produce cordials for sale only in Pecetto and Turin, and, while some of these cordials may well have been those which were employed to turn wine into vermouth, there is no evidence to that effect.

At the beginning of the last century, the Cinzano interests moved from Pecetto to the great "vermouth capital" of Turin, and thereafter the firm's story was one of unalloyed success. Today the name is one of that handful of proud ones that are recognized the world over: Cinzano manufactories, depots, bottling plants and agents cover the globe.

The firm recently enjoyed a big success with *Cinzano Bianco*, though their most famous global product is certainly their traditional red *Italian vermouth*. Like most vermouth firms, they are also major producers of ASTI SPUMANTE.

CIRRHOSIS
A progressive liver disease associated with addictive drinking. But alcohol is not the only cause of it and many heavy drinkers have perfectly healthy livers. However, in FRANCE there are more deaths from cirrhosis than in any other country.

CLARET
The general English word for red wines of the Bordeaux area; a corruption of *clairet*, a light-coloured, unimportant red wine made for local consumption without much ageing. Originally it was probably a mixture of red and white wines.

CLARET CUP
A lemon, an orange, 6 slices of pineapple (preferably fresh), 2 measures each of brandy, Cointreau, sugar syrup, fresh lemon juice. Slice fruit and over them pour other ingredients. Add plenty of ice. Add one bottle of inexpensive red wine and a siphon of soda-water; stir. Decorate with fruit in season.

CLARK & SONS LTD., MATTHEW
An excellent example of a City of London wine and spirit company which, still under Clark family direction, has kept abreast of the times in a type of business notoriously resistant to change. It was founded in 1810 by Matthew Clark, whose father was kidnapped as a youth and sold as a labourer on American plantations. Escaping by swimming to a British warship, he became a substantial figure in City commerce.

The first important overseas company whose representation in Britain Matthew Clark obtained was certainly John de KUYPER, whose gin and other products they still handle. Among other brands they represent are MARTELL and KRITER, and in 1964 they amalgamated with the FINSBURY DISTILLERY, both firms becoming subsidiaries of Matthew Clark (Holdings) Ltd.

CLERKENWELL (LONDON)
Several notable firms being listed in this work as sited in Clerkenwell, the reader may well ask what is so magical about the district. It boils down to water, and the constant pursuit of it, near the City of London yet outside its contamination, by brewers and distillers. Clerkenwell gave its name to this area of London with good reason.

The Clerks' Well was referred to in Fitzstephen's *Life of St. Thomas-à-Becket*, published in 1174, and is certainly much older. The name comes from the custom of parish clerks assembling beside it from time immemorial to enact a scriptural drama, and this rite may even have pre-Christian origins. The well is marked on the earliest extant map of London (c. 1560). After a varied history of exploitation, for many years the well was "lost", being rediscovered accidently during rebuilding work in 1924. More a spring than a well, being only some six feet deep, the peculiarity of it is that the water level never alters a fraction of an inch.

Other sources of pure water locally were Choice Well (now Chiswell) Street, Goose Well (Goswell) Road, and Sadler's Wells, while Turnmill and Cow Cross Streets give evidence of running water. (Clerkenwell, formerly in the defunct London Borough of Finsbury, is now incorporated in the Borough of Islington).

CLICQUOT See Veuve Clicquot-Ponsardin.

CLIMAT
The French word for a Burgundy vineyard.

CLOS
A term much found in connection with BURGUNDY wines, meaning a vineyard surrounded by a wall (which may or may not have tumbled down).

CLOSURES See Corks; Crown cork.

CLOVER CLUB
Two-thirds dry gin, one-third grenadine, juice of half lemon, white of an egg. Shake with ice very briskly and strain into goblet.

COATES & CO. See Plymouth Gin.

COBBLER
A somewhat archaic term for a "long" cocktail concocted from alcohol, juice and a good deal of fruit garbage.

COCA-COLA (Coke)
It is said that over 80 million bottles or glasses of *Coca-Cola* are sold daily. (These figures have gone up since I wrote). It is advertised in 60 languages. It was created and first sold in Atlanta, Georgia, in May, 1886, by John S. Bemberton. Dr. Bemberton in that year spent $46 on advertising. He died two years later, having sold a substantial share in the business to a local drugstore proprietor, Asa G. Chandler, who later acquired sole ownership. The Coca-Cola Company was incorporated in 1892. By 1904, when sales first topped the million-gallon mark, the product was an American national institution. In 1919, the Chandlers sold the company for $25 million. In 1920 the word *Coke* was established in law as belonging to Coca-Cola exclusively.

During World War II, sugar-rationing restricted sales to the civilian public by 50 per cent, but the company's policy was to ensure that as far as possible servicemen could get *Coke* at 5 cents a bottle, regardless of what it cost to get it to them. To this end 64 bottling plants were established overseas. Over 5,000 million bottles of *Coke* went to combat zones in addition to that served through dispensing machines. Since the war Coco-Cola's expansion has been dramatic, with new bottling plants opening internationally at the rate of one a fortnight. Fresh lines have also been introduced, notably FANTA.

Coca-Cola is what it always has been: a basic syrup of secret formula (formerly only made in Atlanta, but more recently elsewhere as well) which is bottled, or put into dispensers, with addition of sugar, water and carbon dioxide. Most bottling plants are independently owned and operated by local companies.

COCKBURN
Famous port and a semantic trap for the uninitiated: it is pronounced "ko-bern".

COCKTAILS
Mixed drinks have been drunk for millenia. Was not the "wine of Hippocrates" of the Fifth Century B.C. a form of "cocktail"? In the Second Century A.D. the Roman physician, Claudius, made *vini gallici*, a mixture of lemon juice and dried adders (who said a cocktail must be alcoholic?), which Emperor Commodus praised as the best pre-prandial tot. *The London Distiller* (quoted under Rectification) gives a host of recipes for spirituous drinks of considerable complexity which, though medicinal in purpose, could be classed as cocktails. Do we not claim

Cocktails

therapeutic qualities for some cocktails?

But we are here concerned with the peculiar word cocktail itself. I have often written about this, but it is rather a fascinating topic for imbibers, so I will summarize the theories. 1 Because it was once used for horses of mixed stock, not thoroughbreds. These animals had their tails docked and were called "cock-tailed" horses. Thus a mixture of drinks became known as a cocktail. 2 During the American Revolutionary War, Betsy Flanagan had a tavern near Yorktown, used by officers of Washington's army and also those of his French allies. Betsy was annoyed because people said her neighbour, a Loyalist Tory, had better poultry than hers. One day, goaded beyond endurance by a supporter of King George being superior in any particular to herself, she purloined some of his birds and served them to her military customers. They much enjoyed the feast and on repairing to the tap-room afterwards were intrigued to find bottles of ready-prepared "bracers" decorated with feathers. Triumphantly, Betsy explained they were tail feathers from her hated neighbour's roosters which they had just eaten. "Vive le Cock-tail," said one of the Frenchmen, proposing a toast. And the word stuck for a mixed drink. 3 Another American Revolutionary War story, it tells of another tavern and a patriotic landlord who named his prize fighting cock after General Washington. His daughter, Bessie, wanted to marry an American officer, but her father was not willing. Soon afterwards "Washington" disappeared. "Mine Host" offered Bessie's hand to the man who returned the cock, who, hardly surprisingly, except to the delighted and obviously ingenuous tavernkeeper, turned out to be Bessie's intended. A betrothal banquet ensued and the flustered girl mixed up the drinks most unconventionally. But everyone thought them fine, and in honour of the ornithological connection named them "cock tails". 4 American naval officers were paying a courtesy visit to a local Mexican overlord—when is not said—and after successful negotiations refreshments were brought in under the supervision of their host's lovely daughter. The American C.O. said they would never forget her, if only for the splendid drinks she served. Her name was Xoctl, to the pronunciation of which the visitors could get no nearer than "cocktail", which they subsequently transferred to any mixed drinks. (Were this piece of fiction true, it seems more likely to me we would be calling them ox-tails). 5 In the Eighteenth Century, a spirituous mixture (cock-ale) was given to fighting-cocks in training. It was a habit to toast a victorious bird with concoctions containing as many ingredients as the survivor of the bout had tail-feathers. The implication is obvious. 6 At Campeche, Gulf of Mexico, visiting British sailors imbibed local punches traditionally stirred with a wooden spoon. One popular barkeeper, however, used a root, known from its shape as *cola de gallo*. This was translated as "cocktail". 7 A New Orleans physician of French extraction served much-admired mixed drinks to his American friends. As a gimmick, he used double-ended gallic-style egg-cups, *coquetiers*, and the nearest his pals could get to that was "cocktail". (Ouch!) 8 The French again: there was a sort of wine cup known for long in Bordeaux a *coquetel*. It is said Lafayette's volunteers brought the recipe to the United States where it was Americanized to . . . you guess. 9 On Mississippi river-steamers, a successful gambler might call for a tub to be filled with a selection of every liquor in the bar, and glasses were used which were shaped roughly like a cock's breast, while the stirrer, obviously required to blend such a mixture, had a resemblance to tail feathers. The illustration to a ballad, *An American Cock-Tale* published in 1871, gives some credibility to this theory.

Cocktails

We are never going to know why this odd word became associated with a mixture of drinks or the addition of various ingredients with a spirit. "Cocktail" was used in approximately its modern connotation in an American magazine of 1806, and was so used in *Tom Brown's Schooldays* and by the novelist Thackeray. In 1862, Jerry Thomas published a "cocktail book", the *Bon Vivant's Guide, or How To Mix Drinks*. This was followed 20 years later by Harry Johnson's illustrated *Bartenders' Manual, or How To Mix Drinks of The Present Style:* was that word *present* a slight knock at Thomas's book as being out-of-date?

Cocktails were at that time often made before drinking outdoors, at shooting parties and the like. Authors like Thomas, Johnson and, later, Blunier in *The Barkeeper's Golden Book*, did not follow our current fashion of lumping nearly all short, and some long, mixed drinks as cocktails: they employed infinite sub-divisions—*Crustas, Daisies, Fixes, Shrubs, Smashes, Twists,* and so on. Only a few of the old-time names survive, outside highly professional circles, such as *Fizzes, Sours, Collins*. The term cocktail has become fairly all-embracing.

In the 1920s and early '30s, traditional recipes were varied by countless and many absurd additions and established drinks like the MANHATTAN (quoted by Harry Johnson) took on their modern form. Much of this extravagance was due to PROHIBITION in the U.S.A. and the need to hide and freeze the taste of hooch, "bath-tub gin", and adulterated good spirit, but it also fitted the ebullient years before the Great Depression (the "Cocktail Age") with, in England, its "Bright Young Things". Few of the ridulous concoctions of that period have survived, exept those enshrined in the pages of such a classic (recently republished) as *The Savoy Cocktail Book*. Many more are mercifully buried in the files of the United Kingdom Bartenders' Guild. Connoisseurs of exotica would find amusement in the now rare *Booth's Anthology of Cocktails*, which epitomized the current idolatry of celebrities (who were in those days not pop singers or fashion designers) linked with weird cocktail recipes. However, at "Sank roo doe noo" in Paris *(Harry's Bar)* this period gave us the lasting SIDECAR and WHITE LADY.

Typically, it was in a 1925 production of *Spring Cleaning* by that very fashionable playwright, Frederick Lonsdale, that a cocktail was first served on the stage. He just beat the rising young Noël Coward, who in the following year had four cocktails (plus ten glasses of champagne) served during his sensation-making *The Vortex*. Much later, cocktails were, of course, served in T. S. Eliot's *The Cocktail Party* although the favourite drink of the mysterious stranger was plain gin and water (no hang-overs for him!).

Today, people tend to say, at least in Britain, that cocktails are not much drunk. If one means on an American scale, this is certainly true, but the popularity of home bars and the steady demand for books about mixed drinks makes me believe that probably only excessive taxation of ingredients stops Britons from drinking as many cocktails, and as often, as Americans. In the U.S.A. around 50 cocktails are in regular demand. Contrary to popular belief, the COLLINS just beats the DRY MARTINI in the national popularity stakes, both for consumption in the home and away, followed by the SCREWDRIVER, MANHATTAN, SOUR, and OLD-FASHIONED. But regional preferences may be markedly different. Internationally, in cosmopolitan circles the Dry Martini is indubitably king of cocktails; perhaps it is the only truly global one. (I am naturally not including national mixed drinks such as France's vermouth/cassis as cocktails in this context).

Cocktails

Recipes For ease of reference, the most famous cocktails and mixed drinks are entered under their precise alphabetical placings. Those that are associated with a particular dominant base, gin, brandy, etc. are listed at the end of the appropriate sections; that is, there is a list of famous gin drinks at the end of the Gin (History) section, so that if you want a gin cocktail you may refer to the list and look up the recipe of any that take your fancy.

When I feel I have lived long enough I won't wait for illness. I'll take a long walk into the ocean—after cocktails of course.
George Sanders

COCKTAILS (Ready-mixed)

Commercial ready-mixed cocktails are far from a new idea. HEUBLEIN'S were selling them from Hartford, Connecticut, at the turn of the last century. While enjoying little status with serious 'mixologists', they are popular with some women and those who doubt their proficiency in running up cocktails, or are simply disinterested or idle. They have always been vastly more popular in America than Britain and have lately enjoyed a considerable vogue in the United States, particularly through supermarket sales. Individual-sized packs of pre-mixed cocktails are a sales growth item.

Though aesthetically displeasing to many, canned cocktails were an obvious development. Another modern notion (in the United States) is to have powdered mixes, such as *Whiskey Sour Mix* for the easy-making of cocktails by adding these flavourings to the hard liquor. I suppose this is a logical development of the vogue for "instant" powders. It reminds me of the cartoon showing a savage taking a tin from a shelf in his hut: it was labelled "Instant Man".

COCKTAIL SHAKERS

There are basically two types, the standard three-piece shaker, container, top with strainer, and cap, and the professional Boston two-piece, which breaks approximately in the middle and is used with a separate strainer. In the U.S.A. the lower half of a Boston shaker is often in glass, in Britain invariably in metal. Amateurs are advised to stick to the standard model, and unless you are very sure that it closes hermetically, wrap it in a napkin, or you may splutter your renowned *White Lady* over the boss's wife's best dress, which is liable to cast a slight aura of gloom on what looked like a promising evening.

Shakers are needed for cocktails containing heavy ingredients like cordials and liqueurs, or additives like egg, for which robust mixing is necessary. See Bar (Bar equipment).

COFFEY STILL See Patent Still.

COGNAC

This well-defined area of south-western France, to the north of Bordeaux, produces wines in themselves of no distinction but which distil into a brandy considered generally superior to all other grape brandies. The district of Cognac around the town of that name and Jarnac, is divided into zones of descending prestige: Grande Champagne, Petite Champagne, Borderies, Fins Bois, Bons Bois and Bois Ordinaries. "Fine Champagne", the term often found to describe good cognacs, is distilled from wine from both the Grande and Petite Champagne, with not less than 50 per cent of the former. But in France, simply *une fine* can mean any grape brandy; it need not necessarily be cognac.

These divisions originated from the joint visit to the area over a century ago by a geologist and a wine and spirit taster. One sampled the soil, and the other the wines and the spirits made from them. They discovered that those districts which the geologist said should, as the result of his analyses, produce

Plate 7. The rémuage process in making champagne involves turning the bottles to collect the sediment in the bottle necks. Later, the necks are frozen and the sediment is forced out.

Plate 8. These Heidsieck champagne cellars tunnelled in chalk stretch for eight miles below Rheims.

Plates 9 and 10. Overhauling and setting up the wine press takes place before the harvest. The press is one in the Cognac district of France. The vineyards throughout the Cognac area are cultivated by thousands of small farmers. The vineyard at which this picture was taken is owned by Jas. Hennessy & Co. Cognac is doubly distilled by the pot still process (see picture overleaf). The distiller stays by his still all night to make sure the process at no time ceases.

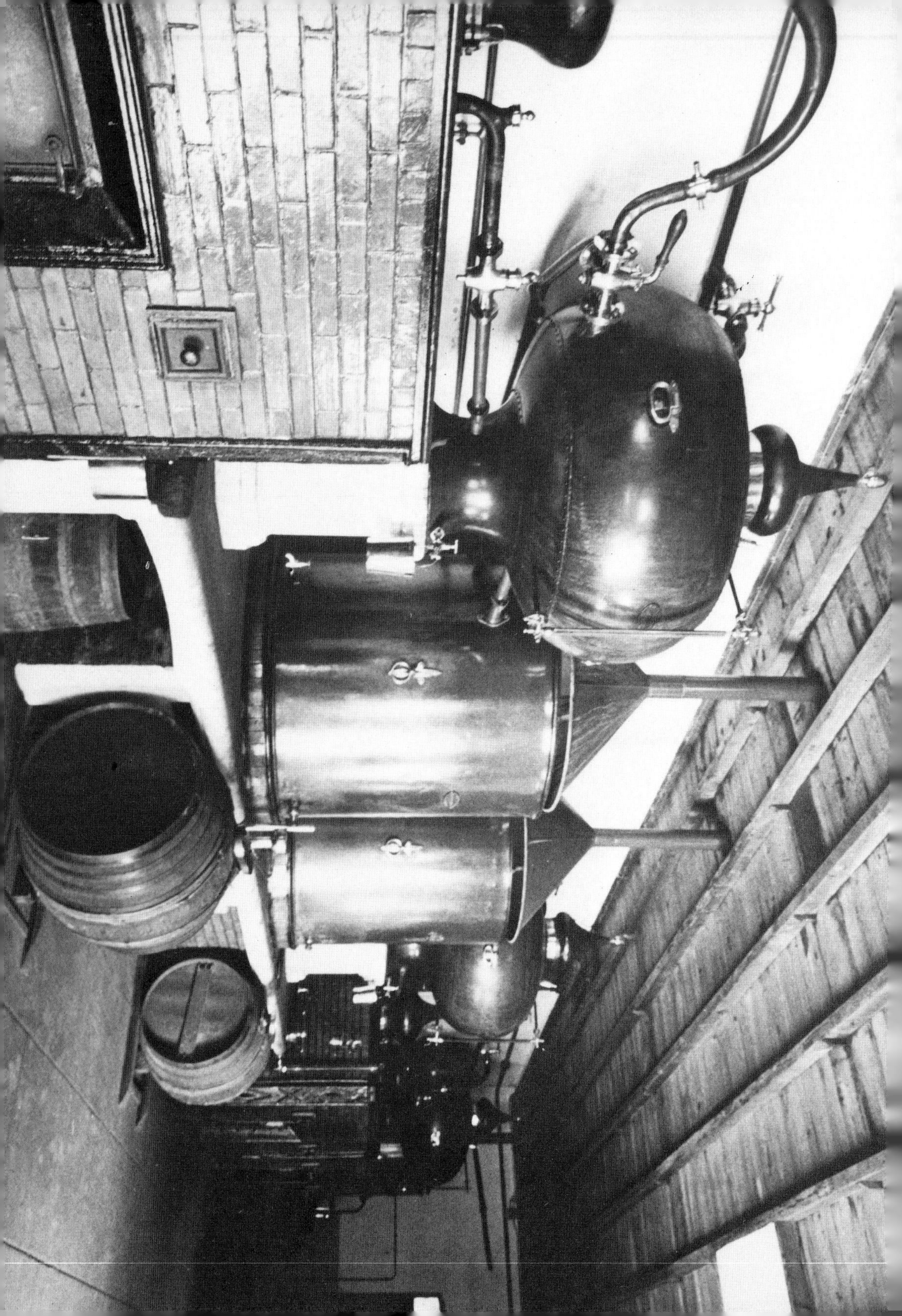

the best brandy, did in fact do so. Soil, plus something in the air borne from the sea, appeared to be the basic reason for the excellence of cognac.

Cognac is double-distilled very much in the same way as Scotch whisky and, like that, needs long maturing. The climate being on the dry side, evaporation in cask is serious: the "angels' share", as it is delightfully called, is greater than in Scotland. To continue the analogy with Scotch, cognac does not go on improving indefinitely in wood, though it may be kept longer than whisky; 50 years is the optimum.

Some very old and specially fine cognacs, having reached their limit of cask age, are transferred to glass vessels where no change in their character will take place. They can then be used for blending; a little very old cognac will make a lot of difference to a blend of younger spirit—just as a little old sherry will blend well with younger sherry.

True vintage cognac (known in the trade as "old landed") does exist but it is a costly rarity. In France a cognac may not be marketed under a vintage label. However, some English shippers will bring over a new cognac in cask and mature it in England. This will be the unblended brandy of a single distillation (the comparison with Scotch single malt whisky is inevitable). When bottled it should carry its vintage (of the wine from which it was made), area (probably Grande Champagne) and date of bottling.

But, to repeat, most cognac is blended; the average age being indicated in various ways with the commonest of which I have dealt under STARS; V.S.O; X.O. See also Napoleon brandy.

Three Star cognacs, and their equivalent under brand names, are suitable for brandy-and-soda/ginger ale and other mixed drinks, and it would not be desecration to use some V.S.O.P.s as a beverage with a little water. But the more expensive grades are obviously for post-prandial delectation. A small balloon glass is the ideal instrument, and the objectionable habit of some *sommeliers* in heating these (and using absurdly large balloons) is to be deprecated. The glass, containing cognac worthy of respect, should be gently warmed in the hand till it gives up its true aroma. Then it should be sipped and savoured very slowly. See also Brandy.

COINTREAU

Most famous of the *Triple Sec* curacaos, made in both France and the U.S.A. Delightful as a liqueur, or "on the rocks" at any time, it is part of the essential stock of a cocktail bar.

COLLINS

The most popular in the U.S.A. of all cocktails, which may surprise those who would have bet on the Dry Martini. It is said to have derived its name from John Collins, of Limmer's Hotel, Conduit Street, London, in the early Nineteenth Century, commemorated in the verse:

My name is John Collins, head waiter at Limmer's,
Corner of Conduit Street, Hanover Square.
My chief occupation is filling the brimmers
For all the young gentlemen frequenters there.

It is probable that one of the "brimmers" he served was what we would now call a SOUR, and in due course, through the use of OLD TOM gin, the *Tom Collins* was born.

With the virtual disappearance of this gin, there was a reversion to "John", though both titles are used today for the same drink. I opine that the correct usage is JOHN COLLINS for a Collins made with dry gin, and here with diffidence I must take a stand in opposition to the almost omniscient David A. Embury of the U.S.A. *(The Fine Art of Mixing Drinks)*, who maintains that a *John Collins* is made with Hollands gin. He says a *Tom Collins* is made with either *Old Tom* gin (hard to obtain) or London dry gin. He lists

Colombia

many *Collins*, amongst them, *Colonel Collins* (bourbon); *Mike Collins* (Irish whiskey); *Pedro Collins* (rum); *Sandy Collins* (Scotch).

To show how confusing the names of cocktails can be: a highly experienced bartender of my acquaintance in London had to admit defeat when asked for a *Peter Collins*. His bafflement proved equally astonishing to his customer, who explained that where he came from, in Australia, it was the usual name for a *Collins* made with whisky.

COLOMBIA

The republic produces annually some 600 million litres of beer (mainly lager style), 17 million litres of AGUARDIENTE and 10 million of rum, plus sundry amounts of BRANDY (the English word is used), gin, liqueurs, etc. Non-alcoholic effervescent drinks run somewhat below beer production. Wine production is not considerable. Rum and aniseed-based liqueurs, for which West Germany seems the best customer, are the main exports. Dutch-style gin is imported from Germany and the country is a good market for Scotch whisky. The liquor trade looks active, and the laws appear to be reasonably permissive.

COLOUR

If there were a demand for blue rum, this could be produced. The taste would be exactly the same. Distillates have no natural colour, and though some may acquire colour naturally, such as malt whisky long matured in sherry casks, where colour is required it must be added, the most common ingredient being CARAMEL. Some VERMOUTH also requires colouring.

Colour may be infused in various ways and may, unlike caramel, be part of the flavouring process, an exotic example being *Zubrowka* vodka. On the other hand, total lack of colour may be the requirement, as with most dry gin, except the unique Booth's.

Colour is largely a matter of fashion; we now drink paler brandy than our forbears, for example. I believe this achromatic era will give way sooner or later to one where flavoursome, well-coloured, "masculine" drinks oust anaemic, light ones.

COMBUSTION (Spontaneous)

It was a myth beloved by early temperance crusaders that heavy drinkers were liable to burst into flames either through the spontaneous combustion of the inflammable spirit in which they were soaked, or by exposure of their alcohol-drenched persons to naked flame. There are many "authentic" stories of such individual pyrotechnics, but despite these pretty legends no toper need fear such a fate for an instant.

COMPARISONS

METRICATION is apparently destined soon to tyrannize over the British potable field. The following extremely limited table gives an indication of how the traditional pint unit will fare.

Pint (Br.)	Fluid oz. (Br.)	Litres	Fl. oz. (U.S.)
1	20	.56	19.2
2 (1 quart)	40	1.13	38.4
Gallon (Br.)			Gallon (U.S.)
1	80	4.5	1.2

Since the U.S.A. and Britain do not use the same pint measure, it follows that their quarts vary. A quart is a regular spirit bottle in the U.S.A. and means a bottle holding 33.3 fluid ounces (Br.), a size unknown in Britain itself. A fifth (of a U.S. gallon) is the commonest spirit bottle in use, and fortunately this coincides precisely with the standard British spirit bottle of $26\frac{2}{3}$ fluid ounces (Br.).

PROOF causes a certain amount of confusion, largely owing to the separate methods of measuring used by Britain and the U.S.A. The table below gives the various equivalents in round figures of degrees proof for Britain and the United States, and in percentages of alchoholic content by volume for the GAY-LUSSAC system.

Proof (Br.)	Proof (U.S.)	Gay-Lussac
175	200	100%
100 (Proof)	114	57%
88	100 (Proof)	50%
85	98	49%
80	90	45%
75	86	43%
70	80	40%
65	74	37%

The most customary strength for spirits in the U.K. is 40% Gay-Lussac.

CONGENERICS (Congeners)
Materials, other than ethyl alcohol, found in spirits. They may be what gives a spirituous drink its characteristic quality, or they may consist of unspecified deleterious matter, the removal of which is desirable.

CONGO
The list of products handled by my local correspondent is of a sophistication that shows that at least in some places in the vast republic a high standard of living prevails. Everything is obtainable for those with the thirst and necessary cash. The most popular beverage is beer, both locally produced or imported, and there is little surprise in the fact that Scotch whisky (I understand Dewar's *White Label* is particularly esteemed) is the principal spirituous import. There appear to be no special aspects of licensing laws or drinking habits worth reporting.

COOPERAGE
In the brewing trade wooden casks have virtually disappeared in favour of bulk containers and metal pressurized kegs. However, the ancient art of the cooper finds vital expression in the production of fine wines and spirits. In Spain I have seen men in JEREZ still fashioning casks, from the sawing of the timber to the finished article, completely by hand with tools the shapes of which have hardly changed for a thousand years. I have also seen casks being made almost entirely by ingenious machines, needing little human skill (though that little very expert indeed).

I found a pleasing mixture of technical aids and supreme craftsmanship when I visited the cooperage of W. P. LOWRIE in Glasgow. Here entirely new casks are made from American oak; charred (an alarming process to the uninitiated, for it seems the casks will be burnt completely) and wine-treated with PAXARETE.

A seven-year apprenticeship is required before a man may become a cooper, and entry to the craft guild is severely regulated. Both as to manpower and raw materials there appears to be a more or less perpetually critical shortage, which fortunately has never yet developed into an insoluble crisis.

The wine trade is somewhat better placed than the Scotch whisky industry; except for fine wines, very large wine vats can be employed for maturing. Scotch whisky production needs those, too, but, for maturing, a vast number of butts are required. These may be newly charred casks, the much prized true sherry casks, or remade AMERICAN WHISKEY casks which arrive dismantled in the form of a number of component staves. (There is a danger that the advent of LIGHT WHISKEY in the U.S.A. may deprive Scotland of some important sources of casks).

Repair work occupies much coopering time: rarely does a whole cask reach the end of its natural life at one time; a few new staves, a fresh hoop here or there, and it is resurrected. It is not my intention to try to describe a cooper's work, but I assure readers that if they can obtain leave to visit a major cooperage they can hardly fail to be fascinated (and temporarily deafened!).

COOPERS' LIVERY COMPANY
We first hear of the cask-makers of the City of London organizing themselves in 1396, though they were not incorporated as a company till Henry VII recognized them in 1501. Like most livery companies they were founded both to prevent abuses in their craft and to perpetuate what we might now call lucrative "restrictive practices".

CORA
Italian aperitif firm; their *Cora* AMERICANO was recently introduced into Britain. It is excellent for those who do not wish to make up their own cocktail.

CORK
For the storage of wine in bottles no stopper can compete with natural cork. Until its general use was adopted around 1550 A.D., the keeping of wine in small quantities was hardly practicable, as wooden plugs or oil-soaked rag were the only stoppers available.

Until cork became widely available in the Seventeenth Century, natural sparkling wines like champagne could not be satisfactorily produced, nor could fine wines be left to mature in bottle. Before then, and from ancient times, bottles or similar articles were little more than handy containers (used rather as we might decanters) and wine was stored in *amphorae* or casks.

The world now uses some 300,000 tons of cork annually (the U.S. taking over half), not, of course, wholly for beverages. Spain alone has about 2 million acres of cork forests, other sources being southern France, Portugal, Italy and North Africa, and small areas of California, Brazil and Japan.

Cork is the bark of *Quercus suber*, the trees having a productive life of over a century. They yield comparatively little until over 50 years old, but in their prime a single tree may give 500 lbs. Climatic conditions affect the rate of bark growth, but within three years or less after stripping, a tree should be ready with another crop.

Ideal for wine, cork is less used for spirits today, as metal closures with neutral synthetic linings are better; a spirit bottle with a cork, if laid on its side for an unnaturally long time, can become slightly tainted through the action of alcohol on the stopper. That is why spirits are traditionally stored upright, while wine is stored lying down so that the cork may not dry out and admit air. Wines long in bottle, and vintage port wine, are sometimes given new corks and returned to the bin for further ageing. Plastic "corks" are now being used for some inexpensive wines that stay only a little time in bottle; they are quite satisfactory.

CORKED
The condition of a wine in a bottle where the cork has become infected through bacterial action or excessive bottle-life (French *bouchonné*). This occurs only in a minute proportion of vintage wines. A "corky" wine can make its malady abundantly clear. When you see an expert smell the cork from, say, a vintage claret, it is not wholly affectation: a good cork will give off no odour but that of its wine.

CORKSCREW
Widespread use of corks inevitably brought an instrument for removing them; first called a "bottle-screw". People have their own prejudices—I prefer a wine-butler's corkscrew, which works on a lever principle, and contains a knife for cutting round the capsule at the lip of the bottle. There are various patent corkscrews which remove stubborn corks with ease. The essential is that the cork be withdrawn smoothly, without, especially when vintage wines are being opened, disturbing the sediment, or breaking the cork. For champagne corks an additional tool may be required: champagne pliers to ease the occasional stubborn cork. The French boxwood corkscrews, including a

counter-screw, have much to recommend them. They have been copied in metal.

Where it is undesirable to touch the cork, experts may cut off the neck of the bottle below the cork with the use of red hot wire or pliers, but amateurs do not need to acquire this esoteric technique. Also for experts is an instrument that slips down opposite sides of the cork, grips it without piercing it, and pulls it out intact.

Two types of air-operated cork-removers are sold: with one you pump in the air which forces the cork out; in another model a "sparklet" compressed-air cylinder is used. There is no effect on the wine, though purists deplore this method, and should a bottle be cracked, the pressure can break it.

CORPSE REVIVER
An alleged HANG-OVER cure. There are sundry versions. This is the Savoy Hotel's: one measure each of cognac, *Fernet Branca* and white crème de menthe. Shake well with ice and strain into large cocktail glass.

CORTON See Burgundy.

CORUBA
An important rum on the British market.

COSSACK VODKA
A brand of English vodka introduced by D.C.L. in 1961, which has proved a great success. It is produced in the oldest-established spirit rectifying distillery in London and is marketed through Buchanan Booth's Agencies Ltd.

COTE
The side of a hill; the term is to be found in relation to many BURGUNDY wines or areas, thus *Côte d'Or,* and *Côte Rôtie* in the Rhône district.

COURAGE LTD. (formerly
Courage, Barclay & Simonds)
The four firms who have come together in the last decade to form the present Courage group, one of the great British brewing conglomerates, can each claim their own chapter in the history of the industry. All four companies were founded in the late Eighteenth Century; oddly enough, all within a decade.

Courage The first step in the setting up of the Courage group was the merger in 1955 of two famous London breweries, Courage & Company Limited and Barclay, Perkins & Company Limited.

In 1780 John Courage came to London from Aberdeen as agent for a shipping line. Breweries then were almost as thick on the ground as London thieves, and in 1787 he bought a small brewhouse on the south bank of the Thames, almost opposite the Tower of London. It cost him £615. He died ten years later, but his brewery lived on. Many other John Courages have since occupied the founder's chair and today the name is perpetuated in a brand of bottled beer that is famous throughout Southern England.

Barclay David Barclay, a banker, had entered the brewing industry a few years earlier. In 1781 he acquired, with his cousin Sylvanus Bevan, the Thrale brewery at Southwark, about a mile up the river from the Courage plant. James Boswell recorded the event in his writings on the exploits of his famous companion, Dr. Samuel Johnson. The gruff doctor, an old friend of the Thrale family, attended the sale. "He was", quotes Boswell, "bustling about like an Excise man, with ink horn and pen," and on being asked the value of the property, replied: "We are not here to sell a parcel of boilers and vats, but the potentiality of growing rich beyond the dreams of avarice". The brewery fetched £135,000, a great sum in those days. As far back as the late 1700s a brew called *Thrale's Intire* was highly respected in many parts of the world (see Russian stout).

Courage and Barclay In 1903 Courage ac-

Courage

quired their brewery at Alton in Hampshire, the water there being especially suitable for the brewing of pale ales, particularly *John Courage*. Like most other brewery companies, Courage, after the First World War, were seeking means of expansion and consolidation and increasing their output. In the years that followed they acquired interests in other brewery companies increasing the number of their tied houses to some 1,200 in an area covering Greater London, North Kent, Surrey, Berkshire and Hampshire.

Barclay Perkins were also expanding fast during this period and associated themselves with other breweries, and by 1955 their tied houses could be found in Greater London, Essex, Kent and Sussex. The merger of Courage and Barclay meant that the new company controlled some 2,500 tied houses as extensive free trade interests.

Simonds The House of Simonds was founded late in the Eighteenth Century by Mr. William Blackall Simonds, and as early as 1790 trade had increased to such an extent that the brewery had to be moved to a new site in Reading.

In 1815 the victory at Waterloo was toasted at Sandhurst Military Academy in Simonds beer, and the connection continued through the Crimean and Boer Wars and led to the establishment of Simonds branches in many parts of the world before N.A.A.F.I. (the British form of PX stores) came into existence.

In spite of great growth and activity on the home front, Simonds kept a firm hold on their bases on the battle fronts. After N.A.A.F.I. came on the scene the Simonds branch in Malta was merged into the firm of Simonds-Farsons-Cisk, with a brewery at Hamrun; a controlling interest was secured in Saccone & Speed in Gibraltar; and an interest was also obtained in East African breweries in Kenya.

In 1960, when Simonds joined the Courage and Barclay group, they controlled some 1,200 tied houses, hotels and catering establishments, as well as a chain of retail wine and spirit shops.

Bristol Brewery Georges In 1788, a year after John Courage invested his £615 in the overcrowded brewing industry in London, Philip George and six other notable Bristol merchants took a similar plunge in the West Country. The brewhouse they acquired had been built in the middle of the Eighteenth Century by a partnership headed by a Mr. Isaac Hobhouse, and history records that they made this investment from the profits of slave-trading, then still regarded by many as a respectable and very profitable activity.

During the early period trade was confined mainly to Bristol, with exports to Ireland and Liverpool, but the Irish trade was abandoned after a few years, because, it is recorded, "no one in Ireland ever seemed to pay their bills".

The most serious rival of Georges was Bristol United Breweries, and side by side with the Georges expansion Bristol United were acquiring other breweries in the West Country.

It was not until 1956, however, that the two south-western brewery giants finally got together, and when in that year the two companies merged they had a combined strength of some 1,450 tied houses.

In 1961 Bristol Brewery Georges & Co. Ltd. was welcomed into the Courage Barclay and Simonds fold, bringing the whole of the West Country into an operational area that already encompassed the central and eastern sections of Southern England.

See also Smith's (John).

COURVOISIER

This famous brand of cognac has an equally famous motto: "The brandy of Napoleon" (not to be confused with NAPOLEON BRANDY)—but why should a French product rejoice in an English description? The origin in anecdotal. The emperor, though abstemious, always had cognac with him on his campaigns, and perhaps found it comforted his notoriously weak stomach. After his abdication in 1815, Napoleon thought for a short time of leaving secretly for the United States, and Fouché, the minister of police, arranged to victual two ships.

Among the supplies was cognac provided by Emmanuel Courvoisier. Napoleon abandoned this project and decided to surrender to the English. He sailed for the Island of Aix, near Rochefort, to board the British man-of-war *Bellerophon*. His effects were so voluminous that a second ship was required to carry some of them. On these ships, and subsequently on H.M.S. *Northumberland* which took Napoleon to St. Helena, British officers had the opportunity to taste the special cognac which they dubbed: "the brandy of Napoleon". Courvoisier was subsequently appointed official supplier to Napoleon III. The company was taken over in 1963 by Hiram Walker.

CRABBIE'S

Well known in the industry for their Scotch, so far as the public is concerned Crabbie's *Green Ginger Wine* is their most celebrated product. To my taste it is the best of ginger wines.

CRACKLING

The English word for PETILLANT, more used in the U.S.A. than elsewhere.

CRADLE

A wine cradle, which is specially associated with claret and is sometimes understood as such, was used as an instrument for bringing aged wines from the cellar without disturbing the sediment; it was not a piece of equipment for serving the wine. Unfortunately, this is what it has become. Cradles have been elaborated and decorated out of all reason, and are widely used with wines that have no cause to throw a sediment. As to their use with old wines, while it is possible to let the bottle rest in them and expertly to withdraw the cork without shaking, it is extremely hard to pour without a rocking motion that will cloud the later glasses. Pretentious use of cradles is a curse of restaurant usage, and has recently become a form of domiciliary ostentation.

CRAWFORD'S WHISKY

The firm of A. & A. Crawford was established in 1860 at 8 Quality Lane, Leith, by the brothers Archibald and Aikman Crawford. On the death of the partners, Archibald and Aikman, in 1880 and 1885, respectively, the business was under the supervision of Mr. David Ireland who became the senior partner. Mr. Ireland was also entrusted with the training of Archie and Harry, sons of the original partners, who had by this time come into the business. It is Mr. Ireland's signature for the firm which appears on the *Three Star* label to-day. (*Crawford's Five Star* is a splendid "premium" Scotch). In the 1890s the young Crawfords were taking a bigger part in the business and extending the wine and spirit trade. It was probably about 1900 that the modern *Three Star* label was created.

After the First World War the business was really developed and *Crawford's* whisky became known in Britain, and established in world markets. In 1922 the firm moved to its present offices at 93 Constitution Street and David Ireland retired from the partnership, the firm being carried on by Archibald and Harry Crawford. In 1928 Mr. W. W. Winton was taken on as a partner; and by 1937 he was left as sole partner. In 1942 A. & A. Crawford became a limited company with the Winton family as directors, and in 1944 it was taken over by The Distillers Company Limited.

Today *Crawford's* is well known in such markets as France, Switzerland, Belgium, Holland, South Africa, United States, South

Cream Sherry

America and New Zealand. On the home market, sales of *Crawford's* have increased and today it is one of the top sellers in Scotland.

CREAM SHERRY
At its best this is Spanish oloroso, but the term may be equally applied to any sweet sherry.

CREME
There is a vast list of *crèmes*, more syrups than liqueurs, of which only *crème de cacao* is much seen outside France. Crème de menthe is, however, a true liqueur and may be fairly dry.

CROFT & CO.
The firm is nearly 300 years old and is noted for its vintage port. Also from Croft's comes a distinctive pale "cream" sherry called *Croft's Original*.

CROWN CORK
The most universal of closures consisting of a metal cap, enclosing a cork or plastic lining, which grips the lip of a bottle. It is most frequently used for soft drink and beer bottles. Though a familiar object to millions of people its origins are scarcely known. This beneficent invention was designed in its present form in 1891 by William Painter, an ingenious man of English descent, who lived in Baltimore, U.S.A. The British patent, granted the following year, illustrates a closure virtually indistinguishable from the one we know today. This was the final chapter in a long search, in the later stages of which Painter was active, for a practicable and cheap disposable stopper for bottles that protected the pouring surface.

The end of the Eighteenth Century saw the introduction of bottled beer and of soda-water on a commercial scale. The simple cork, which needed to be wired to the bottle, was the first solution, and survived into our own times with (in normal commerce) the regrettably defunct old-fashioned brewed ginger beer. Subsequently, umpteen designs were made for closures designed to have a life equal to that of the returnable bottles.

The system employing a durable glass ball, captive in the neck of the bottle, which gas pressure forced against a rubber washer, was invented by H. Codd in 1870. An objection to this application, which one does not have to be very old to remember, particularly in association with fizzy lemonade, was that the pouring edge was unprotected and the exposed washer a potential source of infection. Also, small boys liked to smash the bottle to obtain the "marble".

In 1888, W. J. King produced a captive closure with a lever, of which many forms subsequently came on to the market. The familiar loose screw top found its modern form with H. Barrett's patent of 1879. At the same time various systems were tried for keeping corks in bottles of gaseous fluids without wiring, but none was truly practicable, and in 1878 came the first forerunner of the crown cork which Painter finally perfected. Today, it has no real rival, though non-returnable bottles of mineral waters now tend to have screw-tops so they may be resealed if the contents are only partially used.

CRU
Literally "growth" in French, and a word that can be misleading and may be abused. Should denote a wine from a high-ranking vineyard. There has been much controversy on the *crus classés* (classified growths) of Bordeaux (see article on Bordeaux for this).

CRUST
The deposit that forms after long storage of red wines in bottles (principally port). Port is particularly prone to throw considerable crust, and this is considered a merit.

CRUSTED See Port.

Cyprus

CUBA LIBRE
Invented in Havana in the '30s when it was a tourist paradise for Americans; but the popularity of the drink has survived both right-wing and left-wing Cuban dictatorships. In a tall glass, over ice cubes pour generous measure rum; top with *Coca-Cola*; add slice of lemon.

CUCUMBER
This is an interesting variation on lemon rind or rounds in some long drinks: it is virtually essential in correct preparation of *Pimm's No. 1 Cup*.

CUP
Cups, difficult to define separately from PUNCH, will be found under appropriate main ingredient headings, CLARET CUP, etc.

CURACAO
Originally made on the Dutch island of that name in the West Indies from rum flavoured with a local type of orange. As *Triple Sec* it is manufactured widely, but its best form is Cointreau or *Grand Marnier*.

CURACAO (Netherlands Antilles)
This territory gave its name to that most versatile of cordial liqueurs, originally made from a light rum base and flavoured principally with a special type of local orange. Orange curacao finds proprietary form in Cointreau and *Grand Marnier*, these being based on cognac, and various firms put out *Triple Sec*, which is similar, though usually of lesser quality than proprietary brands.

Dutch beer (*Amstel*) is produced in the colony and is widely exported in the region, curacao liqueur having a considerably wider market. Very high proof rum is imported, mainly for making into liqueur; so is bottled beer from Holland and the ubiquitous Scotch whisky. Licensing regulations are liberal.

CUSENIER
French liqueur brand-name, particularly noted for its *Freezomint crème de menthe*.

CUTTY SARK
A leader of the "light" (light in colour) Scotch whiskies, and off and on the single biggest selling Scotch in the U.S.A., though far less prominent in the U.K. Owned by BERRY BROTHERS & RUDD, of London, and marketed in America by the Buckingham Corporation. There is a slight variation from the normal terminology in the instance of *Cutty Sark*, as it is correctly termed Scots whisky. See also McCallums.

CUVE CLOSE
The system employed in making various sparkling wines by which the secondary fermentation, which produces the effervescence, takes place not in bottle but in large pressure tanks. See Vin mousseux, Asti, etc.

CUVEE
The wine from the contents of a single vat. In champagne it may mean a special wine, but it is another word tending to mislead the unwary: *special cuvée* (a mixture of English and French is frequent in the wine industry) really means nothing unless allied to a reliable name.

CYPRUS
This is a wine country of great antiquity; Cyprus sherries have become a major export, and table wines, brandy and unfermented grape juice are also a major trade. Beer, brandy, wine and ouzo (*arak* to Turkish Cypriots) are the most common local drinks, with Scotch, vodka, dry gin, champagne and liqueurs being imported. Liquor is sold retail until 23.00 hours and bars can sell till 03.00 hours. Drinks are normally accompanied by a variety of *meze* (snacks) and, my

correspondent adds, "One might say that Cypriots drink for the sake of eating."

Wines The wine peculiar to the island is *Commandaria*, which is thought to be the oldest named wine still in commerce. *Commandaria* is dark, extremely sweet, and made from sun-dried grapes. It owes its name to the Commanders of the Knights Templar, to whom Richard Coeur de Lion gave the island in 1191. Its nearest Greek equivalent would be *Samos*. It is a fine dessert wine, though locally relished with pre-prandial snacks.

About a third of the population is concerned in the wine and related industries, and there is a considerable production of table wines of many varieties, the whites tending to be on the sweet side and the reds robust.

Cyprus is the third largest supplier of wine to Britain, largely in bulk for blending and bottling in the U.K., and is best known for its extremely successful fortified wines, which benefit from preferential Commonwealth tariffs and are thus competitive in price. Cyprus sherries are mainly on the sweetish side, corresponding to the taste in the mass market, though it is expected that superior types of dry Cyprus sherries will shortly be available (see Imported Wines Ltd.).

CZECHOSLOVAKIA
Beer is popular as one would expect in a country which produces the wonderful PILSNER URQUELL lager. *Schnapps* of various sorts are drunk, and excellent wines, particularly whites, are made, though the country is a net importer of wines from her Balkan neighbours and Russia. Imported liquors are largely confined to use by the tourist trade.

D

DAIQUIRI COCKTAIL
The finest of white rum cocktails, and one of my own favourite choices. It is said to take its name from the Daiquiri nickel mine in the Oriente province of Cuba. The manager once ran out of imported liquor, so his manservant made him up a mixture using Cuban rum (then of little except local repute), fresh lime juice, and sugar, all abundant in the vicinity.

Opinions differ on exactly how a *Daiquiri* should be made; my own version is 2 ozs. of white light rum; 1 oz. of fresh (unsweetened) lime juice; 1 oz. of grenadine. Shake; serve very cold. The same drink is sometimes called a "Bacardi", *Ron Bacardi White Label* rum then being absolutely mandatory.

In *The Fine Art of Mixing Drinks*, Mr. Embury gives both praise and space to the *Daiquiri*, of which the excellence is little appreciated in Britain owing to the difficulty in obtaining fresh LIME. He quoted slightly but distinctly different *Daiquiris*, as made in Cuba by the late Constante Ribalagua, known as *El Rey de los Coteleros*, the "Cocktail King", who is said in his career to have squeezed 80 million limes and made 10 million *Daiquiris*. Ribalagua used an electric blender, and strained very finely lest any ice chips get into the glass. Mr. Embury lists a further six variations, really too far removed to qualify as *Daiquiris*. The classic recipe should satisfy all but the most jaded palate.

It is permissible to make a *Daiquiri*, in Britain at least, with fresh lemon juice: double

Denmark

the amount you would use had you procured fresh limes.

DAISY
Virtually an archaic term for a long spirituous cold drink flavoured with fruit. It is made by filling a goblet with cracked ice. In shaker mix 1 oz. lemon juice, 2 ozs. preferred spirit, ½ oz. grenadine. Pour over ice, add soda, decorate with mint and fruit.

DAME-JEANNE
In France a large storage bottle, often wicker-covered. Called a "demi-john" in English.

DAO
Sound Portuguese red wines; also some white.

DAVENPORT'S
Important and exceptionally progressive Midlands brewery based on Birmingham, England.

D.C.L.
See The Distillers Company Ltd.

DECANTING, DECANTERS
Only certain wines positively require decanting—vintage or crusted port, and old vintage red wines that have been long in bottle. These also aesthetically need decanters of the correct type, stoppered in the instance of ports, but not necessarily so in the case of table wines that will shortly be consumed. The decanting of spirits is purely a decorative matter. So far as sherries are concerned it is a question of taste. There is a distinct danger from a social viewpoint that you may be thought to be giving a spurious wine a cut-glass cachet it does not deserve.

Where decanting is vinously essential, the operation should be conducted over a strong light, shining through the neck of the bottle so that one may perceive the point at which the undesirable sediment is about to arrive, then stop pouring. A clean wine funnel is an aid (it need not be a silver George II one) and in the case of the rarest old wines some experts would add a piece of fine muslin, to catch any odd bits or cork or other detritus, as an additional filtering agent. With careful cork-drawing, minimal disturbance and maximum care, I think this is unnecessary.

Decanters tend to discolour at the base. They may be cleansed with a mixture of vinegar and ammonia, rinsing out plenteously afterwards with hot water, of course.

DEGORGEMENT
The removal of sediment from the neck of a bottle during the making of CHAMPAGNE.

DE KUYPER
The famous Dutch "Geneva" gin, traditionally known from the shape of the bottle as *Old Square-face*. See also Cherry brandy.

DELAFORCE
Celebrated for vintage port and a powerful name in the industry.

DELAMAIN
A great name in cognac; shipped to England by Mentzendorff's.

DE-LUXE
One should learn how to treat this word, for it may be descriptive of superior quality; i.e., *Buchanan's (de-luxe) Scotch Whisky*. Or it may, since it is not a legal definition, be applied to quite ordinary potables which I cannot instance for obvious reasons.

DEMERARA See Rum Guyana.

DEMI-SEC
This literally translates as "semi-dry", but in fact on a bottle of sparkling wine it means that it is decidedly sweet: a typical example of the semantic confusion that has grown up in the wine trade.

DENMARK
A lot of excellent beer is produced and drunk, and CARLSBERG lager is a notable export. Akavit (aquavit) is popular, as in all Scandi-

Dent & Reuss

navian countries, and so is *Kijaffa* (which sounds as if it ought to have something to do with oranges, but is a cherry-flavoured cordial). *Cherry Heering* is another well-known export.

The principal imports are table wines and Scotch whisky which is normally drunk with soda-water. Taxes on potables are very high, with nearly 60 per cent purchase-tax on the wholesale price of alcoholic beverages; plus 10 per cent tax on retail prices and an 18 per cent restaurant and hotel tax. Licensing laws are sensible.

DENT & REUSS LTD.
I owe my introduction to POL ROGER champagne and HINE cognac to this company which, though now in the BULMER group, retains a family and City tradition.

DESSERT WINES
Sweet wines, fortified or not, often, but not always, drunk at the conclusion of meals or with ices, fruit, etc.

DEVENISH
The Devenish Weymouth Brewery was founded in 1742. It was purchased by William Devenish in 1824 from a John Flew and considerable additions were made to the property. The business prospered and expanded over the years and the growth enabled the firm to acquire other brewery businesses in the West of England. Horrell and Sons, Cider Mills, Stoke Canon, near Exeter, were acquired in 1957. This is a wholly owned subsidiary producing cider for the whole of the Devenish Group.

On Sunday, 11th August, 1940, the brewery offices, hop store, and brewer's laboratory were destroyed by enemy action, and the brewing room and coopering house severely damaged. Through the generosity and goodwill of the chairman and directors of Eldridge, Pope and Company and Messrs. John Groves and Sons, the company's houses were kept supplied until June 1942 when brewing was resumed.

On 7th May, 1941, the entire roof of the bottling stores was destroyed by incendiary bombs. The fire was prevented from spreading to the adjoining buildings by the efforts of Messrs. Groves' and Weymouth Town fire brigades, as a result of which bottling recommenced the following week.

In 1964 it was apparent that the public image of the group was confused, with various subsidiary company names still in use. There was no rationalization in the marketing of beers, label designs, etc. In 1965, therefore, the company name was changed to Devenish Weymouth Brewery Limited, the use of the name "Devenish" was established throughout the group, and a completely new image began to be presented.

J. A. Devenish and Company Limited remain the parent company, a public company with a London Stock Exchange quotation, and this controls the overall operation of the trading companies as outlined.

DEWAR & SONS LTD., JOHN
In 1846, Mr. John Dewar, no longer in the bloom of youth, opened an inconspicuous wine and spirit shop in the high street of Scotland's ancient city of Perth. Not until 14 years had passed and he, at the age of 50, had established a modest but sound reputation locally, did he look further afield and engage his first traveller. From such humble beginnings rose one of the greatest names in Scotch whisky, known today as *Dewar's* in Britain, and principally as Dewar's *White Label* overseas where it enjoys a huge success.

The dynastic operations which were to bring the House of Dewar to eminence commenced before John Dewar's death, in 1880, when his son, John Alexander, was admitted into the firm. A John Dewar, direct descendant, is active in the company today. Shortly afterwards T. R. (Tommy) Dewar, a younger brother of John, also joined the firm. By 1896 they decided that the distillery they rented at Tullymet, South Perthshire, was quite insufficient for their rapidly expanding business and they began to develop their distillery interests until they had acquired seven. The age of blended Scotch was commencing and the growth of the English market, for reasons I outline in the Scotch whisky entry, under way. It is worth noting that *Dewar's* was the first important Scotch to be sold in bottle.

The two Dewar brothers were men of outstanding ability in contrasting ways. John, later Lord Forteviot, was the administrator and organizing genius, and also made a mark in public service in Scotland and nationally. Tommy, who was elevated to the peerage as Lord Dewar, was more the extrovert, a great sportsman, wit, and a pioneer publicist. Both were Members of Parliament before their elevation to the House of Lords, John Dewar as a Scottish Liberal and his brother as a Conservative in London, a typical contrast.

Lord Dewar's interests ranged wide: he purchased the famous Raeburn portrait, *The MacNab*, in 1917, for the then very high price of 24,200 guineas. It hangs in Dewar House, Haymarket, London. He also bought the perhaps even more celebrated *Monarch of the Glen* by Landseer, probably the most reproduced of all Victorian pictures. One may be excused for thinking that these shrewd purchases did not exactly harm the Dewar image with the public. There are plenty of Londoners who will remember the first giant electrical mobile advertisement: Tommy Dewar had it erected across the Thames from the Victoria Embankment. It depicted a Highlander drinking his dram of Dewar's whisky. Under Lord Dewar's direction the famous *Spirit of his Ancestors* coloured advertisements were designed. They were published in the Press and they are still used overseas today, notably in France.

Dewar's de-luxe brand is the well-known *Ancestor*, a name taken directly from the advertising slogan. The models for the *Spirit of his Ancestors* picture were all Dewar employees. At the time of writing, one, Mr. Lawrie, was very much alive and had recently visited Dewar House in London.

By his ideas, personality and energy, Lord Dewar has been credited as being the man who did more than any other in putting blended Scotch whisky on the map in London, and throughout the world, though pretty forceful counter-claims could be made on behalf of some of his rivals. When he arrived in the South, the English were drinking gin, rum, brandy; when he died in 1930 Scotch was triumphant. After that there was a continuing story of success in Britain and many other countries, largely under family and family-selected men, later in association with D.C.L.

DIABETIC

Sugar-free and low-calorie mineral waters are increasingly available for diabetics, who should not take alcohol without doctor's advice or with very good knowledge of their condition. As to carbohydrates, the British Diabetic Association puts out a chart adapted from a Medical Research Council report, from which I cull some extracts, set out in the table below.

Fluid	*Carbohydrate* (approx. grams per ½-pint)
Brown ale (bottled)	8
Bitter beer	6
Pale ale (bottled)	6
Stout (bottled)	12
Extra stout	6
Dry cider	8
Sweet cider	12
Vintage cider	21

Diastase

Fluid	*Carbohydrate* (approx. grams per 3 fl. ozs.)
Port	10
Dry sherry	1
Sweet sherry	6
White wines:	
Champagne	1
Graves	3
Sauternes	5
Red table wines	trace
70° proof spirits	trace

Note The Australian Diabetic Association recently recommended that members who were permitted by their physicians to drink gin, should prefer Booth's *High & Dry* brand (produced in Australia), a spirit exceptionally light on added ingredients.

DIASTASE
This is about as technical as I will get. It is an enzyme (which, broadly, means a catalytic agent which changes the chemistry of something into something else). It forms in sprouting cereal and converts starch to sugar, to make ALCOHOL.

DIETING
It is not my intention to obtrude my own opinions into what may be considered purely medical fields. I have dealt briefly with CALORIES and CARBOHYDRATES for those who from inclination or necessity interest themselves in such matters. However, it does seem to me that people with weight problems (which can mean too little as well as too much) should not imagine prematurely that alcohol is the scapegoat, or the cure. There is little doubt that two persons may in practice react very differently to precisely the same drink, one finding it affects them adversely and the other the contrary.

Let us be more precise and, indeed, personal. With me, beer puts on bulk, with very little effect on my actual weight: it makes me measure more without being perceptibly heavier. Spirits, which some people consider fattening, I find not so at all; but with spirits it can well be the additives that cause the trouble. Those of us who fail to rejoice in a perfectly balanced metabolism should not look for facile second-hand answers to our dietary problems nor, without personally proven reasons, deny ourselves sensible spirituous sustenance.

DISTILLERS AGENCY LTD., THE (D.A.L.)
This company started life as the export department of The Distillers Company Ltd., when the latter company was first incorporated in 1877. But it was not until the early 1920s that D.C.L. absorbed other big Scotch whisky companies. At this stage it was decided to form a separate company to take over the blending and exporting business of The Distillers Company Ltd., and The Distillers Agency Ltd. was incorporated in 1924.

The newly formed company took over export marketing of KING GEORGE IV *Old Scotch Whisky* and *Highland Nectar Rare Old Scots Whisky*, which had been originally registered in the 1880s, and also placed KING GEORGE IV on the British market for the first time in 1924.

D.A.L. took over the blending and bottling establishment at South Queensferry, Edinburgh, which had a history of distilling and bottling dating back to the 1850s, and the premises were extended to compete with increasing business. Further plans for expansion were stopped by World War II. A disastrous fire in April 1949 completely destroyed the premises, and a fine new bottling and blending plant was erected and came into operation in September 1952. Even this was not big enough to cope with the increasing volume of business, and extensions were completed in 1967 to enable the company to compete in the ever-increasing bulk handling of whisky in casks.

DISTILLERS COMPANY LTD., THE (D.C.L.)

In 1877 the owners of six Scotch whisky distilleries combined to form The Distillers Company Limited, with a nominal capital of £2 million and registered offices at 12 Torphichen Street, Edinburgh. In the words of the prospectus issued three years later, when the shares were offered to the public, these firms were all old-established houses, several of them having been in existence for about a hundred years. They all possessed large connections, and carried on a highly prosperous trade. Their main object in amalgamating was to secure the benefits of combined experience and the advantage (which manufacturing and trading on a large scale alone can command) of reduced expenses.

Six years after the original merger, they were joined by a seventh company, which brought with it a London-based gin rectifying business. This modest stake in gin production was gradually strengthened over the years by the acquisition of further interests, and eventually by the establishment of gin distilleries in many overseas markets.

Meanwhile, between the two World Wars, some of the leading Scotch whisky blending houses had merged their interests in the enlarged group of The Distillers Company Limited. The D.C.L. group of companies has since continued to grow by expanding the sales of its many brands and developing interests in other industries. Its sales operations are carried on by a number of subsidiary companies which trade on a very large scale throughout the world. It is one of the largest commercial undertakings in the United Kingdom in terms both of total assets and total turnover, and the largest organization engaged in the production, marketing and export of Scotch whiskies.

DISTILLERS' LIVERY COMPANY

An institution of the City of London founded by Sir Theodore de Mayerne (see Rectification) to bring some order into a commerce then in little repute. It was granted a charter by Charles I, which was abrogated by Queen Anne, with unfortunate effects on the trade. This worshipful company took the first steps that were eventually to give the London gin-distilling industry a unique repute.

DISTILLING

That alcohol may be separated from the water in any fermented brew (wash) of vegetable matter, or from wine or other spirit-bearing beverages, was known in principle in many parts of the world long before the scientific principles governing the operation were understood. In modern terms, the whole concept is based on the fact that ALCOHOL boils at $78.3°$ C ($173°$ F) and water at $100°$ C ($212°$ F). Even a non-technically minded person may readily comprehend that if an alcohol-bearing liquor be heated in excess of $78°$ C but under $100°$ C, then the alcohol will be vaporized but not the water. Distilling consists in doing just that. The process then simply involves trapping the alcoholic steam, cooling it, and returning it to liquid form. I say "simply", but great expertize is required to obtain good distillations.

According to the method used and the degree of heat employed, the resultant spirit will be of higher or of lower spirituous content. At the same time, the spirit will have carried with it flavourings from the original mash which may be highly desirable, as in whisky or cognac, or they may be unwanted CONGENERS. The latter can be removed by redistillation, that is RECTIFICATION (e.g., gin), or by maturing in wood (e.g., whisky).

There are two types of still in general use today, the pot still (known as an *alembic* in most non-English-speaking countries) and the patent, or continuous still, invented in Scotland in 1826 and perfected by Aeneas Coffey who gave his name to it. The pot still, derived from the earliest types of distillation, is used to produce malt whiskies and cognac; the continuous still for grain or other spirits to be made into grain whiskies or to be used for, say, gin. However, in the case of the best of gins pot stills will probably be used for flavouring during rectification.

That spirit could be distilled from fermented matter was undoubtedly independently discovered (possibly by accident) in many parts of the world then totally out of touch with each other. When northern Europe was still barbaric, the Chinese were probably distilling from rice wine and by 800 B.C. distillation was being practised in the sub-continent of India and Japan. The Arabs were noted chemists and certainly had the secret at an early date. Distillation (from mead?) came to England around A.D. 1000, Ireland a century later, and some authorities place its introduction into Spain in A.D. 1200 (the Islamic Moors may have discouraged it); France in A.D. 1300; and Scotland in A.D. 1500.

But these dates are of doubtful significance, and by no means relate to the use of spirits as popular drinks in those countries nor to any particular degree of distilling expertize, though a fairly sophisticated still was illustrated in a German book of 1512. Primitive stills were discovered by explorers in places as far apart as Tibet, Peru and Tahiti.

DOG'S NOSE
Traditionally this is sweet stout with gin and nutmeg. In modern times it has become the name for a mixture of beer and gin: an offence against both ingredients.

DOMAINE
The (mainly) Burgundian equivalent of CHATEAU.

DOMECQ, PEDRO
One of the greatest names in sherry; I specially relish their very dry, pale *La Ina*. Their *Celebration Cream* is among the best in its class in the popular market, and their *Double Century* a highly reliable sherry in the medium-dry range.

DOMINICA (West Indies)
Local rum and imported Scotch are the most favoured drinks, plus beer, but the usual drinks are also imported. Import duties are high. There are virtually no restrictive licensing laws. Rum is far and away the leading drink, but none is exported.

DOP
A rough brandy of the MARC type once popular in South Africa, made from fermented residue of grape pressings.

DOSAGE
Part of the process of making CHAMPAGNE.

DOUBLE
The smallest measure in England with which a serious drinker need concern himself. Twice a SINGLE.

DOURO
The grapes for port are grown in a defined area in the hills surrounding the valley of the River Douro. The vineyards, on the steep hillsides, are terraced to conserve the soil from erosion. The vintage takes place at the *quintas* (wine estates) and the new wine is stored on the *quintas* until the following spring when it is racked and transferred to the wine lodges at Vila Nova de Gaia. See also Offley Forrester Ltd.; Port.

DOUX
Literally soft, but meaning very sweet as applied to some unimportant French wines, as opposed to fine sweet sauternes, etc.; and to some sickly VIN MOUSSEUX mercifully restricted to the domestic market.

Plate 11. After winding through the vineyards of northern Portugal, where the grapes for port are grown, the River Douro reaches the coast at Oporto, the outlet for shipping port to the rest of the world. The lodges where port is matured and blended are at Vila Nova de Gaia on the opposite side of the river facing the point in the foreground of the picture.

Plate 12. An habitué of bars and a connoisseur of cocktails, the author of *Drinks and Drinking* appreciates a Dry Martini made by Peter Burbridge, head bartender of the Britannia Hotel, Grosvenor Square, London.

Plates 13 and 14. Above: the hospice of St. Esprit at Beaune, built in the 1400s (see Beaune); below: an old wine press at Beaune.

Plate 15. The traditional cooper's tools illustrate the skill needed for this ancient craft. The implements shown are used in France for making cognac casks (see Cooperage).

DOW'S

One of the great names in VINTAGE port. A new style of port was recently introduced to the British market: *Dow's 1962 Reserve* (bottled 1969). This differs from vintage or vintage character port because it has been aged in cask six or seven years before bottling. It also differs from "tawny", a blend of several years, since it is a quality single-year-in-wood port. It is intended to offer Dow's *Reserve* in all good years; but to avoid confusion, never in years when Dow's declare a "vintage". Being matured in cask, the wine needs no decanting, and it is not intended it should be kept in bottle like a vintage port. Dow's is controlled in Portugal by Silva & Cosens Ltd., Oporto, and is handled in Britain by George Idle, Courtney & Co., London.

DRAFF

The residue of vegetable material from the MASH process of SCOTCH WHISKY distilling, the sale of which as cattle food is a valuable sideline.

DRAM

Colloquial Scottish term for a tot of Scotch whisky. "A wee dram" is often far from wee.

DRAMBUIE

The name derives from the Gaelic *an dram buidbeach*—the drink that satisfies. One of the most popular liqueurs in the world. Its legendary origin is the gift of the recipe for it from Bonnie Prince Charlie to the Mackinnon family for saving his life after the 1745 collapse of the Stuart cause. Traditionally the basic elixir is compounded by the head of the family who alone knows the secret. It is based on fine Scottish whiskies (I was surprised to see butts of 15-year-old malts when I visited the production plant near Edinburgh), honey and herbs.

DRIVING AND DRINKING

Each country has its own rules, ranging from the debatable severity of some to the highly permissive of others. I must be concerned mainly with those of Britain, where the permitted level of alcohol in the system of a driver who attracts the attention of the police through an accident or by a road rule infringement is 80 milligrams per 100 milli-litres of blood. This is around the middle in the international league table: a British compromise.

In an article in *The Sunday Telegraph*, Dr. Ronald C. Denney, lecturer in Analytical Chemistry at Woolwich Polytechnic, and author of *The Truth About Breath Tests*, was critical of current British practice, but he gave some incidental good advice for motorists which has some relevance in these pages. Partly to summarize: a motorist is best advised to take his breath test (should he think he is over the limit) at the police station rather than the kerbside; a request for a roadside test may only be made by a uniformed police officer; if he be hospitalized, as a hospital patient the motorist cannot be asked to take a test without consent of the doctor in charge; a blood or urine sample can only be requested if the test has shown the motorist is above the prescribed limit or has refused a test; a blood sample may only be taken by a qualified doctor; a proper legal warning must be given before a blood or urine sample is requested, and the person supplying such a sample is permitted to demand a sealed portion of the sample for private analysis if he so wishes.

For technical reasons, under the current law it is probably best to give a blood rather than a urine sample, though in fact most drivers opt for the latter. Dr. Denney also suggested, though there are other factors involved, that the "average" man (a theoretical entity) with reasonable legal impunity can consume during seven hours one whisky or one half-pint beer per hour (not exactly a riotous party). Two double whiskies or two pints within a "short time" will take him over the limit within a half-hour. Women's limit

Dry

is lower. Fat men can take marginally more than slim ones. Dr. Denney, and other independent authorities, are highly critical of details of present British legislation, both in relation to fairness to drivers and on other grounds. I have my own view. It is simply expressed as, "Don't drive—Drink"!

DRY
I have often been asked to define this word. I would say that it means a spirit that is light in flavour and completely lacking any taste of sweetness, but not necessarily colourless. In a wine it denotes absence of sweetness. But it must not be confused with sharpness or bitterness.

The generic term *London dry gin* does indeed, as far as quality brands are concerned, indicate an unsweetened gin though it may apply to one that is strongly flavoured. The issue is slightly confused by the French use of the word *sec* which in literal translation means dry but in practice denotes something quite different in wine, or in *triple sec* liqueur which is decidedly sweet. Three of the biggest selling medium-sweet sherries have *dry* in their brand names. Dry is a "selling word", carrying a smartish connotation, but it must not always be taken literally.

DRY FLY
One of the big-selling medium dry sherries, by Findlater Mackie Todd. Their premises at 92 Wigmore Street, London, are worth visiting to see the collection of wine bottles.

DRY MARTINI
There has been a certain amount of nonsense talked about the origins of this legendary cocktail. I will dispose of this right away. My friend J. Maxtone Graham has more than once gone into print with the explanation that it was invented around 1860 by Jerry Thomas, the Californian bartender who wrote the first of all cocktail recipe books. The tale goes that Jerry refreshed a traveller with a cocktail which he later codified as a dash of bitters, 2 dashes of maraschino, one ounce of *Old Tom* gin, a wineglass of vermouth and 2 small lumps of ice. All he could remember about the man for whom he first made it was that he was on his way to the town of Martinez. So he thus named the drink, and it was later corrupted to Martini.

Now, Jerry may indeed have invented a vermouth cocktail, but emphatically *not* a Dry Martini. Look at his ingredients. His vermouth would certainly have been sweet Italian vermouth at that time. Maraschino is hardly a dry liqueur, and *Old Tom* gin (no longer much made) was sweetened. It was a positively sickly cocktail that Jerry Thomas made. Right?

Now I have in my possession a tape recording made by my good friend James Porter. It records the voice of the famous Luigi, head bartender at the Savoia Majestic hotel in Genoa. Luigi gives what I am prepared to accept as the origin of the Dry Martini cocktail. Luigi went to the United States in 1912 (only by a freak of circumstance avoiding working his passage on the *Titanic*). He got a job with his fellow-countryman, Martini di Arma di Taggia, bartender at the fashionable Knickerbocker Hotel in New York City. Luigi recalls that his master was then making, indeed invented at the Knickerbocker, a cocktail which was named after him, and it consisted of dry gin and dry vermouth with a touch of orange bitters. This would certainly qualify as a Dry Martini, and in default of other entrants, I declare that Signor Martini, who retired in due course to his native land and is buried in Genoa, was the true and first mixer of a cocktail that was destined to sweep the world.

A customer for these early Dry Martinis was John D. Rockefeller the first, who must have enjoyed them for occasionally he left as much as 25 cents as a tip! Luigi recalls that the mixture was about half-and-half gin and

Dry Martini

vermouth (*Noilly Prat*), and in fact it is only comparatively recently that Dry Martinis have been made with the minute proportion of vermouth that is now fashionable.

At the height of the "Cocktail Age", the Dry Martini held its own against the many more complicated and frequently revolting mixes that proliferated (fortunately soon to expire) in the world's bars (or speakeasies). In 1928, at the smart casino at San Remo (is it possible that Signor Martini passed that way?) all Dry Martinis were being made with Martini dry vermouth, the first known special association of this famous product with the cocktail that many people think was named for it. This is understandable, if incorrect, for indeed there are today probably more Dry Martinis made with Martini dry vermouth than any other: personally I insist on it.

The Dry Martini is essentially an American cult, but its devotees are to be found everywhere that gracious living means something. Not that excessive addiction to Dry Martinis necessarily makes for gracious living. American columnist Bob Considine quoted the famous Toots Shor as condemning the drink as an "A-Bomb". Said Toots, speaking in his celebrated eatery: "A guy comes in here and he looks like he's fresh from taking his lessons as an altar-boy. He has one Martini and he wants to clean out the joint. A loving couple comes in; you never saw such a happy couple. Then the guy or the dame drinks a Martini and you've got to get the waiter to separate them". Mr. Considine ended his report by saying Toots offered him a drink. He asked for a Dry Martini. "Make it two", said Toots.

A good, large Dry Martini (there is no such thing as a small Dry Martini in my vocabulary) is strong and to be treated with respect. I have previously gone on record as saying "there is no such thing as one Dry Martini", but I do not really believe more than four are a good thing before dinner (or lunch). It is a very clean, appetite-provoking cocktail, and no two addicts totally agree on how it should be made.

I think you need a large mixing glass and plenty of ice; you need a very dry gin (I use *High & Dry*; in the United States I would opt for *House of Lords* or *Tanqueray*); Martini dry vermouth; a washed lemon; adequately large, stemmed glasses in the refrigerator. Whatever proportions of gin to vermouth you use, mix briskly and only sufficient for the number of drinks you intend pouring. Do not fill the glasses completely: you do not know how steady your guests' hands may be. A piece of rind pinched over the finished drink; not immersed. That is all there is to it. I do not go for olives.

There have been all sorts of variations: people have tried substitutes for vermouth—saké, Pernod, grenadine, dry sherry, orange juice, anchovies and even Chanel No. 5 are ones I have listed. That is not how to make a Dry Martini. Whether a *Martinisicle*—a Dry Martini deep frozen on a stick like a lollipop—is a cocktail at all is a matter of opinion. I opine that a Martini "on the rocks" qualifies, but there must be both gin and vermouth, in whatever amounts, before you are in the league. If you want to make a very dry Dry Martini try adding lots and lots of vermouth, which you must then throw out of the glass before adding the gin!

In *Fifty Years Decline and Fall of Hollywood*, Ezra Goodman wrote that when William Holden was less than a global star, but already pretty well known, he was the only film actor allowed by his then boss, teetotal Y. Frank Freeman, to have a bar in his dressing-room. Holden used to say to his stand-in (who rejoiced in the name of Sugar), "Warm up the ice cubes", which was the code for "mix me a drink". Holden once set fire to a Dry Martini (we do not know how) and dubbed it a "Hot Martini".

The Martini has given rise to a host of

Dry Martini

stories. I quoted several in my *Booth's Handbook of Cocktails and Mixed Drinks*, and do not intend to repeat them here, but I forgot the daddy of them all, of which there are several versions. Most readers will have heard it but it is worth recording. It is said that part of the survival kit of American flyers is a Dry Martini kit. One pilot had to bail out over the Sahara. There was nothing around him but miles of sand, and, as he awaited rescue, he unpacked his kit, prepared the dehydrated vermouth, the gin concentrate, the ice, and was about to mix himself a much needed morale booster, when a Bedouin popped up from behind a dune and said, "That's no way to make a Dry Martini".

It is strange that this is one field in which everyone considers himself an expert. Brian Page of London's superb Empress restaurant, told me of two allegedly smart devotees of the Dry Martini who gave him specific instructions, in itself not a bad idea if you do not know your bartender. One said, "Want it really dry—but dry; don't overdo the gin." The other insisted, "It can't be too dry for me. I like 'em as dry as can be. Be sure you use dry ice."

John Perosino of the May Fair Bar, London, recalled for me how two ladies, mother and daughter, came into his bar. They ordered and said father would be along and he would like a very dry Dry Martini. John made one (he is good) and when the man had finished it, he said he would have another, but drier. That was hardly possible, but John did the wave-the-vermouth-bottle-act when the shadow of it falls on the gin. Excellent, said the man, but he would like one more—and this time really dry. This nonplussed John, but he had a brainwave. Instead of leaving out the vermouth, he omitted the gin. "Now that's what I call a wonderful Martini," commented the customer. How can you win?

Speaking of professional bartenders, I find opinion about equally divided between those who think a classic Dry Martini should have a dash of orange bitters and those, like me, who consider this practice archaic: I have almost come to blows on the subject with my old friend Gerry Kelly of the splendid little *Vine* in Piccadilly Place, an olive's throw from Piccadilly Circus.

I was quite tickled by the tale of the man who ordered a Dry Martini in a bar where he was not known. Having finished the drink he ate the glass, except the stem. He had a replacement and repeated the performance. Another customer said, "I can't understand you leaving the stem; I think that's the best part".

A Martini to be worthy of the name must be made with the very finest Vermouth and positively sublime Gin. Otherwise it is a sell and a swindle and incompetent to set the mood for a meal.

Frederick Birmingham
in *The Esquire Drink Book*

DRY MONOPOLE
A fine *grande marque* champagne from HEIDSIECK & Co., founded in 1785.

DRY SACK
Probably the biggest-selling quality medium sherry sold in Britain, by WILLIAMS & HUMBERT.

DUBONNET
The very popular French aperitif made from sweetened fortified wine and sharpened with quinine. It comes in both red and white form.

DUFF GORDON
Celebrated name in sherry, notably *El Cid* amontillado; also Duff Gordon's *Cream Sherry*, notable for being bottled at the bodega in Jerez.

DUTCH GIN
This type, which is not only made and is popular in the NETHERLANDS but in several adjoining countries, is undoubtedly

much more akin to the first gins than is the comparatively light-flavoured London dry gin. It is usually based on a barley or maize grain spirit. This is rectified at a lower strength than is normal for London and flavoured with the essential juniper and other botanical ingredients, the taste being different too, and much stronger than, London gin. Dutch gin is essentially a schnapps, to be drunk cold and straight and it hardly lends itself to mixed drinks. Its devotees claim powerful medicinal merits for it. The best Netherlands varieties are of high quality as spirits. The principal brands known outside the Netherlands are BOLS in the stone bottle and DE KUYPER (*Old Square-face*).

Dutch (Geneva) gin is drunk in Quebec province, Canada, and in New Zealand for some reason, apart from Scandinavia in general, Belgium and Germany, and, naturally, those parts of the world where Dutch traditions are historically preserved. It was certainly made in New York when the Dutch ruled it as New Amsterdam, though for some reason this production has been largely referred to as whiskey. The popularity for Dutch gin in Britain has declined dramatically since the Second World War.

E

EAU DE VIE
Any spirit in France, but virtually meaning ones which have no special name nor distinction: strong, anonymous, rough distillations like the cheapest MARC. Some are pretty appalling and contribute much to the country's health bill: described as "water of life", they would be better dubbed *"eaux de mort"*.

EGG NOG
Combination of hot sugared spirit with an egg beaten into it. Made with wine or beer it is usually called a *Flip*.

EGGS
Whole eggs, or yolks, are quite often used to produce satisfying mixed drinks like NOGS. Egg whites are a feature of a number of cocktails. Ardent fans of mixed drinks may find it convenient to separate some egg whites, which will keep fresh a considerable time in bottle under refrigeration. Some professionals use dried powdered egg albumen.

EGYPT
In antiquity Egypt was renowned for her wines, but her modern wine industry is of quite recent origin, efforts only having been made in this century to recapture some of the ancient reputation. Despite the Islamic principles of the country, consumption of spirits, imported and domestic, is high—so is taxation. A crude, powerful molasses distillation, *tafia* (sometimes mixed with superior spirits, but more often drunk neat), is the drink of the masses. The rich prefer whisky and cognac.

EISWEIN (Ice wine)
TROCKENBEERENAUSLESE, but made from grapes picked while still frozen by the frost, and even sweeter. Occasionally made—some is thought to have been produced in 1969. It requires very long maturing to reach perfection, and is something of a rarity, including the price.

El Cid

EL CID (Amontillado)
Fine medium sherry from DUFF GORDON.

ENGLAND See Great Britain.

ENTRE-DEUX-MERS
Large wine-making area in the Bordeaux region producing a huge amount of ordinary table wines.

E.P.L.
"Excessive Product Loyalty", an expression coined by the author for a HANG-OVER.

EPLUCHAGE
The ancient practice, now reserved for a few great French wines, by which each bunch of grapes is examined and any grapes less than perfect are snipped off.

ETHIOPIA
Virtually the whole range of drinks is imported, and beer, wine, brandy and ouzo are produced in the country. Licensing of imports is fairly strict and duty runs at around £2 a bottle. In sophisticated circles international drinking customs prevail.

EVERARDS BREWERY
An important Midlands concern, based at Leicester where it owns around 130 public houses and numerous retail shops. Starting in 1849 as ale and porter brewers, the firm has been known under various titles, but has during four generations remained an Everard concern. In an age of conglomerates, this retention of personal family control makes for good beer, contented tenants and satisfied customers.

EXSHAW
Firm noted for exceptionally fine old cognac.

F

FACTORY HOUSE
The old, and still used, name of the headquarters of the British port industry in Oporto though it is more correctly called the British Association. Only wholly British-owned firms belong. The name stems from the time when British traders (factors) overseas established extra-territorial posts in various parts of the world, enjoying special privileges and monopolies.

FANTA
Claimed to be the world's largest-selling orange drink. Owned by Coca-Cola.

FEINTS
In distilling, the "rough" or uninteresting spirit, which it is not desirable should go into the final spirit. They are found in the second distillation of Scotch whisky, or the "heads" and "tails" of the redistilling (RECTIFICATION) of gin. Broadly, feints are the strong alcohol that comes off at the beginning of a run through the stills or weak alcohol that comes at the end. Feints need not be wasted; they are mixed with other spirit and water and rectified into pure alcohol.

FERMENTATION
The production of alcohol and carbon dioxide by the breaking down of sugar in a MASH of vegetable matter, the action being started by the natural yeast that forms on ripe grapes or by yeast purposely introduced.

FERNET BRANCA
Famous medicinal Italian proprietary bitters,

which some people actually like for the taste. Many more people dislike the flavour but believe firmly that it is good for HANGOVERS, on the assumption that the best medicines are the most unpleasant to take. I think its claims to soothe the stomach are well founded. Italians drink it as an aperitif.

FIASCO
1 Italian straw-covered bottles, much associated with chianti. 2 A disaster; i.e., a party where the drinks run out too early.

FILTERING
The filtering of wine is mainly done by highly sophisticated techniques though older methods of FINING persist for really good wine. It is an essential part of VERMOUTH manufacture, and spirits and beers are filtered before bottling. Modern filtering machines are often very large to cope with mass production.

FINE CHAMPAGNE See Cognac.

FINING
The clarification of wine, etc., by addition of a number of materials (finings) which will carry to the bottom of the vessel any particles that may remain suspended after maturing is completed. In the case of wine aged in bottle these particles remain, and others form, which is the sediment. Beer normally used to be delivered unfined, the landlord himself clarifying it, a part of the lost art of innkeeping since the introduction of PASTEURIZED beers. See Filtering.

FINLAND
This splendid country enjoys its liquor enormously, and has extremely tight licensing laws. For a long period, until abolition in 1932, Finland had total prohibition. I need hardly say that this laid the foundations for a major alcohol problem. After a period of chaos, in 1937, Oy Alkoholiliike Ab, which has been translated into English as "I Like Alcohol", was established and all private distilleries were absorbed into this state monopoly. Its constitution is not unlike that of some nationalized British boards (e.g., British Railways Board).

Alko, to give it its short name, is said to contribute some 7 per cent of the national revenue. It operates as a limited liability company and though all shares are held by the state, it is not necessarily subservient to government policy—within, of course, its constitution. Under this, Alko must divert a proportion of its revenue into temperance propaganda, placing it in the peculiar position of being forced to attack its source of profit. (However, this is no odder than American cigarette companies being obliged to preach the allegedly dire effects of smoking their wares).

Alko is extremely efficient, produces first-class spirits, and is a major manufacturer of industrial as well as potable alcohol. Through private-enterprise agencies, Alko imports, on an approved list, Scotch, gin, cognac, etc. Alko is a considerable customer for fine wines, of which the Finns are moderately fond, and which it is Alko's job to promote in preference to spirits.

I believe there is a mild move towards increasing their number, but when I was in Finland there were only 110 state liquor stores in the whole country, 30 in Helsinki. These stock, or will obtain, any liquor on the official list. Each drink has a number and it is by this —never by name—that brands are ordered. They are open from 10.00 hrs. to 17.00 hrs. and are wholly functional in atmosphere. No sales on Sundays or public holidays. The legal age for purchase is 21, which entitles one to a permit to buy alcohol, up to a limit of 2 litres a day. This seems adequate, but provision is made for extra purchases for special celebrations if the police authorize it. Helsinki residents may only buy in the store where they are registered; other Finns may buy in any

Fino

store. These are scattered on a pattern laid down over 30 years ago and leave some recently developed areas without a store. Only in the remotest parts may deliveries be made, or people buy more than their daily ration at one time.

The problem of alcoholism, which is fairly acute, is not helped by the absence of taverns. I have seen men come straight out of a liquor store, tear the top off a half-litre of vodka and start drinking it then and there, and public parks contain their quota of boozers. Unfortunately, there is really nowhere for them to go, except home. Outside a few luxury restaurants, and the handful of smart bars that were allowed to open in 1952 for the Olympic Games, and some licensed hotels, even with meals there is nowhere for the Finn to go for a quiet drink. According to my latest information, and I doubt if Alko has since been allowed to open any more restaurants itself or grant additional licences, there were only 250 public places of any type where, under any conditions, the consumption of alcohol is permitted.

FINO
Driest of the types of sherry.

FINSBURY DISTILLERY LTD., THE
Founded in the middle of the Eighteenth Century by the Bishop family in the CLERKENWELL district of London. It remains essentially a family business, though recently amalgamated with Matthew CLARK & Sons. The distillery's most celebrated product is STONE'S *Ginger Wine*, but they also make a range of British wines, including such long-esteemed bucolic beverages as cowslip and elderberry wines.

FIRKIN
A 9-gallon English beer BARREL.

FISH HOUSE PUNCH
This originated in Philadelphia in the Eighteenth Century and there are innumerable versions of it. Blend thoroughly 2 bottles of Jamaica rum, 1 bottle of brandy, $\frac{3}{4}$ lb. of brown sugar, 3 pints of water, 2 teaspoons of peach bitters (the more common orange bitters will do). Pour over a large block of ice in suitable bowl.

FIZZ
Archaic and rather non-U slang for champagne. See also Gin Fizz.

FLEISCHMANN
Well-known U.S. spirit company, influential in gin and whiskey, and major importers.

FLIP See Egg Nog.

FLUID OUNCE
In Britain, one ounce of clinically pure water at a temperature of 62° F (17° C) and an atmospheric pressure of 60 inches. A better description for our purposes is a "5-out", referred to towards the end of the Great Britain entry.

FLUTE
Short, stemmed, narrow glass from which good champagne should be drunk. The finest are absolutely plain and very thin; they should not be heavy and cut or decorated, though antique ones are often fluted. Rare, very old champagne flutes will be found frosted. This was because the original champagne had the natural effervescence all right—it also had the sediment. So it might have tasted alright but it looked awful. This is why other types of old glasses were coloured. See Glass.

FORTIFIED
Wines to which grape brandy, or other spirit, has been added. The most noted examples are PORT, SHERRY and MADEIRA, though there are numerous other localized types. One might include vermouth, despite controversy as to whether "manufactured" wine-based drinks are truly wines.

FOSTER'S
Best known of Australian LAGER, and sales

France

efforts are being made for it in the British market. It is made by Carlton & United Breweries, Melbourne, who control 10 breweries, export *Foster's* to 40 countries, are Australia's largest beer exporters, and make the country's only truly "national" beers.

FOUR ROSES
A big-selling blended AMERICAN WHISKEY (Seagram's).

FOX & CO. LTD., PERCY
Few firms can have had a stranger beginning than this one, whose founder, Percy Fox, took over an agency from someone he only glimpsed and all as the result of an advertisement in *The Times* of 1885.

The advertisement asked him to present himself to Monsieur Lanson, the grandfather of the present head of the firm, in Rheims, as an applicant for the agency in this country of LANSON champagne. After what must have been a mutually satisfactory interview he was given an address in the city of London, and advised to discuss the question of this agency with a gentleman who was at that time acting as distributor for the firm of Lanson. Arriving at the latter's office, he was shown into a waiting-room. The gentleman he was seeking looked in, and said he would receive Mr. Fox within a few minutes: but was heard going down the stairs a minute or two later. Whether he went home or left the country has never been known but the fact is he never came back. Thus the firm of Percy Fox came into existence, 78 years ago. Mr. Fox assumed the chair and re-engaged the secretary, and so started the connection which still remains between the two firms today.

Two other famous brands on the present list of this well-known agency are WARRE'S port and GARVEY'S *San Patricio* sherry.

FRAISE
Strawberry-flavoured cordial liqueur, not much seen outside France.

FRAMBOISE
A sweetish EAU DE VIE, flavoured with raspberries, worth drinking in France if the house recommends it as a speciality.

FRANCE
By the nature of this volume's title, this section must start with the rather lugubrious reflection that France appears an unhappy exception to the almost universal rule that alcohol as a national problem exists in inverse ratio to the repressiveness of the licensing laws. One can buy and consume wines and spirits in France at virtually any time local demand for them exists, which is accepted by the French as their right and particularly enjoyed by visitors from less permissive lands, who may never appreciate that beneath the Gallic culture and *joie-de-vivre* lurks a menace of sinister proportions. To state the simplest of figures, the French annual per capita consumption of *pure alcohol* is 28 litres, compared with 20 for Italy, 14 for Germany, 11 for Switzerland, 10 for the U.S.A., Britain, and Belgium, and 7 for Sweden.

Though 70 per cent of this national thirst is slaked with comparatively innocuous wine, this indicates an addiction to alcoholic beverages of dangerous dimensions. Nor do the French ignore the situation. Like most civilized countries, France has taken her problems concerning alcohol with a varying degree of seriousness. Libertarianism being a French tradition, there has been little resource to legislation on the sale of alcoholic beverages in the sense of licensing restrictions. Edicts against drunkenness there have been, and in recent times a prime minister tried to push milk in place of stronger stuff, and instituted spirit-less days. This failed.

In the last century the problem of alcoholism was appreciated, and Zola's brutal exposure of Parisian working-class inebriation (notably in *L'Assommoir*) troubled some consciences. Yet it has probably been more rural

France

than urban intoxication that has been France's prime evil, certainly since *absinthe* was outlawed. In wine-growing districts, rough wine is downed in stupendous quantities, and the long-established custom of allowing the smallholding vine-grower to distil, or have distilled for him, a quantity of very strong and inexpensive spirit for his own consumption, is a major source of endemic local addiction.

Cirrhosis of the liver alone causes the death of some 14,000 French citizens a year (ten times the British rate) according to French sources. However, the World Health Organisation in a 1969 report put the figure at 23,000, adding that for every death from this disease ten more people were treated for it in hospital, later to die from another cause possibly connected with it. The latest French figures at my disposal gave 25,334 as the number of admissions for alcoholism to psychiatric wards of state hospitals (not private treatments), some 40 per cent of all admissions. The number of alcoholics in France is estimated by the World Health Organisation as 4.5 million; a more conservative French figure is 2 million; 400,000 are women.

Adding the deaths officially listed as directly due to alcohol to a third of the 13,000 road accident fatalities (this being the proportion attributed to intoxication) the *Haute Comité d'Etude et d'Information sur l'Alcoholisme* recently gave as 50,000 the annual toll attributable to excessive use of alcohol. It compared this to the yearly annihilation of the inhabitants of a town the size of Vichy (an interesting simile since Vichy is noted for the salubrious state-owned spring waters that bear its name). The committee's publicity matter, including three pages of advertising in mass-circulation *Paris Match*, has rightly been addressed equally to men and women. The emphasis is wholly on moderation, not teetotalism. The French Academy of Medicine suggests three scales; one for men in sedentary occupations (7.5 centi-litres of pure alcohol per day); one for women (5 cl.); a third for outdoor manual workers (10 cl.).

In simple terms of wine (the *vin ordinaire* most commonly drunk in France) these amounts are broadly translated into three-quarters of a litre for men, half-a-litre for women and one litre for heavy workers. To allow people to judge their consumption, a fairly ingenious system of "cubes" has been introduced. For instance, what we might consider a substantial "double Scotch" rates 2 cubes, and so does a large glass of strong *vin ordinaire*, while a normal wineglass of fine wine rates 1 cube, as does a normal portion of aperitif wine. Broadly, a "cube" equals 1 cl.; thus the drinker is encouraged to adjust his daily "cubic capacity".

This seems a sensible approach to the problem. Its pragmatic reasonableness can hardly affect the addicted imbiber, nor will it stop the dangerous habit of the stiff early morning *eau-de-vie* which is one of the customs of French proletarian industrial life, but such a campaign could make intelligent people look at their own drinking habits. It has been noted that heavy drinking in France is climbing up the social ladder: no longer is it almost wholly a proletarian vice. The "cube system" may have an educational value, if it catches public imagination, yet it is not being unduly cynical to suggest that officially inspired propaganda is unlikely to make much long-term social impact—anywhere.

It is a pity that I have felt impelled to deal candidly with these unpleasant subjects, which seem incongruous when writing of a country whose contributions to good drinking have been unique, but it would be less than honest to do otherwise.

There are few more conservative and patriotic a people than the French, so there is one well-publicized phenomenon in connection with France and drinking on which I must touch—the Scotch whisky invasion. Until comparatively recently, the Frenchman

SOME FAMOUS FRENCH DRINKS AND WINE DISTRICTS

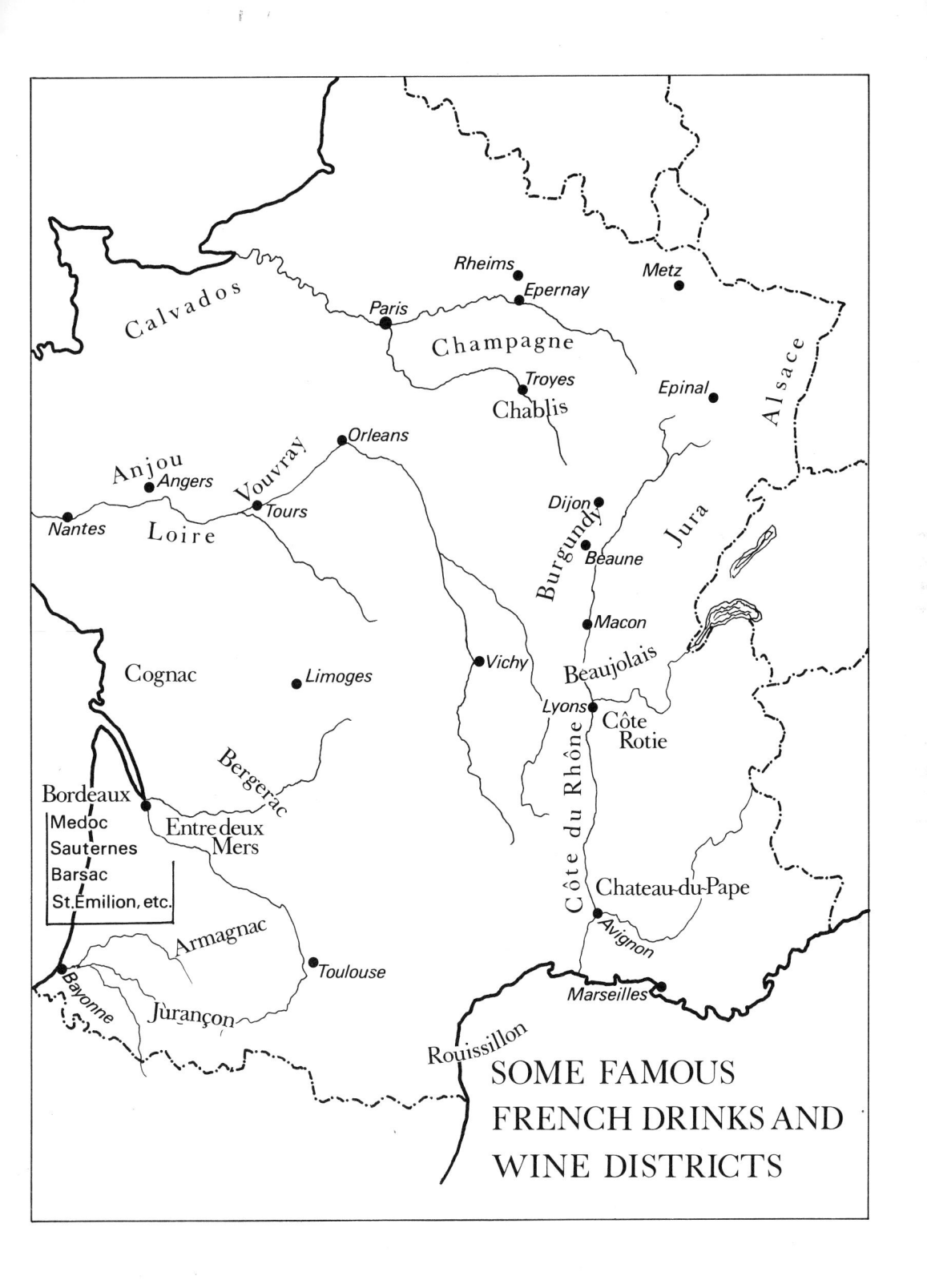

France

was almost totally impervious to foreign drinking fashions, content with his wines, his French beers, his liqueurs and vast range of spirits and aperitifs. (I do not consider the vogue for *Le Pub*, selling British beer at fantastic prices, to be more than ephemeral).

The ties between Scotland and France are traditionally of long-standing, but it is only recently that the French have taken with enthusiasm to drinking Scotch. It must be more than simple *snobbisme*, the sales are far too large (any figures I might now give would be wrong by the time you read them). Every *bistro* has its bottle of Scotch; in a comparatively humble roadside restaurant in the depths of the country I was faced with a choice of five brands. I believe France is now the second most important export market for Scotch. It outsells cognac in cognac's homeland. The French are known to cook *Homard Thermidor* with Scotch instead of brandy! I think they have simply acquired a taste for it, and perhaps the spread of drinking this pure matured spirit in place of some of their odder mixtures will have a beneficial effect on French livers.

Wine In the rather rudimentary manner which is acknowledged as typical of this volume's approach to the vast subject of wine, sections of varying length are dedicated to a superficial or more detailed examination (plus some personal observations) of ALSACE, BORDEAUX, BURGUNDY (including BEAUJOLAIS and RHONE), CHAMPAGNE, and LOIRE plus sundry cross-references.

The French produce, by general consent, probably the most and certainly the best wine in the world—though when it comes to supreme white wines the Germans have a considerable claim to pre-eminence. Yet the country's attitude to wine is ambivalent. The French are so proud of their wines that, to take one instance, army units passing the historic Clos Vougeot vineyard in Burgundy are required to salute the vines, yet on the other hand they drink as much awful wine as any people in the world and they are incontestably the largest wine consumers. I reckon that, apart from those engaged at the upper end of the wine trade, there are more Britons who truly appreciate and have knowledge of fine French wines than there are equivalent Frenchmen.

Except for the coastal north-western part and the high centre of the country, wine of sorts is produced virtually all over the country, some of it so poor that even the locals will not drink it and it is, as an agricultural support project, expensively turned into industrial alcohol. On the other hand, there can never be enough of the finest champagne or vintage first growth bordeaux. About a sixth of France's working force is employed directly, or indirectly (cooperage, distilling, glassware, etc.), in the wine industry.

FRAPPE
A drink frappé means that it is served with finely crushed ice (sometimes called snow); the best known frappé being with crème de menthe. It is not the same as GLACE.

FREE HOUSE
A PUBLIC HOUSE in Britain not controlled by a brewery.

FRUIT
Fruit, particularly citrus fruits, used in preparing drinks should be washed. Much fruit is sprayed with a preservative, *Dyphenil*, which, while innocuous, may impart unwanted flavour to delicate mixed drinks. Try to obtain fresh, untreated fruit.

FULLER, SMITH & TURNER LTD.
Any observant traveller between central London and Heathrow Airport may notice this company's premises at Chiswick—the Griffin Brewery. Their brewery house is the oldest in England. Some of their buildings

and cellars are of great antiquity, though the oldest actual relic, a leather sign "Griffin Hock Brewery", is dated 1745. This has no vinous origin, for hock in that connotation is of much later date. But it is an indication that brewing took place at Chiswick centuries before, for *hock* is an ancient English word for "harvest" (it was thus used by Chaucer). Presumably local harvesters, in the days when the area was utterly rustic, were regaled with ale brewed at Chiswick. *Fuller's Mild Ale* is still known as hock. Why a griffin insignia was first used by the brewery is obscure. Perhaps it has something to do with the fact that in the Seventeenth Century the property on which it stands was owned by the father of Matthias Mawson, a famous bishop of Ely. The diocese of Ely owns and has jurisdiction over a strange little enclave in the City of London, Ely Place, and the griffin is the badge of the City (far-fetched?).

In due course John B. Fuller, from a family of Wiltshire landowners came into the business by providing a much-needed loan. He eventually took over, and in 1845 brought into partnership Henry Smith, part-owner of Ind & Smith of Romford, and the latter's head brewer, John Turner. Thus the firm acquired its present title (of which there is a ribald and totally unjustified Cockney parody too vulgar to sully these chaste pages!). Ind & Smith became Ind & Coope (see Allied BREWERIES), and the two breweries carved up the London area between them so as not to tread on each other's toes. This continued until the rise of the tied-house system.

Fuller, Smith & Turner remain a small, highly efficient, independent concern, a rarity in London, with only a few pubs in the centre, the West being their special domain. They are notably popular with their tenants. Fuller's beers are first-class and in cold weather their unique *Winter Bitter* is something I particularly relish.

Under the direction of the late Charles Williams, ably succeeded by his son David, the company established a subsidiary, Griffin Catering. This forward-looking firm reconstructed a well-known West London hostelry, *The Master Robert*, and, without destroying it, established London's first, and still probably most comfortable, motel. Apart from other enterprises, Griffin Catering foresaw the changing pattern in pubs—the need to attract youth without antagonizing the mature. They successfully converted the *Red Lion* at Brentford—virtually on the site of Sir Felix Booth's distillery—to appeal to all ages. More particularly with the younger set in mind, though they do not lack older patrons, they opened "Country and Western" type bars, with appropriate and changing folk bands, one of the latest to open being the Nashville Room, carved out of a vast former "gin palace" in West London.

FUSEL OIL
The general term for some displeasing CONGENERICS that are found in distillations. These are removed by redistillation or, say, in the instance of whisky, they disappear during the essential process of maturing. Prior to 1915, maturing was not necessarily as complete as today, and fusel oil would sometimes accumulate mildly at the top of a bottle of whisky standing upright in store. Hence the habit of giving a bottle of whisky a couple of shakes before opening, which one still occasionally sees done, though it is nowadays quite superfluous.

G

GALE LISTER & CO.
Well-known Leeds firm owning hotels and restaurants; proprietors of BRONTE liqueur and the MALDANO products.

GALLIANO
Distinctive pale yellow liqueur from Italy; popular in the U.S.A.

GALLON
The British gallon equals 4.5 litres or 0.83389 American gallon. Put the other way round, there are 1.2 American gallons to each English one. See Proof (gallon); Wine (gallon).

GANCIA
One of the biggest exporters of ASTI spumante, and in Italy renowned for vermouth.

GARVEY
In 1780 William Garvey left Annagh Castle and the shores of his native Ireland for Spain, where he hoped to buy cattle. Whether he ever succeeded in buying his cattle is open to question, but we do know that in Spain he met and married a local girl, settled in Jerez, and founded a business which was quickly to become one of the world's greatest sherry houses. Today, over 180 years later, the House of Garvey is still a family concern and every shareholder a descendant of William Garvey.

It is interesting to note that Garvey was the first firm ever to export fino sherry from Jerez; Patrick Garvey, the founder's son, was the man responsible for this far-sighted decision. Today, of course, Garvey's reputation as shippers of sherry is unsurpassed and it is fitting that our gratitude to Patrick Garvey's courage, and indeed to his native land, is recalled in *San Patricio*, much admired by those who like a really dry sherry.

The bodega in which Garvey mature their fino *San Patricio* is the largest in Spain, a vast cathedral-like structure rising to a great height and able to house 10,000 butts with a total capacity of 5 million litres of sherry.

GAS CHROMATOGRAPH
An instrument which automatically analyzes the chemical content of samples submitted to it and records the results on charts. Thus, in a case of alleged SUBSTITUTION of, say, one spirit for another, the suspect spirit will show a different chemical pattern to that of the one it purports to be. In a British court of law in 1966 gas chromatography was successfully used by the Government chemist, at the request of the police and H. M. Customs, to prove that stolen gin had been bottled and sold under a famous brand name.

GASTON DE LAGRANGE
A fine cognac, in *Three Star* (in this instance a meaningful designation) and V.S.O.P. range, the reputation of which is certain when we know the brand is controlled by MARTINI & ROSSI. Not always available, but much worth remembering. See Stars.

GAUGER
Term for a customs officer, particularly in Scotland, who performs the technical work of measuring accurately the strength and content of casks.

GAY-LUSSAC, JOSEPH (1778-1850)
This French chemist contributed much to the wine and spirit industry, and not least of his achievements was the logical system, named after him, for establishing the al-

Germany

coholic strength of spirituous beverages. Unfortunately the British were wedded to their own PROOF spirit notions and too chauvinistic to adopt a Continental one. See also Hydrometer; Comparisons.

GENEVA See Dutch gin.

GENEVER (GENEVA) See Dutch gin.

GENTIANE

Aperitif liqueur based on alcohol and gentian root. The French *Suze* is the best known proprietary brand. Also distilled in Switzerland.

GERMANY

The country's great contribution to mankind's refreshment apart from its wine is, of course, beer. As far as exported German beer is concerned, *Lowenbrau* and *Holsten* must rate very high in any list. Dark and powerful Munich beer is perhaps best drunk from a stoneware flagon in a beer-cellar of the city of its origin.

After beer, the beverages in most general demand are brandy (German brandy is gaining a certain reputation overseas), Genever gin, wines and *Coca-Cola* and other soft drinks. Tonic-water is a comparative newcomer but seems to be making headway, to the benefit of sales of London dry gin. Almost needless to say, Scotch whisky is increasing its hold. Perhaps it would have been simpler in dealing with national habits if I only mentioned countries where Scotch is *not* growing in popularity! Cognac and vermouth are other major imports.

Apart from traditional exports, German sparkling wines (*sekt*) are doing well: those made by the champagne process are of high quality. "Schnapps" may be colloquially used to cover all straight spirits, particularly when they resemble whisky, dry gin, vodka, but are not necessarily the true product.

Wine It will be generally admitted that the principal wines of Germany are predominantly the white Rhine wines, numbering several of the greatest wines in the whole world. Fritz Hallgarten's *Rhineland, Wineland* is the ultimate authority, and I am humbled in writing about such wines to the extent that I shall do no more than outline certain outstanding points about them of which some features (BEERANAUSLESE, RHEINGAU, SEKT, MOSEL, NAHE, RUWER, SAAR, for instance) are elsewhere mentioned.

Virtually all German wine is white; the reds play almost no part in Germany's considerable wine export trade. The types principally known overseas are the Moselle wines, notably light and fragrant, and the wines of the RHEINGAU and RHEINHESSE; the Franconian and PALATINATE wines, which are mostly more robust, do not feature to anything like the same extent in export commerce. German wine laws are very strict. Names of wines are based on the localities whence they come; thus wine from Johannisberg is called *Johannisberger*. Invented brand names may not be used with names indicating place of origin, but may be used in conjunction with, say, LIEBFRAUMILCH which is not a place at all. As an indication of quality the grape variety from which the wine is made may be put on the label, such as RIESLING, SYLVANER or TRAMINER.

German wine is more costly to produce than the wine of neighbouring countries. Some vineyards are extremely small, and it is often these that produce the finest wines. The rarest of them are probably the most expensive wines in the world, such as the fabled EISWEIN. Points to remember: *Original* ... with various suffixes means a wine made and bottled by the vineyard-owner; CABINET (or *Kabinett*) indicates a specially selected wine; *Schlossabzug* is estate-bottled. German wine lore is possibly

THE WINE DISTRICTS OF WEST GERMANY

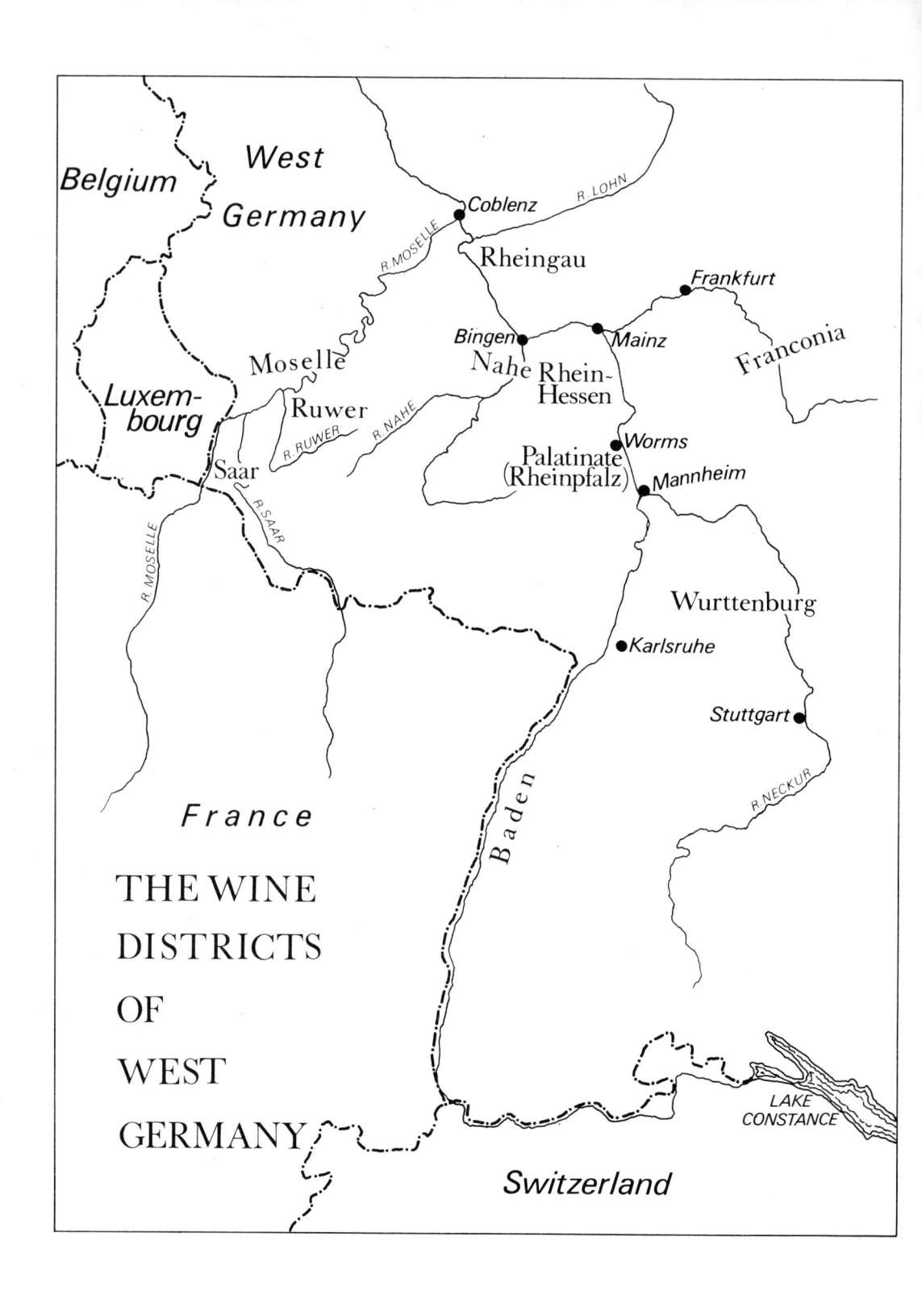

Plate 16. The picturesque region of the river Mosel is one of Germany's famous wine districts.

Plate 17. The Munich beer festival takes place in October each year.

Gin

harder to understand and more esoteric than French.

GEVREY-CHAMBERTIN
Notable BURGUNDY.

GIBSON
A Dry Martini with a pearl onion in it on a stick. This is said to have come about through a certain American ambassador named Gibson, who was teetotal. To avoid embarrassment at diplomatic cocktail parties, it is said that an ingenious aide suggested the envoy carry a glass of water in which an onion was placed, giving the impression that the envoy was in fact enjoying a version of the Dry Martini with his guests.

GILBEY'S
This is one of the famous English names in both the wine trade (notably port) and distilling. It is in the latter context that it has become especially well known to the general public in connection with gin—perhaps even more so overseas than in Britain.

Gilbey's started distilling gin in London in 1872. They now do so outside London, at Harlow. Their square, frosted bottle dates from American Prohibition days, when a great deal of fraud was practised by bootleggers, and the bottle was intended to make deception and imitation more difficult. They were pioneers of granting licences to make gin under their name to reputable firms overseas, and themselves have several foreign subsidiaries. They are now a cornerstone of I.D.V., within which their gin is probably the group's single largest selling international brand. (Within the International Distillers & Vintners group there are listed ten home or overseas companies containing the name Gilbey, which is why I have simplified the heading to this entry).

GILBEY VINTNERS Ltd.
A marketing rationalization of some of INTERNATIONAL DISTILLERS & VINTNERS' major interests. At its inception in 1970, it was estimated G. V. would have a yearly turnover of £50 million.

GILL
Quarter-pint; the measure upon which legal OPTIC and spirit-serving devices used in public places are based in Britain. Notices are required stating how many "out" of a gill is the standard measure of the house.

GIMLET
Invented by British colonial administrators in the Far East, and from its tangy taste named after the sharp carpenter's tool. Strictly, half-and-half dry gin and *Rose's* lime-juice cordial, but may be made with less lime. Shake well.

GIN FIZZ
One measure of dry gin, juice of half a large lemon, half tablespoon of powdered sugar. Shake well, strain into wine-glass and top with soda-water.

GINGER WINE See Crabbie's; Finsbury Distillery.

GIN (History)
Gin must have special interest for the social historian. No definitive work on this subject has been produced, in contrast to the vast bibliography of Scotch whisky, and it is not my intention here to remedy this deficiency. However, it is a subject meriting considerable space.

The tracing of its origins can be a trifle more precise than for the other great spirits of the world. Gin appears to have been first made around the middle of the Sixteenth Century at the medical faculty of the University of Leyden; and the "invention" is widely (but not unanimously) credited to one Sylvius. Certainly the Dutch were known for their experiments in distilling and had for some time been producing crude AQUAVITS. During times when the Low

Gin

Countries were a constant scene of battle, soldiers found these ardent spirits excellent before fighting, when even minor wounds were likely to cause lingering deaths. Since they were probably fighting for a cause of which they were ignorant against an enemy whom they had little reason to dislike except for being there their morale needed boosting. From these pre-battle potions stemmed the phrase "Dutch courage".

From its source, we gather that the new spirit, well refined in reasonably equipped laboratories and flavoured with the oil of juniper, long known for its therapeutic qualities, was first made as a medicine. See Gin (Medicinal). We must assume that being purer and more palatable than existing spirits, pioneer commercial distillers in the Netherlands copied this *eau de genièvre* (juniper) and it is likely—though much is conjecture at this stage—that the first to do so was Lucius BOLS whose distillery was established near Amsterdam in 1575. Corrupted to *Jenever* or *Genever* in the vernacular, this juniper-flavoured spirit soon became sufficiently well known in commerce to be brought into England. English distilling was at a primitive stage, for while the Scots and Irish relished their strong drams, the English were mainly drinkers of ale, wine, cider, or, for the rich, "brandywine" from the Continent.

However, production of GENEVA (or Hollands) started in ports such as Portsmouth, Plymouth, Bristol and London, where the demand was initially created by returning soldiers, sailors and traders who had enjoyed it in the Netherlands. It was considered a good "cure all", and not immediately as a social drink; headway was steady but not spectacular. Charles I granted the first charter to the DISTILLERS COMPANY, but these distillers were essentially medical practitioners, not concerned with wholesale manufacture. (Undoubtedly there was a lot of illicit distilling: there was to be a great deal more). When James II lost his throne in 1688, production of gin (the English edition of Geneva, later to gain global renown) was running at around half a million gallons.

Apart from the fact that James's departure for France rendered illegal the importation of French spirits, the advent of William of Orange brought in as monarch a king from the home of gin itself. This set a seal of patriotic approval on gin, and, as has been elsewhere remarked, to this combination of patriotism and inebriation the metropolitan masses, particularly in London, responded with alacrity and unbounded enthusiasm. The national thirst was also abetted by one of King William's first Acts, designed to encourage the use of home-grown grain for distilling spirits, which must have ensured support for the new sovereign from the landed gentry and yeoman farmers. A further purpose of the Act was to make the smuggling of French brandy less profitable.

Queen Anne gave further fillip to English distilling, but for some reason at the same time abrogated the charter of the Distillers Company who alone had the power, at least in London, to exercise some quality control. The results of such an inept governmental measure one would have thought foreseeable.

By 1727 gin consumption was running at 5 million gallons; six years later the London area alone produced 11 million gallons, and in the next decade this virtually doubled. These were simply the declared quantities: no one could compute how much more was illicitly distilled. When it is probable that properly declared and taxed gin was none too pure by today's standards, it seems likely that the illegal stuff would have been refused as undrinkable even by a modern "meths" drinker.

The aristocracy and gentry despised gin as a lower class intoxicant and preferred to

Gin

befuddle themselves on portwine, or smuggled cognac. It was an age of intemperance. But, as I have stated elsewhere: "During the considerable period when a large number of the labouring masses were apparently in a state of permanent intoxication, and their rulers steadily inebriated on costlier potables, these two social extremes—aided by a by no means abstemious commercial class, and with a hard-drinking literary and artistic coterie to record their prowess—were building up the greatest empire known to man. It does not seem that sobriety and national greatness are necessarily synonymous." The British are a comparatively temperate people nowadays, or is that just the result of taxation?

Gin was immensely popular. It provided quick oblivion for an urban proletariat whose conditions could hardly have been worse. Undoubtedly there was great abuse, but I feel that Parliament decided it must act less on social and humane grounds than through a long-standing idea of legislators the world over that there must be something inherently wrong with that which is popular. This peculiar notion is virtually universal and assails democratic and totalitarian regimes alike.

Perhaps the British Gin Acts of the first part of the Eighteenth Century were a reaction against the exceptional permissiveness of previous legislation. However, the mob had been encouraged to drink gin, had found it to their liking, and were now finding the powers-that-be—over whom they had no control except through civil insurrection —were taxing and discouraging their tipple. An early Act was quickly evaded, as were most of the Gin Acts, for it clearly defined what gin was in order to tax it. So the distillers stopped making gin and put out different, and presumably coarser, spirit which (not technically being gin) escaped the duty. This became known generally as *Parliamentary Brandy*, with scores of "brand names" to evade the Act: *Cuckold's Comfort, Last Shift, Ladies' Delight, Gripe Water*, etc.

At this time there were over 7,000 dram-shops in the cities of London and Westminster, wherein it was estimated that in one way or another one in five houses sold gin. It was quite customary to offer a dram of it, particularly to the ladies (early appreciators of gin), during a shopping transaction. It was sold by "barrow boys" and hawked door-to-door, and a "gin concession" in a prison was well worth having. Much quoted has been the sign on a grog-house in Southwark: "Drunk for a penny; dead drunk for tuppence; clean straw for nothing," and this was certainly typical of the attitude to strong drink and indicative of contemporary "public house" amenities.

It was the 1736 Gin Act that was the most concerted blow against the gin trade and one of the most ineffective pieces of social-fiscal legislation to date. It imposed a tax of £1 a gallon on gin, a retail licence of £50 and prohibited the sale of less than 2 gallons at a time. The idea was that cost plus quantity would put gin outside the scope of the poor. In effect it was a form of prohibition. Only two licences were applied for. The subterfuges previously used proved effective enough in keeping the populace supplied with "gin" and the next 15 years were to see the macabre gin era in its full flourishing.

The apex, or nadir—according to one's viewpoint—was reached in 1743 when a population of $6\frac{1}{4}$ millions drank over 18 million gallons of gin! And, of course, only a section of the English drank it. As was proved in the U.S.A. in our own times, try to prohibit liquor and you end by encouraging it. The fact that gin was largely illegal made it the more attractive and undoubtedly this fact alone caused some who would not otherwise have touched it to be tempted to try it, and possibly thus to

Gin

become addicted to it. Illicit gin-shops flourished, and though some 12,000 persons were found guilty, it was difficult to enforce fines: the prisons were too crowded anyway. Informers, who alone could provide evidence, tended to suffer mysterious and often fatal accidents. The law was brought into contempt, always a bad thing.

An infamous character of this time was Captain Dudley Bradstreet. After making good money as an informer, he appreciated that not only was the likelihood of his living to enjoy the loot diminishing with each fresh case, but there was more money on the other side, plus even a spurious popularity. So to quote the book he later wrote in ill-merited and prosperous retirement, *The Life and Uncommon Adventures of Captain Dudley Bradstreet* (1775): "Having got an acquaintance to take a house in Blue Anchor Alley ... I purchased in Moorfields the sign of a cat and had it nailed to a street window. I then caused a lead pipe, the small end about an inch, to be placed under the paw of the cat: the end that was inside had a funnel to it. I got up early next morning ... at last I heard the chink of money and a comfortable voice say: 'Puss, give me two pennyworth of gin'. I immediately put my mouth to the tube and bid them receive it from the pipe".

This pioneer "coin-up" machine garnered 200 guineas in a month. Moving around, a sort of mobile "speakeasy", Bradstreet made a fortune. A cat may have been used for Bradstreet's sign because OLD TOM was one of the names used to evade the Gin Act.

Such a failure was the 1736 Act that it was repealed in 1742. This did encourage reputable distillers of the time (Booth's alone remains in business) to produce good gin in opposition to the hooch in general commerce, but it did nothing to control excessive drinking.

Further Acts, in 1751 and 1756 were alike unsuccessful, and Hogarth could paint his celebrated *Gin Lane* as an all too valid commentary on the London scene. It was London that was the main gin-drinking and distilling scene, though it was also something of a menace in other cities. The countryside was mainly loyal to beer, ale and cider.

The Industrial Revolution was just around the corner. With sensational rapidity factories were flung up beside the canals, and to work in them people came in their thousands and then in their tens of thousands, fugitives from the picturesque poverty-stricken cottages. They came for the money and for the comfort of the "New Model Dwellings", where one did not share the space with farm animals and where, with luck, the roof never leaked at all. These back-to-back houses are, of course, the slums of our times which we are tearing down to erect on the sites the vertical slums of A.D. 2000.

In they flocked from the Dales, the Welsh mountains, the valleys of Ireland. They had a little more money, they worked hard in bad conditions, their expectation of life was just as low as ever, perhaps lower. One thing they did miss; the rustic tavern, the farmhouse ale, the simple bucolic pleasures and pastimes. It was not long, however, before their social activities gravitated to the street corners where those remarkable edifices grew up which were quickly, and for obvious reasons, to be known as "gin palaces". Easy for the rich to deride them. They offered often the sole refuge from an overcrowded home; they were a vast improvement on the sordid groggeries of yore, and soon they were to justify their title of "palace". The interiors had gaslights, mirrors and gleaming brass, and there was the pleasant barmaid, and the jolly publican, who was more important to the local resident than the mayor and only slightly less important than the pawnbroker and undertaker.

The young novelist Charles Dickens,

perhaps already obsessed with the joys of coaching inns he pictured so wonderfully that one doubts their existence, wrote scornfully of "gin palaces". Later his famous illustrator George Cruikshank, attacked them, and especially gin, with a vigour explained by the fact that he was a reformed boozer.

The fact that the urban populace were enjoying themselves in the "gin palaces"—which also sold much else—incensed the do-gooders, prodnoses and the temperance movement in general, supported by funds largely subscribed by the more puritanical elements among the new plutocracy. Gin was an easy item to single out among the increasingly catholic and bibulous repertoire of taste of the urban working class. It had the advantages of lending itself to caricature, a solidly bad reputation from the previous century, and, being a lower-class drink, to attack it was unlikely to upset the wealthy. Lord Byron ("gin and water is the source of all my inspiration") was not the sort of ally to help a product in England. He probably only made the remark in a mood of iconoclasm to annoy the conventional.

Gin was indeed to be found in homes of the gentry, for the delectation of their womenfolk. But the latter, delighting in euphemisms, would hardly refer openly to the spirit which they found salubrious and stimulating: it was called "white wine" in genteel circles, and there existed decanter labels inscribed with the word *Nig*. No incipient racialism this, but a means of avoiding the naughty word and, it is said, intended to deceive illiterate servants: it is sometimes erroneously quoted as being just back-slang, but had more than a lower-class connotation.

In an attack on the plethora of public houses springing up across the land, and in apparent disregard for the fact that a growing population required an increasing number of social resorts, in 1871 Mr. Gladstone, whose liberalism often displayed itself in peculiar ways, brought in a Bill which would have halved the pubs in England and Wales. It was not a popular measure. The House of Lords, then frequently the protectors of the common man against the follies of the House of Commons which nominally represented him, opposed the Bill. One bishop, certainly not a frequenter of "gin palaces", said the act was an iniquitous attack on civil liberty and he "would better see England free than England sober". This noble episcopal appeal was successful, and Gladstone withdrew the measure. Despite the fact that suffrage was by no means universal, his action did not save him from defeat at a general election three years later. Commenting on his failure at the polls, which he certainly did at some length, he mentioned, *inter alia*, that he had "been borne down in a torrent of gin".

Over the next three decades gin began to acquire a respectability to match its popularity and was to start crossing the social barriers. There were many reasons. "Unsweetened gin" began to make its appearance, a lighter more delicate spirit than the pungent distillations of the past and marking the final separation between London gin and its Dutch forbear. This unsweetened gin later became London dry gin. Gin was taken up by the Royal Navy, whose prestige was colossal. We do not quite know when naval officers started drinking PINK GIN. "Bitters" (ANGOSTURA) were originally a medicine, a specific for sundry fevers such as the Royal Navy might encounter on, say, the West Indian station. Since PLYMOUTH was, and is, a distilling centre, it is reasonable to assume that a puncheon of gin found its way aboard a man-of-war and that an officer of experimental turn of mind tried taking his bitters with gin, thus inventing a drink destined to go far outside service circles.

The successors to those inebriated ad-

Gin

venturers, soldiers and administrators, to whom earlier reference has been made in connection with the building up of the British Empire, in many places took quinine (also a compulsory Royal Navy medicament on certain parts of the African coast). This was later made up as *Indian Quinine Water*, and undoubtedly proconsuls found that this "tonic water" was more agreeable if London gin was added to it. Some of those who survived to retire to Cheltenham or Bath brought back the habit of drinking "gin and tonic-water", and if a former governor-general of "Gombo-Bomgo" knighted and well-to-do, drank gin, it ill-behoved any local stay-at-home tradesmen, or member of the landed gentry, to decry the habit, rather to emulate it.

As the railways pushed to the farthest corners of the United Kingdom, bringing untold benefits, the first of the truly grand hotels were built in the main cities. The St. Pancras Station Hotel, London, was the pride of them all though its fabulous interior now houses nothing more romantic than the offices of British Rail, inglorious bureaucratic progeny of the mighty independent lines of the past. These mighty edifices had great dining rooms, and, apart from using them when breaking the family's journey from York to Paris, Londoners actually took their wives to them for a dinner "out", instead of taking someone else's to older and more discreet establishments. Indubitably these lucky people (both the women and their escorts would have been the "trend-setters" of their time) would want a pre-prandial drink. American habits were fashionable, and American women more emancipated than English ones. Americans had long drunk sundry mixed drinks, indeed knew them as cocktails, while the English were much more conservative. So the English women would have been interested in American drinks, and in came the gin-and-Italian, for example. In the '80s, an American opened a bar near the Bank of England, specializing in mixed drinks—*Fogcutter*, *Gin Smash* and so on—quite new to London. While women would not have been served there, some men must certainly have introduced these drinks to wives and girl-friends, and since gin is particularly suitable for mixes, this would all have added to its acceptability. Additional encouragement came in the first decade of this century with London's first American bar, the *Criterion*, with a long list of gin drinks.

One indication of gin's comparative respectability by the end of the Nineteenth Century has been pointed out to me by Mr. Charles Miller of Morecambe, Lancashire, who found in his 1894 edition of Mrs. Beeton's famous book a "beverage" reference to two cocktails, a MINT JULEP and a GIN SLING. Mrs. Beeton would hardly have concerned herself with a totally disreputable product. A Victorian *Gin Twist* was equal parts of gin and water with sugar and lemon, and it was sufficiently well-known to be the source of an adage: "Truth should be like *Gin Twist*—half and half."

Oddly enough, one of the most famous of gin drinks did not have its origin in the home of COCKTAILS, the U.S.A., but in the last century in the home of dry gin, London. This was the JOHN COLLINS.

The First World War gave a tremendous boost towards the freeing of women from the social yoke of the past. In society, women led the "bright young things" of the Cocktail Age, drinking cocktails, mainly based on gin, of appalling complexity. The "Cocktail Age" was a stupid period, only affecting a handful of people with too much time and money and itself stemmed from the stupidity of U.S. Prohibition; but the "Cocktail Age" and Prohibition combined give the final seal of approval to gin.

After the "Cocktail Age" came World War

Gin

II, which for most people put paid temporarily to social drinking. With the return to normality, gin assumed the position of an international spirit of great purity; see Gin (Production). It was equally appreciated by men and women, mainly drunk in Britain with simple mineral additives, and in the U.S.A. in somewhat more varied mixes. Gin has been referred to as the "Cinderella spirit"—quite rightly. Once despised, gin has come from rags to riches, from pub to palace, from nonentity to notability, from pleb to peer.

Recipes in this book are being confined to "classics", ones of international repute. Gin is more associated with mixed drinks than any other spirit, so I feel obliged to itemize rather more recipes for drinks based on it than with any other spirit. See entries under the following: Bronx; Clover Club; Dry Martini, Gimlet; Gin Fizz; Gin Rickey; Gin Sling; Gin Sour; Horse's Neck; John Collins; Negroni; Pink Gin; Silver Streak; Singapore Gin Sling; White Lady.

GIN (Medicinal)

We are aware from the previous entry that gin had a medicinal start to life. There is no knowledge when the salubrity of the juniper berry's oil was discovered; long before the Dutch invention it had been compounded in France with wine, being known as "the wine of the poor". Obviously, the French poor knew a thing or two. Oil of juniper is a prime diuretic, relieving some disorders connected with acute acidity. It might be said that it is unnecessary to take alcohol with it; may be, but its far more pleasant that way.

To get the full therapeutic benefit of gin one should not, of course, take it with anything but pure water since pleasing additives may themselves be acid-causing. Not many people drink gin and water today; formerly it was a common drink. (It is sometimes taken with peppermint as a specific for indigestion).

However, I make bold to opine that the acquisition of a gin-and-water habit can bring considerable benefits to health, and, incidentally, to pocket. A near total devotion to *Booth's Gin* and water (*Malvern* water if available) has, with me, kept at bay, without further medication, a GOUT condition that was threatening to become chronic. (Gout is directly allied to acute acidity).

In passing we may note that at the beginning of the Nineteenth Century, the London Hospital started using gin in place of brandy; but this may have been out of patriotism as much as medicinal preference. A rather sombre association with gin is the cocktail known as the *Brompton* (presumably from Brompton Hospital, London), which is sometimes given to the fatally ill: it consists of gin, morphine and honey. It is sometimes lugubriously called the "terminal cocktail".

The *New Era Illustrated* in 1934, said, "Gin is recommended by many important physicians. It has very beneficial effects on disorders such as gout, rheumatism and any form of bladder or kidney complaints, and women have for many years appreciated the necessity of taking gin as a remedy for the minor ailments to which their sex is subject." But this sort of endorsement does not mean that anyone *seriously* ill should try to prescribe for themselves. One brand of gin was officially recommended recently, the only instance I know of this happening. See Diabetic (Note).

There is little doubt that gin (all brands of repute) is the only spirit in daily international use that contains an active medicinal additive: the restorative powers of others are not in dispute, but whisky, brandy, rum or vodka (the Russian and Polish types might claim beneficial herbal ingredients) do not have such additives.

Gin, probably "Geneva", played an unexpected role at the Battle of Waterloo.

Gin

During his famous march to support the Duke of Wellington, the Prussian Marshal Blücher was thrown from his horse: a massage of gin and onions revived him and he continued. I do not suppose the Iron Duke knew about this. But he may have had occasion to reflect on the qualities of the spirit when the London mob, angered by his opposition to the Reform Movement and certainly not a little excited by gin, summoned enough courage (Dutch variety) to break the windows of the town mansion of their former hero.

It has recently been suggested that a modicum of gin eases childbirth. And in the veterinary field, a dog breeder has recorded that one of his prize-winning show dogs would not mate until he received a double gin.

GIN (Production)

The late André Simon, who told me he did not like it, has described gin as "the purest of all spirits". I hold the *maestro* to have been correct when he wrote that, in the sense that gin (the best London dry variety) is the most highly rectified (redistilled) spirit in general commerce. It is, of course, flavoured, but this does not invalidate M. Simon's statement, since these additions are salubrious.

There are other ways of making "gin"—and some extraordinary "gins" are to be found (and should be avoided) in many countries. The following description of gin distilling will broadly cover London dry gins bearing the handful of truly famous brand-names. However, practice in the main gin distilleries does vary in detail. See also Dutch Gin.

An already carefully distilled and relatively pure GRAIN or CANE spirit (sometimes mixed together later) comes into the distillery at around 140° (U.K.) proof—about 80° per cent pure alcohol. Together with water (as in brewing, technically referred to as "liquor"), which reduces the spirit to some 100° proof, measured quantities (in the 2,500 gallon range) are put into flavouring pot-stills, together with carefully measured botanical ingredients: juniper, coriander, cassia, orris, etc. The first distillations are not of the highest quality, being excessively flavoured. These, the "heads" (feints) do not go into gin receivers but are directed into feints receivers. When the distiller in charge gauges, through "nosing" the spirit and reading the strength, and finds that the gin is of the correct standard, he directs the flow from the condensers into gin-receiving tanks.

In some distilleries, both flavouring stills and purely rectifying stills are used. The two types work in tandem, each flavouring still being linked to a rectifying one. The highly flavoured gin from the pot-still marries with the rectifying still, the flow from each being directed into a single receiving tank. Some hold that this refinement produces a superior gin.

Towards the end of the day's run through the stills, the spirit becomes weak in flavour and strength: eventually the still will contain no more alcohol, only water. This latter distillation, the "tails" (feints), is also directed into feints receivers. In due course, these feints will be run through a still reserved for this purpose, and the best part of this rectified spirit will be added to fresh spirit and go into gin. The finest gin rectification consists of taking only the best from each day's production, a continuous process of selection. (In lower quality gins, the presence of feints will make themselves apparent by a distinctive "pong").

In Britain, gin is rectified under duty-paid conditions, as distinct from Scotch whisky, and a great deal of money is tied up while the spirit is on the premises. While it is quite accurate to say that gin can be made in the morning and drunk in the afternoon, in effect this does not happen. Again to quote from the best practice; gin from several days distillations is distributed through a number of blending vessels and is agitated with compressed air, thus perfectly marrying the product of several days' runs through the stills. This is to ensure complete standardization of the blend in question.

The gin, which is now around the strength of the original spirit taken into the distillery, is moved in bulk to the bottling warehouse which is duty-free; thus the brand-owners get back the money paid out in duty, and will pay it out again when the gin is sold and despatched from the bonded warehouse. Before bottling, the gin is reduced to the required strength, which depends on the final market, and is filtered. Bottling and labelling procedure is similar to that for Scotch whisky.

GIN RICKEY
Over ice in tumbler pour 2 measures of dry gin, juice of half a fresh lime, teaspoon of grenadine syrup. Add the entire squeezed lime. Top with soda-water. (A *Rickey* may be made with any spirit, but gin is probably the best for it. Lemon is here not a really satisfactory substitute for lime). An excellent version may be made with SLOE GIN. See also Rickey.

GIN SLING
Juice of small lemon, heaped teaspoon of powdered sugar, 2 measures of dry gin, dash of Angostura. Mix in tumbler with ice, top with water.

GIN SOUR
Two measures of dry gin, one measure of lemon juice, teaspoon of powdered sugar, dash of orange bitters. Shake, strain into large cocktail glass. (Proportions are an individual matter. *Sours* may be made with any spirit, or served as a long drink by the addition of soda-water).

GLACE
A drink glacé means that it is very cold, by refrigeration or by addition of ice cubes ("on the rocks"); but this is not technically the same as FRAPPE.

GLASSES
Only in comparatively modern times has everyone taken to drinking from glass; ceramics, metal, leather, wood have been used much longer for containers. Gradually, a mystique grew up—part aesthetic, part whim of fashion—which resulted, not necessarily sensibly, in certain glasses being used for certain beverages.

At one time, Rhenish wines were often discoloured and contained bits of straw and other extraneous matter. It was pleasanter, therefore, to drink them, and many other unfiltered wines for that matter, in heavily cut coloured glasses. Hence the coloured modern "hock glass", which serves no purpose (unless decorative which many are not), and in fact hides the lovely modern Rhine wines' limpid beauty. Blue Bristol glasses served the same function. Engaging to the eye, I think them totally unsuited to appreciation of wine, which is partly visual.

The question of glasses for CHAMPAGNE I deal with separately. As with much wine lore, a great deal of nonsense is uttered about "correct" glasses. Any stemmed glass of adequate capacity, having a mildly tulip shape to conserve bouquet, is fine for red or white wine—to try to differentiate between a "claret glass" and a "burgundy glass" is pointless. The "hock glass", inconveniently long-stemmed, if uncoloured is a harmless affectation (the stem is only so you do not warm the wine by handling, an invitation to careless elbows). Cut glass can in itself be attractive (so is some of the finest Victorian moulded glass); it gives extra sparkle and can add grace to a traditional table setting. But give me a paper-thin "baccarat" glass,

Glasses

a thing of beauty in its shape, and never ornamented, and you have the ideal functional, yet superbly attractive, wine glass. Never fill a wine glass more than two-thirds full. Exaggeration of shape spoils some modern crystal of high quality in material and manufacture, but which appears to have been made to the design of a teetotal industrial designer.

Exaggeration has been marked in the case of brandy-snifters. What should be a logically-shaped bulbous glass, comfortably to be warmed in the hand, has often contracted elephantiasis and become a vast balloon, which demands enormous measures if the spirit is not simply to cling to its mountainous sides. At the other extreme, in pursuit of the desirable concentration of aroma, there are brandy-glasses the apertures of which defy one actually to drink the spirit without cutting the bridge of one's nose.

Apart from all-purpose wine glasses, the well-equipped household needs glasses for sherry or port, liqueur glasses (not excessively tiny), tall tumblers for long drinks, and cocktail glasses. Now it may be argued that cocktails are "fun" drinks, but really some glasses being used for them are absurd. As far as I am concerned, the end was reached when I was served a Dry Martini in a *square* glass! All too often, in places that should know better, a cocktail is served filled to the brim: not every cocktail-drinker's hand is that steady. And a habit has grown up of serving "king-size" cocktail in a saucer-type goblet, which may make it look bigger than it is, but certainly makes it harder to drink. A normally shaped 4-oz goblet is about right for a Dry Martini or a wine-goblet for a man's-sized one.

The dumpy "old-fashioned" tumbler is admirable for many drinks: I use it for many mixed drinks "on the rocks" or even for whisky or a gin-and-tonic. Squat old cut-glass whisky tumblers are lovely for that spirit, but the trouble is that a "double" does little more than wet the bottom of most of them. The stubby shortstemmed, tall, narrow-waisted "illusion" glass used in various sizes from "liqueur" to "schooner" is just about what its nickname indicates.

There is, of course, a fantastic range of professional glassware, for wine, beers, mixed drinks . . . you name it, someone has, or will, invent a special glass for serving it. I am on the side of clarity, simplicity and sanity.

GLAYVA
A $70°$ proof Scotch-based aromatic liqueur, from Edinburgh.

GLENFIDDICH
See Grant & Sons Ltd., Wm.

GLEN GRANT See Glenlivet.

GLENLEVEN SCOTCH
A fine vatted malt whisky from HAIG'S.

GLENLIVET
As may be read in the SCOTCH WHISKY section, George Smith of Glenlivet, Speyside, was the first man to have the temerity to take out a licence when in 1823 the Duke of Gordon promised Parliament that, in return for realistic regulations, he would bring order to the chaotic distilling business of Scotland. Smith was harried by the illicit distillers of the glen where it was thought 200 illegal stills operated. But he always carried two pistols and made it clear he would not be worried if he had to use them.

He prospered, his Highland malt whiskies becoming so famous that, when the situation settled down, many rivals wished to cash in on Glenlivet's reputation. This led to the Glenlivet Case of 1850, which established in law that only whisky produced in the parish of Glenlivet itself might be called *The Glenlivet*, but other distillers might use the word "Glenlivet" provided it was preceded by another name. Many distillers jumped on this bandwagon (and a few still quite legally do so) so that the Livet became known as the "longest glen in Scotland" (it is actually short).

None of this affected George Smith, who died in 1871 in his 80th year, with an estate of 20,000 acres and a reputation for making the finest malt in the Highlands. Following his son, a nephew, Colonel Smith Grant, came into control of the company. In 1953 the Smith of Glenlivet business amalgamated with that of Glen Grant (Glen Grant-Glenlivet Distillery), to become the Glenlivet-Glen Grant Distillery Co. Grant is a very common and honoured name on Speyside, and one must not, therefore, confuse the Grants mentioned here with the Grants of GLENFIDDICH.

The Glen Grant Distillery (there is geographically no such glen) was started in 1840 by John and James Grant, the prestigious word "Glenlivet" later being added to the distillery's title. *Glen Grant Malt* stands on its own feet beside *The Glenlivet*.

GLOGG
A Scandinavian winter drink, much used in Sweden. Simple version: bottle of medium-sweet sherry; 1 bottle of brandy; 3 ounces of powdered sugar; teaspoon of powdered cinnamon; 8 dashes of Angostura; half-bottle of red wine. Heat without boiling. In warmed mugs place a few raisins and an unsalted almond, and pour mixture on top.

GLUHWEIN See Mulled wine.

GOLDEN GUINEA
Sparkling French muscatel wine (made by the *methode champenoise*) from Saumur, and celebrated abroad years before the current fashion for similar wines.

GOLDWASSER
One does not see much of this liqueur, of ancient origin in Danzig, these days. Semi-dry, lemon flavoured, a feature is tiny flecks of gold dust in the bottle which, when shaken, rise and shine.

GOMME
French for heavy sugar syrup.

GONZALEZ BYASS
Producers of many notable sherries but specially famous for the internationally best-known very dry sherry TIO PEPE. Gonzalez Byass & Co. Ltd. is the largest vineyard owner in the sherry-producing area of Spain. The company owns 1,800 acres of vineyards and has over 9 million gallons of SHERRY maturing in the soleras of the firm's bodegas.

The enterprise was founded by Don Manuel Maria Gonzalez in 1835. Shortly after sherry exports to Britain expanded rapidly, and Mr. Robert Blake Byass became a partner in the firm with an office in London.

GORDON'S See Tanqueray, Gordon.

GOUT
Goût (taste) will often be seen on champagne bottles for the French market, less often overseas. *Goût anglais* (English), dry but not as dry as BRUT; *Goût américain* (American), slightly sweeter; *Goût français*, decidedly sweet. In some parts of France, rough EAU-DE-VIE is, presumably, with Gallic irony, referred to as *goût*.

GOUT
The tradition dies hard that this extremely painful complaint (probably the only one which induces hilarity in nonsufferers) is brought on by addiction, or parental addiction, to portwine. There has not been a great deal of research into gout, possibly due to the fact that while it is much commoner than most people suppose, it is not a killer, but there appears to be no real evidence that wine of any sort, or indeed, alcohol in any form, induces gout. Research in Spain

Graham & Co.

proved the contrary. However, there may be gouty subjects who find that certain alcohols, though much more often, certain foods, tend to trigger attacks. Having found the drug, and there are many, that best relieves or staves off gout, the sufferer may normally drink what he likes. The alternative, which I follow, is to go easy on drinks I find bring on my gout. See Gin (Medicinal).

Gout is an extremely personal complaint; no two persons appear to have it in the same way nor for the same causes, nor do they respond to the same medication. It is no respecter of classes, and it is entirely fallacious to think that only the rich and idle suffer from it; it is a prevalent cause of industrial absenteeism. There is a likelihood that heredity plays its part. Treatment today is pretty sure. In the past it must have been piling agony on agony to wrap the offending foot in a sort of poultice. Nothing could be more wrong. While the extremities, and particularly the big toe, are the areas mainly affected, gout in the nose and even the throat is not unknown. Nor, contrary to belief, are women unaffected though it is far less common with them than with men. See Salmon and Trout; Champagne (Digression).

Note Supporting the theory that alcohol is not in itself a prime cause of gout comes news that those living at the delightful Cotswold village of Bourton-on-the-Water are exceptionally prone to gout, and they attribute this to the hardness of the local water.

GRAHAM & CO., W. & J.

This is an old family firm with a long and interesting history connected with vintage port. The firm of William Graham & Co. was engaged in general trade in Glasgow from 1784 onwards, and the strong connection with port came about very much by chance. John Graham, a son of the founder of the firm, sent home from Oporto a large consignment of port which he had received in settlement of a bad debt. This was in the 1820s, and it was the first time a shipment of port had ever arrived in Glasgow. Up till then Leith had been the accepted centre for port, but *Graham's Port* caught on and the trade continued.

The port business was split off from the rest of the firm's general interests in the 1880s, and a separate company was formed. The business has always been managed by a Graham, and the present chairman, Gerard Graham, is a great grandson of the original William. The agents for the firm in England are Reid, Pye & Campbell.

GRAIN SPIRIT

Neutral alcohol from a cereal base, probably maize, but barley and others are used, such as is employed for making some gin, vodka, alcoholic cordials; and certain liqueurs, etc. It carries more prestige than CANE spirit, but at a sampling of good quality of both types which I attended, I unhesitatingly picked the "drier" spirit and, in my then ignorance, said it was obviously grain spirit. It was cane.

GRAIN WHISKY

Though all whisky is made from grain (principally barley), this means whisky, distilled mainly from maize, by PATENT STILL (continuous) distillation. The term applies almost exclusively to grain whisky made in Scotland (as opposed to grain NEUTRAL spirit made elsewhere) for eventual blending into brands of Scotch whisky. But apart from distilling grain whisky, Scottish grain distilleries produce a great deal of potable alcohol for other purposes.

Choice Old Cameron Brig is a mature straight grain Scotch sold in bottle.

GRAND MARNIER

By some standards a comparative newcomer

among liqueur brands but widely esteemed today; it is a type of CURACAO, based on fine cognac.

GRAND VIN
Literally "great wine" but much more likely to be seen on the label of an indifferent one. Without other more definite indications of origin and quality, such a phrase as *grand vin de Bourgogne* is meaningless.

GRANT & SONS LTD., WM.
William Grant pulled himself up by his own shoe laces. Humbly born in 1839, not until 1886 had he acquired enough money and expertize to set himself up as a Highland distiller, buying equipment for £120 from an old distillery and the next year founding Glenfiddich Distillery. *Glenfiddich* pure malt, or slightly older straight malt, are much relished by connoisseurs. In general commerce the firm's most celebrated product is Grant's *Standfast* (the name is based on the old battle-cry of the Grant clan) in its unusual triangular bottle. (This Grant company should not be confused with *Glen Grant*, see Glenlivet).

GRANTS OF ST. JAMES'S
See Allied Breweries.

GRAPEFRUIT
The rind may provide a slightly exotic variant to lemon. I have tried it squeezed over a Dry Martini; an offence to purists but a harmless and amusing change.

GRAPE JUICE
Pure pasteurized grape juice is available in an increasing number of brands and types and its use has much expanded in France recently. It is most useful in the preparation of NON-ALCOHOLIC mixes.

GRAPES
The fruit of the vine from which wine is fermented. The best grapes produce the best wine, and as in other things the smaller the quantity the greater the quality. Generally speaking vines which naturally produce small harvests yield the finest grapes for wine. All the parts of the grape (pulp, seed and skins) contribute to the quality of the wine. But it is important that the seeds should not be broken open during fermentation as this would be deleterious to the wine.

With certain exceptions white wines are made with white-skinned grapes, and the skins are removed at the beginning of the proceedings. Red wines are made from dark-skinned grapes, and the skins of these grapes are used to colour the wine.

There are literally hundreds of varieties and hybrids of grapes, and it is not within the compass of this book to examine them in detail. Any authoritative work on wine will provide you with this kind of information. Sometimes a wine is named after the grape from which it is made, e.g., RIESLING.

GRAPPA
Italian version of MARC.

GRAVES See Bordeaux.

GREAT BRITAIN
British laws concerning the sale and manufacture of alcoholic drinks have grown up over centuries, some statutes going back nearly 600 years still obtain, while others are as new as Parliament's last session. There is widespread demand, which it is singularly unlikely will be met, for a radical rethinking. The secretary of the London Central Board of the Licensed Victuallers' Protection Society has gone on record as saying the British retail liquor trade is "handicapped and harassed by legislation of a burden and complexity that has no parallel in any other walk of life".

Although many of the regulations covering the *manufacture* of alcohol have remained unaltered for centuries, regardless of changing techniques, H. M. Customs and Excise

Great Britain

do try to interpret them with commonsense. By no means is this the case with laws affecting the licensing of premises for the sale of intoxicants. This is not necessarily to blame the law enforcement officials; *Patterson's*, the definitive legal tome on licensing legislation, needs over 1,600 pages and a vast index to try and explain all the complexities to trained lawyers. What hope for the licensee or simple consumer?

For the guidance of visitors to the United Kingdom, it may in outline be said that one can purchase strong drinks in authorized places between 11.00 hours and 15.00 hours and about 17.30 hours to 23.00 hours; Sundays (if at all) 12.00 hours to 14.00 hours and 19.00 hours to 22.30 hours. But these represent about the most liberal regulations. There are many variations from one place to another. Outside major urban areas, a considerably earlier morning opening often pertains, for the law was made when a farm labourer, after working since sun-up in the fields, might want to break for a flagon of ale.

Thus it comes to pass that the old country inn that has been transmogrified into a sophisticated country hotel and restaurant must open its bars at the unholy hour of 10.00 hours, and stop sales of intoxicants sharp at 14.00 hours, just when some of its clients are starting lunch. One could list indefinitely anachronisms and absurdities, which serve no useful purpose, in no way reduce real or imagined abuses, confuse visitors, bedevil an important trade, annoy the general law-abiding public, disturb the police in more vital functions, and tend to breed evasion and contempt for the law.

A post-war socialist home secretary, to his credit since he was an abstainer, removed certain legal vagaries (particularly concerning London). As a result, to give one example, such ridiculous if delicious peculiarities as the following were obviated.

Previously, "permitted hours" in Chelsea, ended at 22.30 hours, while adjacent Westminster enjoyed an extra half-hour. This caused a stampede across the dividing line around the magic hour, and in the case of one tavern in Sloane Street, the saloon bar was in Chelsea but the public bar in Westminster! At the same time hours for consuming alcohol in restaurants and clubs with music and dancing were extended to 02.30 hours. But that became the final hour, and a gloriously British legal quibble "the bottle party" (clubs lawfully staying open all night) disappeared, with a depressant effect on "London After Dark".

More recently club law, which is a separate aspect of British licensing confusion, was revised and complicated, making it harder for holiday-makers or other celebrants to obtain liquor in the afternoon and giving impetus to illegal dives.

Another fairly recent change in the law made it legal to take away liquor from a licensed shop during normal store hours, where previously that could only be done during the "permitted hours" of the locality. Prior to the change, at other times one had to have the goods delivered, and no one could define "delivery". Did it mean to one's home or to one's car?

The granting of liquor licences rests with licensing justices, making for vast localized differences between liberalism and harshness. There are two basic types of licence, "on" for bars, and "off" for stores, most public houses being licensed for both "on and off" sales. Liquor may not be consumed in a shop or store having only an "off" licence. New licences in either category are obtained with difficulty, except in the case of adequately equipped restaurants, which may receive a conditional "on" licence, that is, drinks are only for customers eating there. A "beer and wine" licence does not give the right to sell spirits.

Great Britain

A feature of the British wine and spirit trade has been the development of self-service, or self-selection, through the increasing grant of liquor licences to supermarkets. There has been considerable opposition from existing outlets, but this appears to be less effective than previously. At the same time there has been massive reorganization of formerly traditional off-licence stores. The number of lines stocked has been drastically rationalized (i.e. reduced), in many instances self-service and "own brands" have been introduced, and there is a fierce price war. However, well-run individual off-licence stores, giving superior service, continue to prosper despite mainly higher prices. Delivery of small orders and credit facilities are their attraction. Nor have all the personal, often family, wine and spirit retail businesses disappeared though many have a hard fight: they must finance big stocks since to offer a large choice is part of their edge over the mass trade.

On the wholesale side, "cash-and-carry" warehouses proliferate; extremely active is the Trademarkets consortium. They buy in large quantities to gain maximum rebates and can undercut the conventional wholesalers. They are used by the many retailers to whom cash transactions appeal. There is a considerable temptation for public house tenants to buy from them, as prices are often cheaper than those of the brewers from whom they should buy under their agreements: they risk losing their pubs by so doing.

It is illegal to serve strong drink to anyone under the age of eighteen which, with some fourteen-year-olds looking very adult, sets predicaments for owners of licensed premises. On the other hand liqueur chocolates (subject to regulations as to amount of content) can be sold to all over 16 years old.

Drink may legally be ordered in an hotel at any hour the management are prepared to deliver it to a room, and sometimes residents are served in public rooms after the bar has closed. Visitors to Britain, unless exceptionally experienced, had best familiarize themselves with local peculiarities on alcoholic refreshment by enquiry. To complicate the issue, the rules that apply in England vary considerably for SCOTLAND, WALES, and NORTHERN IRELAND (some of the variations and oddities are listed separately), and for the ISLE OF MAN and the CHANNEL ISLANDS which are considerably more Continental in their outlook.

Note Towards the end of 1970, the Government stated it was setting up a review body under Lord Erroll to study the whole matter of licensing laws in England and Wales. A separate body would report in regard to Scotland. The clear intention is a further relaxation of restrictions. The question is highly controversial, and even after reports are made it seems likely that there will be much further discussion before fresh legislation is enacted.

Social drinking patterns While the breathalyzer looks like having a permanent effect on British drinking habits, a majority of the British drink at the pub, an institution of great antiquity. While the ordinary pub of many industrial conurbations still leaves much to be desired in amenities, on the whole the brewing trade (controlling most of Britain's public houses) is to be congratulated on the way it has improved many establishments. In the past ten years in particular a vast capital outlay has been poured into pubs. Aesthetically we may be appalled by some rebuilding efforts, yet they represent in amenities as vast an improvement over the premises they replace as the Victorian "gin palace" (see Gin) did over the sordid grog-shop it superseded.

The social importance of the pub—"the

Great Britain

local"—may not loom quite as large as it did before television came in, but it is still far from negligible. Added to which, an affluent class that formerly despised public houses now regularly frequents them. The best type of pub both serves and represents its area. On a new council housing estate the call may be for brashness, pop music, a room to park the kids; in the stockbroker belt it may be for discreet lighting, a grill room, mock oak beams and old pewter. And Britain is still well supplied with carefully preserved picture-postcard inns of historic renown and unique charm: they are part of the country's heritage and are lovingly described in many guidebooks.

While remote, expensively renovated houses may be ruined by BREATHALYZER legislation, the true "local" pub may take on a new lease of life. The "regular" who motored thither may disappear in favour of the true "regular" who lives nearby but has hitherto been motoring elsewhere. Many a British drinker has discovered he possesses feet (see also Public houses).

Apart from his "pub" (the social manifestation of the British way of life most obvious to the outside observer) the Briton likes to drink in his club. This ranges from the poshest of West End London clubs in St. James's to the vast and ebullient workingmen's clubs, which are by no means new but are a virile feature of the British scene in various parts of the country. A club has a strict legal connotation, and runs the gamut of the social and economic classes. There are clubs afternoon, bridge, dancing, dining, factory, gambling, gentlemen's, industrial, luncheon, night, political, professional, racial, religious, social, sporting, strip, trade and even drinking... the Briton is highly clubable. There are, of course, temperance clubs but for the most part sociable consumption of alcohol plays a notable part in a club's activities and certainly in its finances.

A feature of the British drinker is his marked lack of brand awareness when ordering by the tot in pub or club (see Brand), as opposed to his almost complete awareness of the brand of spirit he wants when buying for his home. This may stem from a reluctance to "make a fuss", but it makes no sense not to be particular about brand preferences at all times. One must admit, the attitude sometimes comes from ignorance ("they're all the same"): they emphatically are *not*.

Traditionally the Briton drinks beer, with cider regionally important. In Scotland and Northern Ireland he traditionally drinks whisk(e)y, and in metropolitan England gin. However, traditional regional patterns are today very blurred. For instance, some 40 per cent of U.K. vodka sales are in Scotland, and *per capita* Scotch whisky sells almost as strongly in Ireland as in England. Gin and whisky are sold everywhere.

While British sales of wine are still tiny compared with, say, France, they are growing yearly. Sherry is in vast demand, though port barely holds its own. Rum came back on a wave of interest in light rums, and foreign travel has increased a demand for potables formerly considered exotic.

The range of drinks in a well-stocked British "off-licence" store rivals any in the world. The Briton is as omni-bibulous as any civilized person elsewhere, though his most usual potion continues to be draught bitter (or bottled) beer, lager, Guinness, cider, gin-and-tonic (or other additive), whisky and water (or soda), sherry, port, and brandy (now being priced out of the daily market). Those are what you are most likely to be offered in his home (see also Cocktails).

The restrictions on motorists' drinking may lead to more domiciliary imbibing; the home bar is a status symbol, and I foresee this as increasing the range of British

Plate 18. A customer chats over a beer at London's "The Australian" public house in Chelsea.

Plate 19. A quiet game of crib is one of the sociable pastimes enjoyed in British pubs.

Great Britain

drinking habits. A liking for strong drink is an ineluctable part of the national character. Gluttony and drunkenness were factors in the British make-up much noted by foreign observers during the time when Britain was building the world's greatest empire.

Taxation To what extent a more temperate Britain is due to improved conditions of life is arguable; it seems just as likely that it is due to the enormous cost, through taxation, of alcoholic beverages, which produces almost 20 per cent of the country's internal revenue. Only in a few places outside Britain are the two basic British spirits, Scotch whisky and real London dry gin, more costly than in their homelands. In a volume intended as a fairly durable reference, it can be misleading to give precise figures, but in 1970 taxation of spirits (domestic or imported) had certainly reached an extremely high level, with a levy equivalent to 220p per standard bottle at normal strength (but do governments recognize extremes?). Since then producers have slightly increased their prices; to their credit, for only the second time in 10 years.

It has been suggested that were a British producer of a branded full-strength (70° proof) spirit drink to rely entirely on the home market for his livelihood, he would as like as not be out of business, unless the brand had a near monopoly. Without substantial exports, and they are very substantial (with D.C.L. way ahead) there could hardly be a worthwhile home trade in spirits for, without overseas earnings, the profitable domestic price would not simply be excessive but prohibitive. Exports of spirits subsidize the home market. (Spirits are excessively taxed on their alcoholic strength as compared to wines and beers).

Retail prices of all drinks are uncontrolled, though it is technically illegal to use a line as a "loss leader" in order to encourage sales of more profitable items. Thus there are wide local fluctuations in retail prices of alcoholic drinks. This applies both to retail outlets and bars of all types; it is thus impossible to give any useful information on prices, but the visitor must be prepared to pay pretty stiff prices in smart places. The "on" sale mark-up ranges from under one hundred to as much as 400 per cent, mainly to suit "smartness" of the establishment.

Sundry U.K. considerations Dependent on a vast internal revenue from intoxicants, British governments nevertheless seem intent on enforcing a type of prohibition through price. As a result people begin to turn to making their own stimulants at home. It is thought there are 750,000 homes making their own "wines", and additional ones making beer, which is quite legal. To distil privately, however, is a penal offence and brings down on it the full weight of the law. Occasional cases come to light, an interesting one recently being a brewery employee who for some time quietly distilled spirits on his firm's premises. He got rumbled in the usual way; unable to keep his duty-free nectar to himself, he sold some and his secret leaked out. There is no evidence that illicit distilling exists in any quantity in England, though it is an Irish tradition. To distil on any scale produces odours detectable at some distance, and revenue men are adept at noticing unwonted local exhilaration incompatible with personal budgets. There can also be considerable dangers in amateur distillation; private enterprise in this field in an English prison let to the death, insanity or loss of sight of its perpetrators. Yet while taxation remains excessive, the temptation to manufacture illegally will be there, and it also makes it easier to dispose of stolen liquor; the highjacking of spirit consignments is a regular feature of yuletide crime.

Great Britain

Alcoholism (see Alcohol) is not the problem in Britain it is in some countries, and it is arguable that publicity it has recently received may be due more to growing awareness and diagnosis than to any serious increase in the disease. But, of course, it does exist in all social strata, its most pathetic manifestation being in the methylated spirit drinkers, sometimes mixing this vile semi-poison with cheap red wine, "red Biddy", or rough cider, a potent concoction which leads to addictive degradation.

The International Council on Alcohol and Alcoholism recently estimated there are 300,000 people in Britain suffering from varying stages of alcoholism. This is not an alarming figure compared with that of some countries, though it has been claimed that there is a tendency for industry to "hide" its alcoholics. The British Medical Council on Alcoholism noted a more sinister trend, an increasing addiction by teenagers; also growing inebriation among housewives. Unfortunately, much alleged "data" on this subject is inclined to be tendentious and blurred by temperance propaganda.

The normal measures in use in English bars are defined by law and must consist for whisky, gin, rum or vodka (brandy was omitted through a bureaucratic oversight) of one-quarter, one-fifth or one-sixth of a gill, colloquially a "4-out", sometimes called a "club measure"; a "five-out", or a "six-out". In England the "six-out" is the most usual, in Scotland the "5-out" which is a British fluid ounce; fractionally smaller than the American fluid ounce, and equivalent to 2.8 centi-litres. Northern Ireland favours the big "4-out". Licensed premises must display notices stating the sizes of measures they use and must employ officially sealed or stamped measuring devices. For a "cocktail", which lacks precise definition, official measures are not required.

The standard British spirit bottle contains $26\frac{2}{3}$ fluid ounces (see Bottle sizes). Cognac is sold in 24-oz. bottles. The normal strength of spirits is 70° proof, (80° U.S.; 40 per cent Gay-Lussac), except domestic vodka which is usually 65.5° proof.

Wine It is likely that the grape was introduced to England by the Romans, for they would have wanted a regular supply of wine, and supplies from the Continent must have been erratic. Certainly the vine was well established in Saxon times. There is nothing climatically wrong with southern England, and although it was very heavily forested until oaks were needed for warships in vast quantities, there must have been sufficient southern-facing slopes to provide adequate vineyards.

The importation of French wines is of early origin, from the Norman Conquest onwards, and particularly when through the marriage of Henry II to Eleanor of Aquitaine the Bordeaux region was brought under English rule. A body blow to English wine production was dealt by Henry VIII when he dissolved the monasteries, which were certainly the main wine producers. Thereafter there was a steady decline. There is no evidence that British wines ever enjoyed much reputation.

Wine (fortified wines and vermouth) is produced in Britain in large quantities, but this is from imported grape must (unfermented juice), or other vinous materials. It is a major industry, mainly in the hands of Vine Products Ltd., and supplies the inexpensive end of the market with perfectly acceptable products which are labelled so none but an idiot will mistake them for anything superior. There are a handful of private vineyards, where wine is made, but commercial exploitation of these is virtually nil.

However, in 1967 the English Vineyards

Association was formed; more vines are being planted, and there is hope that, particularly if some form of excise tax relief is granted (for which the association is pressing the government) English grape wines may eventually find their place in the market.

Hambledon wine is a good white wine made from grapes grown in Hampshire by Sir Guy Salisbury-Jones. It can be bought from Peter Dominic, the London wine merchants.

There is a growing interest in amateur winemaking, using a remarkable selection of bases: one of my daughters makes a tolerable spinach wine. Production of English country wines on an industrial scale is active, the principal makers being the FINSBURY Distillery and the MERRYDOWN Wine Co.

Drink because you are happy and never because you are miserable.
G. K. Chesterton

GREECE

As most people know, whether or not they have been there, the most popular drink is OUZO. It accounts for 80 per cent of the spirits drunk in the country. The *bon ton* drink Scotch. While it is fashionable abroad to accuse the Greeks of lack of governmental liberalism, this criticism certainly cannot be levelled in the context of this book. Anyone can sell alcoholic beverages at any time of the day or night.

The other notable Greek speciality is RETSINA, a taste for which there is little acceptance overseas. Ouzo and Greek brandy are considerably exported, the U.S.A. being much the best market. There is also considerable production of *eau-de-vie* from the copious wine output.

The Greeks being addicted to cafe life, there is much sociable sipping of ouzo; customarily extra-diluted with ice and soda, or plain water in the hot weather, with which most of Greece is blessed for a major portion of the year. A volatile people even when sober, the Greek in his cups is rarely a nuisance, working off his energy in extremely acrobatic dances, and songs accompanied by vigorous hand-clapping. The cost in glasses sometimes comes high.

Wine The first taste of retsina is enough to put a visitor off Greek wine for life, but there are plenty of others and it seems a pity that export of Greek wines to Britain has lagged, though a substantial amount of wine goes to European countries and to the U.S.A., possibly because of the considerable number of citizens of Greek origin there. I have drunk excellent sound red wine from Corfu, and when visiting Greece had no difficulty in obtaining good table wines at very reasonable prices: for white, the best were perhaps from Rhodes. Controls are rather lax as to naming and blending, except for Samos wines which may only be made on the island. They are sickly sweet to many people; I enjoyed them more in Greece than when trying them in London. Some effort is being made to reorganize the Greek wine industry and get producers more interested in making more quality wines.

GREENALL WHITLEY & CO. LTD.

In August 1786, William Orrett, Thomas Lyon and Thomas Greenall formed a partnership to trade in South Lancashire and Cheshire under the title of "Orrett Lyon & Greenall". William Orrett was commissioned by the partners to acquire suitable premises that could be used as a central brewery to supply a number of public houses they had acquired or leased in the district. The premises chosen by William Orrett was the old *Saracens Head*, Wilderspool Causeway, Warrington, and the first brew produced by the newly

Greenall Whitley & Co.

formed partnership was made there on the 10th January, 1787.

In 1804, William Orrett died and three years later his family sold their interest in the business to the surviving partners, who continued to trade under the title of Lyon & Greenall. Following the death of Thomas Lyon in 1859, Gilbert Greenall became the sole proprietor of the concern trading as Greenall & Co. Shortly before the death of Thomas Lyon, Gilbert Greenall brought his nephews John William and Peter Whitley into the business, and in 1867 Gilbert Greenall formed a new partnership with his nephews trading under the name of Greenall Whitley & Co. The partnership continued until October 1880, when the company was incorporated by a memorandum of association under the present title.

In the early days of the business the beer was delivered by sailing "flats", which were a special type of barge equipped with sails. At this particular time certain members of the Greenall family were also directors of the Mersey & Irwell Navigation Canal Company. This particular canal system enabled them to distribute their beers in an easterly and westerly direction, but with the subsequent introduction of the railways distribution was extended to embrace areas north, south, and south-west of the brewery, thus opening up a widening field for the brewery's products. Here again the Greenall family at that time enthusiastically encouraged this new form of transport and became instrumental in furthering the development of it and eventually erecting a siding into the brewery itself.

The town of Warrington is situated like a hub in a wheel with the roads from the town forming the radial spokes of the wheel. Thus, the brewery was ideally situated geographically for the widening distribution of its products, and with the coming of firstly the steam wagon and later the internal combustion engine, the company was eventually able to undertake deliveries to Holyhead in Anglesey, the Caernarvon peninsula, and as far south as Shrewsbury and Wellington in Shropshire. At the same time it was extending its activities to embrace parts of Staffordshire, and central and southern Cheshire.

Today, the brewery at Warrington is the headquarters of the Greenall Whitley Group, which is the largest independent brewing concern in the country and which now embraces seven breweries, a distillery, and a soft drinks manufacturing plant.

GREENE, KING & SONS LTD.
Important independent brewery company with its main business at Bury St. Edmunds, Suffolk, and a major subsidiary at Biggleswade, Bedfordshire. In an age of brewing conglomerates, private companies like this enjoy special prestige in the eyes of many customers.

GRENADINE
The best known and most useful of all syrups, and an essential for stocking a cocktail bar, as it is a gracious sweetening agent. It is normally non-alcoholic and thus by no means a LIQUEUR.

GROG
Sometimes the word is used for mixed spirituous (hot) drinks or for a tot of spirits, but it is principally associated with the Royal Navy's discontinued rum ration. The name came from Admiral "Grogram" Vernon who instituted the practice of having the immensely strong daily rum ration diluted. "Grogblossom" is a somewhat old-fashioned and deplorable name, since the condition may not have anything to do with alcohol, for a person with an exceptionally inflamed proboscis. See also Slang.

GROUSE SCOTCH WHISKY
A connoisseur's blend from the independent

family firm of Matthew Gloag & Son, founded in Perth in 1814, and therefore distinctly one of the oldest whisky houses.

GUINNESS

Guinness was founded in 1759 by the first Arthur Guinness, who signed a lease for about an acre of land at St. James's Gate, Dublin, for a period of 9,000 years at a rental of £45 per year.

For the first few years the brewery at St. James's Gate brewed ale and table beer, but the new porter from England was growing in popularity in Ireland, and in 1799 Arthur Guinness made the decision that in future they would brew only porter.

In the 1820s the first English agencies were established and an advertisement in the *Morning Post* of June 27, 1829 confidently and prophetically states that "Guinness Dublin Stout must from its age, purity and smoothness ensure the approbation and support of the Public". The public did, in fact, approve and support it, and in 1837 no less a person than Disraeli was dining off "oysters, Guinness and broiled bones".

In 1933 a 120-acre site at Park Royal, Middlesex, was bought, and work was started on a new brewery. It was designed by the late Sir Giles Gilbert Scott, R.A., and completed in 1936, when the first brew was made.

At the same time there was a popular misconception that water from the Liffey for brewing was sent to Park Royal from Dublin. There are still occasions when Guinness have to point out that even in Dublin the water from the Liffey is not used for brewing—it comes from the springs of County Kildare and at Park Royal from the Metropolitan Water Board!

Guinness is a naturally conditioned beverage. Its ingredients are barley, water, hops and yeast. The yeast which gives the famous head today is a direct descendant of the yeast used for the brewing of the first Guinness nearly two centuries ago. A portion of the new yeast produced during each day's brewing has always been reserved for the following day's brew, thus maintaining the family line unbroken.

A supply of this directly descended yeast was sent to Park Royal for the first brewing there, thus enabling Guinness to be produced with all its distinctive qualities in England as well as Ireland.

The position of Guinness in the brewing industry is unique; the company has only one licensed house of its own in England. Stout is supplied in bulk to bottlers and brewers all over the country.

Although all the company's advertising is well known, perhaps it is most famous for its posters. At the time of the coronation of Queen Elizabeth II, a poster appeared with a zoo-keeper holding, above the heads of a crowd, a park seat on which the sea-lion, the ostrich, the kangaroo, the toucan and the pelican waved Union Jacks. Few people can have been in any doubt about who issued this wordless coronation poster. The "girder" poster, showing a Guinness-drinker lifting a girder, which first appeared in 1934, was probably the most popular. It gave rise to the expression in public houses of "have a girder".

In recent years, Guinness has diversified its interests. In 1951 they acquired William Nuttall, the parent company of Callard and Bowser and two other confectionery concerns. In 1960, together with Philips Electrical Industries Ltd., they acquired Crookes Laboratories and also in 1960, K. G. Corfield Ltd., camera manufacturers in Northern Ireland.

In 1961 Irish Ale Breweries Ltd., an Irish consortium of Guinness and Ind Coope, was formed to obtain greater efficiency of production and marketing of *Phoenix* ale and *Double Diamond* in Ireland. Later, Irish Ale

Guinness

Industries Ltd., acquired Bulmer's Ltd., of Clonmel, the only Irish cider makers. Following this, an agreement was reached between Irish Ale Industries and Showerings for the production at Clonmel of Showerings' brands (*Babycham, Coates* and *Gaymer's* ciders, etc.) in addition to other ciders and other products manufactured there.

In November 1961, in conjunction with Courage, Barclay and Simonds, Mitchell and Butlers and Scottish and Newcastle Breweries, Guinness launched *Harp* lager on a national scale in Britain. It was first brewed at Dundalk and put on sale in Ireland in July 1960, and introduced to the north-west of England in the spring of 1961.

On June 28, 1963, Earl Mountbatten of Burma opened a £2½ million *Harp Lager* Brewery at Alton in Hampshire. This is the first brewery on a new site to be built in Great Britain since the war, and indeed since the building of the Guinness brewery at Park Royal. It is the major brewery for the production of *Harp* in the United Kingdom in which Arthur Guinness, Courage, Barclay and Simonds, Bass, and Mitchell and Butlers have joined forces. These companies are the proprietors of Harp Lager Brewery (Southern) Limited, the group which built the new brewery. All the *Harp* lager required to supply the market in the southern part of Great Britain (south of a line drawn from Merioneth to the Wash) is brewed here. The daily capacity of the brewery is 1,000 barrels (36,000 gallons).

Arthur Guinness Son & Company Ltd., over two centuries, have built their prosperity upon the sale of one product: Guinness—and today the company looks back on a continuous growth of output. In spite of their diversifications Guinness is still of overriding importance to the company.

The company has the largest overseas sales of any brewery in the British Isles. In 15 years of the most dynamic growth overseas the company has known, exports of Guinness have risen vastly. Today overseas sales are at the £6 million mark and the product is sold in 125 different overseas markets, the largest market being West Africa. Two breweries, each capable of producing over 100,000 barrels a year, have been built at Ikeja near Lagos, Nigeria, and at Sundei Way in Kuala Lumpur, Malaysia. Guinness is also brewed under Guinness supervision in South Africa, Kenya, Sierra Leone, New Zealand, Canada, Australia and Trinidad.

Digression Guinness has always been headed by a member of the Guinness family, the present chairman being the great-great-great-great grandson of the founder. A good story is told of Edward Cecil Guinness, 1st Earl of Iveagh (1847–1927), which I heard many years ago and for the truth of which I will not vouch. Guinness sales were soaring and it was decided to advertise. A slogan was required. As is customary various agencies were invited to submit proposals. Lord Iveagh saw various advertising men, armed with formidable charts and schemes. Then came in one who had nothing with him. "Before I say anything," he told Lord Iveagh, "can you tell me what you yourself think of Guinness?" "Well," replied the Earl, "I know Guinness is good for you." "There's your slogan and the basis of your advertising campaign", said the man. No longer employed, for years variations on the "Good-for-you" theme was a Guinness advertising hallmark.

GUYANA

Very important rum producing country. Light white rum is the most popular local drink, and is often drunk with water. *Guyana* comes from the American Indian name meaning *Land of Waters*. It is also drunk in the form of *Rum Punches*. Licensing laws are liberal, and bars are known as "rum shops".

Recently, the increasingly prosperous multi-racial society has started to patronize licensed beer gardens, which also sell rum. Excellent gin and vodka are produced under licence from well-known firms. See also Rum (Guyana).

H

HAIG & CO. LTD., JOHN

Haig's, quite apart from their present world renown, have two special claims to fame: they are certainly the oldest name in Scotch whisky and they played a very important role in its emergence as a mighty industry. Without delving unnecessarily into the past, for those of historical bent (and I admit I am) it may be worth recalling that when the Normans continued their conquest into the Lowlands of Scotland a knight known as de la Hage (and umpteen other spellings) took over as his fief a domain along the River Tweed, and erected a fort at Bemersyde. He came from the Cherbourg area still known as Cap de la Hague. A late Twelfth-Century manuscript indicates a Petrus del Hage established in the district and a century later was written the much-quoted prophecy: "Tide what may, what'ere betide, Haig shall be Haig of Bemersyde".

The Haigs were thereafter a part of Border history. Haigs fought in the Crusades, one fought with Wallace, one fell at Otterburn, another at Flodden. The family had a pretty turbulent history (it is well told in James Laver's *The House of Haig*), and their fortunes declined. It was Robert, driven by his family from Bemersyde in 1627, who first attracts notice as a distiller. Before settling as a tenant farmer in Stirlingshire, he had studied distilling in the Netherlands. We know he was a distiller because in 1655 he was hauled before the kirk session, a church body with formidable legal powers, for using his still on a Sunday. He got off with a rebuke: distilling itself was no crime, but the kirk disapproved of Sunday work. Robert's son, Alexander, was certainly a distiller (it was part of a farmer's normal activities) and a law-abiding one, for in the revenue accounts for 1699-70 he is recorded as having distilled 128 gallons and six pints between 1st March and 1st June, 1699. Admittedly it was far harder for Lowlanders to evade officialdom, either then or after union with England, than for the Highlanders in their mountain fastnesses.

The next fact worthy of recall is the marriage of Alexander Haig's great-grandson, John, to Margaret Stein, daughter of John Stein, in 1751. It directly affected the development of the whisky industry. The couple set up home near the Kilbagie distillery (no longer making whisky) in Clackmannanshire. This was owned by the Stein family, pioneer exporters of whisky to England and the biggest distillers of their day. John Haig died in 1773, and his five boys were taken into apprenticeship, four of them founding the various parts of the House of Haig. (Margaret Haig's great grandson, Douglas, was the British Commander-in-Chief in World War I and later Earl Haig of Bemersyde).

Margaret's brother Robert Stein had become interested in the PATENT (continuous distillation) still which he is credited with inventing. Though the idea was perfected by Aeneas Coffey and patented by

Hallgarten

him, the Steins were not put off and continued, in association with the Haigs, to employ this new way of mass-producing grain whisky. At one time all the Lowland whisky distilleries were in Haig-Stein control, and in due course, when blended whisky came into vogue, they were in a leading position to exploit the demand for the essential grain whisky, even though efforts to sell straight grain whisky were not very successful. Thereafter the Haig story was one of conspicuous expansion.

Markinch, not far from Edinburgh, is today's headquarters of the Haig empire. In London their offices are in Distillers House. Haig joined D.C.L. in 1919. Haig is the largest-selling Scotch in the U.K.: it has a vast export. The de-luxe brand is the famous *Dimple*, called *Pinch* in the U.S.A. Fairly recently, Haig's introduced a vatted straight malt whisky, *Glenleven*.

HALLGARTEN

S. F. & O. Hallgarten are one of Britain's leading importers of German wines, their most celebrated brand being *Kellergeist* liebfraumilch, a name to be found on many lists and another of those quality guarantees to which I attach importance. Their *Niersteiner Domtal* (Domgarten) is equally reliable. Apart from many other lines, they are U.K. agents for *Royal Mint* chocolate liqueur: Peter Hallgarten is author of *Liqueurs*, the best book devoted to this subject. Fritz Hallgarten's *Rhineland, Wineland* has run into several editions (including paperback) and is widely considered the definitive book on the wines of Western Germany. The company owns Arthur Hallgarten of Mittelheim, Rheingau.

HANG-OVER

I do not see why anyone who has *never* had a hang-over should be reading this book. To appreciate moderation one must have experienced the tribulations of excess. A hang-over is induced at its simplest by over-indulgence; it is a form of poisoning, when the body contains too much ALCOHOL. It cannot eliminate it fast enough; therefore you are ill. Any surfeit sickens: one can get a type of hang-over from eating too many herrings; or smoking 80 cigarettes of an evening.

It is not always a question of how tight you were last night that regulates the acuteness of your hang-over (see E.P.L., P.A.G.) or whatever euphemism you may employ. You can drink a great deal of straight spirits and water, for instance, if that is your tipple, and be a boozy nuisance, and wake up as fresh as paint. Or you can get the same way on wine and beer and brandies-and-ginger-ale, and feel awful. Too many mineral waters or synthetic mixers are hang-over-inducing, but true fruit drinks tend to be beneficial.

The whole business is fraught with old wives' tales. Mixing your drinks does not make you more inebriated; you may think you are and you may feel worse next day, but you will be no drunker clinically. The favourite old wives' tale is the "Hair-of-the-Dog" one: the notion of having a stiff drink of the same type you were mainly on the night before as a hang-over cure. Looked at logically, it is only adding alcohol to a system distressed because it already contains too much. But psychologically, it does work; and you may feel better. It is all very personal, but I think champagne works wonders. However, do not have anything else for the rest of the day and do not have too much. The established patent cures contain alcohol, FERNET BRANCA and UNDERBERG (I rate the latter highly), but they are also herbal. Morning-after cocktails and other drinks include HEART STARTER, PRAIRIE OYSTER, CORPSE REVIVER, and, though excellent on any occasion,

BULL SHOT and BLOODY MARY are also recommended.

If you are in the West End of London, noted breeding-ground of hang-overs, you might pop into Perkins, the chemists, in Piccadilly (conveniently close to the American Club), explain your particular malaise and try one of their special pick-me-ups—pretty marvellous. If you are able to get it, a couple of whiffs of pure oxygen brings remarkable results, for oxygen-starvation and dehydration are characteristics of the hang-over. Drink masses of water.

As to prevention, there is no doubt that milk, cream, oil, slow up the intake of alcohol, but as you will not get plastered so fast, you may in the event drink more and have a worse hang-over. One should certainly not drink heavily on an empty stomach, which is better appreciated in countries where they serve substantial snacks with drinks, for which an occasional olive or potato crisp is no substitute. At first alcohol stimulates the appetite, say, three Dry Martinis, but after that it kills it (say, six Dry Martinis), and one is set for an almighty hang-over if one omits to eat. It is not a particularly pleasing notion, but if you can be sick before you go to sleep and drink plenty of water, with lime juice cordial if possible, you may escape even after a smashing evening; but only if you get adequate sleep. Before retiring is the time to take SELTZERS, much more effective than when the damage has been done during the night as you lie awash with alcohol. See also Smoking.

HARP (Lager)
Owned by GUINNESS; the brand leader in Britain.

HARPER, I. W.
Fine bourbon whiskey, owned by SCHENLEY'S.

HARVEYS OF BRISTOL
In 1796, in Denmark Street, Bristol, William Perry established his headquarters as dealer in port, sherry and other commodities. That is still the firm's main address. Perry took in a Thomas Urch as junior partner, whose sister, Anne, married Thomas Harvey. This man had a father of the same name, both notable sea captains in the employ of John Maxse, who was not only a shipowner but a wine importer in competition with Perry. The older Thomas Harvey was a great Bristolian character: children of the city were cowed into obedience by the mention of his name, more fearful to them even than Bonaparte's. He was drowned at sea with his wife and entire crew.

The younger Thomas Harvey became a rich shipowner himself. His second son, John, by his marriage to Anne Urch was apprenticed to his uncle, Thomas Urch. He had a flair for the wine business and in due course became proprietor. John Harvey & Sons built up a huge general wine and spirit trade, but they became specially famous for their sherries and, of course, most notably for unique BRISTOL CREAM.

The company commenced to take giant strides forward after the war and especially after 1956 when George McWatters, great-grandson of the founder, took over the chairmanship. In brief, the company went public in one of the most successful issues on the London Stock Exchange; it acquired other businesses, vastly increased export, and in October 1960, opened a warehouse and bottling plant at Whitchurch, near Bristol, which was revolutionary in design and efficiency. Ultimately, the company's success attracted outside interest and a takeover battle ensued which ended in the acquisition of the Harvey group by SHOWERINGS, and the departure of energetic George McWatters, but the family tie is maintained with the company through his brother, Michael, a director

Haut

of the firm, who was greatly responsible for the Whitchurch project.

Though the Denmark Street headquarters, with invaluable records of this famous company, was blitzed in 1940, the ancient monastic cellars beneath survived and they contain a wonderful wine museum. In them, too, lie some magnums of Bristol Cream laid down in 1953 to mark the coronation of Queen Elizabeth II. They will not be opened until the silver jubilee in 1978: a small quantity will then be sold, at what a price I cannot conjecture.

HAUT
Literally "high", but a geographic and not qualitative expression; e.g., Haut-Medoc is a district higher up the Gironde than Medoc. *Supérieur* has much the same meaning.

HAUT-BRION, CHATEAU
A 600-year-old BORDEAUX vineyard producing very notable wine. It is one of the *premiers crus* of the Bordeaux classification, and the outstanding red wine from Graves.

HEART-STARTER
Reputed HANG-OVER cure, but a little noisy for the ultra-fragile. A large measure of gin; a cup of iced water; a teaspoonful of *Andrew's Liver Salts*. Toss the lot down quickly. Wait.

HEDGES & BUTLER
This long-respected firm of wine merchants, whose premises preserve a charming façade of antiquity in London's Regent Street, is now a vinous linch-pin of the BASS CHARRINGTON empire. Under their name the group markets the *Hirondelle* range of table wines, possibly unique among brand-named blends, in that they come from AUSTRIA.

HEIDSIECK
This is a slightly muddling name in champagne, for there are three important brands bearing it and they should not be confused. They are *Charles Heidsieck*, *Heidsieck Dry Monopole*, and *Piper-Heidsieck*.

HEINEKEN
A Continental lager beer with some 20 per cent of the growing U.K. market for its type.

HENKELL
The largest producers of German sparkling wines. In the early Nineteenth Century, Adam Henkell commenced business as a wine merchant in Mainz. Production of *sekt* (the German for sparkling wine) was started in 1856, and this quickly developed, including a considerable export within Europe and to America. By 1908, the Henkell business moved to palatial new premises in Wiesbaden, capital of the RHEINGAU. Today, Adam Henkell's great-grandson controls Europe's largest sparkling wine business, and that includes champagne. There are many brands of sekt, and many brands bearing the Henkell name, but by far the most important is *Henkell Trocken* (dry) of which the *Extra Dry* variety sells over 8 million bottles a year. In taste the best sekt is akin to good French (*brut*) VIN MOUSSEUX but is perhaps best described as being more mellow and fractionally less dry.

Henkell Trocken is made by the full "champagne method". (Every day except Saturday and Sunday, the cellars at Henkellsfield, Wiesbaden, may be visited between 09.30 and 11.30 or 14.00 and 15.30 hours).

HENNESSY
In 1740, Richard, third son of Charles Hennessy of Ballmacmoy, Co. Cork, settled in COGNAC. He had previously left Ireland to fight in the Irish brigade for the French king and was now a wounded veteran. He chose Cognac since that was the town near which his comrades were stationed. He heard that the local brandy was credited with restorative powers, and he needed restoring. He sent a few casks to his Irish friends and relatives and

they, despite a probable delight in their own island's whiskey, forwarded glowing reports on the reception of this French spirit. So he went into business. In 1765 he founded a company which his son, James, turned into Jas. Hennessy & Co. Hennessy recently merged with Mercier and Moët et Chandon.

Hennessy *Bras Armé* is the standard brand, the mailed arm and battle-axe being the family crest. Hennessy claim the largest stocks of aged cognac: their *V.S.O.P.* is outstanding. The pride of their stable is Hennessy *X.O.* from brandies at least 45 years in cask.

HEUBLEIN'S OF HARTFORD, CONNECTICUT

If only for a single revolutionary event in the world of drinking, this celebrated U.S. firm deserves adequate mention.

The founder of the House of Heublein, Andrew Heublein, began his career in America as a painter and skilled weaver, by trade. Born May 28, 1820, in Suhl, Bavaria, he came to America in 1856. With him came two sons, Gilbert F. and Louis. Settling in Beacon Falls (Conn.), he moved later to New Haven and finally, Hartford, where in 1859 he opened a restaurant, cafe and small hotel.

"Heub's" popularity grew. Its Continental atmosphere, cuisine, domestic and imported brews and liquors attracted the dignitaries of that day. Andrew had a gift for catering fine foods and beverages to fanciers. By 1875 his sons, Gilbert and Louis, were running the business. They branched out, opening the Heublein Café in Hartford's Opera House, becoming "bottlers" on Gold St., emphasizing the importance of choice foods, delicacies, vintage wines and liquors in the restaurant-hotel, and conducting a wholesale wine business.

In 1892, G. F. Heublein & Bro., launched the bottled cocktail. The initial cocktail, called *The Club*, was the Martini (not the Dry Martini of today). The cocktails came about as the result of a request from the governor's footguards. They were to have an outing and they ordered a gallon of Martinis and a gallon of "Manhattans". Came the big day. It rained. No party. The two gallons were put on ice for the following Saturday. Again the party was called off. An order to "throw the stuff out" found a helper tasting the cocktails and reporting they tasted fine. An idea was born: the bottling of ready-made cocktails. Sales initially were to area clubs, thus the name *Heublein Club Cocktails*. Quickly the new products won national and international demand.

By 1914, now a national firm, Heublein had headquarters at 196–206 Trumbull St., Hartford, with branch offices in New York, Frankfurt, Germany, and London. A chief Heublein import, from 1907 on, was Brand's *A.1. Sauce*, originating in the royal kitchens of England's George IV. World War I disrupted importation of the sauce. Heublein acquired the manufacturing rights to it for the United States and began production in Hartford. Meanwhile, the liquor business grew until PROHIBITION caused Heublein to close down its liquor plant. However, *A.1.* sauce sales kept climbing and key distillery personnel were transferred to food operations.

Repeal led Heublein to return to the liquor business. Liquor leaders for Heublein then were the *Club Cocktails* and gin. Later, the company was appointed sole United States distributor for BELL'S Scotches by the House of Bell.

Volume literally burst the firm at its staves by 1938. Strong financially, in personnel, in products and in the ability of its management, Heublein stood ready as a launching pad: its biggest "missile", SMIRNOFF vodka, was on the way.

Smirnoff vodka sold a million bottles a day in 1912 in Czarist Russia. It was brought to America by Rudolph P. Kunett, a Ukranian whose father, in Russia, had supplied the grain and neutral spirits from which it was

Heublein's

made. Mr. Kunett acquired rights to the formula and name from exiled Vladimir Smirnoff in Paris. In 1934, he set up a plant in Bethel, Conn. But the vodka of the American branch of Société Pierre Smirnoff et Fils did not sell. He wanted to get out. No one would buy. He met Heublein's president, English-born John G. Martin. Mr. Martin was enthusiastic. Other Heublein executives less so. A compromise was arranged to pay Mr. Kunett a retainer, make him a company officer and give him a royalty on every case sold. In 1939 Heublein took over the sale and manufacture of *Smirnoff*. It sold no more than 6,000 cases a year.

Then, after the war, came the *Moscow Mule*—the result of brainstorming between Jack Morgan, owner of Los Angeles' Cock 'n Bull Restaurant, and Mr. Martin. By 1947, the *Mule* was a west-coast rage. It spread east. Vodka flowed into every mixer and juice. Different drink names appeared on menus and bar cards: *Bloody Mary*, *Screwdriver*, *Bull Shot*. Heublein's *Smirnoff* vodka blasted off to a climb that by 1961 stood at 2,000,000 cases a year with Heublein's *Relska*, America's second largest selling vodka, and *Popov* vodka vying for third in the mushrooming market.

Today, *Smirnoff* vodka accounts for a major percentage of Heublein income, yet sales for other products in the expanding fine food and liquor line keep gaining in importance. Heublein today manufactures and markets a total of 14 bottled cocktails. See COCKTAILS (Ready-mixed).

The company imports HARVEY's sherries and ports, *Bisquit* cognacs, IRISH MIST liqueur, and a number of other lines.

Around the world Heublein's international division has more than kept pace with the company's domestic growth. Smirnoff plants (operated abroad under licensee agreements) operate in 38 nations, with *Smirnoff* in direct export to the remainder of the nations of the Free World.

HEURIGEN
Young wine, much drunk in AUSTRIA; light and pleasing.

HIGHBALL
Said to have originated in St. Louis, U.S.A., in the latter half of the Nineteenth Century. On many American railroads, if a ball was hoisted to the top of a pole at a station through which a train was passing, it was an indication to the driver to speed up. Hence it came to be used for a fast drink, quickly prepared, a whiskey and water or soda. Now a *Highball* can be any named spirit with ice and various mineral waters, served in a tall glass. A *Highball* made with cider is known as a *Stone Fence*.

HIGH & DRY GIN
A long-established gin, distilled by BOOTH'S Distilleries, but within the last decade completely changed in formula and visual appearance. Produced not only in the Red Lion Distillery, London, but in 30 overseas countries and widely exported. A best-seller in some parts of the U.S.A., where it is distilled, and exceptionally successful in South Africa, Japan, New Zealand and other countries in which it is produced or to which it is exported. Perhaps *High & Dry* is even better-known internationally than in Britain, though it is there becoming particularly appreciated in informed circles as "the world's driest gin", a point of special interest to amateurs of cocktails and followers of the Dry Martini cult.

HIGHLAND QUEEN
The reference is to Mary Queen of Scots. I think this brand of whisky, from Macdonald & Muir, is particularly artistically advertised in a day when to be "with it" is often apparently considered sufficient in itself.

HINE
Before World War II this famous COGNAC (the "H" is pronounced for it is a West of

England, not a French, name) was largely confined to great occasions. It is now, I am glad to say, infinitely more widely distributed. Control of this firm was bought in 1971 by D. C. L., who are interested in its world-wide export potential. Hine 3-Star (5-Star Sceptre in the U.S.A.) is considered the best in its class. Their V.S.O.P. is outstanding, matched by the older "Antique" and "Old Vintage" brands.

HIRAM WALKER

Hiram Walker-Gooderham & Worts Ltd., of Walkerville, Ontario, Canada, is internationally known for its *Canadian Club* Canadian whisky. Its U.K. subsidiary controls a number of Scotch whisky interests, its most famous blend being *Ballantine's*. It also markets *Old Smuggler*, better known in the United States than in its homeland, and the de-luxe brand *Ambassador*. It has many more brands through sundry subsidiaries. Prof. R. J. S. McDowall opines that this very large and important group is analogous to D.C.L., in that it "consists of a number of relatively independent companies".

HOCK

A word brought into use by the English in the last century to describe what had hitherto been usually called Rhenish wines and has enjoyed wide currency for all still German wines. It is said to derive from the town of Hocheim, whose wines enjoyed the reputation of being favoured by Queen Victoria, via Prince Albert doubtless. For another and earlier use of the word hock, see Fuller, Smith & Turner.

The term has come to be disliked as a description by the German wine trade, because it is felt it has become "debased" by being attributed to wines from other countries.

HOLLAND See Netherlands.
HOLSTEN
A superb German LAGER, brewed, matured and bottled in Hamburg. It is of high SPECIFIC GRAVITY and keeps very well. Holsten also produce low calorie *Diat Pils*, amongst other beers.

HONG KONG

With the outer islands and portion of the Chinese mainland on which Great Britain has a lease till 1993, Hong Kong covers no more than some 30 square miles into which are crammed over 4 million people, only 1.25 per cent of whom are not Chinese. The Chinese very rarely drink during the day, confining their intake to the evening meal. They do not drink wine, unless they have become Westernized, as is increasingly happening through travel.

The favourite spirit is brandy, which has long enjoyed amongst the Chinese the fallacious reputation of increasing virility. Whisky comes next and beer is popular. The most popular beverages by volume are *Coca-Cola*, *Seven-Up* and beer. These are produced locally, as is *Vita-Soy* (soya bean milk). Whisky, brandy and beer are re-exported on a considerable scale. Beer from communist China is so cheap that it undercuts the local brews. There are no special laws concerning sale or advertising of liquor, Chinese men mix both cognac and Scotch with *Seven-Up*. There is a tendency even amongst the ultra-conservative Chinese for the rising generation to break away from parental example and thus the young are showing an inclination to drop the traditional brandy in favour of whisky, gin, rum and other drinks.

HORSE'S NECK

Hang continuous spiral of lemon peel in tall glass. Add ice cubes, 2 measures of dry gin, top with ginger ale. (This may be made with any preferred spirit.)

HOUSE OF LORDS GIN

The export name for BOOTH'S *Gin*, having particular prestige in the U.S.A. where it has

100 Pipers Scotch

been known in discerning circles longer than any other imported gin. The origin of the name lies in a certificate of nearly half-a-century ago from the superintendent of catering at the House of Lords appointing Booth's Distilleries as official suppliers to that august assembly. For many years *Booth's Gin* in Britain carried a neck label stating "as supplied to The House of Lords", but in modern times this has been dropped. Recently, *House of Lords* gin for the United States was given a striking new bottle (after years of employing the famous hexagonal Booth's one) and a very distinctive new label, and a refinement of the formula at the Red Lion Distillery, London, has made this gin even drier and of sparkling clarity.

Such changes in a traditional product and in a traditional trade verge on the revolutionary. However, a constant awareness of the requirements of the fickle but very perceptive UNITED STATES market is essential to success with American drinkers, particularly in what I might call the "Dry-Martini belt". The new *House of Lords* label, on a redesigned original "U.S." bottle, is now the pack for this brand in all markets including N. America. This prestigious gin now has a limited distribution in the best of the British market.

100 PIPERS SCOTCH WHISKY

SEAGRAM'S are pushing with this blend in the U.S.A. and U.K., in the latter market introducing it at a price above other comparable blends. According to *Management Today*, Samuel Bronfman, president of Distillers Corp-Seagram, admitted after the U.S. launch that "People weren't exactly standing out in droves for a new Scotch." But the same journal quotes a rival Scotch importer as saying, "despite a lousy name, lousy advertising, lousy packaging, it will within five years be the biggest label in Scotch."

HUNGARY

This ancient wine-producing land is overseas today best known for *Bull's Blood*, a splendidly robust red wine, and its legendary TOKAY has, as a supreme wine, fallen somewhat into eclipse. Old bottles of Tokay "essenz" (*Imperial Tokay*), made from over-ripe grapes from which the juice is extruded solely by the self-pressure of the grapes in the vat, occasionally turn up as a vinous curiosity. It is no longer made for sale, as it would be impossibly costly, but is used for blending.

HUNT'S

Established company of mineral water manufacturers now part of the Beecham Food Products group and entering the British market very competitively with normal range plus TROPICAL LEMON.

HYDROMETER

Perfected by a retired excise officer, Bartholomew Sikes (or Sykes), and named after him, it consists of a metal globe carrying a graduated scale. By a complicated system involving varying weights on the base of the globe, a thermometer and massive charts, it can be used, and has officially been used since 1816, to establish the PROOF alcoholic content of British spirits.

I

ICE
Under the section on WATER, I pass comment on the futility of being fussy about water if one is not equally so about ice. Not that commercial ice is not normally of high purity, but I have seen it most unhygienically handled. (In Soho, London, I have seen a passing canine resident nonchalantly lifting its leg against an ice block deposited outside a well-known restaurant.)

If you find your tap-water displeasing, ice made from it will (though refrigeration reduces flavour) retain that character; then use a bottled spring water for your ice. If you buy a block of ice for a party, wash it. Wrapped in a clean sack it will keep well even in warm weather. An ice pick, or similar tool from your work bench, will hack it easily into large lumps. To reduce these, wrap them in a towel and bang on a hard surface. This ice will be harder and last longer than that you make in a domestic refrigerator.

The "Ice Age" took a long time to reach Britain; now it is here, thus removing one American cause for complaint, I find it necessary to say when I do *not* want it in my drinks. Bars, even quite modest ones, seem intent on showing their modernity by putting ice in everything . . . progress? See also Frappé; Glacé.

ICELAND
Frankly, I have not discovered much about the drinking patterns in this fascinating country, but I am promised more information for the next edition of this book. Iceland seems to be the only non-prohibitionist country in the world which does not allow production or import of beer; until recently, local official spirit measures were the world's largest. Sounds interesting.

ICE WINE See Eiswein.

I.D.V. See International Distillers & Vintners Ltd.

IMPORTED WINES LTD.
This is a group of companies that have been mainly concerned in the importation and sale of wines from Commonwealth countries.

The Emu Wine Co. and P. B. Burgoyne & Co. shared the honour of introducing Australian wines to Great Britain on a commercial basis around 1870. The principal wines imported for half a century were of a very full burgundy character and it is a tribute to their merits that, at about the turn of the century, nearly one bottle in 15 of all imported wines originated from Australia. Today there is a customs preference granted on Commonwealth wines but, from 1860 to 1920 no such inducement existed, so that all the more credit is due to these pioneer importers for successfully overcoming the difficulties of marketing wine produced 12,000 miles away.

Wines originally introduced nearly a century ago, such as *Emu* Australian burgundy and Burgoyne's *Tintara* still have a large sale throughout the United Kingdom. The combined effects, however, of rising costs, such as freight charges and the vast recent rise in Continental holidays have militated against Australia sharing fully in the very greatly increased consumption of European table wines in recent years.

Fifteen years ago, at a period when the duties on high- and low-strength wines were grossly out of balance *Emu Imperial Bond* Australian sherry was introduced to this market. By a shrewd process of blending it made a wine of this character available for the first time since the Second World War, to a

Ind Coope

new wine-drinking public at a price that it could afford. It is today among the large national brands in popularity. However, its value has been lost to some extent, because owing to a subsequent reduction in duty sherry was brought much closer in price. It was not possible to absorb the duty completely on *Emu*.

Probably one of the most dramatic developments in the history of the British wine trade is the phenomenal increase in Cyprus wine consumption during the last dozen years. To be candid, the island's wines were held in low repute until very recent years, when, thanks to close co-operation between Britain and the Cyprus authorities the whole problem of modernizing their ancient wine industry was studied deeply.

The Cypriots responded magnificently and within 15 years they have become widely accepted as being with Germany, the most technically advanced wine makers in Europe.

P. B. Burgoyne & Co. realizing these developments started promoting Cyprus wines quite early and, thanks to the realization of the Cyprus producers that a study of the needs and tastes of this potential market was all-important, the consumption of Cyprus wines today, in Great Britain, is greater by far than that of any other country, bar France and Spain.

IND COOPE See Allied Breweries.

INDIA

To deal with a country of 550 million inhabitants, speaking various languages, spread over 17 states and with diverse national, social and religious affiliations, one must generalize to a great extent. A vast number of people, for economic or religious reasons, touch no alcohol and the main beverage is tea, with coffee, buttermilk, fruit juices and synthetic fruit drinks widely popular. With those who can afford them, proprietary beverages associated with health (*Horlicks* and *Ovaltine* have been quoted to me) are much liked.

Where the use of alcohol is permitted, TODDY leads; it is fermented, according to availability of raw materials, from coconut, palmyra or date palm sap. Where rice is grown, *Pachwai* can be made: it is a fermentation of water in which rice has been cooked. In some backward areas, children are given fresh *Pachwai*. (It is also made from grain on the same principle.) It is said that in some districts if a labourer be given half-a-pound of rice to eat he will tire within three hours and demand more food, but if he is given the *Pachwai* made from the rice water he will work through the day without complaint.

"Country spirit" is a generic term for distillations of the ARRACK type, made from a variety of materials, including a tropical flower, Mahuwa. It is usually pretty crude stuff and in industrial areas is normally sold not stronger than 30 per cent alcohol content. In rural districts it may go up to the same strength as is usual for British spirits. It is often flavoured with spices or local fruit essence. There is a great deal of illicit distilling of "country spirit", said to equal that of licensed manufacture. To quote my correspondent, "The illicit liquor is of very mixed quality and some of it can be quite deadly and there are reports from time to time of serious illness as well as deaths from consumption of execrable lots of such booze. Illicit distillation also results in serious loss of revenue for the state governments but, in spite of vigorous police measures, it has been virtually impossible to stamp this evil out, as profits are high and opportunities many. Most illicit stills are of small size, usually producing 2 to 3 gallons of liquor a day as a home enterprise."

More sophisticated spirits are made, representing Indian endeavours to reproduce the conventional spirits and potables, such as whisky, brandy, gin, etc. Indian whisky is not very successful, nor brandy, but Indian gin, rum and vodka compare, at their best, very

Plate 20. The O'Neill (Brian Boru) harp is the symbol of Guinness products. The original is in the library at Trinity College, Dublin.

Plate 21. Making Irish coffee at Shannon Airport, where, it is said, the drink was invented.

Plate 22. The St. James's Street headquarters of Justerini and Brooks.

Plate 23. "Bols Tavern", off the Rozengracht, Amsterdam, (see Bols).

favourably with imported lines. There are also, however, some poor imitations in these categories. Indian beer can be excellent. I did not know India produced wine, but she does, and though at the moment only making rather ordinary table wines, hopeful efforts are being made to improve them. Wine and fortified wines are made from imported concentrates as well. The alcohol trade is somewhat inhibited by internal taxes on bottles and closures. A good export of fruit drinks is building up.

Eighty per cent of imported alcoholic beverages consist of Scotch whisky, followed by French brandy and some table wines and liqueurs. Imports are on a quota based on individual importers' trade in the immediate pre-war year, and this has progressively been reduced in the interests of conserving exchange till it is only 4 per cent of the 1939–40 value of imports. Special licences are granted for those catering for the tourist trade, and ships' victualling is a free trade under international law. Excise taxes are very high and this, combined with scarcity of quality imported liquors, has forced prices up so that they are the perquisites of the decidedly wealthy.

Licensing laws vary greatly from state to state, most of which, though conscious of revenue considerations, have prohibition as their goal, in principle anyway (though I am sure sane legislators must appreciate what has happened, at least in their own country, where enforcement of prohibition has been tried). There is some ambivalence: a few states, though officially dedicated to the idea of ultimate prohibition, allow any form of advertising promoting alcohol because it aids the exchequer. In other states, the liquor trade has voluntarily agreed (the constitution forbids a ban) not to advertise alcohol. The variety of regulations, dry days, limitations of public consumption, are as enormous as the country. Apart from the prohibitionists, there are those who realize that alcoholic abuse (a result of industrialization and urban slum conditions) cannot be cured by laws, nor morality legislated, but that education on the evils of misuse of strong drink is the answer, partly paid for by taxes on alcohol.

In prosperous commercial and educated circles generally, the Anglo-Indian convention of not drinking whisky before sundown remains in force. If anyone has alcoholic drink before the evening it will be gin-and-tonic or beer. Cocktail parties are part of the smart life of the big cities, and then Scotch-and-soda is the preferred drink. Some legacies of the British Raj are still enjoyed.

INN See Public houses.

INNHOLDERS' LIVERY COMPANY
Known in Middle English as "herbergeours" and then as Haymongers, before becoming Hostelers, the Innholders of the City of London soon drew themselves away from the ordinary run of public house keepers, and came into association to protect their rights well before Henry VIII granted the company a charter.

INN SIGNS
These are a cherished feature of British PUBLIC HOUSES, the most ancient sign being that of the *Bush*—recalling the shrub that marked Roman highway hostelries. With the increase of literacy, inn signs became less important, but there has recently been a renewal of interest in them and brewers are to be congratulated on commissioning ones from excellent artists. Many signs flattered local landed gentry and peers. Queen Victoria's celebrated "we are not amused" stemmed from a misjudged pleasantry connected with an inn sign.

The Crown is the most common sign, either plain or with additional words. There are 1,099 of these. There are 930 *Lions* of various hues and shapes, *The Red Lion* being the most popular. There are 800 *Bells*, and 750

I.D.V.

Royal Oaks (often a reference to King Charles II's legendary hiding place as Prince of Wales during the Civil War). There are 500 *Ploughs* and 460 *King's* (*King's Head* or similar themes). The *Thirteenth Mounted Cheshire Rifleman* is the longest sign. Perhaps the most sinister is *Pity The Poor Straggler*, sign of a house at one time tenanted by England's then public hangman who, it was told me, once had a notice displayed reading "No hanging about the bar, please". A very ancient and frequently found sign is the *New Inn*; the *New Inn* at Gloucester dates from 1450. *Astronaut*, *Telstar* and the *Man In Space* complement in modernity what the *New Inns* have in antiquity. (Origins of many quaint names will be found in the illustrated booklet, *Inn Signs, Their History and Their Meaning*, published by the Brewers' Society.)

INTERNATIONAL DISTILLERS & VINTNERS LTD.

In this important British conglomerate the giant brewing combine of WATNEY MANN holds a very considerable stake, and as part of the deal involving this, Watney Mann disposed of their free-trade wine and spirits interests to I.D.V.

GILBEY'S may perhaps be said to be the most well-known name in this enterprise. Among other brands and firms, I.D.V. controls, or is agent for, such well-known names as HENNESSY, BOLS, SMIRNOFF, JUSTERINI & BROOKS, HEIDSEICK *Dry Monopole*, Bouchard père et fils, CARAFINO wines, Peter Dominic, CROFT, *Justina* wines.

INTOXICATION, INTOXICANTS
See Alcohol; Hang-over.

INVERGORDON DISTILLERS LTD.

This company, which started producing grain whisky in 1961, was the "brainchild" of the late James Grigor, provost of Inverness, and of Sir Max Rayne, the chairman of the London Merchant Securities Group of Companies. Invergordon from the outset has used those same distillation techniques handed down by its predecessors, but coupled with the most up-to-date methods of quality control, spirit analysis and cask movement.

Invergordon grain whisky is to be found at the heart of some of the leading brands of blended Scotch whisky. Invergordon production is in the 10 million proof gallons per annum range, possibly only exceeded by Distillers Company's Carsebridge distillery.

However, pride of place among the company's activities does not go to the fine modern grain distillery at Invergordon. This is reserved for the new malt distillery at Tamnavulin-Glenlivet among the rolling foothills of the Cairngorms by the River Livet, close to the site of an old water mill which provided power for carding the wool brought in by the shepherds for miles around, hence the name *tamnavulin*, which is Gaelic for the *Mill on the Hill*. The distillery went into production in 1966.

IRAN

Pepsi-Cola, *Coca-Cola* and *Canada Dry* ginger ale are produced locally and are popular, as well as other well-known soft drinks. There are three makes of beer. Vodka is produced, as well as wine, from which brandy is distilled, and some of this is exported to the U.S.S.R. Small quantities of Iranian vodka find their way to Western Europe. The principal import is Scotch whisky, followed by French cognac, and fairly small quantities of champagne and other wines and liqueurs. Soda-water is the principal additive to spirits.

Bars normally close at midnight, and the sale to the public of all alcohol is banned during Ramadan and on other Moslem religious holidays. There is no advertising of alcoholic drinks, since the country is officially Moslem. In summer, fruit drinks are drunk in vast amounts; tea and coffee are extremely popular. In practice, alcohol is largely confined to foreigners and highly Westernized "society" folk.

IRELAND
Public houses in the Republic of Ireland open on weekdays, in winter 10.30 to 23.00 hours, in summer until 23.30 hours. Sunday opening is from 12.30 to 14.00 and 16.00 to 22.00 hours. This is a decided improvement on Great Britain. The only days the pubs are (technically) shut are Christmas Day and Good Friday. St. Patrick's Day counts as a Sunday. Hotel residents can drink round the clock. Licensed premises, including clubs, can have 12 extensions a year till 03.00 hours.

The Irish have a reputation as topers. Two American sociologists wrote in 1963, "Drink has been their curse. It has been the principal fact of Irishness that they have not been able to shake". Looked at in American terms this may be true. In New York in a single year, a review based on ethnic groups showed that Irish-Americans provided 25.6 first hospital admissions for alcohol psychoses per 100,000 inhabitants; the next group, Scandinavian, coming out at a mere 7.6. However, in the homeland, it may surprise some to learn, the Irish in fact consume less than half the alcohol drunk in Switzerland, New Zealand, Australia and Belgium; less than a third that taken in Italy and less than a fifth that in France. Over 70 per cent of alcohol drunk in Ireland is as beer, Guinness leading; yet despite their legendary thirst, the Irish can only manage a per capita consumption of 102 pints per head of population, way behind the over-taxed U.K. resident, who averages 164.

Ireland's standing in the alcoholism and cirrhosis stakes is equally low and in convictions for drunkenness per 100,000 population the Irish can produce per annum no more than 105 against Canada's 740; though in fairness to the dominion one must add that her repressive licensing laws have the usual effect of increasing drinking offences. No, we shall have to agree that the Irish are not big drinkers, or not until they get to New York. But they are happy drinkers; none better while away the hours, with a mug of Guinness in hand and a flow of marvellous conversation. See also Irish whiskey; Guinness.

IRISH COFFEE
This attractive and popular potion has done much to re-enliven interest in IRISH WHISKEY. It is said to have been invented by Mr. Joe Sheridan when he was head chef at Shannon Airport, Eire. I give the official recipe. Warm a stemmed glass. Put into it a jigger of Irish whiskey, sugar and *really* hot black coffee. Stir well. Pour pure cream gently on top (or cream, slightly whipped). Do *not* stir after cream has been added.

IRISH MIST
Honey and herbal-flavoured liqueur based on aged Irish whiskey. The name is modern, but it is claimed to have a legendary origin in the "heather wine" known a thousand years ago. In the last century, Daniel Williams of Tullamore Distillery, tried to find the long-lost recipe, which was thought to have been taken abroad, but died before succeeding. His descendants went on searching, and narrowed the field to Austria without any further success. So they tried to reconstitute what they thought the ancient drink might have been like.

Then in 1948, by a strange coincidence an Austrian war refugee turned up at Tullamore, Eire, with a recipe which he said had been for generations in his family: it turned out to be a variation, and mild improvement, on the Williams family's reconstructed one—and that is *Irish Mist* now. It is exported in great quantity.

IRISH WHISKEY
This is indubitably the oldest form of whisk(e)y, the art of distillation having been

Irish Whiskey

brought to the country some 900 years ago when Ireland enjoyed an active cultural life, in advance of the British mainland. Her monastic traditions would have aided the production of *Uisge Beatha*, local rendering of *aqua vitae*, since monks had a virtual monopoly of serious distilling. In the ancient *Book of Leinster*, the spirit is mentioned for the first time. It records that after a feast at Dundadheann, near BUSHMILLS, guests left at midnight after soundly partaking of the local distillation, seeking their way to Louth on the East coast, but never came fully to their senses till they found themselves in County Limerick in the South.

In due course whiskey passed from the cloister to become virtually a cottage industry, anyone distilling without let or hindrance. Evidently, King Henry VIII thought this made his Irish subjects too happy, for an Act restricting production to licensed sources was promulgated, and, as far as the North was concerned, the King's Deputy in Ulster instantly granted himself a licence.

In 1661 whiskey came under taxation, with a duty of fourpence a gallon, but no one seems to have bothered much about this, for in 1784 a survey showed at least a third of the stills were illicit. A census of 1813 indicated 20,000 illegal stills in operation. Some exist today, producing "potheen" (derived from the *pot-still*) which ranges from the rawest unmatured spirit to a tolerable semi-mellowed whiskey. An ingenious method of frustrating revenue officers, who often rely on the tell-tale smell of distilling to discover an illicit still, is for the potheen "moonshiners" to take their apparatus to sea in a boat, the breeze dissipating the odour. An attempt may be made to take advantage of the romance of potheen by launching a *Potheen* brand commercially.

For a long time such whisky as was drunk in England came mainly from Ireland, but around a century ago Scotch began its triumphant descent on the South, and into Ireland herself. However, Irish whiskey ranks among the small number of truly fine international drinks that are a distinctive and famous product of their particular country. The Irish Whiskey Association is active in promotional activities throughout the world, and the industry's commercial strength has in 1966 been augmented by a merger of three distilleries in the republic: John Jameson & Son Ltd., founded 1780; John Power & Son Ltd., founded 1791; and Cork Distilleries Co Ltd., this last having come about through a local merger in 1867. The whiskey named after one of its most popular salesmen, Paddy Flaherty, became its leading brand and is known as *Paddy*. The sole distillery in Northern Ireland is BUSHMILLS. The Irish, north and south, once had their own choice of at least 13 brands of whiskey, now they are reduced to about six.

Irish whiskey is matured for a minimum of seven years. While brands will, of course, vary, the general composition of the mash is barley (half of which is malted for most brands), wheat, rye and oats: Irish whiskey is peculiar in using oats. The pot-still method is usual, employing large stills and three distillations in place of the two customary for Scotch malts. *Tullamore Dew* is a fine light Irish whiskey. See also Irish Mist.

Recipes Irish whiskey can obviously be used, if preferred, for *Whiskey Sling, Rickey, Collins*, etc. Apart from IRISH COFFEE, there are really no celebrated mixed drinks associated with this type. In connection with recent promotions of Irish whiskey, a few cocktails have been dreamed up, of which I select two, SERPENT'S TOOTH and SHAMROCK.

ISLE OF MAN

This autonomous British island pays by choice the full U.K. taxation on drinks, receiving a rebate annually from the British exchequer, one reason for the low income tax. The Manx Parliament (the House of Keys) is 1,100 years old, and has a much better title to be called the "Mother of Parliaments" than that which has existed at Westminster for a considerably shorter time.

In summer, public houses stay open from 10.30 to 22.45 hours on weekdays, Sundays from noon to 13.30 and 20.00 to 22.00 hours. Winter hours are shorter, with no Sunday opening. The casino has a unique licence, granted directly by the governor. The government has a direct stake in this establishment. The casino's bars are licensed from 10.00 hours until 05.00 hours. Drinks and drinking patterns are similar to those of the mainland. The main local brewery is owned by Heron & Brearley Ltd., who are the island's principal supplier of drinks; there is another brewery at Castletown.

ISRAEL

The influx of new citizens from many wine-growing countries has given a considerable fillip to an ancient industry. The hot climate, and local taste, have dictated a dominance of sweet wines, and port, malaga, tokay, sweet sherry, sauternes and champagne were produced. These are now put out mainly under Hebraic brand-names. See also Sabra.

Vermouths are also made, and grape brandy. Most of the production is consumed locally but as production increases so do exports. For export, the wine is produced under religious control, as it is often used on ritual as well as social occasions. A number of new vineyards are not yet fully established so that quality of future wines is still speculative, but conditions are good, the expertize is there, and a ready and loyal overseas market exists.

ITALY

The famous wines of this country include CHIANTI and VERMOUTH. They are drunk all over the world. The Italians themselves have a preference for red wines. In order of importance, I have abbreviated the following list compiled by a leading agent as indicating national drinking habits: Italian wines (including aperitifs such as CAMPARI); Italian beers and soft drinks; imported beers and *Coca-Cola* (made under licence); imported wines (mainly French); brandies (imported and domestic); Scotch whisky; *grappa* and other *eaux-de-vie*; fruit cordials (domestic and imported).

A lot of potables are imported, French wines and champagne leading this field; followed by Spanish, German, Portuguese and Hungarian wines; and then Scotch, brandies, American and Canadian whiskies. Dry vermouth is widely used as an additive for spirits. Italian taste is sophisticated, and one normally finds the whole range of internationally known drinks and brands in well-stocked stores and bars. There are no restrictions on liquor imports and retail and bar licences are easily obtained. There are strong laws to protect the consumer against substitution, false claims and deceitful labelling. There are virtually no restrictions on advertising and promoting alcohol, except in media designed for young persons. An increasing demand for the best known brands indicates the growing prosperity of the country and the education of popular taste.

Under a package of economic measures announced in the autumn of 1970, Italy upped the tax on spirits by 50 per cent, a move which may somewhat inhibit sales of Scotch whisky which is enormously popular.

Wine Production of wine is marginally bigger than that of France though consumption in the latter country is considerably ahead of the Italian. Virtually the whole country produces wine of some type, and of course a fair amount of this is turned into VERMOUTH, is distilled into brandy or *grappa*, or is required for such famous drinks as CAMPARI.

Without in any way denigrating Italian wines, vintage plays a comparatively small part in the vast industry: essentially, the Italians are concerned with sound table wines made for drinking young, or to be blended and pasteurized for export. (In recent times there was a great scandal in the Italian industry when it was revealed that a vast amount of artificial wine, made from an extraordinary range of waste products, was being sold. Why it was economic to go to this trouble in a country bulging with wine I have never discovered, but the disclosures rocked the country. I am sure there will be no repetition).

By general consent the best Italian wines come from Piedmont, home of the splendid robust barolo reds, as well as the totally contrasting ASTI SPUMANTE, and vermouth. On the other side of the country, the Veneto, lie the vineyards near Verona which produce my favourite Italian white wine, the delicate SOAVE. From the Veneto also come bardolino, which is akin to beaujolais, and the better-known VALPOLICELLA. Personally I prefer this to the (normally) harsher CHIANTI, most popular of all Italian table wines: I prefer a chianti bottled in Italy, it invariably seems much better, and, of course, the vast majority is bottled there. Moving southwards, right in the middle of Italy is Umbria whence comes sweet ORVIETO, sharing with chianti the wicker-covered flask.

Frascati, from the town south-east of Rome, is another attractive white wine, on the sweet side, though dry ones exist. Moving towards the toe of Italy, the Naples area is noted for its LACRIMA CHRISTI, which personally I do not put in the same class as the more northerly white wines, though some people do. Sicily is mainly noted for MARSALA. Vintage wines from Brolio, Frescobaldi and Antinori can be first class.

J

JACK DANIELS WHISKEY
This famous American brand proudly calls itself Tennessee whiskey, and is traditionally made by slow filtering through deep charcoal before ageing in cask. It enjoys a high reputation.

JAMAICA
As one would expect, rum, one of the island's great products and exports, leads the popularity stakes. Gin, vodka and beer (lager) are produced locally. *Tia Maria*, the country's own liqueur, is an important export in its own right. Scotch whisky is imported as well as other leading brands of spirits. A type of "Scotch" is being made locally from cane alcohol mixed with a Scotch whisky base. Rum punches and other esteemed mixed drinks are for tourists; the residents tend to take their rum with ice and a little soda-water or plain water. Licensing laws are liberal, but strictly enforced.

JAPAN
The national drink is, of course, SAKE. With beer and Japanese whisky, these are the most popular stimulants. The prestigious drink is Scotch (de-luxe brands particularly) and cognac is also highly regarded; to some extent, but to nothing like the same extent, the Japanese share the fallacious Chinese theory that brandy aids virility. Local production of whisky, of which not a little is now exported, runs at well over 100 million litres a year; gin, rum and vodka run at about $5\frac{1}{2}$ million litres; sundry liqueurs at $16\frac{1}{2}$ million; brandy 5 mil-

SOME FAMOUS WINES OF ITALY

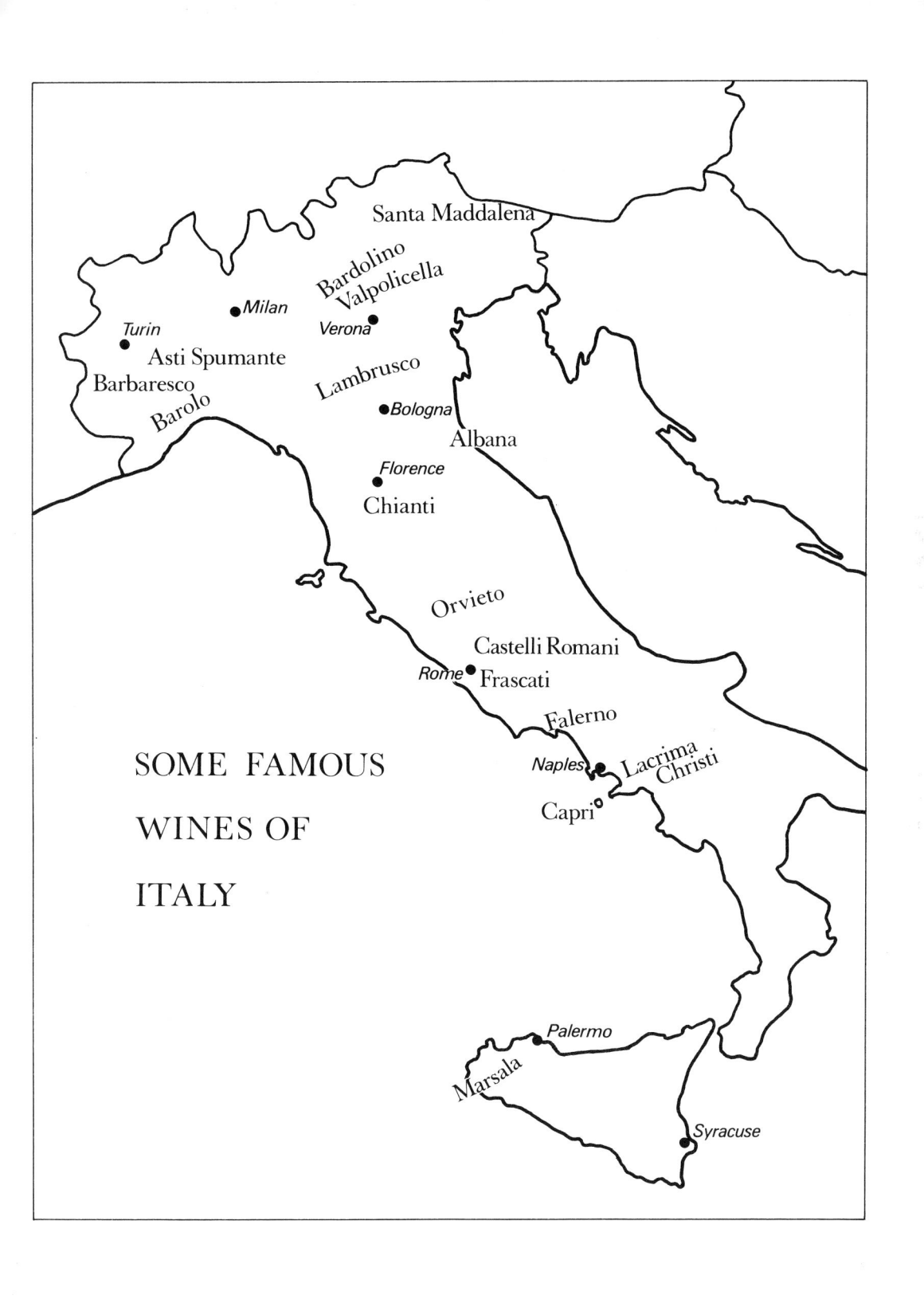

Japan

lion; wine rather over 2 million; beer 2,500 million, and sake 1,400 million. These statistics give a good indication of Japanese tastes. Exports, whisky apart, are beer and saké, mainly to the U.S.A. and South-east Asia. Sale of strong spirits is strictly controlled, and my informants tell me there are "too many definitions and restrictions" about the sale of saké in Japanese law, which repeats the complaints of many countries. Any media may be used for advertising liquor.

In the normal way, Japanese who can afford to, drink saké before every meal, especially in the evening. It appears somewhat addictive and devotees may consume two, or even three, large jars nightly: this is known as *banshaku* (every night boozing). Saké parties commemorate every event from births to funerals. Traditional restaurants normally pay scant attention to Western drinks and concentrate on serving saké; at formal events geishas pouring it. The position is completely the reverse in smart bars and night clubs. Fish dishes are considered the best accompaniment to saké, and it is often served accompanied by little pieces of *sashimi*, sliced raw fish.

Before the Second World War the heavy drinker was considered a pillar of society and rejoiced in the name of *tora* (tiger), but a more temperate attitude prevails today. The tradition of plying guests with saké is still maintained, as many a visiting businessman has found when taken to a restaurant. I am told with frankness from Tokyo that this "usually annoys foreign guests." Well, I know quite a few people who have been to Japan and they certainly have not complained: quite the contrary!

Despite the anti-Americanism of students, American social (dinking) customs strongly influence affluent Japanese, and there is a steady Westernization in this field. The young are taking to such drinks as gin-and-tonic and vodka-and-lime. Scotch retains its great prestige. A bottle of standard well-known Scotch (there are a vast number of brands on the market) costs from £4 upwards. The most prestigious *sukochi* of all, *Joni-kuro* (*Johnnie Walker*) *Black Label* sells for £11·50 a bottle as I write, according to *The Financial Times*. It is *the* snob whisky; if possible no Japanese businessman would demean himself by offering a contact as a New Year present even *Johnnie Walker Red*.

In 1971 the Japanese removed the import quota restrictions on Scotch. However, the 100 per cent *ad valorem* duty applies, as against 35 per cent for American whiskey and 40 per cent for Canadian whisky, plus hefty excise duties. At present Scotch is only some 1 per cent of the Japanese market for whisky, but the signs are hopeful. In the upper end of the whisky market, *Suntory* and *Nikka*, the principal Japanese brands, have fought and eroded Scotch interests and though the aforesaid Japanese businessman would drop dead before losing face by presenting a colleague with a domestic brand, the general consumer is more price conscious.

Japanese Whisky This is decidedly less of a joke than it was. Gone are the days when imitation Scotch bore "distilled in Aberdeen" (it was said that a township was thus renamed); "as supplied to Buckingham Palace", or, I am assured, "pressed from the finest Scottish grapes". Suntory, the best known distillers, have distilled, matured and blended some whiskies which, while indubitably a long way from Scotch, have gone some way towards capturing an aroma of Scotland and have been pronounced tolerable by independent experts. There is a tendency by some distillers to let the tartan creep in, but apart from the global vigilance of the Scotch Whisky Association in such matters, the Japanese authorities themselves are alert to misrepresentation. Suntory's least expensive brand, retailing at around £2 against about £4 for a standard Scotch, is labelled *Finest Old Liqueur. A blend of ancient whiskies. Distillery at Yamazaki, Osaka.*

Japanese whisky is finding its way abroad; it is even considered rather smart to have a bottle in the home in parts of California. The day indeed may come when Japanese whisky stands on its own feet as a distinctive national product, like bourbon.

J. & B. RARE
A leading "light" Scotch whisky, taking its name from JUSTERINI & BROOKS, a subsidiary of INTERNATIONAL DISTILLERS & VINTNERS; not particularly strong on the British market, where there is no great enthusiasm for this type, but the current brand leader in the United States and some other overseas markets.

JIGGER
Bar term for a MEASURE; essential equipment.

JIM BEAM
Established only a decade after the Rev. Elijah Craig "invented" BOURBON, this brand of *Kentucky Straight Bourbon Whiskey* simply claims to be the "world's finest" (why not just the U.S.A.'s, since bourbon may not be distilled elsewhere?). It is, on my latest chart, the biggest-selling whiskey in its field.

JOHANNISBERG
Vineyards of immense antiquity surround this place which produces notable vintages, the greatest being labelled as *Schloss Johannisberg*. See Germany (Wine).

JOHN COLLINS
This is sometimes incorrectly called a *Tom Collins* (which was made with the virtually extinct OLD TOM gin). One measure of dry gin, half-tablespoon of powdered sugar, juice of half lemon. Pour over ice cubes in tumbler. Top with soda-water. For history, see Collins.

JULEP See Mint julep.

JUNGLE JUICE
Originating from "trade gin" and raw African distillations, this term is sometimes used quite affectionately to describe poor quality spirits or hair-raising mixtures.

JUSTERINI & BROOKS LTD.
It is a commonplace to write of the "romance of commerce", but here we have a business literally founded on romance. For if Giacomo Justerini had not fallen in love with the opera singer Margherita Bellino, he would not, in 1749, have followed her to London. He brought more than his heart. He had copied sundry recipes from the archives of an uncle, a distiller in Bologna. Through his lady love's operatic acquaintances he came into contact with one Samuel Johnson (not *the* Samuel Johnson) who had made money in the theatre, and thus obtained the finance to establish himself as a distiller of cordials in Pall Mall, conveniently round the corner from the Italian Opera House in Haymarket.

What happened finally between Giacomo and Margherita is not known; in 1760 Giacomo returned to Italy, leaving the business in Johnson's hands. However the name Justerini was preserved (presumably he retained a financial interest) as is shown in an advertisement in the *Morning Post* in 1779, referring to the concern as a "Foreign Cordial Warehouse". The business was expanding, the first royal warrant, of many, being granted by the Prince of Wales (George IV). Trade was extended into fine wines, by Johnson's son, Augustus, and by the latter's son, of the same name.

In 1831 Augustus Johnson II sold the business to a wealthy young man, Alfred Brooks, who, for reasons unknown, deleted Johnson from the title, added his own name, and retained Justerini's—giving it precedence. The firm has thus been known ever since. Brooks sold the company to his son-in-law, William Cole, a rather dull but worthy person, in 1876. He did not take much interest in the wine trade, but Justerini & Brooks prospered. It was sold in 1900 and became an incorporated company.

It has been, and remains, a fashionable wine merchants, serving the best West End clubs, Buckingham Palace, the great country homes, the wealthy. In 1954 Justerini's bought a rival in the quality field, Chalié Richards. The combined business moved into beautiful new premises in Bond Street, leaving the Pall Mall offices which I can just remember as a boy when my mother stocked her cellar from them: alas, I was too young to taste her choice—or Justerini's. They have since moved again, to St. James's Street, which is really more suitable than the Bond Street of today. Maintaining a highly personal identity, Justerini & Brooks now shine as a star in the I.D.V. group.

The product with which Justerini & Brooks' name is most closely associated in the minds of the general public is one that would have certainly startled Justerini himself or Samuel Johnson, Scotch whisky. *J. & B. Rare*, a pale and very light whisky, has enjoyed an enormous success in the U.S.A. and in many other export markets. It was brilliantly marketed just at the time when American taste was demanding exceptionally light Scotch, and the brand's overseas operations amount to a separate business.

JUSTINA
Brand name for a range of popular blended Portuguese table wines widely sold on the U.K. market (I.D.V.).

K

KAHLUA
An excellent coffee-flavoured liqueur from Mexico.

KAVA
An alcoholic beverage used in numerous South Pacific islands, made from the bitter root of a widespread plant, by an interesting if slightly off-putting method. The local maidens chew the root and then spit it into a common bowl of water.

KEG
Cask, in wood or metal, of no fixed content but normally around 10 gallons. Keg beer is pasteurized beer in strong kegs with the gas to force the beer out already inside the keg.

KENYA
There is no reason to suppose that the withdrawal of colonial power overnight changes social patterns, and the drinking habits of Kenyans are essentially British, with Scotch whisky dominating the spirit scene with an importation of well over 100,000 proof gallons, whilst gin lags with a mere 10,000. Brandy rates higher with some 26,000 proof gallons. Rum is not popular, but vermouth shows a surprising 50,000 gallons; still wines run at 105,000 gallons and champagne at nearly 6,000. These figures seem indicative of prosperity and a good life. Local production of spirits is around 165,000 litres, most of which I assume to be WARAGI. Beer is

extremely popular, with a production of over 60 million litres, some of which is exported. Licensing is strict as to cleanliness of premises.

KING GEORGE IV OLD SCOTCH WHISKY

One of the original blends sold by The Distillers Co. Ltd. When, soon after the First World War, the D.C.L. decided to discontinue selling brands directly, a new company, The DISTILLERS AGENCY LTD., was incorporated to continue the marketing of this excellent blend.

It is interesting to note that when, in 1822, King George IV made the first royal visit to Edinburgh by a reigning monarch for 200 years, he set sail at the end of this visit in his yacht, the *Royal George* from Port Edgar in the Royal Burgh of South Queensferry alongside where, in later years, were built the premises in which the whisky bearing his name was blended and bottled. A painting in oils by John Christian Schetky (1822) recording the departure of the royal yacht hangs today in the managing director's office in London.

The head office of *King George IV Old Scotch Whisky* is at 63 Pall Mall in London, directly opposite St. James's Palace where, on the 12th August, 1762, a son was born to Queen Charlotte and King George III who became Prince of Wales and Prince Regent (better known, probably, as "Prinny"), and ultimately crowned King George IV in 1820. A pendant sign hangs outside "63" showing the monarch in Garter robes, as portrayed on the label on every size of bottle of this famous whisky. In the entrance hall, there is a special display of interesting Regency items, dominated by an original painting by a court painter of the time showing the king in his Garter robes.

In 1962 the company remembered the bicentenary of his birth, and the highlight of the celebrations was the luncheon given to many of its friends in the wine and spirit trade in the Royal Pavilion in Brighton, the residence specially built for "Prinny" and where he spent so much of his time.

The registered office of The Distillers Agency is in Edinburgh, in an elegant Georgian house in Coates Crescent, one of the city's many delightful Nineteenth-Century crescents.

KING'S RANSOM

Premium Scotch whisky from William Whiteley & Co.: well above the average U.K. strength.

KINLOCH & CO., CHARLES

This firm, now an important part of the COURAGE group, was founded in the City of London in 1861, and is among the largest shippers, bottlers, blenders and distributors of wines and spirits in the U.K.

KIR

A mixture of chilled chablis and CASSIS, invented by the celebrated Canon Kir, who died in 1968 aged 92. For a cleric he led an ample life; as parliamentarian, doyen of the national assembly, mayor of his beloved Dijon where he scandalized his church by officially receiving the Russian leader Khrushchev in 1960. A gastronome, to be immortalized by a drink is not a renown he would have despised.

KIRSCH

At its best a brandy made from a cherry base and distilled, either with or without the crushed cherry stones. It is principally a product of the German Black Forest area and adjacent parts of France, also Switzerland. At its best it is not a CHERRY BRANDY in the normal meaning of that term, but a true brandy.

KOBRAND CORPORATION

American selling agents for *Beefeater* gin, they pushed the sales of *Beefeater* on the U.S.

KOUMISS

eastern seaboard for five years before the breakthrough, which made *Beefeater* Britain's most successful gin export. See also Burrough.

KOUMISS

Alcoholic beverage, used in wilder parts of the Balkans and Caucasus, made from fermented milk, the source dependent on the type of animal most available locally.

KRITER

A French brand of exceptionally fine VIN MOUSSEUX. It is an unusual example of a new entrant into a difficult market making good. The Kriter company was only formed in 1962 and within seven years it was selling 3 million bottles a year in France alone and expects sales to go to 8 million. Its impact on the British market, the most important for quality French wines, has also been considerable.

Kriter departs from the normal CUVE CLOSE method, in that the wine undergoes its secondary fermentation in bottles, as with good champagnes. But instead of the costly REMUAGE and DEGORGEMENT, Kriter adopted a process by which, after fermentation and a resting period, the bottles have their contents siphoned into pressure tanks without losing any of the natural effervescence. In a continuous operation, the same bottles are filled with wine from the next CUVEE and the cycle is repeated. In the pressure tank the appropriate DOSAGE is added, followed by a brief refrigeration during which the sediment sinks to the bottom. The wine is then drawn off into new bottles. It is made principally from Aligoté grapes, grown throughout the Burgundy district. This is a remarkable instance of adjusting time-honoured wine-making to mass production, without sacrificing quality, for *Kriter* has all the character of a bottle-fermented wine, the very dry *brut de brut* providing, in my opinion, outstanding value in sparkling wine.

KRONENBOURG

A mass-selling quality strong French lager which is being strenuously introduced to the British market, presumably in the hope of adjusting a considerable imbalance since British beers started flowing increasingly into France.

KRUG

A fine brand of CHAMPAGNE, of which prized vintages quickly become rare. I have been told that on the fall of France to the Germans, the German leader Hermann Goering immediately commandeered for his personal use as much *Krug* as his minions could lay hands on, which shows his good taste for wine, if nothing else.

KUMMEL

Today the Dutch probably make the best type of this caraway-seed flavoured liqueur, though it was originally the Riga version that was most esteemed. Popular in Germany, it is considered a prime digestive. It may be mixed with gin to break down its rather strong taste.

L

LABELS
A label should be informative; its decoration is unimportant except as a marketing operation. Many great wines have quite ordinary labels; some notable other drinks are not very attractively packaged. A wine label should tell you what is in the bottle; what type of wine, by whom made, the country of origin, the year of its vintage, if any, where it was bottled (when it was bottled for some fortified wines), who shipped it. The more important the wine, the more information there will be. It is not difficult to read a wine label, though some rather special knowledge is needed for German wines of pedigree. If it is a simple blended wine, this should be plain.

LACRIMA CHRISTI
A fairly undistinguished Italian (usually white) wine from the Naples area, enjoying a fame from its name (*Christ's tears*) that would otherwise probably not adhere to it.

LAFITE-ROTHSCHILD, CHATEAU
Celebrated BORDEAUX vineyard, not to be confused with that of another member of the Rothschild family, MOUTON-ROTHSCHILD. Lafite-Rothschild is one of the four *premiers crus* in the 1855 classification of Bordeaux wines. Old labels may give this wine as *Château Laffite*.

LAGAR
The big stone vat in which the grape juice for Portuguese wines, notably port, is pressed.

LAGER
Originally a cellar for maturing BEER.

LAMB'S NAVY RUM
Perhaps the best known of traditional pungent rums (United Rum Merchants).

LANG'S SCOTCH WHISKY
Well known in Scotland for over a century, this blend has recently made a big effort to invade the English market, establishing a new London office in Piccadilly. Sales have increased lately in the U.S.A. and the burgeoning European market for Scotch whisky. Lang Brothers were established in 1861, a few years later acquiring the Glengoyne distillery, which started operation in 1833, a decade after rationalization of the industry and virtual elimination of illicit distilling. The firm is now part of the Robertson & Baxter group.

LANGUEDOC
A massive wine-producing area of southern France which makes vast quantities of poor blending wines; the first post-war bulk wine imports to Britain came from here and were welcomed, but would on their own hardly be bothered with today, unless as local beverage wines on holiday. Because of the fierce summers, some tolerable, sweet, wines are made.

LANSON PERE ET FILS
The first member of the family to control the fortunes of the champagne firm was Jean Baptiste Lanson who had no fewer than eight sons of whom two, the eldest, Victor, and his brother Henri, joined their father. At this time, the company's output was relatively small and the bulk of it came to Britain, the only country to which Lanson's exported. But steadily and gradually production was increased until shortly after the Franco-Prussian War of 1870, when Victor was joined by his son Henri-Marie Lanson, the firm was in a position to increase their shipments and when his father died, Henri Marie decided to seek markets elsewhere, as well as in Britain.

Lanson Père Et Fils

With increasing rapidity sales were stepped up until the outbreak of World War I, when the fighting and then the *Phylloxera*, which destroyed thousands of vines, put a stop to the increasing sales. Even so, when the offices of the company in Rheims were razed to the ground by enemy action, a tiny staff working in the underground cellars managed to maintain small but steady shipments to Britain, the U.S.A. and the Netherlands, by keeping their activities secret from the German invaders right up to March 1918.

Once the war was over and the time had come to re-establish the company on a sound peacetime footing, Victor Lanson, the present chairman, and his brother Henri, who had taken over many of their father's responsibilities in 1919, found themselves with a tiny skeleton staff and the whole premises to be rebuilt. They set to work with determination to restore the fortunes of their house and while Victor and his father took the initiative of buying further vineyards when many had decided there was no longer a place for fine champagne in a chaotic world, Henri travelled Europe and France and spent nearly 20 years in the U.S.A. rebuilding the company's overseas trade.

The reorganization of the company was nearly completed in 1939 when World War II brought another halt to their fortunes. By this time, they had vineyards in Sillery, Verzenay, Ambonnay, Bouzy, Mareuil s/Ay, and Dizy, from which the red grapes were obtained, and at Oger, Avize, Cramant and Chouilly, from which they obtained their white. These vineyards normally supplied about half the company's requirements, but the war brought two major catastrophes, a lack of manure which resulted in greatly reduced crops, and wholesale requisitioning of their champagne by the Germans, which left their stocks extremely low by the end of 1945. It took five years to make good this damage and in 1950, when rebuilding of export sales began, Victor Lanson made the world tour.

More recently, with only small crops in 1956, 1957 and 1958, sales in France herself had to be cut down by half in order to meet export demands, but since then Lanson have been able to carry on and expand sales, especially of its *Black Label*, an extra-dry non-vintage champagne, which is becoming more and more popular all over the world every year. This represents some 85 per cent of the company's champagne sales and is known by the same name everywhere. I rate it high amongst non-vintages. The British agents are Percy FOX & Co.

LAPHROAIG
Best known of the malt whiskies from the island of Islay, off the Scottish Atlantic coast.

LA TACHE
Outstanding BURGUNDY wine.

LATE BOTTLED See Port.

LATOUR, CHATEAU
Excellent claret, whether or not château-bottled. Incidentally, it is highly unlikely to be anything but château-bottled. There are a host of other "Latour . . . this-and-that" in the BORDEAUX country. *Château Latour* is one of the four *premiers crus* in the 1855 classification of Bordeaux wines.

LAURENT PERRIER
An excellent champagne which, having for some time not been very active in the British market, is making a strong and deserved comeback.

LEBANON
Aniseed-flavoured ARRACK is the most favoured drink. The usual spirits and wines are imported, in wines *rosé* being specially popular. There are no licensing restrictions, and as one would expect there is virtually no drunkenness. It is worthy of note that though half the population of 1,500,000 are Moslems and (at least officially) forbidden strong drink,

consumption of whisky is some 700,000 litres a year. Arrack is customarily drunk in the afternoon or evening to the accompaniment of a multitude of appetizing little dishes. A friend tells me he was intrigued during a visit by the habit of serving drinks in restaurants and nightclubs, accompanied not just by the usual "nibbles" but also strips of raw carrot.

LEES
Dregs left in a wine vat or other vessel; the residue of flavouring stills used for gin rectification, or other similar sediments.

LEMON
The amateur "mixologist" should always have lemons to hand; it is a most important FRUIT. A good lemon/orange press is extremely useful. Though fresh juice is best, I consider it permissible to make use of the convenience of unsweetened *P.L.J.* lemon or frozen orange juice. I have also employed concentrates with success for certain drinks requiring a lot of juice and for non-alcoholic mixes.

LEMON GIN
ORANGE GIN, substituting lemon rind.

LIEBFRAUMILCH
This means about as much as HOCK does. It is simply any German Rhine wine. In Worms, Rheinhesse, there exists a church, surrounded by a vineyard, called Leibfrauenkirche: this is the legendary origin of the name. *Liebfraumilch*, if allied to a well-known name, can indicate an excellent wine: otherwise, it may mean nothing. Among excellent wines in this category I include *Hans Christoff* from Deinhard & Co., a firm with other fine wines. CAPITAL WINE AGENCIES LTD. have unusually good value in their German-bottled *Rheinkapelle*, from M. Meyer of Rudesheim. See also Sichel, for *Blue Nun*. I would also mention *Crown of Crowns*, an excellent brand by Langenbach, a firm represented by Percy FOX and Co. Ltd.

LIGHT WHISKEY
This should properly be in quotation marks, for what it may eventually be called, in addition to the over-all description "American whiskey", is not known. We are here dealing with the future, and it is a complicated matter. Since we shall be hearing quite a lot on this subject, I will try to simplify the question.

Regulations did not, until comparatively recently, permit American whiskey producers to mature their product other than in new casks, in order to claim they were aged. Further, bourbon and rye whiskies must be distilled below 160° proof (U.S.) and are customarily distilled at considerably lower proofs. This produces a whiskey with a high CONGENER content, which is reinforced by "extractive" from the new barrels. To this is due the distinctive and fairly strong character of bourbon and rye whiskies.

Probably because of the marked success of Scotch whisky, and Canadian, in the U.S.A., the American Distilling Co. Inc., submitted to the alcohol and tobacco tax division of the internal revenue service that they wanted permission for their proposal "to add a new standard of identity for a whisky which has been distilled at more than 160° proof but at less than 190° proof, aged in oak barrels seasoned by prior use, and to permit such whisky to bear a conventional age statement."

What the company wished to be allowed to produce was a "light whiskey", and the reasons why it wished to employ previously used casks were these. First, it was permitted to distil at the higher proof mentioned (over 160° proof) and such a product would legally be whiskey under U.S. laws: but unless it were aged in new casks it would be unlawful to give this whiskey a stated age. Secondly, the new whiskey the company wanted to make would have only half the congeners (call it flavour if you like) of bourbon. But from new casks the whiskey would extract just as much as would the lower proof bourbon or rye. In

Lillet

that event, the final product could not be the very light whiskey that was the object of the operation. (There would also be an economy in the employment of re-used casks, but that was not an important point in the submissions of the company.)

The company's submission made it very clear that this was not to be an imitation of any existing whiskey but a new product altogether, though the competitor clearly in mind is Scotch and particularly the "light" brands that have enjoyed popularity in the U.S.

The experiment was allowed, and 200m. gallons of "light whiskey" are maturing, the first batch scheduled for release in mid-1972 after 4 years in cask.

A "light whiskey" should not be confused with "white whiskey". For instance, Brown-Forman have introduced a white whiskey on the American market. However, it may be remembered that all whiskies, including Scotch, are white in colour prior to maturing. After maturing most whiskies require some colouring to appeal to the market.

Once the initial furore has settled, the ultimate fate of "light whiskey" will not be known for some time. American Distilling Co's vice-president Joseph C. Haefelin has indicated a big U.S. demand with the affluent and trendy under-35's. Stanley Giraitis of Schenley Affiliated Brands has suggested four-fifth of the new spirit will go into American whiskey blends and that Bourbon, Scotch and Canadian whiskies will not suffer, though Vodka might. *On verra.*

LILLET

An admirable aperitif which I hope may again become as well-known outside France as it used to be when I was younger. It was launched by two brothers of that name in 1872, and remains the principal product of a firm which is still essentially a family one.

Lillet is based on wines from their estates, some 40 miles up the Garonne from Bordeaux. The wines are matured a year and then blended to ensure consistency. After a further two years' maturing the blended wines are flavoured with sundry herbal ingredients, one being quinine. Not until after another three years, during which ingredients and wine marry completely, is *Lillet* aperitif ready for the market. There is a *Red Lillet*, but at present only the *White* is on the British market. It is a distinctively "different" drink served very cold, with a twist of lemon, with or without the addition of a little water or soda. It does splendidly with gin.

LIME; LIME JUICE (Cordial)

Limes, which can play an important part in mixed drinks, are only seasonally available in Britain, and then not widely. One may instead have to use fresh lemon juice which is not the same thing; use about twice as much as you would for lime. Overseas one can sometimes obtain *Rose's* unsweetened bottled lime juice, but unfortunately not at the moment in Britain. *Rose's Lime Juice Cordial* is indisputably the best in its field.

LIQUEUR

1 Sweetened *eaux de vie*, of which there is an enormous variety. I think that similar but lower strength alcoholic drinks of this type, such as cherry brandy, are best described as cordials, though that phrase is used in the U.S.A. to describe many liqueurs. Not to be confused with *sirop* (syrup), such as GRENADINE, which are normally non-alcoholic, nor with CREMES.

2 For whisky, cognac and so on, "Liqueur" is a prefix or suffix broadly applied to more aged and costlier spirits, and is something of a misnomer. It is not usually mentioned on labels but is rather a popular trade and consumer description, meaning the spirit is so smooth that it merits drinking when one would otherwise have a liqueur, at the conclusion of a repast. On the other hand, if one could afford it, one would presumably drink "liqueur" whisky at any time. Another ex-

Plate 24. Vineyards line the hills on either side of the River Douro (see Offley Forrester Ltd.).

Plate 25. Workers harvest grapes at Croft's Quinta (*wine estate*) da Roeda, in Portugal.

ample of the rather senseless words that have come into common usage.

LIQUID GALLON See Wine gallon.

LIQUOR
In a distillery or brewery, this word means WATER. Colloquially, and even in legal parlance, it connotes (including throughout this book) alcoholic beverages in general.

LITRE
With metrication in Britain we shall have to start thinking about this. A litre equals 1.7 English pints (1.7608 pints, if you want to be pedantic, which I do not). Or 0.2 gallons. Fortunately, the standard English bottle of 26⅔ FLUID OUNCES is almost equivalent to .75 litres, the same as the average wine bottle. See Comparisons.

LIVERY COMPANIES
There are five livery companies of the City of London traditionally concerned with the wine and spirit trade, the BREWERS', COOPERS', DISTILLERS', INNHOLDERS' and VINTNERS'. One must be careful not to confuse ancient city guilds with modern organizations: viz., the Distillers' Company is not The DISTILLERS Co. Ltd., nor is the Brewers' Company the same as the Brewers' Society.

LODGE
The dominance of English interests in port and madeira is indicated by the employment of this word for a place for storing wine.

LOGAN'S DE-LUXE SCOTCH WHISKY
Premium blend put out by WHITE HORSE.

LOIRE
A large and important French wine district leading north-west from BURGUNDY and at the conjunction of the two areas producing very similar wines; thus the Loire's *Pouilly Fumé* to Burgundy's *Pouilly Fuissé*. It is broadly divided into Anjou and Touraine. It is essentially a region of delicate white and *rosé* wines, many of them *pétillant*, and some sparkling, which are extremely attractive though hardly *grands crus*. As with the beaujolais, they are for drinking young, fresh and cool.

Apart from *Pouilly*, the best known names are *Anjou* (particularly *Rosé d'Anjou*), *Vouvray*, *Sancerre* and *Muscadet*, all of which are broadly in commerce in Britain, and *Saumur* which is better known in France. *Muscadet* is something of a vogue wine in Britain, appealing by its lightness and low alcohol content to much the same consumers who like Portuguese *vinho verdhe*. I consider it desirable to obtain French-bottled Loire wines, despite the extra cost, but the often misused phrase "doesn't travel" does tend to apply to the best Loire wines and they certainly seem very much better when drunk near where they are made.

LONG JOHN
Well-known Scotch whisky owned by SEAGER EVANS.

LOWENBRAU
A strong and expensive German lager which has enjoyed considerable success in Britain. Mr. J. C. McLaughlin, has been specially active promotionally, and his *Bier Kellers* have proved popular.

LOWRIE LTD., W. P.
Through BUCHANAN's a D.C.L. subsidiary company. When James Buchanan first established himself in London, it was to his friend Mr. Lowrie to whom he first turned for supplies for use in his own blend, and Lowrie's still operate the same Convalmore Distillery, Dufftown, as then. They are agents in Scotland for some notable wine firms and also operate two very important cooperages. I have visited the one in Glasgow, a memorable experience. COOPERAGE is a vital

Low Wines

ancillary activity to the production of Scotch whisky.

LOW WINES
Nothing to do with wine at all, this term is nowadays principally used to describe the first distillation of Scotch whisky.

LUXEMBOURG
A considerable producer of Moselle wines, most of which are consumed locally, and a small importer of wines from neighbouring France. Main production is light white table wines, with a limited amount of fine wine closely defined by law. KIRSCH, QUETSCH and MIRABELLE are made. After World War II, under government control, quite a lot of Luxembourg "champagne" (the quotes were not then required by British law) was imported into the U.K.: it was better than many substitutes for champagne. It appears to have, unlike some of its rivals, disappeared from general commerce. The wines, and drinking habits, of the Grand Duchy are very similar to those of Germany, with French undertones.

M

McCALLUM'S SCOTS WHISKY
Please note the variation from the normal "Scotch"; a blend by the firm founded in 1807 by Duncan and John McCallum, which only joined D.C.L. in 1953. There is a deluxe variety.

McEWANS
Famous Scottish brewery, now incorporated in SCOTTISH & NEWCASTLE BREWERIES.

MACKENZIE
Big name in vintage and other ports, and also sherry. The firm is based on Oporto.

MACKESON'S
Possibly the only stout on the British market that on a national scale is even in the same league as GUINNESS. Brewed by WHITBREAD's.

MACKINLAY'S SCOTCH WHISKY
See Scottish & Newcastle Breweries.

McMULLEN & SONS LTD.
Well-known family brewers of Hertford. In 1940 I was a fellow officer in an army mess in Hertfordshire with Captain (later Lieut.-Colonel) R. P. McMullen, who now heads the business. He saved Christmas for us by obtaining already scarce wines and spirits from the brewery: it was a yuletide I have never forgotten.

They are the only independent brewery left in Hertfordshire. The brewery was founded in 1827 and the works and warehouses, etc., cover four acres. The firm produces some fine ales, and its *Olde Time* ale won a diploma at the London Brewers' Exhibition in 1960. It owns nearly 200 licensed houses in the surrounding area, imports wines and spirits for bottling and controls a chain of off-licences.

MACON
Fairly robust red and white BURGUNDY wines. From a reliable shipper, usually an excellent buy in the less expensive end of the market. (The "C" is hard.)

MADEIRA
Though I am not optimistic, I hope that the

Madeira wine industry is successful in its not inconsiderable efforts to repopularize the very distinctive wines of the island which, formerly rivalling sherry and port, suffered a steady decline in esteem since the PHYLLOXERA ravaged the vineyards.

Madeira is peculiar in being a "cooked" fortified wine, which gives it an unusual, indeed unique, robustness, so that it has no known age limit and, unlike other wines, appears to improve unceasingly in cask and to last indefinitely in bottle.

It is a wine of great antiquity, the vineyards having been planted by the pioneer Portuguese empire-builders of the Fifteenth Century. The island's volcanic soil was enriched by the incineration of the huge forests that originally covered it.

Again Madeira is unusual in growing vines on rich soil, for wine grapes more usually grow on soil unsuitable for other crops.

The cask-ageing of madeira was probably accidental, in that sending the wine to distant Portuguese colonies meant long sea voyages; there is no evidence that it actually benefited from sea travel, but certainly did from the prolonged sojourn in wood. Later it became the custom to send madeira round the world. Madeira also benefited from the heat of the tropics where Portugal was rich in possessions: this would kill most wines; again, madeira's extraordinary robustness relished the treatment.

Today, the same effect is achieved by leaving the wine, fortified with spirit, to rest in wood at fairly high temperatures for a year or more; this is what gives madeira its special character. The finest dessert malmsey madeira (*Bual*)—in a butt of which the unfortunate Duke of Clarence met *his* deserts—is treated under the sun; the others are stored in specially heated *estufas* (stoves), aboveground cellars. The other types of madeira are *Sercial*, dry and an admirable alternative to sherry, and *Verdelho*, medium-dry. These two should be served mildly chilled, not iced and not, in my opinion, "on the rocks", the best are too interesting for such frigid use. Malmseys of great age, a century or even more, are still in normal commerce. Blandy's list madeiras of 1826 and 1835.

MADERIZATION See Oxidation.

MAGNUM
Double bottle, mainly seen for champagnes. It is also used for claret and burgundy. Wine will keep better for a longer time in larger than normal bottles.

MALAGA
Like MARSALA, this FORTIFIED Spanish sweet wine has suffered a great decline overseas from its former popularity.

MALAYSIA and SINGAPORE
Brandy is imported, principally for the Chinese population with whom it is extremely popular (see HONG KONG). Beer and *samsoo* (rice spirit) come next. Toddy (fermented palm sap) is a speciality: it does not keep and must be drunk fresh, so its sale is limited to specially licensed toddy shops. The popularity of brandy is shown by the import figures (1969), 214,030 gallons, against 92,288 gallons of whisky. Alcohol may not be advertised on TV, but there are no other restrictions. A large amount of toddy is made in Singapore, which seceded from Malaysia in 1965.

MALDANO
Large-selling popular wine cocktails, *Green Goddess* and *Late Night Final*, plus *Egg Flip*.

MALT
1 Grain, usually barley, that has briefly germinated and then dried. This process, by the formation of DIATASE, turns the cereal's starch into sugar, which in due course will be turned into alcohol during FERMENTATION. 2 A description of pure malt Scotch

Malta

whisky; whisky made from only malted barley, not blended with GRAIN whisky. It is sold either as *Single Malt*—product of distillation from one distillery; or as a *Straight Malt*, sometimes called *Vatted*, a blend of aged malts from more than one source.

MALTA
As a growing tourist resort, the George Cross Island will become an increasingly important market for liquor. At present the inhabitants drink wine (there is a local production), beer, spirits and *Kinnie* (a domestic soft drink). Wine is imported from several countries and beer from Italy and Libya. Spirits come principally from Britain in the form of Scotch whisky and gin. *Schweppes* mineral waters are available. There are sensible licensing laws. Alcohol may be advertised by all means, but on T.V. only after 8 p.m. (20.00 hours).

MALVERN WATER
A very pure bottled water from the neighbourhood of the town of that name in Worcestershire. I recommend its use for those who like their gin or whisky with plain water, are fussy about the quality of the ice they make, and whose local tap water is excessively doctored.

MANHATTAN
One of the great American mixed drinks, this is said to have been evolved in 1846 in Maryland, when a bartender stirred up a quick drink of whiskey, syrup and bitters to revive a wounded duellist. Moving to New York in the '90s, vermouth replaced syrup and the cocktail took its name from the fashionable central section of the metropolis.

Most usual recipe today: 1 oz. of American whiskey; ½ oz. of dry vermouth; ½ oz. of sweet vermouth; dash of Angostura. Stir; strain into cocktail glass; decorate with cocktail cherry. This is what the erudite Mr. David A. Embury calls a medium *Manhattan*, and he also lists a sweet variety (only Italian vermouth) and a dry one (only French); also a "de-luxe" version, employing fine bourbon whiskey. In all, this savant of mixed drinks gives a lot of space to the *Manhattan* in his famous *The Fine Art of Mixing Drinks*, classing it as one of the six great basic cocktails. On the other hand the equally authoritative Bernard De Voto once called the *Manhattan*: "an offence against piety", which does not seem to have affected its great popularity.

MARASCHINO (DRIOLI)
Maraschino is distilled from Marasca cherries, and is sold in distinctive straw-covered bottles. The demand for this liqueur, as a digestive and for the use in cooking and cocktails, has resulted in many similar products being produced in various countries where the Dalmatian cherry is not available. This is reason enough to record facts about the first maraschino in the world, made by Drioli, the leading quality brand.

The firm of Drioli was established in Zara, a port on the Adriatic coast, in 1759; there still exist business books from 1766 onwards. From these books, and the remaining correspondence itself, one can see the reputation that Drioli have enjoyed throughout Europe. Towards the end of the Eighteenth Century, exports to England increased to such an extent that some orders had to be refused for want of stock.

In the early days, one of the best customers was the English Government of Malta and Corfu, which every now and again, used to send some "Public War Vessels" to load hundreds of cases of maraschino Drioli, to be afterwards forwarded from Malta to London, as the Prince Regent, George IV, was very fond of the liqueur.

One of the earliest friends of Francesco Drioli was the ancient house of Justerini and Brooks, of London, and the *Morning Post* of June 1779, carried their announcement advertising this liqueur from the Drioli Distillery.

Maraschino Cherries, the fruit being preserved in the liqueur, vary considerably in quality: the best dignify certain drinks; others are no more than cherries in syrup. Use only the best, or none.

MARC
Distilled wine, but emphatically not cognac, and not necessarily matured. There are some good ones, and the best *Marc de Bourgogne* is widely relished, but the majority are firewater. Vineyard owners are allowed to distil a certain quantity of spirits for their own use, and itinerant distillers come round to do this. It would be difficult to stop this long-established practice but there would be fewer CIRRHOSIS deaths if it were abolished.

MARGARITA
Perhaps the only TEQUILA cocktail with any age behind it. Said to have been named by a bartender in Virginia City in memory of his "gal" who died in his arms after getting in the way of a bullet during a shooting. Use 1½ ozs. of tequila; ½ oz. of Cointreau; 1 oz. of lime or lemon juice. Shake; strain into glass of which rim has been wiped with citrus rind and dipped in salt.

MARGAUX
One of the great names of BORDEAUX. Normally any *Margaux* wine will be in the upper echelon, while those of the ancient Château Margaux are outstanding, being one of the four *premiers crus* in the 1855 classification.

MARSALA
Sweet Sicilian fortified wine, formerly extremely popular in Britain, and many other countries, but little regarded now.

MARTELL & CO.
Even in the wine and spirit trade, where family influence is often long-lived, the vast Martell cognac concern is notable for having, come revolution or war, remained a Martell-controlled business since 1715. In that year, Jean Martell came from the Channel Islands and set up in business in Cognac whence, via La Rochelle in particular, brandy was already being exported in considerable quantities, largely to England (legally in time of peace, illicitly when England and France were pursuing one of their wars).

Jean Martell died in 1753. His widow, who survived till 1786, took their sons Jean and Frederic into partnership. In 1807 they established the firm of J. & F. Martell. A worldwide business, Martell's representatives in London for well over a century have been Matthew CLARK & Sons.

The size of the Martell empire can be gauged from the fact that it is estimated that the equivalent of 1,200,000 bottles of their cognac are lost yearly through evaporation from casks, the poetically named "angels' share". The company owns or controls over 50 distilleries and the cellars normally carry some £25 million worth of cognac at current market prices.

MARTINI & ROSSI
The foundation of perhaps the greatest of all names in VERMOUTH does not date from as early a period as some other famous ones. However, the firm from which Martini & Rossi stemmed was the first to receive the royal accolade in the form of No. 1 certificate when, in 1840, protection was given to vermouths made in Turin. It is from that year that Martini & Rossi trace their story, although the original business is undoubtedly of longer antiquity. Starting as Martini & Sola, with the accession of Commandatore Luigi Rossi as co-owner, followed by his four sons, the Rossi family established a control which saw the company on its way to world renown. There are now Martini & Rossi companies spread across the globe.

A new generation took over from the founder's sons—another four, the Counts Theo, Napoleone, Metello and Lando Rossi.

Mash

In Italy, Count Metello founded the Italian Wine Federation and is now its honorary president, and the late Count Lando was president until 1967.

Advertising has played a major role in Martini & Rossi's success, apart, of course, from the quality of the company's products. Count Metello has, from its inception, been president of U.P.A., an association for the protection of advertisers' rights and he was the founder of the International Union of Advertising Associations.

In recent years, Martini & Rossi introduced a prestigious form of public relations activity, the establishment of the now celebrated and beautiful Martini Terraces in Milan, Genoa, Paris, London, Barcelona, Brussels and Sao Paulo. These form the social hub for Martini & Rossi's diverse sporting, cultural and charitable activities, linked by the Martini International Club.

At Pessione, near Turin, the Martini Museum has an unrivalled collection of articles, from ancient wine-presses to containers nearly 10,000 years old, illustrating the history of wine. It is open free every day 09.00–12.00 and 14.30–17.00 hours.

Martini & Rossi's great reputation rests primarily on their celebrated red *Italian* vermouth, but in modern times they have come to be dominant in dry *French* vermouth to the extent that there are some who believe the DRY MARTINI cocktail was named after them: that is not correct—see the section concerned with this drink. They also produce *bianco* vermouth and Martini *Asti* (spumante), and have diversified into other related vinous and spirituous activities.

MASH
Crushed MALT and hot water ("liquor" if you want to be technical) from which is extracted the liquid (WORT) from which, after fermentation, spirit can be distilled or beer produced. The equivalent liquid, unfermented grape juice, for making into wine, is called MUST.

MASSON, PAUL
A leader among American wine producers and a name, though I am not suggesting there might not be others, likely to become familiar in Britain if American (particularly Californian) wines succeed in a current export drive.

MASTER OF WINE
The ultimate vinous accolade in Britain. There are over 70 Masters of Wine. Only two or three pass the tremendously stiff practical and theoretical examinations each year; sometimes none succeeds.

MATEUS ROSE
The light *pétillant* (crackling) Portuguese wine that has been the outstanding success among the generally very successful Portuguese wine industry. I believe it sells a million cases in the U.K. alone.

MATURING
Wines of any real character and fairly high alcoholic strength will improve on maturing in wood, or, as we know, in the case of high-quality wines, in bottle. Some fortified wines improve in wood or bottle, notably vintage port in the latter instance. In sherry there is a continual blending system. The new wine is added in succeeding years, and the wine is bottled when the blend has reached the required standard. Certain types of sherry will continue to improve in the bottle, but not those of normal commerce.

Wines which have been PASTEURIZED will not improve in bottle. Spirits do not improve in bottle in any way, and may even eventually deteriorate: ancient bottles of cognac are collectors' pieces, not drinkers'! Precisely what happens to wines and spirits while maturing in wood has not been established; it remains something of a mystery.

MAURITIUS

Beer, stout (odd how well stout seems to go in warm countries), wine and rum are produced locally and are also imported, plus Scotch, champagne, brandy, gin and cider and *eau-de-vie*. Soft drinks are extremely popular—*Coke*, *Pepsi* and lemonade are made on the island. Soda-water and fruit juices are the main additives for spirits. Strong alcohols are sold in restaurants until 23.00 hours every day and in stores till 19.00 hours on working days only. The middle classes drink local products mainly and the richer folk go for imported drinks. All tend to prefer strong drinks, even in the torrid summer, whisky being the "in" drink. Spirits must be aged at least 5 years and not be of lower strength than 20 per cent alcohol.

MEAD

A drink of great antiquity, particularly associated with the Ancient Britons though some kind of fermented honey or honey-flavoured wine was drunk in Greece during centuries B.C. Tacitus, visiting the Roman army in Britain at the beginning of the first century A.D., compared mead unfavourably with the wine to which he was accustomed. There are sundry early mentions of mead (*meeth*, *meathe*), as an intoxicant, medicine and aphrodisiac. Samuel Pepys refers to Charles II drinking METHEGLIN in place of wine at a banquet, but by that time it had become comparatively rare and expensive. Mead had been largely made by monks and the dissolution of the monasteries by Henry VIII, coupled with a steady decrease in the number of wild bees as more and more of the land was put to arable use, caused a shortage of honey, which was too precious as a sweetening agent to allow much to be turned into a drink.

Mead is today made commercially in Cornwall and Sussex. The only place where I know it is regularly used is at the Elizabethan Rooms of the Gore Hotel, London, for their "Tudor Feasts". It continues to be rated an excellent specific for colds, 'flu, asthma and hay fever. Apart from being taken neat, mead mixes with conventional spirits, or minerals.

"Mead" has been called the "honeymoon wine", from Babylonian Laws of about 2000 B.C. which stipulated "wine of the bee" as the drink for wedding banquets and that the bride's family should keep the bridegroom supplied with as much of it as he required for the lunar month following the marriage; hence "honeymonth" (honeymoon).

MEASURES

Where necessary I use the simple word "measure" to indicate quantities, e.g. (in a recipe), "3 measures of gin". In order to measure ingredients, a JIGGER holding a fluid ounce is essential for anyone making mixed drinks, and a double, 2-ounce one is a useful addition.

MEDOC See Bordeaux.

MERCIER

Founded in 1858 by Eugène Mercier, whose great-grandson heads this CHAMPAGNE house, which is among the largest of all shippers of this wine. They have some 12 miles of cellars under the vineyards opposite their premises at Epernay which, for the ¼ million visitors who come each year, are equipped with electric trains. Lady guides conduct the visitors on a tour of the cellars and premises. See also Hennessey.

MERRYDOWN WINE CO. LTD.

This company was only established after World War II, at Horsham, Sussex, and I remember in the '40s making acquaintance with the delectably strong vintage ciders with which it established a reputation: this was before any cider was taxed. This is now called "vintage apple wine" and is still strong, containing 22 per cent proof spirit. It all started

Mescal

in 1937, when two men, Jack Ward and Ian Howie, started experimenting in making fruit wines with crude equipment and a German manual in a house called *Merrydown*. They got together again after the war.

Things were humming along nicely when a bombshell exploded: in 1956 the government put a tax on all ciders over 15 per cent proof alcohol. Should *Merrydown* bring down their strength and try to compete with the giant cider makers or keep the strength? They doubled their price—and increased the strength. Sales fell dramatically. But despite further tax increases Merrydown fought its way back in the following decade and is now well established, a small firm, but a profitable one, besides its famous "apple wine", producing 12 quality English country wines, MEAD and vinegar.

MESCAL
The cactus type plant from which is made *pulque*, the Mexican intoxicant from which TEQUILA is distilled.

METHEGLIN
Old name for MEAD, but probably, from its derivation, from an ancient Welsh word for "spicey potion"; also a medieval "cocktail" containing various herbal additions.

METRICATION
The Continental metric system is probably going to be thrust on a largely unconsulted and certainly unwilling Britain by 1975. In the potable field this means the established pint unit (and less comprehensible fluid ounces) will be eventually superseded by a totally alien unit based on the LITRE. There is a case for moderate decimalization, as the Americans understand (e.g., PROOF), though they will wisely not have anything to do with metrication. See Comparisons.

MEXICO
The poor drink PULQUE and beer and, when they can afford it, TEQUILA of varying degrees of refinement. The wealthy tend to drink in the cosmopolitan American manner, somewhat disdaining tequila. But the Americans are increasingly taking to tequila.

MINERAL WATERS
This term originally covered natural spa waters with a distinctive and medicinal mineral content, but "minerals" is now used to describe manufactured soft drinks such as tonic-water, bitter lemon, etc.

MINT JULEP
This great American drink, raising memories of beautiful colonial mansions in the Deep South, is one of infinite variety and it is surrounded by a mystique rivalling that of the DRY MARTINI. Apparently the name *julep* is of ancient Persian origin, the medicos of the time using a similar word to describe tasteful additives employed to make palatable, noisome and allegedly curative mixtures. How on earth it reached the Deep South is wrapped in historical mystery. I have taken this recipe, to be safe, from The Bourbon Institute's book. Four sprigs of mint; 1 lump of sugar; 1 tablespoon of water; 2 measures of bourbon whiskey; crushed ice. Muddle the mint, sugar and water in a tall glass. Fill it with ice. Add the bourbon but do *not* stir. Garnish with fresh mint sprig.

MIRABELLE
A liqueur flavoured with Mirabelle plums, particularly associated with the Alsace and Lorraine districts of France. The best are truly distilled plum brandies. This is the type of liqueur which, while it travels perfectly in the literal sense, tastes so much better in its native land.

MISE EN BOUTEILLE (au château)
French for "bottled" and usually associated with a Bordeaux CHATEAU or a Burgundy DOMAINE bottled wine; thus indicative of a superior wine. The German name for it is the equivalent of the English "estate bottled" or, maybe, *Kabinet*.

The term indicates that the wine has not been subsequently blended or "tampered with". One should bear in mind, however, that in many instances a blended wine has nothing wrong with it. In addition, English bottling has been improved.

MOET ET CHANDON
Founded 1743, and the biggest sellers of champagne on the British market. Moët et Chandon reintroduced their *Dom Perignon* de-luxe vintage champagne to Britain in 1953 to mark the coronation of Queen Elizabeth II. It was first made shortly before World War II. The term *Dom Perignon* (the "inventor" of CHAMPAGNE) is exclusive to the company. The bottle is modelled on that used for early champagnes; similar ones have been introduced for other firms' de-luxe brands. See also Hennessey.

MOLASSES See Cane spirit.

MONTILLA
A fine, light, dry, fortified SPANISH wine, made some distance from JEREZ and thus not qualifying, in legal estimation, for the title sherry. It deserves to be better known abroad. To be called *Montilla*, the wine must come from bodegas in the town of Cordoba or certain designated other places. The wine need not have been grown in the area but may come from outside: Montilla district wine also goes to Jerez and becomes sherry by there being fortified and put through the solera system. A marked peculiarity of Montilla is that the bodegas do not contain casks but giant ceramic *tianajas*, with wooden lids, modelled on the ancient Greek amphora.

MONTRACHET See Burgundy.

MOONEY'S
Owners of "Irish Houses", pubs noted for conviviality and the quality of their Guinness, which enjoy a celebrity quite out of proportion to their numbers. Founded in 1863, when James G. Mooney took premises in the centre of Dublin. He opened in London in 1890, and in 1900 opened in the Strand, at No. 395 (more or less opposite the Savoy Hotel). This house has been extensively modernized.

MOROCCO
Promotion of alcohol, the use of which runs contrary to the kingdom's official religion, is forbidden. Naturally, there is a good deal of evasion. Moslems of sufficient eminence and claiming descent from the prophet have been known to drink alcohol on the assumption that, because of their ancestral saintliness, it turns to water on touching them. On the border with free-wheeling Tangiers, smuggling of contraband liquor into Morocco is an active local occupation, rendered lucrative alike by illicit drinking by Moslems and the very high taxation, since the independence of the country, levied on alcoholic imports for consumption, officially, by unbelievers.

Whisky, gin and vermouth are also counterfeited for the Morrocan market by little factories in the Casablanca suburbs. Wine, beer, whisky and Martini vermouth are the most esteemed drinks. Wine, vermouth and distillation from figs and dates are made in the country. Red and white wines are exported to France (for blending), and to West Africa whither Martini also send vermouth. Principal imports are beer, champagne, whisky, cognac. The truly faithful prefer green tea to any other beverage.

MOSCOW MULE
Said to have been first mixed by Jack Morgan in his *Cock 'n Bull Tavern*, Los Angeles, around 1948 and to have been the actual beginnings of the VODKA vogue in the U.S.A. It is composed of vodka and iced ginger beer, plus lime or lemon juice.

MOSEL (Moselle)
Starting in the SAAR and passing through the RUWER and Lower Moselle before join-

Moshi

ing the Rhine at Koblenz, the wine district taking its name from the river is long and narrow, with very steep vineyards growing almost entirely RIESLING grapes. This gives an instant clue to the type of wines produced. The vineyards are laboriously covered with local slate which both retains rainwater that would otherwise rush downwards without penetrating and, on disintegration, acts as a fertilizer. It also gives a specially pleasing character to much of the wine: the best known are *Bernkasteler* and *Piesporter*.

MOSHI See Waragi.

MOULIN-A-VENT
One of the better BEAUJOLAIS wines.

MOUSSEC
Well-known British effervescent wine.

MOUSSEUX
General description of any French sparkling wine, other than champagne. See Vin Mousseux.

MOUTON CADET
A relation of the great MOUTON-ROTHSCHILD in so much as it comes from the same paramount *commune* of the BORDEAUX district, Paulliac, and is produced under the supervision of the cellar-master of the château. It is said to be the largest selling CLARET in the world. There is also a white *Mouton Cadet*. It is often found on British restaurant wine lists, and the inexpert will not cause any social gaffe by ordering it.

MOUTON-ROTHSCHILD, CHATEAU
One of the best of all wines of BORDEAUX, and one of the most sought after and costly of clarets. Under the 1855 classification of Bordeaux wines *Mouton-Rothschild* was relegated to the "second division" on a technicality. Hence the family coined the motto, "First I cannot be; second I disdain to be; Mouton I am."

MULL
The best way to mull a wine or ale is the traditional one: by putting a red hot poker into it.

MULLED WINE
Two bottles of strong inexpensive red wine, one-third bottle of ordinary port, quarter bottle of brandy, a lemon stuffed with cloves, peel of 2 lemons, teaspoon of powdered nutmeg, 3 cinnamon sticks. Bring the lot to near boiling very slowly, adding brown sugar to required taste. Serve in mugs.

MUMM
Highly esteemed champagne firm; *Cordon Rouge* is their best-known brand. G. H. Mumm & Co. own over 300 acres of vineyards. The firm has ten miles of cellars and modern machinery for the various processes at its works at Rheims, where thousands of visitors flock to see champagne in its various stages of production.

MUSCADET See Loire.

MUSIGNY
Alone or in association with other names, the name is borne by some of BURGUNDY'S greatest wines.

MUSIGNY; CHAMBOLLE MUSIGNY See Burgundy.

MUST
Unfermented grape juice.

MYER'S RUM
Famous brand produced on SEAGRAM'S Trelawny estate in Jamaica, which extends to 20,000 acres and is the home and workplace of approximately the same number of people engaged in cattle raising and other types of farming, as well as sugar cane production. A quarter of the estate is planted with sugar cane which provides half the sugar factory's requirements, the rest being bought from independents. The distillery makes not only *Myer's* but some rum for blending elsewhere.

N

NAHE
A wine district which takes its name from the River Nahe which joins the Rhine at Bingen and has its source in the Hunsruck Mountains. The best Nahe wines are among the finest of German wines.

NAPOLEON BRANDY
This is a much abused term for old cognac; sometimes referring to one dating from the time of Napoleon III, sometimes to a cognac from a cask started during his reign or even that of Napoleon Bonaparte. But also I have elsewhere quoted a modern list with a *Three Star Napoleon* cognac.

Genuine bottles of what one may call "true" Napoleon cognac do exist, notably *Fine Champagne Impériale 1811*. Writing about this in *Harper's Wine and Spirit Gazette* (24.3.67), M. P. Gratacos of Lucien-Foucauld & Cie, Cognac, gave the story below.

In 1811, on the birth of the King of Rome, the ill-fated son of Bonaparte, M. Lucien-Foucauld, presented the emperor with a small cask of cognac and set aside a large quantity for sale as "1811 vintage". This was eventually shipped almost entirely to England. Contemporary bottling would have had an imperial "N" seal. Collector's items apart, "Napoleon" tends to be a suspect term in connection with brandy, but I must again mention this casts no aspersions on the famous *Brandy of Napoleon* slogan of the ancient and celebrated house of COURVOISIER: they are only saying that the emperor drank their product.

NASSAU ROYALE
A fine and unique liqueur: see Bahamas.

NATURE
Obviously this means "natural", and in normal commerce applies to *champagne nature*, that is to say, wine that could be turned into good champagne, but, instead, has been matured and bottled as a still wine. Unfortunately, very few firms bother to do this today (for the results can be splendid). It is commercially more profitable to make the wine into champagne. It may have been listed in England in recent years, but it is not widely known.

NEGRONI
Two measures of dry gin, 1 measure each of sweet vermouth and CAMPARI. Pour over ice in tall goblet, top with soda-water, add slice of orange.

NEGUS
Old-fashioned spiced hot wine drink popularized in Queen Anne's time by Col. Francis Negus. Associated with port, but any heavy wine may be used, whether fortified or not. The technical difference between this and a MULL is that the latter should properly be heated by insertion of a red-hot poker in the mixture, and the "Negus" warmed in a pan.

NELSON'S BLOOD
British Royal Navy term for rum, the issue of which has now been lamentably terminated.

NETHERLANDS
The Dutch gave gin to the world, "Hollands" being for long a synonym for gin in Britain before London started making the London dry gin which gained international fame. *Genever*, or "Geneva" (see Dutch gin), beer (lager style) and brandy (called *vieux*) are the principal potable productions. Dry

155

Neutral Spirits

gin is also distilled, and cosmopolitan circles like imported London dry gin, while Scotch whisky is, of course, ever increasing in popularity. Table wines, vermouth and fortified wines are the most popular imports. The new generation tend to go in for "long" drinks in place of the established drinking of chilled "Geneva" in schnapps glasses.

For some time there has been severe limitation of outlets for spirits, but a fair measure of extension of spirit licences is envisaged under laws passed in 1967. The Dutch are great home entertainers, and in general the drinks at celebrations will be beer, "Geneva", vermouth, sherry and long mixed drinks.

NEUTRAL SPIRITS

Unflavoured potable spirit such as is used for rectifying and flavouring gin, for making vodka, or, in the U.S.A., for adding in massive proportions to the cheaper brands of "blended rye", etc. Also known as "silent spirit".

NEW ZEALAND

Beer is extremely popular, consumption running at about 65 million gallons annually. Tea is drunk in great quantity, the country taking nearly $6\frac{1}{4}$ million pounds. Several notable London gin companies produce their brands in the country. A small amount of beer is exported, mainly in the form of ships' stores, with a little going to the Pacific islands. Scotch whisky and brandy are the principal imported spirits, with the customary additives. Vodka has made some impact. PIMM's and similar mixes are popular in summer. Licensing, under the Licensing Control Commission, is strict, new licences being obtained with difficulty and only on proof of real need. Alcohol sales are prohibited on Sundays, Christmas Day and Good Friday.

Other than for New Zealand wine, no licences exist for the sale of single bottles of alcohol. These can only be purchased through existing licensed premises; i.e., licensed hotels. Wholesalers may, however, sell to the public in quantities of not less than 2 gallons (a case). Some areas have a system of trust controls, which means that the whole liquor trade in a trust area is controlled by the residents of the area who elect the members of the trust. There remain several areas in Auckland and Wellington which, through a system of local option, have elected to remain dry since the early part of this century. Alcohol may not be advertised on television, and no advertisements may imply that alcohol confers medicinal benefits. Between 1917 and 1967 all licensed premises, as in Australia, closed at the ridiculous hour of 18.00 hours, just when many people felt they had earned a noggin. This has now been extended to 22.00 hours.

Hokonui This is something local to New Zealand. It is a whiskey-type drink illicitly made on the more isolated parts of the west coast of South Island, particularly during an era of local prohibition during the first quarter of the century. Occasionally, illicit stills are uncovered today. *Hokonui* has, according to New Zealand House, London, "an aura of romantic fascination to most New Zealanders, who regard it as a symbol of the 'good old days', when not quite everything was under the control of the law".

Wine There seems every chance that we shall in the future hear more about New Zealand wine, emphasis in the past having been heavily placed on fortified dessert wines, up to four-fifths of total production, the balance being light white table wines. There is growing interest in making premium wines, and "champagne" styles which have been almost totally lacking in the past. Local demand for table wines grows apace, and the balance-of-payments situation encourages expansion of the New Zealand wine industry.

New Zealand's first vines were planted in 1818 by Samuel Marsden, who brought them from Australia. In 1833, James Busby, who had done so much for the burgeoning Australian wine industry, was producing wine in the Bay of Islands.

NICHOLAS
The huge French wine business, with some 600 branches, selling every type of wine from *ordinaire* to great wines, and with its own proprietary brands that are household names. Some of these have been successfully marketed in Britain by Allied Breweries; they are excellent sound table wines, and good value.

NICHOLSON & CO. LTD., J. & W.
An old-established British gin company. The Nicholson family first became associated with the gin trade through their cousins, the Bowmans, who were gin rectifiers in CLERKENWELL. In 1731 Ann Bowman married John Nicholson and sometime later the Nicholsons joined their cousins at the distillery. The firm became Bowman and Nicholson, but by 1806 the name Bowman had dropped out and the partnership of J. & W. Nicholson was established. Over the years some 20 Nicholsons covering five generations have taken part in its management and control of the business has remained in the hands of the Nicholsons.

In 1966 it was decided to move the gin distillery to a new one at Three Mills, London, which had been bought by the Nicholson family in 1872. There had been corn mills there probably dating back to the time of the Domesday Survey. When Nicholsons bought it they used it for grinding corn, which was then distilled into alcohol and then sent to the rectifying plant at Clerkenwell. In 1941 milling and distilling was stopped because of the war. As the bomb damage then suffered was so great, it was decided not to rebuild as a distillery but to convert the site to bonded warehouses. In 1966 a consortium of Nicholsons, Metropolitan Bonded Warehouses and Charrington Vintners was formed to operate this bond.

NIGERIA
Licensing laws are almost identical to those of Great Britain, for imperial habits die hard (personally, I would have thought relief from British-style licensing regulations would have been one of the first joys of national independence!). The most popular of all beverages is Guinness which sells throughout the country. In poorer areas palm wine is much drunk. This toddy is made by tapping the heart of a palm tree. The sap is not intoxicating when entirely fresh, but it quickly ferments into a fairly potent brew. The tree dies a few years after first being tapped. Beer, including Guinness, the leading soft drinks, and a number of whiskies and gins are produced locally. Imported spirits come in bulk, for local bottling or blending.

NOBLE ROT
In French, *pourriture noble*, a fungus forming on excessively ripe grapes left on the vine after the normal harvest and used for making very sweet wines, notably sauternes.

NOG
More popular in the U.S.A. than Britain, there is no precise definition of this word, but I think a "nog" must always contain egg, and a basic edition is RUM NOG (also Egg Nog).

NOILLY PRAT
This is a French (dry) VERMOUTH, which was included in the class of drinks known as *French* (e.g., as in gin-and-*French*), before Italian and French vermouths lost their national identities. It was almost certainly the type of dry vermouth used in the first Dry Martini cocktails.

NON-ALCOHOLIC DRINKS
None would expect this volume to contain a

Non-Alcoholic Drinks

great deal about beverages devoid of all alcohol, though I pride myself on having given sufficient prominence to some famous non-spirituous brands that may be taken alone or used as mixers. However, there are occasions when imbibers themselves require an interesting mixture devoid of added stimulant, be it only for a children's party. In that context, I would remind you of the merit of making ice cubes with a few drops of flavourless food colouring added, whereby enchantingly polychromatic effects may be given to the plainest soft drink. (I have also experimented in producing purple gin-and-tonic and crimson vodka-and-lemonade; it is amusing to see the effect on recipients. See Colour.)

To cover some non-alcoholic drinks I invented the word "Mocktail" and hearing this, Pamela Vandyke Price, the charming, erudite and catholic-minded editor of the beautiful *Wine & Food* magazine (a publication unfortunately killed by economic pressures of publishing and now incorporated in *House & Garden*), commissioned me to write a feature for her on the subject. It is from that article I cull three of the four following recipes, which are simply basic ideas on which to work.

Pussyfoot This is perhaps the only classic non-alcoholic "cocktail", consisting of half-measures each of lemon juice, orange juice, unsweetened lime juice (or more lemon juice); dash of grenadine (or half-teaspoon sugar-syrup); yolk of one egg. Shake well with ice, strain into wine-glass; top with soda-water, serve with cocktail cherry. (This drink has no set recipe.)

Slim Jim Three measures each of grapefruit juice, tomato juice; dash of Worcester sauce. Shake with ice and strain.

Tea Punch Three cups of very strong tea; 2 pints of fresh orange juice; 1 cup of lemon juice; 2 cups of raspberry juice (from canned fruit); 1 cup of crushed pineapple cubes. Pour over ice block in punch-bowl. Stir. Add sugar to taste, if required. Before serving, add siphon-chilled soda-water. Decorate with fruit available. (For an alcoholic TEA PUNCH, see separate entry.)

Cardinal Punch In suitable container over ice cubes, pour 2 pints of tinned cranberry juice, 1 pint of fresh orange juice, juice of 2 lemons, 4 bottles of *Canada Dry* ginger ale.

There are a number of non-alcoholic wines, such as *Wundebar*. Excellent pure grape juice, apple juice and other bottled and tinned juices are also widely available today. The better-stocked self-service and department stores offer a fascinating selection. They all go wonderfully with alcohol! (See also LEMON, which applies to orange, regarding some time-saving advice).

NORTHERN IRELAND

This part of the U.K. produces its own special product, BUSHMILL'S Irish whiskey, of which the aged liqueur brand deserves to be drunk neat. Opening hours differ from England. Pubs are open from 10.00 hours to 22.00 hours, and closed on Sundays, though clubs are open. Without lengthening weekday permitted hours, the trade is agitating for an hour off the morning and an additional hour in the evening, plus Sunday opening on an English basis. Prices are similar to those in England in relation to the larger local standard ($\frac{1}{4}$ gill) measure.

The local hotels and caterers' association has approached all Members of Parliament at Stormont for support in amending anomalies in licensing. At present, for example, a visitor to an hotel or restaurant may not drink, even with his meal, after 22.00 hours, though if a resident in an hotel he has a further hour, but not his guests. On Sundays, even if resident, he cannot drink after 22.00 hours, and that must be with a meal, and again his guest has an hour less. On Sundays non-residents may not drink at all, even with meals. Such laws obviously cannot be carefully observed without the difficulty of having to explain to a bewildered tourist on a Sunday why he cannot have a drink with his meal, when he sees a bottle of wine being served at the next table whose occupier happens to be staying in the place.

The favoured local drinks are Guinness, local beer, Irish whiskey and a considerable amount of Scotch.

Postscript As I revise my text, but some time before publication, comes news that while retaining Sunday laws, Northern Ireland may be intending to adopt normal English opening hours, extending evening imbibing till 23.00 hours.

NORTON & LANGRIDGE LTD.

One of the largest of old-established City of London wine and spirit merchants, founded in 1837, operating in Mitre Court from cellars known to have in part existed from 1557, and which were part of the crypt of an ancient church or monastery. These became Wood Street Compter, a prison where inmates existed under terrible circumstances which can be judged by visitors today. There are many reminders of penal horrors of the past. The worst part of the Compter was known as "The Hole". Minor relief could be purchased by prisoners retaining some cash and there was a bar of sorts where oblivion could be bought. The jail closed in 1791.

However, conditions unsuitable for human survival are splendid for wine and thus in subterranean chambers, where men and women lingered in darkness and misery for petty crimes or debt, fine wines now mature. The firm makes a speciality of keeping customers' stocks: few private folk today enjoy access to an ideal cellar in their own homes. Traditionally, Norton & Langridge are considerable suppliers to City livery companies. Apart from fine vintage and other wines, they are agents for some sound Greek wines that are excellent value.

NORWAY

With half the country's Members of Parliament teetotallers, it is hardly surprising retail sales of alcohol in Norway are confined to a mere 65 outlets operated by the state-controlled Vinmonopolet. Only 5 per cent of total sales are in such licensed bars and restaurants as exist, the rest being bought from the monopoly for consumption at home. Public serving of spirits is forbidden on Sundays, public holidays or on the preceding day. Alcohol may be advertised, but the importing agent's name must not be mentioned nor may drink be promoted in connection with sporting events nor in such a way as to encourage drinking; i.e., one may promote a brand but not the merits of a type of drink.

The main local production is AQUAVIT, plus beer, and aquavit is exported to other Scandinavian countries. Aquavit and brandy are the most popular drinks, largely taken with soda-water, and Scotch whisky and brandy are the main liquor imports. Not surprisingly, in view of high prices and very poor distribution of alcohol, illegal production of home-made spirits is of awesome proportions; it is thought to constitute one-third of the country's entire consumption. Thus again do we see how restrictions and legislation by taxation may induce an industrious and honest people to despise their laws.

NOVAL

Quinta do Noval L.B. is a superior late-bottled PORT. After the PHYLLOXERA scourge nearly all European vines were grafted on American rootsticks. Noval, however, kept the ungrafted national vines of Portugal, taking enormous pains to preserve them. This continued until 1931, when the Quinta made its last vintage on a commercial scale entirely from national vines. It is now a celebrated wine and commands record prices at wine auctions. According to Mr. Michael Broadbent *Quinta do Noval* has realized up to 2100 shillings per dozen at auctions at Christie's.

At Noval only about 10 per cent of the vineyard is planted with ungrafted vines of the famous Nacional variety. These make magnificent wine and it is *Quinta do Noval Nacional*, loosely referred to as pre-*phylloxera* Noval, which fetches exceptionally high prices. The reason that all the wine is not made from ungrafted vine stock is that the vines are still susceptible to the *Phylloxera* disease. Their life span is limited and their production is uneconomical.

NUITS ST. GEORGES
Important and prolific *commune* of BURGUNDY, producing some fine wines, but since the name carries particular cachet in England with those not vinously educated, it is one of those subject to some misrepresentation. Again, know your shipper.

NY KA PY
Chinese "whisky" made from a millet base and flavoured with herbs.

O

OBSCURATION
I hate technical terms, but we had better have a brief definition of this one: roughly, the difference in the PROOF spirit content of a spirit made by the adding of colouring opposed to the actual alcoholic content measured by SPECIFIC GRAVITY.

OCTAVE
Eight small glasses of different types of sherry, drunk one after another with a dry biscuit or cheese between. Once a pleasing way of whiling away the time in London wine bars, but I think now totally disappeared.

OENOLOGY
The technique and science of wine production, which has no place here except as a definition. A MASTER OF WINE *could* be an oenologist, but an oenologist is by no means necessarily a Master of Wine.

OFFLEY FORRESTER LTD.
The name of this famous firm in the port trade goes back in Oporto well over 200 years, and the firm is still going strong. In the last century it was a Forrester, notably the eccentric Baron de Forrester, who stirred up the port shippers and producers. Joseph James Forrester, born in 1809, a young Yorkshireman whose family came from Scotland, went to Portugal to join the firm in 1831. After immersing himself in the port trade for 12 years he gave birth to novel views on the subject. His first pamphlet *A Word or Two on Port Wine* was an outspoken attack on the adulteration of port with elderberry juice and other anomalies in its production. This first blast was followed by many others. Some of his ideas were wild (he was against brandy being used in the making of port), and like most outspoken men he made enemies. Nevertheless, he undoubtedly helped to make port into what we know it today.

He could not have been without intelligence for his talents were recognized by the Portuguese government who made him a baron for his work in charting the course of the River Douro and mapping the wine districts through which it flowed. The River Douro was his downfall. He died in a boating accident in its raging torrents in 1861.

Plate 26. Sunday lunch-time at the "Old Bull and Bush", London.

Plate 27. "Dirty Dicks" is a celebrated "spit and sawdust" tavern in the City of London.

OFF-LICENCE
A licence in Britain to sell wines and spirits by the bottle to take away. A PUBLIC HOUSE is normally licensed to sell both "on" and "off" the premises. The term is also loosely applied to shops or departments of stores retailing liquor; these are not licensed for consumption on the premises.

OJEN
Spanish PASTIS.

OKOLEHAO (Oke)
An Hawaian spirit from a mash of sugar-cane, rice lees, and taro root. Requires maturing to be palatable.

OLD CROW
One of the biggest-selling straight BOURBON whiskeys, and, according to my latest figures, the sixth biggest-selling spirit in the U.S.A.

OLD-FASHIONED
A long-established American cocktail, first prepared for race-goers in Louisville's Pendennis Club. Became very popular during Prohibition with extra fruit to disguise hooch. Now made in a distinctive tubby "old-fashioned" glass, it consists of 1 teaspoon of sugar; 3 dashes of Angostura. Dampen with water and stir. Add two ice cubes; 2 ozs. of American whiskey; stir. Top with $\frac{1}{2}$-slice of orange and cocktail cherry.

OLD GRAND-DAD
Bonded or straight BOURBON; this brand is one of the big sellers in the U.S.A., and among the best-known bourbons overseas.

OLD RARITY SCOTCH WHISKY
A light de-luxe 75° proof blend from Bulloch Lade & Co. Ltd. (D.C.L.).

OLD TOM GIN
It is possible that this name was used to evade the Gin Acts, and a (tom) cat was the sign used by the notorious Captain Bradstreet. See Gin (History). It is also just possible that his feline association caused some people to start calling gin by that name. Not very likely, however. One tradition is that at a certain distillery an old cat fell into a vat, thus giving the gin a novel flavour!

Historically, the question of *Old Tom* gin came to light in a lawsuit of 1903 concerning the existing *Cat-and-Barrel* trademark of BOORD'S of London (now a D.C.L. subsidiary), established in 1726 and still exporting gin, though they no longer own a distillery. Obviously the *Cat-and-Barrel* sign meant "gin" at an earlier period when literacy was by no means universal. Boord's established that in fact *Old Tom* derived from Thomas Chamberlain, an experimenter with gin flavourings, and at one time their labels had carried a picture of "Old Tom" Chamberlain.

Old Tom gin came to be a generic term for any very pungent sweetened gin. The demand for such gins declined with the coming of unsweetened London dry gin, but it was in commerce in Britain until comparatively recent times. There is a certain overseas demand for it, notably in Lapland, but exports from London have been affected by the production of an *Old Tom* gin by the Finnish alcohol monopoly.

OPORTO
The town from which port is shipped, which gave the wine its name; it is the headquarters of the port trade, but the wine is stored at the twin city Vila Nova de Gaia on the other bank of the River DOURO.

OPTIC
Measuring device (for spirits mainly) to be seen in all British pubs. There are two authorized types. The most common is the "non-drip" where pressure upwards by the glass on a bar releases a measure of the required spirit. While in theory a clean glass is used for each serving, in practice this is not so, which renders this system obviously unhygienic. The

Orange

now rarely seen "tap" or "pearl" optic is superior on hygiene grounds and others. In Britain optics are government-sealed to prevent tampering and can only be cleaned by authorized dealers. "Le non-drip" has done much to destroy the cheerfulness of French *bistros* where formerly the barman poured by eye alone, but a small-tot version, *le bébé* has been potent in aiding sales of whisky in France, notably *Johnnie Walker*.

ORANGE
Same considerations apply as for LEMON.

ORANGE GIN
A cordial made by infusing orange peel (not the pith) and sugar with London dry gin. Not widely sold in commerce today, though once much used, it may easily be made at home ... once you have bought the gin.

ORGEAT
An almond-flavoured syrup which I occasionally see mentioned in American recipes, but have not for a long time seen in other ones.

ORVIETO
Sweet white wine from central Italy. It is produced by exceptionally long fermentation which reduces all the sugar to alcohol, which is slightly contradictory in view of the fact that orvietos are never truly dry. The best known is *Orvieto Abbaccatto*, which is rendered specially sweet by the addition of a sugary wine made from dried grapes. Best drunk decidedly cold.

OTARD
This celebrated cognac is notable in that for well over 150 years its cellars have been beneath the castle of the town of Cognac itself. It is now controlled by SCHENLEY.

OUZO
Greek PASTIS.

OXIDATION
The spoiling of wine by excessive exposure to the air, as in an insufficiently filled cask or bottle, as you will notice if you keep a half-finished bottle too long. White wines are susceptible to this, when it is sometimes called "maderization", as they darken and take on a flavour faintly resembling madeira. It can happen from too long maturing or bad cellar temperature.

P

PAARL
The name refers to the town and area around it in Cape Province, South Africa. Paarl is the accepted centre of the South African wine trade, and the Co-operative Wine Growers' Association of South Africa Ltd. (K.W.V.) has its headquarters there. Excellent red and white wines and grapes for South African sherry are grown in the area. Fortified red wines, which can be confused with port, are also produced.

The K.W.V. headquarters is an attraction for wine producers from other parts of the world, and for tourists.

P.A.G.
Personal Alcoholic Gastritis, i.e., a euphemism for a HANG-OVER.

PALATINATE
The wine-growing district of GERMANY, south of the RHEINHESSE, producing excellent wines, particularly sweet wines, in great quantity. The Middle Palatinate produces fine wines which command good prices in export markets.

PANAMA
Rum is made and exported in the area, and beer and *sece* are also produced. These three form the principal local drinks. For the wealthy and for numerous expatriates connected with the canal, Scotch is popular and forms the principal potable import. Gin is drunk largely with Angostura bitters, which were evolved for tropical climates. The attitude to alcohol is typically permissive of Latin America.

PARFAIT AMOUR
A cordial liqueur of exceptional sweetness (which, in view of its name, makes it a joke with many people).

PASSION FRUIT
A slightly exotic juice (in Britain it is not always easy to get it) that is wholly admirable in cups, punches, and splendid (iced) with gin. I am told the Australians have turned it into a liqueur. Good on 'em.

PASTEURIZED
Wines thus treated by the process evolved by Louis Pasteur—who may be said to have "invented" germs and thus given birth to legions of hypochondriacs—are incapable of further improvement, but it has greatly helped production of wines for the mass market. The process is simply the brief heating to high temperature of the liquid, thus rendering it sterile. This killing of all bacteria renders it unsuitable for fine wines that will continue for long to improve. Pasteurization is an important part of VERMOUTH manufacture. The majority of beers are pasteurized, not with any improvement in their flavour but to the great convenience of the trade.

PASTIS
The aniseed and liquorice flavoured, plus other herbs, alcoholic (often very strong) drink particularly associated with the Marseilles district. It is very similar to the ABSINTHE it replaced. It has the peculiarity of clouding when, as is usual, it is diluted with cold water, customarily in France filtered through a lump of sugar on a special spoon that rests across the glass. The two best known brands are *Pernod* and *Ricard*, but there are many others. It is virtually the same as the ouzo of Greece, the *ojen* of Spain, and some types of ARRACK. A whole range of anis drinks are roughly in the same category.

PATENT STILL
Also known as Coffey still from Aeneas Coffey who patented it in 1832 after he had improved

Paxarete

the system for continuous distillation invented in Scotland by Robert Stein a few years previously. The system is used to produce unflavoured alcohol in large quantities at high strength, as opposed to the POT STILL. Continuous distillation may be used to produce grain whisky.

Semi-technical note A patent (Coffey) still is a rather complicated piece of equipment. To describe it as simply as possible, it consists of two columns: an analyzer and a rectifier. The alcoholic wash comes into the top of the analyzer and falls down through a succession of compartments. Steam is forced in at the base of the analyzer and this separates the alcohol from the wash which, when it drains away at the bottom of the column, has been divested of spirit. The spirituous vapour comes out at the top of the analyzer and goes over to the base of the adjacent rectifier column. There it rises through compartments divided from each other by perforated plates, and through the column zigzags the incoming cold spirituous wash. The hot spirit vapour from the analyzer heats the wash on its way to the analyzer whilst the cold wash condenses the spirit vapour. By the insertion of unperforated plates at a given level a certain standard of liquid spirit can be drawn off into a receiver. This gives excellent flexibility of control. This type of still can produce great quantities of alcohol without the interruptions for refilling the still inherent in the pot still procedure.

I do not suppose this explanation will satisfy the expert and will not much enlighten the non-technician: it is the sum total of my knowledge, and as scientific as anything in this book was ever intended to be.

PAXARETE
Fortified concentration of sweet, coloured sherry, used to strengthen sweet sherries, and employed in the "wine treating" of casks for maturing SCOTCH whisky.

PEDRO XIMENEZ See Sherry.

PEPSI-COLA
This now immense business—it is estimated that over 80 million people drink *Pepsi-Cola* daily in 115 countries—started in the 1890s when Caleb (Doc) Bradham started serving a bracing thirst-quencher of his invention in his tiny pharmacy in New Bern, North Carolina. The locals called it "Brad's Drink", but Bradham had other ideas, dreamed up the name *Pepsi-Cola* and registered it as a trademark in 1903. The popularity of the drink grew fast. By 1916, more than a hundred bottlers held Pepsi-Cola franchises, the system under which the company operates today.

However, giant leaps forward were not in view till 1931 when a candy store chain, Loft Inc., bought control of the Pepsi-Cola Co. The customary soft drink bottle then was of $6\frac{1}{2}$ fluid ounces capacity. Pepsi-Cola brought out a 12-ounce bottle priced at 10 cents. It did not go. So the company halved the price to 5 cents and coined the advertising slogan "A Nickel Drink, Worth a Dime". This was incorporated in the first radio singing commercial, the words of which, even in the interests of commercial history, I cannot bring myself to reproduce. However, this did the trick. The economic Great Depression was then deep; anything that was a bargain was gratefully received. Pepsi was on its way to do battle with its till then all-powerful rival, *Coke*.

After World War II, direction of this fight from Pepsi's end came into the hands of a dynamic man, the late Alfred Steele, whose fame should rest securely on his great success in pushing *Pepsi* sales but who in the public mind gained greater celebrity by marrying the actress Miss Joan Crawford. This remarkable lady, in whom beauty and brains are subtly allied, was active in the company's interests and became perhaps the most potent ambassador by whom any product has been represented. (In the official *Pepsi Co Story* there is a mysterious reticence about Miss Crawford.)

Looking for diversification, the company first introduced the successful low-calorie diet *Pepsi-Cola* and a couple of other variants, and in 1965 merged with the big snack and convenience food firm, Frito-Lay, whose own story is a romance of American industry—but I am not concerned with "solids". Pepsi Co Inc. is now in transportation, food, and leasing services as well as soft drinks, with a gross income approaching 1,000 million dollars.

PERELADA
Quality Spanish sparkling wine which was the centre of the famous "champagne" lawsuit in the British courts, which established that no wine other than that from the designated district of France may be called champagne in the U.K. (This does not apply universally.) *Perelada* continues to do well under its own colours.

PERFECT
A measure each of dry vermouth, sweet vermouth and dry gin. Shake with ice and strain into cocktail glass.

PERNOD
The best-known in the U.K. of French PASTIS, imported into the U.K. by J. R. Parkington & Co.

PERRIER JOUET
This champagne has a fine 1961 extra dry *cuvée reserve* (Grants of St. James's).

PERRY
Pear "cider". Perry is made from pears on the same lines as cider is made from apples.

PERU
Devaluation and increasing duties are making imported drinks too expensive except for a minority who serve Scotch whisky at their parties as the prestige potable. Also of importance are gin (Booth's produce dry gin locally), rum, and the indigenous PISCO, a brandy distilled from the wine of the country. Pisco may be of fine quality, for it is not from wine that is good to drink that the best brandies are made. Straight grape and cane spirits are also produced. There are no oppressive regulations.

PETILLANT
The French term applied to "prickly" or CRACKLING wines, that are neither still nor truly sparkling—and thus, it may be argued, are vinously neither one thing nor the other. Prime commercial examples are the Portuguese *rosé* wines that are now so popular in many parts. The effect may be produced by allowing gas to escape during secondary fermentation in the CUVE CLOSE operation or, of course, it could be achieved by mild artificial carbonating. The Germans call the same thing *spritzig*, which is almost onomatopoeic.

PHILIPPINES
This is the only country about which my informants unhesitatingly name gin as the most popular beverage, and I trust that this intelligent choice does not have anything to do with the political violence which is a feature of these islands. Gin, rum, beer and a sort of whisky are produced locally, the beer being exported in the Pacific area and to the U.S.A. All types of drinks are imported, Scotch being relished by the well-to-do. The principal additives are *Coca-Cola* for gin and soda-water for whisky. Licensing laws are rather similar to the overall pattern of the U.S.A., though with a rather wider and more permissive pattern of retail sales.

The local popular spirit, *lambanog*, is distilled from TODDY and tastes something like KIRSCH. Celebrations in the province of Quezon involve considerable imbibing of *lambanog*. A gallon jug of the spirit is circulated by the hosts round a group of guests, men and women drinking straight tumblers of it. Says my informant, "The jug and tumbler are passed around until 2 to 5 gallons are consumed, depending on the celebration and the mood of the guests (which must be pretty mellow after a few rounds). No one knows the alcoholic strength of the drink but a good guess is about 90° proof (U.S.)."

PHYLLOXERA
Rather over a century ago, the *Phylloxera* aphid was introduced to Europe through the importation of American vines, themselves highly resistant to the indigenous disease (popularly called after the parasites). Within 20 years it seemed that the wine industry of Europe was doomed. The *Phylloxera* moved into Africa and reached Australia, almost wiping out the vines of Victoria, but for no known reason leaving the great wine-growing areas of South Australia alone. France was the worst sufferer of all. Eventually the cause became the cure. European vines were grafted on to American roots, almost wholly resistant to the parasite, which attacks roots. The industry was restored, but a close watch still has to be kept.

PIAT
This name, all else apart, to my mind means BEAUJOLAIS at its best, and it is well worth paying a little more for that pot-shaped bottle with the *Piat* label.

PICHET
A French, wooden or ceramic, handled container, serving the same function as a CARAFE.

PILSNER URQUELL
The famous, powerful yet delicate Czech LAGER which, provided it be bottled in its country of origin, I rate my preferred beer of this type.

In 1295 King Wencéslas, not the one who spent some time looking out "on the feast of Stephen," granted the burghers of Pilsen the right to brew beer, and they have been taking advantage of it ever since, so they have got a certain experience. They used to do it at home, but in 1840 a lot of them decided this was inconvenient, perhaps the women objected to the smell in the kitchen, and so they employed a master brewer to do it for them; thus the industry was born.

PIMM'S
One of Britain's distinctive contributions to the world of drinks and drinking, and its background is very much a City of London one. A stone's throw from the Bank of England, Pimm's original house in Poultry stood on the site of what was the *Hogshead Tavern* in 1499. It was known as the *Three Cranes* on August 26th, 1661, when Samuel Pepys paid it a visit and later recorded: "Here we drank a great deal of wine, I too much, and Mr. Fanshaw till he could hardly go." By 1841 the old place was famous again as James Pimm's Oyster Bar. James invented the recipe for his cup—the world's first gin-sling.

Old Pimm was dead and gone in the '70s when his successors decided to bottle and supply the cup to bars and restaurants. The first case sent abroad went to the Galle Face Hotel in Colombo, Ceylon. *Pimm's* travelled up the Nile to the Sudan in 1898. It was at Omdurman and Khartoum. A little later it was on the South African veldt.

The present firm of Pimm's Limited (acquired by D.C.L. in 1969) concerns itself solely with *Pimm's Cups*, and the international reputation which *Pimm's No. 1 Cup* enjoys says much for the foresight of Sir Horatio Davies, London's Lord Mayor in 1897/98, who had immense faith in the future of the cup.

The world-famous and unique *Pimm's No. 1 Cup* is based on fine gin; the other ingredients are very much a trade secret.

On joining the firm every employee has to sign an undertaking never to divulge the recipe should it come to his knowledge. It rarely does, for the formula is known to only six of the Pimm's top men: two directors, two senior office executives, and two of the men who supervize the works where Pimm's is compounded by a small specialist staff. Periodically, each blend is tested against the hundred-year-old recipe of James Pimm to see that it conforms absolutely to standard. Conducted by various firms of analytical chemists, the tests cover specific gravity, alcoholic content by weight and volume, quantity of proof spirit and solid or mineral matter.

All the cups are sold in compound form, requiring the addition of aerated lemonade and the company suggests a garnish of lemon and cucumber rind, with the alternative in the summer of the old English herb, borage. It should be served with plenty of ice. I suggest serving in a pint or half-pint tankard (glass or silver) and deplore this habit in "smart" pubs of adding a lot of unwanted fruit, cocktail cherries, etc. I think a sprig of mint can replace borage. Personally I find a pint of *Pimm's No. 1* is improved by a slug of dry gin and a measure of Cointreau: now that is a noble tipple!

PINK GIN

Associated originally with PLYMOUTH GIN, this is just as often now made with any good London dry gin. The correct way to make it is to put four or five dashes of Angostura bitters in a suitable glass and shake out all but that which clings to the surface (unless you wish the drink to be specially aromatic). Using ice cubes, or not, to taste, pour in the gin, adding soda or plain water to individual liking. There is a gimmick version in which the bitters are fired. See Gin, history, for possible origin.

PIPE

The term is almost wholly associated with PORT nowadays, although previously (in varying sizes) applying to other wines. It describes a cask containing approximately 115 gallons (British), and was a traditional gift for a son or godson in the more spacious British past. The wine would be vintage port and would be laid down against the boy's 21st birthday. It would not be excessively expensive to repeat this lordly gesture today if the wine were stored in bond, and it would be quite an investment, the only trouble being that with duties rising all the time it is doubtful if the recipient would be able to afford the customs levy to release his wine. He could always sell it, but that is not really the object of this particular operation.

PIQUANT

On hearing this word for the first time some people might assume it is the name of an exotic wine. They would be wrong for this is the insulting French description for a harsh, acidulously unpleasing wine. Vinegar-like wines are also called *piqué*.

PISCO

Peruvian brandy. A highly esteemed variety, of which I have seen an example in London, contains in the bottle a large, presumably non-venomous, genuine snake.

PLANTER'S PUNCH

This celebrated rum drink—as is often the case with "classics"—has no fixed formula. Traditionally, its composition is one of sour (lime), two of sweet (sugar), three of strong (rum), four of weak (water, ice). Mr. C. R. Hammersley, well-known hotelier of the British VIRGIN ISLANDS and *Planter's Punch* connoisseur, tells me he prefers to reverse the lime and sugar proportions, for the latter using a syrup boiled from semi-refined West Indian brown sugar. He prefers golden Barbados or Trinidad rum. Into a shaker he puts cracked ice equivalent to some

Plonk

5 large cubes; 1 oz. of syrup; 2 ozs. of freshly squeezed lime juice; 3 ozs. of rum (or 4 for hardened imbibers), and a dash of grenadine.

Pour entire contents into tall pre-frosted tumbler. Garnish with rind of half a lime and sprinkle with grated nutmeg. Mr. Hammersley opines that rum punches are spoiled by "hunks of pineapples, cherries and other garbage." I concur heartily. (Britain suffers from a more or less chronic lime famine: lemon is a just acceptable substitute but about double the quantity of this juice is required than for lime).

Mr. Harold J. Crossman lists another recipe, calling for 1 oz. of lime juice, 1 teaspoon of sugar (granulated), and 2 ozs. of Jamaica rum. He suggests considerable "garbage", including mint. Mr. David A. Embury quotes the Myers' company's "American formula", as 1 sweet, 2 sour, 3 weak, 4 strong: a potent concoction. Mr. Embury's personal choice is for the traditional proportions, but he adds Angostura and tops the tumbler with soda-water. Trader Vic's own recipe employs lemon juice in addition to lime. His *Bartenders' Guide* lists three other *Planter's Punches*: Cuban, where the mix is finally topped with orange juice; Trinidad, with lemon as optional to lime; and *Sloppy Joe's*, employing both curacao and grenadine, appropriately this is served with fruit garnishings. You will find sundry other variations. There is no definitive ruling on this splendid mixed drink: it depends on how sour and strong you require it.

PLONK

Slang for any cheap table wine, red or white. Considerably used nowadays as affectionate jargon for undistinguished blended wines, of varying palatability, often sold from cask or in flagons. A "Château Plonque" has been recorded as a merchant's joke. Most popular theory of origin is World War I army slang "plink plonk" (typical old-style Cockney) for *vin blanc*, abbreviated to "plonk". Also attributed specifically to Australian soldiers in France. Mr. Brian Fisher, during a correspondence on the subject in the London *Daily Telegraph*, suggested an onomatopoeic source derived from the noise made when a cork is withdrawn from a bottle.

PLYMOUTH GIN

A distinctive and famous gin long made by Coates & Co. in the Devon port which gives it its name. More aromatic than London dry gin but much less so than Hollands. Specially associated with PINK GIN, and the British Royal Navy, though what remains of the latter has shown lately more broadly patterned drinking tastes. The distillery was bombed during World War II and production elsewhere caused dissatisfaction with many devotees. The firm was acquired by Seager Evans & Co. who in turn are controlled by Schenley Industries Inc. of New York. The quality of *Plymouth Gin* has for some time been restored to its old standard. In the West Country, where local patriotism dies hard, it is often drunk with those additives elsewhere mainly reserved for London dry gin.

POLAND

Essentially a vodka-drinking country, which may have been where that spirit was first made. Outstandingly fine vodka is distilled and widely exported; also cordial liqueurs, notably *Wisniowka*, from black cherries.

POL ROGER

A notable brand of CHAMPAGNE, and the favourite of Sir Winston Churchill, who preferred a vintage *Pol Roger* of considerable age. (Other connoisseurs have shown similar taste for fine champagnes no longer over-bustling with youthful exuberance.) When the great man died, *Pol Roger* placed a mourning band round their labels, a delicate and permanent tribute to a genius too many-sided to ignore any civilized adjunct to human felicity.

POMACE

The residual grapes, apples, etc., from which the juice has been extracted. It can be reconstituted into a sort of wine from which *eaux-de-vie* of widely varying quality may be distilled, notably MARC. From pomace, pectin is made; it is widely used to set jellies, jams and confectionery, industrially or domestically. The residue is a valuable animal feed.

POMEROL

This district produces some of the best red BORDEAUX wines, but has never been quite so esteemed as MEDOC, perhaps because of the famous 1855 classification which did not include Pomerol wines.

POMMERY

Pommery & Greno brut non-vintage is a splendid one in its class. They also make a fine 1962 vintage wine and a 1961 rosé. Pommery is one of the four great CHAMPAGNE houses headed by widows, following the footsteps of the legendary Veuve Clicquot. Even in a business noted for family continuity, that four women of similar status should be in such prominent positions is extraordinary. Honorary chairman of Pommery & Greno is the Princess Henri de Polignac, grand-daughter of that first Madame Pommery who brought her champagne successfully into the vital English market. (The other firms in this category are those controlled by Madame Lily Bollinger, Madame Odette Pol-Roger and Madame Camille Olry-Roederer.)

PONTET-CANET

A very large BORDEAUX vineyard (Médoc).

PORT

It is customary to date Britain's great trade interests in, and consumption of, port wine from the famous Methuen Treaty of 1703, which gave Portuguese wines a favourable import duty as against those of France and Germany: to this treaty port owes its legal protection in the U.K. as a name. Similar wines, not from Portugal, must be called "port-style" or "-type". In fact, Britain had been bringing in wine from Portugal for infinitely longer, and the first commercial treaty between the two countries was signed in 1308. It was not, however, until the last quarter of the Seventeenth Century that the wines of the Douro area (later to be exactly demarcated as the only one whence port could come) became popular in England. These were not fortified wines, nor were those of the first half of the Eighteenth Century, which accounts for the phrase "three bottle (or more) man". When fortification started is not precisely known. It would have come about by the addition of brandy to help the wine "travel". From this probably came the idea of introducing fortification to stop fermentation earlier and produce a sweeter wine. Around the 1780s this was regular practice and inside another decade recognizably vintage port was being produced, and port generally had firmly taken on its present overall character.

Production of Port The vines in the Douro valley are planted on terraces subjected to occasional torrential rains and to intense summer sunshine. Production is equivalent to around 160,000 PIPES, of which the Portuguese government allows only a proportion to be sold as port, in order to eliminate overproduction of indifferent wine. The quantity allowed for port will be between 40,000 and 60,000 pipes according to the average quality of the year's wine. The remainder becomes table wine or is distilled into grape brandy.

The harvesting is done towards the end of September, mainly by itinerant harvesters. The grapes are taken to huge stone tanks and are traditionally pressed by bands of men trampling the fruit to the accompaniment of music and assisted by the stimulus of local brandy. Mechanical pressing is inevitably increasingly used. During fermentation con-

Port

tact is maintained with the pressed grape skins so that maximum colour is extracted. Fermentation will probably last no more than three days, after which the wine is drawn into vats and mixed with a fair amount of quality grape brandy (never highly rectified spirit) of considerable character of its own. This instantly stops fermentation while the wine still contains a high proportion of sugar.

The fortified wine rests in the vats till the year's end, when it is drawn into casks. These were formerly taken by oxcart to the Douro river, on whose swift and turbulent waters special craft speeded them downstream, but like as not today they will go by road and rail. From the *quintas* (vineyards) where it has been made the port wine goes to Vila Nova de Gaia, opposite Oporto, where it is stored in "lodges", not unlike the Spanish bodegas. Oporto, which gave its name to port, is the industry's home and the place whence the wine is shipped. It does not actually house or blend any port: that is all done in Vila Nova.

Vintage port Fairly recently the Portuguese government redefined two classes of vintage port. Vintage port itself is a wine of one single year bottled not more than three years after the vintage and matured in bottle. Late-bottled vintage port is a wine of one single year bottled in Oporto after at least five years in wood and matured in bottle. A vintage year for port is when a shipper—only exceptionally do all shippers agree—decides that his wine is exceptional. He will then "declare a vintage". He will blend wines of that year alone, and put them aside in his lodge.

After about two years they are sent to England and bottled, the corks being sealed with sealing wax. Britain is virtually the sole market for vintage port. It is quickly sold, though far from ready for drinking. Because of the fortification, it would in any event only mature slowly in cask. In glass the process is further retarded. Its lack of cask-life also means that it will throw a considerable deposit that would otherwise have remained in the wood. It really will not be fit for drinking until it is 20 years old and will go on improving virtually indefinitely.

Vintage port is sold for laying down. Because of high excise duties, this will normally be done in bond (i.e., duty free store) and as this costs money, the vintage port's value will increase at least proportionately. In fact, a lot of vintage port is bought as an investment, the purchaser having no intention of drinking it himself but of reselling in bond at a profit. For great vintage ports are very much at a premium. When one does obtain a fully matured vintage port (and you can buy it from the better wine merchants) you must rest it for a considerable time before most carefully DECANTING it, for movement will have disturbed the crust, the sediment clinging to the side of the bottle. Or ask the wine merchant himself to decant it into a new bottle for you.

Late-bottled vintage port develops further in the cask and thus throws much less crust in bottle and requires less bottle maturing, though you will still have a decade to wait if you buy it when it lands in London. But you can purchase a matured late-bottled vintage port and pour it from the bottle. It is usually free from deposit, though I suggest you do decant it. After opening, vintage ports should not be kept longer than a few days: it is very unlikely they will be. It should be drunk at a sensible room temperature.

A crusted port is of vintage quality and character, matured long in bottle—hence the description—but of no declared year.

Other ports Several important shippers are now putting out vintage character ports, which are in effect blended wines of different years of high quality. They are attractive wines, with the smoothness, but not the full richness of a vintage wine, and require no decanting. See Dow's; Taylor's.

"Ruby" is the least expensive port, matured in wood only as long as is required to make it ready for drinking. "Tawny" is superior, paler, and will have spent up to 15 years in cask. Both are blends of various years suitably "married" in cask. They do not improve in bottle, will keep moderately well after opening, and require no decanting.

"White" port is made from white grapes, exactly as is traditional port. It is gaining in popularity in Britain due to the vogue for light-coloured drinks. It is very popular on the Continent: in Belgium about 60 per cent of all port sold is white, and in France some 30 per cent. It is usually used, chilled, as an aperitif. This habit is growing elsewhere, and not only with "white" port. While it would be wasteful to treat a fine old port with less than due respect, a "ruby" may well be taken "on the rocks" or with the diverse additives suggested by the publicists of the Port Wine Trade Association (the trade is almost wholly dominated by British names). Indeed, port is more versatile than traditionalists believe. See also Boat; Bishop.

One of the disadvantages of wine is that it makes a man mistake words for thoughts.
    Dr. Samuel Johnson

PORTUGAL
One need hardly say this ancient wine-producing country is most celebrated as the home of PORT, which has enjoyed enormous popularity in Britain since the Anglo-Portuguese Treaty of 1654, which made Portugal Britain's oldest-established ally. Brandy, vermouths and gin are produced, but port and table wines are the most popular local drinks. The principal potable import is Scotch whisky. Fizzy lemonade and tonic-water are the main additives with spirits. The Portuguese are enormous drinkers of coffee. A sensible people, who like to live well, the Portuguese neither require nor impose excessive regulations on the sale of alcohol.

Wine Apart from port, Portugal has made enormous strides in getting her wine overseas. Britain in particular, has recently gone crazy for VINHO VERDE which has an unusually low alcoholic content. Most of the large production is made to be drunk extremely young. It is mainly produced by a very large number of small-holders, and it is amusing to note that the trade is based on Oporto, which in popular estimation is associated with a wine which could not be more unlike *Vinho Verde*. *Vinho Verde* is excellent as a beverage wine in warm weather, drunk well chilled; it goes splendidly with Portuguese food. Personally, I am at a loss to discover why it is so popular with "roast beef and two veg" in English restaurants.

Portuguese rosé is enormously successful; MATEUS is the leading brand. The Portuguese reds are as good as anything Spain produces, but we do not seem to see them to the same extent as the white and rosé: in reds, Dão is the regional name to remember.

POTHEEN (Poteen) See Irish whiskey.
POT STILL
The traditional still, unchanged in principle for centuries: basically, a vessel for DISTILLING, in which an alcoholic wash is heated to the point where the alcohol separates from the water and in vaporous form rises into condensers where, on cooling, it liquidizes and falls as alcohol into receiving vessels. The pot still method retains the essential character of the mash and hence is essential to the production of fine Scotch malt whisky, cognac, and other spirits of intrinsic merit.

POUILLY
Pouilly Fuissé is a dry white BURGUNDY; the quality will vary greatly with the shipper. *Pouilly Fumé* is a Loire wine, somewhat similar, but because it is less common in

Pousse Café

Britain, perhaps enjoying a superior reputation for no good reason.

POUSSE CAFE
An extraordinary concoction that I have not seen made in years and only worth including as a bibulous curiosity. It means liqueurs so layered that they remain separated in the glass. Traditionally—if it was ever popular enough an oddity to establish a tradition—the ingredients should be odd in number. Here is a version called *Rainbow*. Over the back of a spoon pour, very carefully, exactly equal amounts of crème de cacao, crème de violette, yellow Chartreuse, maraschino, Bénédictine, green Chartreuse, cognac.

PRAIRIE OYSTER
This is said to have been evolved in the "Wild West" of the U.S.A. by a pioneer, one of whose mates became sick and in delirium cried out for oysters, as unlikely a comestible at that time and place as could be conceived. However, his chum produced an egg (wild turkey's?) and put it with some whiskey and gave it to the sick man, who thought it was an oyster, and duly recovered. Well, that is one version I have heard.

The *Prairie Oyster* is essentially a HANGOVER cure, and some people gag on it, but I think it is not a bad idea: it may be the only breakfast you can face. There are a number of views on how it is made, so you will just have to string along with my version, pardner. Mix, without ice, 1 ounce cognac, 1 teaspoon each of wine vinegar and *Worcester* sauce; dash of cayenne pepper. Pour over the yolk of an egg and drink the lot without breaking the egg in the mouth.

PREMIUM
This term is used colloquially, largely in connection with Scotch, to describe brands which are older, often stronger, of superior quality, and generally costlier than the normal blends.

PROHIBITION
The suppression of the manufacture, sale and consumption of spirits, or of all alcoholic drinks, has been variously tried at national level, in Russia (1914–25), Finland, some Moslem states, and many times on a local scale (even in Scotland). It has always been a failure. The word Prohibition has, however, become forever associated with the "Great Experiment" in the U.S.A., which in retrospect seems amazing as an event. It had disastrous effects which have entered both American folklore and history, and the facts concerning Prohibition have, for many people, become blurred.

The extremely active temperance movement in the U.S.A. (by no means moribund today) had by 1906 persuaded 18 States to adopt Prohibition. Maine went "dry" in 1846, but the temperance movement went back 20 years before that. The militant Women's Christian Temperance Union was founded in Ohio in 1874. The Prohibition Party had been established in 1869, and the Anti-Saloon League and other bodies swelled temperance ranks, though there were fierce arguments between advocates of total abolition of alcoholic drinks and those only hostile to spirits as such. 1906 was a high tide for the prohibitionists. Within a few years only Maine, Kansas and North Dakota remained officially "dry". On the other hand, use of local option meant that large portions of some "wet" states were effectively "dry"—or not so effectively, according to their proximity to "wet" areas. Liquor traffic across state borders was naturally rife. The District of Columbia was also "dry"; so were Indian reservations.

The First World War accelerated Prohibition. By 1918 over half the states were "dry", and that year Congress outlawed the manufacture of potable alcohol (except for export) until the conclusion of the war and of demobilization. But before that, a resolution to amend the constitution by introducing Prohibition had been passed through both houses of congress by the required two-thirds majority and was submitted to the individual states. By January 1919, this, the 18th constitutional amendment was ratified by the required three-quarters of all states and had legal application as federal law one year later, applying to all states regardless of whether they ratified the amendment or not. Eventually all states bar Connecticut and Rhode Island ratified. In October 1919 congress passed the Volstead Prohibition Act (bringing into effect the 18th Amendment) over the veto of President Wilson. This prohibited all drinks having an alcoholic content above one half of 1 per cent. As a result Prohibition is sometimes called the Volstead Act as well as the 18th Amendment, quite apart from other pejorative names.

It is not my intention to recapitulate the results of Prohibition. The evasion, corruption, gangsterdom, drunkenness, adulteration, criminality, stupidity, smuggling, loss of revenue, contempt for law, of the ensuing years left scars on the American scene not yet effaced. On 20th February, 1933, Congress repealed the 18th Amendment and passed the 21st, which restored states' rights in control of the liquor trade. It was submitted to the states the next day, and was ratified by early December, just in nice time to allow millions of Americans to equip themselves for the first wholly legal yuletide festivities they had enjoyed for well over a decade.

PROOF

I am not one of those who entirely favour the metric or decimal system, but I must admit that I shall be delighted when we in Britain adopt the French Gay-Lussac method of indicating the alcoholic content of drink. If a spirit says on its label that it contains 40° Gay-Lussac, it means precisely that it has 40 per cent of pure alcohol in it. If in Britain the label says 70° proof (or, more technically, 30° under proof or U.P.) it also means it contains 40 per cent pure alcohol. Which is the simpler and most convenient, not only for the consumer but for the trade?

As most people know, the word "proof" originated from testing spirits by mixing them with gunpowder. If, on the application of fire, the mixture ignited it was deemed "proved"; if it simply spluttered or extinguished the flame it was considered unproved or "under proof". After some efforts at improving the more primitive way of finding the alcoholic content of liquor not much ahead of the ale conners' leather breeches (see Beer), Bartholomew Sikes (Sykes) perfected the HYDROMETER. For reasons of his own Sikes gave the figure 175.25 as ABSOLUTE ALCOHOL (in practice taken as 175) and that for proof spirit as 100. The Americans in due course decided on 200 for absolute alcohol and 100 for proof, which is more sensible but still does not have the complete logic of the French system. However, it is obvious that one has only to take half the U.S. proof figure to arrive at the actual alcoholic percentage by volume of a spirit. If it is labelled, say, 98° proof U.S. it contains 49 per cent alcohol. No such ready calculation is available to the Briton, nor the Canadian for that matter.

Apart from using a Sikes hydrometer and tables, which will show proof spirit to contain 57 per cent alcohol by volume (round figures), you may care to use the calculation that proof spirit is $\frac{12}{13}$ of an equal volume of water at 51°F. (See also Comparisons).

PROOF GALLON

I asked an expert to define this expression:

'Definition of a proof gallon must be related to the expression "proof" and PROOF spirit. Technically the expression proof represents a standard, and proof spirit relates to a standard of alcoholic content or strength.

Public Houses

'Proof spirit is a mixture of absolute alcohol and water in approximately equal quantities by weight (50/50). One imperial gallon of this 50/50 mixture represents one proof gallon.

'If this proof gallon is increased in bulk by the addition of water (i.e., contains less than 50 parts of absolute alcohol by weight) the alcoholic strength will be reduced and it is said to be "under proof", but in terms of the expression proof, which represents the standard, it is still the equivalent of one proof gallon.

'If a mixture contains more than 50 parts of absolute alcohol by weight, then it is said to be "over proof", and one imperial gallon of this mixture will represent more than one proof gallon.

'In brief, a proof gallon is a mixture of absolute alcohol and water in any proportion, the quantity of which is either more or less than one imperial gallon, but being the equivalent of one imperial gallon containing 50 parts of absolute alcohol by weight and 50 parts water by weight. The precise proportions of the mixture are 49.28 per cent absolute alcohol by weight; 50.72 per cent water by weight; at a temperature of 60°F.' Now *you* know all about it!

PUBLIC HOUSES

The English pub is a noble institution, the envy of many countries, two of which at least —France and the U.S.A.—have tried to copy it: "le pub" in France is a costly parody of the true English institution and bears as little resemblance to it, as a London *bistro* fails to resemble the real thing. (The native pubs of Scotland and Ulster, except when copying their English counterparts, tend to be comparatively drab institutions without national identity, for the purveying of drinks, but some Irish taverns have a "Stout" personality).

Though the English were brewing ale before the Roman occupation, the civilized invaders from the south certainly brought the island its first inns, the *mansiones* or *stabulae* that were a feature every 20 miles or so along the great Roman roads for the refreshment of travellers. Though no remains have been found, we may also justifiably assume that in the towns the Romans built would have been the tavern, *bibulium*, such as has been uncovered in Italy, with marble counter in which were cut holes to stand the wine jars. Ivy-wreathed hoops, in honour of Bacchus, indicated all such establishments, sometimes simply a bush on a pole, which presumably gave rise to the saying "good wine needs no bush". The use of this sign survived into Saxon times and even into medieval England; one is depicted in the Bayeux Tapestry.

As towns came to have several taverns, there was no way for the illiterate to designate one from another, and thus grew up at least seven centuries ago the habit of adding a special illustrative carving or sign, the birth of the celebrated English inn signs. For some reason, while other trades drew on recognizable emblems of their craft, some ale brewers chose quite random ones, *The Bull*, *The Cock*, etc., or even expressions like the famous *Trip To Jerusalem* or the *Goat and Compasses* (corruption of *The Good Lord Encompasseth Us*) or *Pity The Poor Straggler*. There are a host of odd names.

Flattery of the sovereign or other royalty, or royal patronage, obviously account for the prolificity of *King* this and that, and local peers or lesser squires have their names on pub signs. The *Crown* is the commonest of all signs. There has recently been a revived interest in inn signs, brewers commissioning well-known artists to paint them, and the rebuilding of a pub often means its renaming; thus modern heroes are sometimes commemorated and one inn sign celebrates the first moon landing. See Inn signs.

A very early inn (it is impossible to establish precisely which is the oldest in Britain)

Public Houses

is the *Angel* at Grantham, at which King John held court in 1213. Its name probably indicates a monastic origin, since the first hostelries as opposed to ale-houses, were run by monks, who did not charge but whose foundations waxed fat on the donations left by pilgrims for whom the establishments were maintained. The very early existence of taverns is proved by the edict of Ecbright, Archbishop of York, around A.D. 750, in which he forbad priests to frequent them. The licensed trade has always been prone to be overregulated, and King Edgar (959–975) restricted ale-houses to one per village. He also ordained that communal drinking vessels should have pegs inside and, as they were passed from drinker to drinker, no draught was supposed to exceed the distance between two pegs. This does not appear an unenforceable rule, but it gave rise to the phrase about "taking someone down a peg".

The Magna Carta laid down that there "shall be standard measures for wine, ale . . ." and price control was a matter of governmental concern by 1266. Ten years later a gallon of ale was set at three farthings, or one penny for a superior brew. What price inflation!

Ale-houses brewed their own ale, and in a village it might be a farmhouse kitchen that was the "pub". In the Sixteenth Century unlicensed "tippling houses" came into towns, where retailed ale was bought from a brewer; they were eventually suppressed after much evasion, yet showed a pattern that was to be repeated much later. From the middle of the Seventeenth Century, ale, the main English drink, began to face competition from BEER from the Continent. This kept better than ale, and caught popular fancy, but it was some time before brewers were allowed to make it and it was not taxed till 1660. Brandy was another competitor of ale, and to stop its importation, in 1690 a law was passed permitting any Englishman to distil spirit from English corn. This was the beginning of the GIN era. Coffee houses were another competitor to ale-houses, but it was the gin shop that really got at the brewers, some joining the opposition and going into gin production, like the Booth family, and some sticking to their last. (See Jane Lane's graphic novel *Gin and Bitters* for a description of this brewer-distiller antagonism). In 1739, of 95,968 houses in London, 15,288 sold drink, much of it gin.

The first modern regulations of public houses came with the Ale House Act of 1828 which laid down certain sensible elements of consumer protection. The century saw a decided swing away from the traditional ale-house with attached brewery and a separation of the functions of brewer and licensee of pub; in a commercial sense they have come together again in our times. Only three English pubs still brew their own beer. The period also saw the full flowering of the "gin palace", the finest of which represented the epitome of the metropolitan public house. In the country, this apogee was reached in the heyday of the mail coaches, but with the coming of the railways these splendid places, on the comfort and cuisine of which many foreign visitors commented, declined to mere local pubs, only to find a new career in the age of the automobile.

At the outbreak of World War I, drunkenness was still rife in cities, English opening hours for pubs being 5 a.m. (05.00 hours) till half-an-hour past midnight in London, and 8 a.m. (08.00 hours) to 10 p.m. (22.00 hours) elsewhere. In August 1914, at the request of the army, in much of central London closing time became 11 p.m. (23.00 hours), which it has remained ever since. During the First World War, under the Defence of the Realm Act (commonly hated as "Dora"), there were increasing restrictions on pubs, and the experiment (a failure in customer appeal, but long maintained) of the state taking over

Public Houses

the breweries and pubs of Carlisle. King George V renounced alcohol for the duration, his patriotism being applauded but his example not widely emulated, and there was talk of bringing in PROHIBITION, which mercifully, in view of what happened elsewhere, did not happen.

In 1921, the regulations under "Dora" were largely consolidated by some inept legislation which persisted until a slight liberalization and rationalization in 1961. For instance, up till 1961 it was entirely legal for a publican to serve a pint of beer in London at, say, five seconds to 11 p.m., but it was illegal for the customer to drink it at 11 p.m. Now ten minutes "drinking-up time" is allowed.

I do not much care for statistics, but the change in the pub scene this century is shown by the fact that there are currently some 75,000 "on" (pub) licences in England and Wales, or around 15.7 per 10,000 head of population, against 102,000 licences in 1900, or 31.7 per 10,000. In contrast to the decline in the number (though not of the quality) of pubs the number of "off" (shop) retail licences has risen, by only 1,500, to about 26,500.

At the moment there is a vast investment by the brewers, who own a majority of the pubs, in rebuilding, remodelling, or building new pubs in areas where they are permitted. Distribution of pubs in anarchic. What were once highly populated areas may now be sparsely inhabited and yet full of pubs, while a new town or modern sprawling suburb may have scarcely any. There are basically three types of pubs. Firstly, the "free house" which is not owned by a brewery and sells what the proprietors like. Secondly, there is a "tied tenanted" house, where the licensee may have some control but agrees to a rent to be paid to the brewery and buys only such beers as the brewery wishes to sell. In addition he must agree to buy other goods from the brewery or its subsidiary companies, and sometimes to stock and push certain of the brewery's own brands of wines and spirits. Thirdly, there is the "tied managed" house, where the "landlord" is a direct salaried employee of the brewery, with virtually no control over decoration, amenities, etc. There are occasional instances of a brewery granting a lease, the purchaser buying the house for a term of years, usually only with a tie as to beer, a position somewhere between that of being "free" and a "tenant". The bulk of public houses come into the second category, but there are an increasing number of managed houses.

There has recently been considerable debate on the question of managed versus tenanted pubs and at least one proposed revolt by tenants fearing eviction in favour of managers. At the time of writing the principal British BREWERIES had approximately the following percentage of managed houses:

Bass Charrington	30%
Whitbread	18%
Allied Breweries	30%
Watney Mann	15%
Courage	16%
Scottish & Newcastle	79%

The proportion of managed houses is, in the present climate of the trade, almost certain to rise.

Pubs face competition, the T.V. in the home may not be as strong a menace as it once was, but that from clubs is formidable as in some areas these offer remarkable facilities and entertainment. The pubs are fighting back (see Great Britain).

Note The terms are colloquially interchangeable today, but the legal difference between an inn and a public house (tavern) is that the former offers food, drink and accommodation for travellers and must, subject to certain provisos, provide them. A public house may turn away anyone, and people are "barred" from time to time as undesirable, without

Plate 28. A malt whisky distillery on Speyside shows the characteristic type of ventilation tower.

Plate 29. Blending is the combining of many single malt whiskies with single grain whiskies. It is a great art, the secrets of which are jealously guarded by the individual blender, who carefully follows a formula of his own to produce a blend of consistent quality and character.

explanation. Though if the person concerned has a grievance, it is open to him to object to the renewal of the house's licence.

PULQUE
The Mexican drink, from the sap of the AGAVE plant, which may be distilled into TEQUILA.

PUNCH
The word comes from the Hindu *pantsh* (five), for the original mixture concocted in India by the British expatriates in the Seventeenth Century traditionally had five ingredients: tea, water, sugar, lemon juice and arrack.

There seems a mild revival in mixing punches, hot or cold, for entertainment, quite an elegant custom providing it be not the sole contribution to party stimulation. Punches come in two categories, individual and "bowl" punches for making in large quantities. The most famous of individual punches is PLANTER'S PUNCH. It is difficult precisely to separate punches from cups, juleps, etc. Under their own headings I give recipes for Baccio Punch, Booth's Party Punch (my own invention), Champagne Punch, Fish House Punch, Red Wine Punch, Tea Punch, Tom & Jerry, White Wine Punch. Again I stress that these recipes are not mandatory; they are guide-lines for your own inventiveness. See also Rum.

PUNT (Kick)
This is the indentation at the base of a bottle, which is found in certain wine BOTTLES.

PUNT E MES
A rather special type of VERMOUTH, from Carpano. The origins of this odd name go back to the time of Antonio Carpano, who had a bar in Turin towards the end of the Eighteenth Century. It was then the custom to add one's own *vermout* flavouring to wine according to the customer's requirements, who would specify that he required so many "points" (punt) of the additive. The pleasing legend runs that fluctuations in a particular stock on the Turin Stock Exchange were one day running at one-and-a-half points either way. This was the subject of discussion at the Carpano establishment. In the middle of the discussion, one broker turned to give his order and, instead of specifying the usual one or two "points" or vermouth flavouring, requested "punt e mes"—in the Piedmontese dialect "one and a half". This was found highly satisfactory, and as a result Signor Carpano started blending a vermouth to this formula, thus coining a trademark.

Quite possibly this is not true, yet it is a happy anecdote, and *Punt e Mes* is a distinctively different bitter-sweet vermouth, which, I am glad to say, I find increasingly available in Britain: it has also a following in the U.S.A., less fickle than in the U.K. I think this vermouth is best taken on the rocks (not too many rocks), with a slice of lemon and, optionally, a dash of soda-water. A slug of gin does the mixture no harm; but I would not use this vermouth for a Dry Martini.

PUSSYFOOT See Non-alcoholic.

Q

QUEEN ANNE SCOTCH WHISKY
From the old-established firm of Hill Thomson.

QUETSCH
The plum brandy of Alsace-Lorraine; similar to SLIVOVITZ.

QUINTA
Portuguese for a wine estate.

R

RACKING
To remove wine from a cask, leaving the sediment behind, and put it into a fresh one for further maturing.

RAYA See Sherry.

RECIOTO
Sweet VALPOLICELLA.

RECIPES
There is a note about these at the conclusion of the COCKTAILS section. The experts vary in their opinions on many recipes for cocktails and mixed drinks, even about their correct names. I have given what I think are the best and most sensible recipes, appending notes on origins, legends, disputations, as applicable. For an inexpensive book of recipes that also has background chat, I suggest you buy my own *Booth's Handbook of Cocktails & Mixed Drinks*. For great detail, much background matter, and extremely individual approach, *The Fine Art of Mixing Drinks* by David A. Embury is wonderfully readable. It is an advanced student's book. For recipes alone, without further information, *The Savoy Cocktail Book* is authoritative.

RECOLTE
Grape harvest in France. To employ it when speaking English is an affectation indicating wine snobbishness.

RECTIFICATION
The redistilling of spirit in order to purify and/or flavour it. This may be done to produce specially "clean" flavourless alcohol, but its main application lies in the production of high quality dry gin. In that instance, an already highly distilled spirit of around 145° proof is partly broken down with water (distilled or demineralized) and then run through a pot still which also contains flavouring botanicals. Thus the original spirit is both purified and flavoured. In some leading gin distilleries it is the practice to rectify half the required spirit without flavouring and blend it with flavoured spirit, two different types of rectifying still being used, this being considered technically conducive to an even more refined product.

The importance of rectification (for spirits not by their character requiring storage in wood) has long been recognized. A book published in London in 1652, carrying the authority of Sir Theodore Mayerne, founder of the DISTILLERS' COMPANY of the

City of London (physician to Henry IV of France and subsequently to James I, Charles I and Charles II of England), quotes rules for London distillers forbidding the sale of "low" spirits—weak distillations from questionable sources. These, the rules laid down, must be converted by rectification "into strong proof spirit, whereby they may be corrected and cured of their natural, harsh, distasteful, unsavoury, or evil qualities, before they be compounded with ingredients, or extracted and drawn into rich or high spirits, strong-waters, or *aquae-vitae*..."

For the historically minded, it is interesting to note that when this tome was published, during the Protector Cromwell's reign, the said rules of the distillers' livery company refer to penalties under the "Laws of the Commonwealth" but the book also refers to the previous era. The volume starts off with the charter granted the company by Charles I (beheaded 1649). This indicated a strange lapse, or unexpected liberality on the part of anti-royalist censorship, which certainly did not prevail in other spheres. I was so much taken by this that I could not refrain from this digression. So I may as well give the charming full title of the work—*The Distiller of London: with the Clavis* [keys] *to unlock the deepest Secrets of that Mysterious Art. With many Additions Of the most Excellent Cordial Waters which have been pen'd by our most able doctors and Physicians, Ancient and Modern, Foreign and Domestick. Now published for the Publike good.*

RED BIDDY
Originally a mixture of rough spirit (methylated or not) and cheap sweet red or fortified wine. The wine took a little of the edge off.

RED HACKLE SCOTCH WHISKY
Considerable promotional activity has recently gone into this brand, owned by Hepburn & Ross (Highland Distilleries Co. Ltd.).

RED WINE PUNCH
Two bottles of robust cheap red wine, 1 bottle of ordinary port, half bottle of cherry brandy, juice of 6 oranges and 4 lemons, quarter pound of powdered sugar. Mix ingredients in large bowl, and add a large lump of ice (better than a lot of cubes). Add siphon soda-water and float rounds of fruit on top.

REFILLING
A complaint internationally endemic in the liquor trade, particularly where high prices or scarcity encourage substitution of lesser-quality liquors for costlier good ones. Some countries, such as the U.S.A., forbid the reuse of bottles; others insist on spirits being sold in non-refillable ones. But the practice persists and it is not unknown in Britain for lesser-valued more profitable brands to be sold through bottles originally containing famous ones.

The fraud is principally effected with spirits but covers fortified wines, even liqueurs. In some countries there is great temptation to use local products as substitutes for highly taxed imported ones. Most authorities are aware of the situation and many countries can employ strong penalties, particularly loss of permits to trade, against offenders.

In the U.K., difficulties of legal proof of known substitution have for long inhibited prosecutions except in flagrant instances. The department of the government chemist has now evolved a GAS CHROMATOGRAPH which can establish with clinical certainty whether a substitution malpractice has taken place. The knowledge alone that this can be done, if sufficiently broadcast, should do much to stop an abuse which is a blot on an otherwise notably well-conducted commerce.

REH & SOHN, FRANZ
Producers of quality German wines which

Relska

lately have been more widely advertised in Britain than any wines in their class.

RELSKA
A brand of vodka of Belgian origin, fairly well-known in the U.S.A. and Great Britain, where it is also made. Called *Relsky* now in Britain (as it is on the Continent) and believed to be the first brand to make a name change in anticipation of Britain's possibly joining the Common Market.

REMUAGE
The turning by hand of maturing bottles of CHAMPAGNE or other quality sparkling wines.

REMY MARTIN
A fine cognac of which one heard little in pre-war Britain but which is today a big number. They make no *3-star* or equivalent grade, only *V.S.O.P.* and a de-luxe *age inconnu*, in numbered bottles, a notable *grande champagne*.

RETSINA
The celebrated resin-flavoured wine of GREECE. Only a long sojourn in the country would allow the average foreigner to acquire a taste for the common retsina drunk in taverns. However, it is possible to come to enjoy the better qualities, that are less resinous, in the right Attic setting. To make sure of getting non-resinous wine, ask for *Aretsina*.

RHEINGAU
The most important of the wine districts of Germany, on the right bank of the Rhine, producing the finest wines.

RHEINHESSE
More or less opposite the Rheingau, this major wine-producing area does not enjoy quite the same high reputation.

RHINE See Germany (Wine).

RHONE
Because of its contiguity with BURGUNDY, and a basic similarity of style, the wines of the Rhône are mentioned under that heading.

RIBENA
Proprietary blackcurrant syrup; may be successfully used where CASSIS is indicated.

RICARD
The biggest-selling French PASTIS.

RICCADONNA
This remarkably successful company was established as an independent enterprise by Ottavio Riccadonna in 1921, and in 1932 built its headquarters in Canelli, near Asti. It is thus a comparative newcomer to the VERMOUTH industry. In 1935 a second factory was constructed. After the Second World War, it became a joint stock company with Angelo Riccadonna as its head. The plant is extremely modern, Signor Angelo being very keen on obtaining the most up-to-date equipment from anywhere in the world. The plant is certainly impressive.

Not least of Signor Angelo's achievements was the sale to Russia, great producers and drinkers of sweet vermouth, of 8 million litres of *Riccadonna* vermouth. He told me that the Russian Sojuzplodoimport of Moscow were utterly businesslike and their payment, in hard currency, exemplary. Though less well-known outside Italy than it may be in the future, *Riccadonna* vermouth outsells in Italy possibly any other brand and it is in that market way ahead of many brands of greater international celebrity. It is also a major force in the growing ASTI SPUMANTE trade.

RICCADONNA PRESIDENT
A particularly good *Asti Spumante*. A special *Riccadonna President Brut* is reserved for the U.S.A.

RICHEBOURG
An exceptionally fine BURGUNDY of

which production is small, since the vineyard is little over 10 acres in extent.

RICKEY
The name is said to have come from "Colonel Jim" Rickey, whose actual name was Joe and who certainly was not a real colonel. He was a well-known lobbyist of Congress, and an habitue of Shoemaker's restaurant, Washington, D.C., at the beginning of this century. The restaurant was much frequented by Congressmen. The bartender at Shoemaker's made the first experimental "gin rickey" for "Colonel Jim", who adopted it as his usual tipple. His friends transferred his popular name to the mix. See also Gin Rickey.

RIESLING
The Riesling grape is a standard grape in many countries. For example, some of the finest German wines are made from Riesling, But it is also used for making wine in such countries as Australia, Hungary, Romania and Yugoslavia. As wines are often named from the grape used to make them, one can have a South African riesling, etc.

RIOJA
The popular strong wine of Spain.

ROB ROY
Half and half Scotch whisky and sweet vermouth. Shake with ice; strain into cocktail-glass.

ROEDERER, LOUIS
One of the major names in champagne. Of special distinction, and rarity, is Roederer's *Cristal*. This came into being because the Tsar of Russia did not care to have his champagne come in green bottles with dimpled bases just like anyone else's. His cellar master was despatched to Rheims to tell Monsieur Roederer that he had better buck up his ideas if he wanted to keep the Russian imperial custom. So champagne for the Russian court was put into clear bottles with flat bases and the Tsar could know that no one else in the world had his wine so bottled. This very distinguished champagne is now available for plebs who can find and afford it.

ROMANIA
The excellent wines of the country, beer and *tuica* (pronounced "tzuica")—a plum brandy—are much esteemed. In the cities, notably Bucharest, cognac, Scotch, vermouth, rum and gin are available. A friend of mine said he was served with the largest gin-and-tonic he has ever drunk in an hotel in the capital. Romania is essentially Latin in culture and this is reflected in notably permissive licensing laws; in fact my official informant says there are none.

Drinking is principally done in inns, but almost any occasion will provide an excuse for drinking, the Romanians being a gregarious and ebullient people. Wine is often mixed with soda-water (*sprit*, pronounced "sphritz"). Both red and white wines are usually chilled. When it comes to spirits, Romanians like them strong as possible. Some wines and brandy are exported to Eastern bloc countries, and in a small way to Germany and the U.K., and to France and Italy where it is thought they are used to "stretch" local production.

At wakes for the dead, local custom demands that guests spill some wine on the floor before drinking so that the departed may participate: a charming habit. Unfortunately the government tends to frown on untrammelled individualism, such as the former tradition in small private vineyards of selling wine not by glass or bottle but "by the bellyful". For a small sum one could drink literally one's fill until sated or insensible.

I must say my Romanian correspondent has been wonderfully candid. "There is a sign in all inns that no alcohol is sold to people already drunk. However, this sign is always disregarded as drunkards make the best customers." Few wines achieve any real age: they are all drunk as early as possible, and after the harvest much partly fermented grape juice is drunk. The breaking down of wine with seltzer enables Romanians to go on drinking for as long as possible. For a toper, I must say Romania sounds absolutely delightful.

Wines The wine industry is highly organized, with a very active export, producing excellent table wines. Romanian reisling is rated highly by some experts; I have only tasted her burgundy styles and found them very good for the money.

In the pursuit of sound blended wines for the British market, three types of Romanian wine are being imported by Coleman's of Norwich.

ROOM TEMPERATURE (Chambré)

One hears people say something like "it's not sufficiently *chambré*", by which they usually mean that the burgundy has not been boiled. There is an odd idea, in Britain at least, that red wine should always be served very warm. Let us consider what room temperature means. (I see no need to perpetuate the gallicism, and doubtless, with the growth of "Franglais", the French will shortly be referring to "le room temperature"). It is based theoretically on the notion that certain wines should be served, as indeed clarets and burgundies usually should be, at the temperature of the room in which they are being drunk (though hardly so in a house in the tropics which is not air conditioned).

The wine should be uncorked and sampled for quality and allowed to rest in a clean atmosphere in, presumably, the dining room. An hour should suffice for this. However, it may be that the wine is already rather warm, or possibly excessively cold. In which case this method, designed for ideal conditions, does not work. Also, if the room be centrally-heated, the wine may indeed reach room temperature but will be positively hot rather than pleasantly tepid. A torrid wine is a horrid wine, though a MULLED wine may be agreeable enough.

I remember, a long time ago, engaging a room in one of those charmingly Victorian flats in the St. James's area. Supply of accommodation then exceeding demand, they were happy to let it for intimate luncheons. I had ordered two bottles of burgundy and gave instructions they were to be served *chambré* (I was showing off my French then). When I arrived with my luncheon companion, the wine was gently steaming, and I use the word advisedly, in front of the gas-fire in the sitting-room. It almost put her off!

There are also plenty of otherwise delightful British homes in which the dining room is, in winter, a chamber of arctic frigidity that is quickly brought up to a condition conducive to human existence a few minutes before dinner. That is no place in which to rest a wine. Better then to keep it temporarily, without agitating the bottle, in a temperate climate like a corner of the kitchen, away from stove odours.

ROSE See Vin rosé.

ROSE-HIP SYRUP

An excellent substitute for grenadine as a sweetening agent in cocktails and mixed drinks.

R.S.L.

Important and extensive range of South African sherries, marketed in Britain by Rawlings & Sons, London.

RUBY

1 See Port. 2 See behind the bar at the *Red Lion*!

RUINART

Claiming foundation in 1729, this is the oldest champagne firm in the world; noted for its BLANC DE BLANCS.

RUM

It is a trifle odd that a spirit so widely used should have a name of which the precise origin is such a subject of controversy. It could be that it is a contraction of "rumbustion" which formerly meant not just an "uproar" but a "strong liquor". "Rumbullion", a Devon word, has been put forward but more from local pride than reasons based on evidence. It seems to me it is not improbable that the Spaniards were distilling in their West Indian colonies before the British or French (who call it *rhum*) came into the picture, and therefore it is reasonable to opine that rum is a typical anglicism for *ron* just as the English, notoriously unable to manage alien sounds, corruped *jenever* to gin. Derivation from the Latin *saccahrum* is another theory. Enough of semantics.

While distillation of spirit from sugar cane must have commenced earlier, not until the middle of the Seventeenth Century does the spirit called rum (not yet so named) appear recognizably in print under the unpleasant appellation of "kill-devil", and as a "hot, hellish and terrible" spirit. It was considered suitable for slaves. By the first decade of the next century, rum, so named, appears in happier guise as ". . . very wholesome and has therefore lately supplied the place of brandy in punch." This indicated that rum was being exported to, and appreciated in, England. It was, too, enormously popular in England's American colonies. It is said that Paul Revere, on his celebrated ride, did not commence his resounding cry "the English are coming" until he had stopped for a dram or two at a rum distillery. (New England still produces rum in small quantities from imported molasses, but most rum drunk in the U.S.A. now comes from Puerto Rico or the U.S. Virgin Islands).

Rum and the slave trade went hand in hand and many a great American fortune, as many a Bristol one in Britain, was founded on the joint traffic. From the middle of the Eighteenth Century rum was both popular and fashionable, forming a main spirituous alternative to gin for the masses and providing the basis of elegant punches for the upper classes. Though styles and usage have changed, rum has continued to grow in popularity. During Prohibition in the U.S.A. it gained immortality in "Rum Row", the 12-mile limit of territorial water within which bootlegging craft ran in defiance of coastguard forces.

Rum is produced by distilling fermented molasses, the residue left after the production of sugar from cane.

Both pot still and patent still are used, the former producing the most pungent and the latter the least-flavoured types. In 1909 rum was defined in English law as a spirit distilled from sugar cane in sugar-producing countries, thus ruling out production in the U.K. Rum, so defined, is produced in many countries but virtually all rum drunk in Britain comes from Commonwealth countries in the West Indies, principally from Guyana and Jamaica. Trinidad and Barbados are the other main British producers.

There is a tendency to distil various types of rum in the main producing countries; i.e., light rum is made in Jamaica which is traditionally associated with heavy dark spirit. Basic characteristics are becoming very blurred, but they may be summarized.
Barbados A light rum, with a flavour somewhat reminiscent of Irish whiskey.
Demerara See Guyana (below); see also Cabaña.
Guyana This is often called "Demerara" rum and was formerly dark and nearly as pungent as classic Jamaican, yet one of the lightest, almost flavourless and totally colourless rums I know is also classified as "Demerara".
Trinidad A rum which is decidedly on the light side.

Rum Nog

Cuba The island has produced a style of rum which is typified by the great BACARDI.
Puerto Rico The island is the world's largest producer of rum.
Virgin Islands The rum tends to be slightly heavier than Puerto Rican.
Martinique The island is a large producer; understandably most of its rum goes to France.

In the West Indies rum is often drunk, particularly that made by continuous distillation, without maturing—as a spirituous addition to fruit juices or coconut milk. For the British market it must, of course, be matured for a minimum of three years and is brought into the country both in cask and bottle, the latter applying mainly to superior well-aged rums. Colour is a matter of market preference. The vogue for ultra-light rums means that in some instances, if the spirit has taken some colour from its cask, it is necessary to remove the colour. These "white" rums, of which brands are proliferating, are sometimes referred to as "Bacardi", as if that were a generic description. This is quite wrong: *Bacardi* is a universally respected brand name. But it has some worthy, less costly competitors of high quality.

The most famous of all rum drinks is certainly PLANTER'S PUNCH, and the DAIQUIRI cocktail is one of the "classic" short drinks. Other celebrated mixes are TOM & JERRY, TEA PUNCH, CUBA LIBRA, FISH HOUSE PUNCH, RUM NOG; and for a basic party rum punch, APPLE RUM PUNCH.

There's naught, no doubt, so much the spirit calms As rum and true religion.
                    Lord Byron (*Don Juan*)

RUM NOG
Two measures of dark rum; an egg; teaspoon of powdered sugar; half-pint of milk. Shake thoroughly with ice; strain into tall glass and top with grated nutmeg.

RUSSIA See U.S.S.R.

RUSSIAN STOUT
This is possibly the strongest beer brewed in Britain, *Russian Imperial Stout*, to give it its full title, is a product of Barclay Perkins, now within the COURAGE Group. In 1796 a diarist recorded: "I drank some Porter Mr. Lindoe had from Thrale's Brewhouse. He said it was specially brewed for the Empress of Russia and would keep seven years." Today *Russian Stout* is matured for two years. It comes in "nips" (three bottles to the pint). I have used it warmed and with the addition of a glass of port as a cure for the common cold. Three such potions and no bug stands a chance, and you will be lucky to be able to stand! It really did work.

RUSTY NAIL
Digestive amalgam of DRAMBUIE and Scotch whisky.

RUTHERFORD, OSBORNE & PERKIN LTD.
Well-known City of London importers of wines and spirits, holding, among others, the whole or part agencies for *Duff Gordon* sherries, *Da Silva* port, *Cruse & Fils* (Bordeaux), *Roederer* champagne, *Exshaw* cognac and National Distillers' (U.S.A.) rye and bourbon. They recently were taken over by MARTINI & ROSSI which will put much added sales power behind the brands they handle.

RUWER
A river which flows into the MOSEL (Moselle). The best Ruwer wines are like the finest moselles. Like those of SAAR district they are known in Britain and the U.S.A. as moselles, and are important in the German wine scene.

RYE See American whiskey.

S

SAAR
A river which flows into the MOSEL (Moselle) and the name of a wine district providing some important German wines.

SABRA
This is possibly the world's newest liqueur, only evolved in 1967. It is distilled by International Distillers of Israel (Seagram's) from Jaffa oranges and is further flavoured with chocolate. It comes at 52.5° proof (Br.). The extremely attractive pack is based on a Phoenician wine flask of 2,000 years ago as exhibited in the museum of glass and ceramics at Tel Aviv. *Sabra* (which means *cactus*) is only now being exploited in such countries as Britain (where it is handled by Cock Russell & Spedding Ltd., London). It has already had a remarkable success in W. Germany.

SACK
There is a long-established notion that this word, "Falstaffian" by association, in Elizabethan times applied to sherry. Spanish wine it may indeed have been, but it is impossible that it was what we would recognize as sherry, which has changed with changing British tastes. The late H. Warner Allen opined that the word derived from *sacar*, Spanish approximation to "export". Sack did not only apply to Spanish wines. There is a discredited theory that sack comes from *seco* (dry). Elizabethans certainly would not have drunk wines that were dry by our standards. *Dry Sack* is a brand name for a medium dry sherry.

ST. RAPHAEL
One of the most famous French aperitif wines.

ST. VINCENT (West Indies)
RUM is both the principal local production, most popular drink, and leading potable export. Punch made with rum is also highly esteemed. Bars' opening hours are more or less at the discretion of their owners, and drinking habits are permissive and in keeping with the sociability that pertains throughout the Caribbean.

SAKE
The traditional "rice wine" of Japan and China. It is not actually a wine but a doubly fermented brew from a rice base. The strength is about that of a strong sherry. It is distinctly an acquired taste.

In JAPAN saké is sold in large bottles. Before drinking it is put into a porcelain jar, a *tokkuri* or *chosi*. This is placed in hot water to warm the liquid, which should be around body temperature. Saké is served in small porcelain cups, *sakazuki*. (Today saké is sometimes served chilled).

SALADIN
Named after the Frenchman who invented them, saladin boxes are long troughs in which sprouting barley is agitated by mechanical means, obtaining the same effect as the old laborious hand-turning of the germinating grain. They are considerably used in malting barley for SCOTCH whisky.

SALIGNAC
I once sampled a 30-year-old unblended London-matured *Salignac* Cognac: I think it was the finest I have ever tasted.

SALMON AND TROUT
Old Cockney rhyming slang for GOUT. The author is chairman of the Salmon and Trout

Samos

Club, an exclusive body of the charitably bent, whose members are drawn from persons in the licensed and allied trades who have a tendency to suffer from this affliction but retain their sense of humour in the face of the hilarity with which non-sufferers greet their occasional attacks.

SAMOS See Greece (Wine).

SANDEMAN & Co., GEO. G.

Member of a very old Scottish family, George Sandeman founded the House of Sandeman in London in 1790. He had a loan of £300 from his father and it was his declared intention to make his fortune in not more than nine years in order to retire in comfort to his native Perth. He stayed South. At first his brother David was his partner but after a few years the latter went back North to found the Commercial Bank of Scotland.

The time was particularly ripe for expansion of the wine trade with Portugal as Britain and France were at loggerheads, and improvements and changes were taking place in PORT wine; true vintage port was just evolving as we understand it. In 1805 George Sandeman was trading at 20 St. Swithin's Lane in the City of London, still the company's address, and the inventory for that year includes a "capital patent crane", which remains in position. (A good thing it was retained: in the blitz of 1940 its hydraulic successor was put out of action and the ancient crane was invaluable in removing precious stocks of port and sherry from the cellars).

Gradually, succeeding Sandemans expanded the firm's interests in Oporto and Jerez until they became, as they have remained, very much among the leaders in both fine ports and sherries. Still run as a family concern, the company went public in 1952, to combine modern merchandizing with the best of traditional trading practices. From among their various brands, and ignoring their fine vintage ports, I would pick out *Dry Don* sherry and Sandeman's *Partner's Port*, as being specially good in the categories of dry sherry and above-average non-vintage port at sensible prices.

SANDERSON & SON LTD., WM.

Vat 69 Scotch whisky has become so renowned as, in the public mind, almost totally to obscure the company behind the brand. Yet the founder of that firm played an outstanding role in promoting blended whisky and was an early propagandist for proper maturing, before the time when this became general practice.

William Sanderson was born in Leith in 1839 and in 1852 was apprenticed to a wine and spirit trade manufacturer who also concerned himself with making cordials, and it is here that Sanderson became interested in compounding spirits. In 1863 he set up his own business as a "British Wine and Cordial Manufacturer", but the subject that preoccupied him was clearly indicated in the very first entry in his record book: "Mixture Whisky—10 gallons Glenlivet, 10 gallons Pitlochry, 5 gallons reduced mixed Aqua, 8 gallons Grain, 4 gallons water, ½-gallon Aqua Shrub, 8 gallons Grain Aqua".

Aqua was a usual word for whisky at the time. *Grain* presumably refers to neutral grain spirit as opposed to "grain aqua" and "aqua shrub". The latter name, derived from the old-time drink, SHRUB, can only mean a sweetened and spiced whisky. In fact, Sanderson was making a whisky liqueur. He continued to make a wide range of cordials, but his interest in whisky increased as his business prospered and while he travelled the British Isles he noted what type of whisky his customers preferred and started blending it for them. This was a period when whisky had started its journey south, when things Scottish were fashionable, and when the *Phylloxera* was about to cause a dramatic decimation of cognac and help switch English taste to whisky. Yet the true nectar of Scotland was generally a little too pungent for "sassenach" palates and Sanderson's interest in blending grew.

In 1880, William Sanderson's son, William Mark, joined him, and quickly showed his business acumen and flair for the whisky business. It was then the custom to send out whisky in casks, both to households and public houses, or to wholesalers who might or might not blend it (or adulterate it for that matter). It was only twenty years since it became legal to send whisky in bottle to England but some blenders had started doing so. Seeing that Leith was famous for its glass bottles, of which William Sanderson made great use for his cordials, William Mark persuaded his father, who did not at first like the idea, to send out Sanderson's whisky in bottles: this was to be of immense importance when it came to launching *Vat 69*.

William Sanderson came to the conclusion that it should be possible, instead of having a variety of blends, to make up one which would epitomize Sanderson's. Late in the Nineteenth Century, William Sanderson produced, by patient work, several superior blends of fine Scotch whiskies. Altogether he made up nearly a hundred different "vattings". Skilled blenders and tasters were invited to sample them all and to select the one which they considered to be the ideal blend of Scotch whiskies. The choice was unanimous, and as the "vatting" was numbered "69" he named it there and then: VAT 69. (He was not to know how visually fortunate this choice was to be, for today, when much sale of whisky by the tot is from bottles up-ended, *69* stands out wonderfully).

The next step was to choose a suitable bottle, and again his, or William Mark's, choice was a happy one. With minor technical alterations, the elegant and distinctive *Vat 69* bottle is unchanged since its inception, possibly the least altered of all whisky packaging and getting on for a century old. The seal which is a feature of the dressing of the bottle carries the Sanderson crest, the *Talbot Hound*, with the motto "*Sans Dieu Rien*" (Nothing Without God).

William Sanderson died in 1908, his business at home flourishing and commencing to spread overseas, and was succeeded by William Mark. After World War I, he in turn was joined by his son, Kenneth, who took over the chairmanship when his father died in 1929. He was approached by Booth's Distilleries with a view to amalgamation, and this took place in 1935, Sanderson's soon dropping their other interests to concentrate on *Vat 69*.

The Booth's-Sanderson combine controlled considerable whisky stocks and distilleries, since the ancient gin company had diversified into Scotch for some time. This made them attractive to The Distillers Company Ltd. which they joined in 1937.

The U.K. marketing of *Vat 69* was effectively rationalized in 1969.

SANGAREE (Sangria)
Heaped teaspoons of powdered sugar in tall glass, dissolve with a little of your preferred type of wine. Add two ice cubes and top with same wine. Stir. This may also be served hot, in which case top with powdered nutmeg.

SANGRE
Mexican version of the BLOODY MARY and thus made with tequila.

SANTIGO
White rum from UNITED RUM MERCHANTS, replacing their "Daiquiri" brand.

SAUCER GLASS
Though there exists a glass or cup of this shape said to have been modelled on the breast of Madame de Pompadour, such shallow glasses, while deemed the right thing

Sauternes

for champagne in some circles, are totally wrong. They dissipate the effervescence which it has taken nature years to put into the wine. The only mildly acceptable saucer glass, and they are hard to find, has a hollow stem.

The correct champagne glass is a FLUTE. Otherwise, a simple wine GLASS is almost entirely satisfactory. The saucer glass is in evidence at weddings. Admittedly it has the advantage of not holding very much as it is also easily spilled. Mercifully, there is a growing revolt against the saucer glass.

SAUTERNES

The renowned sweet white wines of the BORDEAUX area, ranging from the cheap and sickly to the rare and wonderful. A few years ago I was given a bottle from a French cellar which was "liberated" during the invasion of Normandy, its owner having been summarily executed by the French *resistance* movement for collaboration. It was known that nothing had been added to this cellar since the outbreak of the previous war. The bottle in question had no label but contained a wine of golden hue. I pulled the cork, which was in perfect condition, and found it was marked *Kressman 1908*. A fantastic bouquet filled the room. It was a truly memorable sauterne.

In the classification of sauternes and BARSAC in the 1855 BORDEAUX classification, only *Château* d'YQUEM was included as a *Grand Cru*.

SAZERAC

1 Proprietary name of a bottled cocktail produced in New Orleans for over a century.
2 A cocktail with many versions. Dash of Pernod in a small tumbler, swilled round and flicked out. Stir together with ice and a teaspoon of sugar syrup, 2 measures bourbon or rye whiskey and 2 dashes Angostura. Strain into prepared glass.

SCHENLEY INDUSTRIES INC.

This company's story is largely that of Lewis S. Rosenstiel, its founder.

Mr. Rosenstiel was born of pioneer stock. His forbears emigrated to America from Germany late in the Eighteenth Century. They settled on the frontier, in what is now Indiana, at a time when it was Indian territory. They were the kind of people who willingly risked the dangers and hardships of the frontier for the rewards that go with personal freedom.

So the attributes of the pioneer—risk taking, daring, enterprise, courage and, above all, self-reliance—were inborn parts of his character when his connection with the distilling industry began in 1907. In that year, at the age of 16, he left his home in Cincinnati to accept a "temporary" job with the Susquemac Distilling Co. in Milton, Kentucky. But the job turned out to be far from temporary. In 11 years with the distillery Mr. Rosenstiel progressed from meal-room helper to plant superintendent and finally manager.

That was in 1918. Two years later, following ratification of the 18th Amendment, total peacetime U.S. PROHIBITION began. But even at its beginning Mr. Rosenstiel, a firm believer in freedom of human rights, thinking of America as a land of opportunity and freedom of competition, publicly predicted that it would end within 15 years.

His foresight was not shared universally. Many people felt that the alcoholic beverage industry had come to an end for all time. Skilled workers were seeking other outlets for their talents. The sales organizations of distillers disintegrated. The bungs, yeast cells and hydrometers were stored away for another day, or were sold outright, in despair. Warehouses bulged with stocks that could be marketed only in trickling quantities through drug stores, on prescription from physicians.

Aware of the costs of warehousing, the

Schenley

limited market, and the loss of stocks through evaporation and leakage, most distillers sought bulk buyers. Representatives for some of the largest distillers came to Mr. Rosenstiel, one of the few business leaders at that time to be on the buying side. Mr. Rosenstiel obliged these distillers by purchasing their bulk holdings. Throughout the Prohibition era he and a few courageous associates made long-range plans for the day when the pendulum of public opinion would swing back in the direction Mr. Rosenstiel expected.

Mr. Rosenstiel had good, sound whiskey, and now he proceeded to round up the salesmen and executives needed to take responsible appointments when Prohibition was ended. Another far-sighted move was the acquisition of exclusive distribution rights in the United States for a complete line of fine European whiskies, wines and liqueurs.

Meanwhile four distilleries had been purchased: one at Schenley, Pennsylvania; two in Kentucky, at Frankfort and Lexington; and one in Lawrenceburg, Indiana. As a final preparatory step, Mr. Rosenstiel and his associates formed Schenley Distillers Corporation in July, 1933, shortly before Prohibition passed into history on December 5, 1933.

Just when everything was going well for the fledgeling company, the horizon was darkened by two non-related major setbacks. Firstly, the Commonwealth of Pennsylvania adopted a tax on whiskey that would have cost Schenley $6.3 million on its stocks in that state. Secondly, a disastrous fire swept the Jas. E. Pepper plant at Lexington, Kentucky, destroying five warehouses and 18,000 barrels of aged whiskey. Insurance covered the financial loss but it would not replace the priceless whiskey.

The tax levied so unexpectedly by Pennsylvania was payable in cash. Schenley management, convinced that the tax was unconstitutional, resolved to test it in the courts. It took four years to obtain final adjudication. The highest court in the state found the tax to be indeed unconstitutional.

By 1936 the company had soared to a commanding position in the domestic industry and its overseas operations also were on the march. A small yet significant step toward product diversification also goes back to 1935 when Schenley acquired the New England Distilling Company at Covington, Kentucky, the world's largest producer of industrial rum. In 1938, the company added to its reserves of Kentucky whiskey and to its productive capacity through the purchase of the famed Bernheim Distilling Company plant in Louisville. Bernheim had a solid reputation for making fine bourbon under two brand names, widely known then and now, *I. W. Harper* and *Old Charter*.

Eight years of uphill going culminated in 1941 as the company's net sales climbed to nearly 122 million dollars. The long road that had been traversed since repeal, was commemorated by the company in three memorable days in Cincinnati during that year. A month after the Cincinnati meeting, Mr. Rosenstiel announced a nine-point conservation programme with proposals for the production of alcohol for national defence. Even before the fateful December 7, 1941, some of Schenley's distilleries were manufacturing high-proof industrial alcohol needed for the nation's preparedness, particularly for the synthetic rubber programme. By October 1, 1942, all beverage alcohol plants in the country were engaged in war alcohol production. Conversion of Schenley's plants had been speeded up immeasurably by means of a special device invented by one of its engineers known as the Schenley "packed column". This innovation was offered free of royalty to all other U.S. distillers. In all, Schenley made over 200 million proof gallons of war alcohol.

Schenley

In 1945 Schenley acquired production facilities outside the United States for the first time. The company bought Quebec Distillers Inc. with a distillery in Valleyfield, Quebec, and offices in Montreal. The subsidiary was renamed Canadian Schenley Ltd. Schenley's most important international expansion occurred in 1956 when the company purchased SEAGER, EVANS & CO. Ltd., the British distilling firm founded in 1805. In 1958, Seager-Evans acquired Coates & Co. (Plymouth) Ltd., thereby adding to its list the distinctive and world-renowned PLYMOUTH gin which dates back to 1793. A substantial minority interest was obtained in 1962 by Seager-Evans in D. Johnston & Co. (Laphroaig) Ltd., producers of *Laphroaig* and *Islay Mist* Scotch whiskies.

Schenley's newest U.S. distillery was built in Tullahoma, Tennessee, to meet the rising consumer demand for Tennessee sour-mash whiskey, a distinctive product. In 1964 Schenley made an investment in Buckingham Corporation by the purchase of 1,527,225 shares, a majority, of that company's common stock. As I go to press, Schenley's agreed to sell their majority holding under U.S. anti-trust laws. Buckingham is the sole importer into the United States of *Cutty Sark* Scotch whisky, under long-term agreements with two British companies.

Schenley was responsible for founding The Bourbon Institute in 1958 to open new markets for bourbon whiskey abroad, to win increased preference for bourbon among U.S. consumers and to protect the reputation of bourbon by keeping products produced abroad from coming into the country labelled as bourbon, just as Scotch can only be made in its native country. Through Schenley's efforts, the institute has become an industry organization of leading U.S. bourbon distillers.

Today, Schenley plants are located in many areas of the Free World. Most of the company's distilleries are sited in the traditional "blue-grass oval" of the central Ohio River Valley. Several of them are among the oldest in Kentucky. The Schenley distillery at Frankfurt, for example, first opened in the 1860s. Other major company distilleries are located in Indiana, Pennsylvania and Tennessee, and it has outstanding wineries in California. Outside the continental United States, there are two distilleries in Canada... five distilleries in Scotland... distilleries in Brazil, Chile, England, Mexico and New Zealand... and rum distilleries in Puerto Rico and the Virgin Islands. The company, in addition to sales coverage of the United States, has representation in 97 countries, U.S. possessions and territories throughout the world.

SCHIEDAM
An ancient town, now a suburb of bustling modern Rotterdam, which is traditionally and actually the main home of DUTCH GIN: "Schiedam" is sometimes used descriptively for this type of gin.

SCHLOSS
German equivalent to château and equally broad in its implication.

SCHNAPPS
The Germans tend to call all spirits by this name; in other countries variants of the word cover various flavoured aquavits.

SCHWEPPES LTD.
During the second half of the Eighteenth Century, chemists got to work to try to reproduce the "spa" waters that were so popular with those who could afford to travel thither. By 1789, Nicholas Paul of Geneva, had developed a method of manufacturing carbonated waters in bulk. A partner of Paul's, Jacob Schweppe came to England about four years later and manufactured soda-water, with a chemist's shop next to this factory, for even soda-water was then drunk

for health rather than a pleasing additive to spirits. I suppose the first purely social use of soda-water was "hock and seltzer". Some time later Schweppe established a second factory in Bristol. The medicinal nature of mineral waters at the time is underlined by the fact that they carried the large tax of threepence a bottle, being classed as patent medicines. Schweppe retired in 1799, but the firm carried on, and much expanded under his name until it became a public company under its present title in 1897.

Schweppes is now a giant in its field. I suppose if one had to name a single one of its products, it would be the world-famous, often imitated as to label but never as to taste, *Schweppes Tonic Water*. The firm produces and bottles mineral waters, fruit drinks and preserves through 40 companies scattered throughout the world. It owns *Rose's Lime Juice*, the premier quality brand, and the Apollinaris Company (natural sparkling spring water bottled in Germany). It also holds an important place in the PEPSI COLA organization.

SCOTCH WHISKY

There have been various endeavours to describe this greatest of all spirituous beverages the fame of which has spread from the glens of Scotland to the remotest parts of the world. It has often been imitated but never successfully copied. One may tell its story, praise its merits, but eventually all of the many writers about Scotch whisky have to admit that there is some special mystery about it, which some ascribe to air or water or soil, or the very folk who make it, but which I am content to leave as the mystery it is. There are many fine books about Scotch. It is not my intention to pretend to render here a digest of them, but to give such basic facts as may encourage interested persons further to pursue their studies in this fascinating field. (For a start one could do much worse than obtain the highly informative and well set out booklet *Scotch Whisky—questions and answers*, published by The Scotch Whisky Association, Edinburgh.)

History Aqua vitae—uisge beatha—usquebaugh—usky—wusky—whiskey—whisky: such was the evolution of the sound and spelling of the actual word. It came to Scotland from Ireland at a time unknown. The Irish started colonizing Scotland around the Fifth Century, which considerably antedates the "invention" of whisky in Ireland. Its first existing written mention was in 1494; it was at the court of King James IV by 1500, and we may assume that its use was general some time before this, for in 1505 a measure of control was deemed necessary in Edinburgh. To such an extent had home distilling become a popular pastime, that supervision of spirits was placed in the hands of the Royal College of Surgeons. But it was probably pretty crude stuff. One theory for the proliferation of stills is that the difficulty of drying grain after wet harvests, not uncommon in Scotland, produced much naturally fermenting grain which, rather than waste it, the notoriously thrifty Scots turned into alcohol.

We do not hear much about whisky until 1644 when the Scottish Parliament made an attempt to tax it, which produced the inevitable (as when the British Parliament considerably later tried to tax gin)—evasion, illicit distilling and increased insobriety. After the Union of England and Scotland (1707) a proper board of excise came into being, but the Highlands remained wild and inaccessible and there were stills in abundance.

Only after the crushing of the 1745 rebellion were serious attempts made to collect taxes and destroy illicit stills. The customs men, gaugers (a name persisting into our own era), followed the military

Scotch Whisky

engineers who were opening up the country with strategic roads, but discovering illicit stills was a formidable task in rugged and unfamiliar terrain where the inhabitants knew every nook and cranny. The war between gaugers and Highlanders was to go on for a long time.

There were sundry well-known dodges. One was to wait till the gaugers had approached and send off one of the "distillers" with a bag on his shoulder that might be presumed to hide the tell-tale malt. By the time he had been chased and captured and found to have nothing illegal on him, the still would have been dismantled and hidden.

A crucial part of the still was the copper condensing coil and the replacement of this was a matter needing cash, a commodity with which the Highlander was not richly endowed. However, the reward for informants leading to the uncovering of an illicit still almost exactly coincided with the going price for a new coil (or worm). Hence, and "informer" would apprise the gaugers of the whereabouts of his own still where they would duly find an unserviceable coil and other equipment of minimal importance. The reward would be paid and the "informer" was back in business shortly afterwards in another location.

There is the almost certainly apocryphal anecdote of the farmer in whose possession the gaugers found some distilling equipment but no malt or spirit. Informed he would be arrested, he protested and was told it was sufficient evidence to have the equipment. "While you're at it then you had better add rape to the charges," he said. "What on earth for?" queried the officer. "Well, I've got the equipment," answered the farmer.

The farmer-poet Robert Burns, who so wonderfully sang the praises of whisky, somewhat surprisingly became a gauger, but his heart could not have been in the job.

In 1777 there were eight legal stills in Edinburgh and an estimated 400 illicit ones. So it can be guessed what sort of numbers existed in the countryside. In 1823, when the situation had become chaotic, 14,000 illegal stills were uncovered, an indication of the vast number there must have been.

It was then that the 4th Duke of Gordon, a huge landowner and man of immense power in Scotland, decided that it would be best to sweep away an accumulated mass of decaying and impractical regulations. He stated that in return for a realistic licensing and taxation system he and his fellow magnates would make every effort to suppress illegal manufacture of whisky. The proposal was received with relief by a distraught government. This did in fact reduce, though could not stop, illicit distilling. The first man to take out a licence, George Smith of Glenlivet in 1824, incurred the odium of his fellow distillers and suffered persecution for some years. What did stop illegal practices, today extremely rare, was the coming of large-scale commercialization of the Scotch whisky industry.

In 1822, King George IV paid a state visit to Scotland and despite a certain sartorial flamboyance he made a bit of a hit. He did insist on drinking whisky, which may have had its effect a year later and would certainly have brought Scotch to the notice of many southerners: the visit was widely publicized and illustrated.

Not until 1860 was Scotch whisky sent to England in bottles, and that decade saw the real start of blending, Usher's of Edinburgh being leading pioneers. This was to launch Scotch on its all-conquering invasion of the world. It involved the co-operation of the POT STILL malt distillers of the Highlands with the PATENT STILL grain whisky distillers of the Lowlands, who had hitherto been mainly antagonistic, and were to be so again before combining interests. Another factor aiding Scotch was the vogue for

Plate 30. Taking samples from a spirit safe at the Red Lion gin distillery, London.

Plate 31. A French cellarman samples wine from his silver *tastevin* and spits it out.

Scotch Whisky

Scotland established by the novelist Sir Walter Scott, made even more fashionable by Queen Victoria with her delight in Balmoral and her widely read books about her life there. The queen is said to have horrified Mr. Gladstone by drinking a mixture of whisky and claret. The scourge of the PHYLLOXERA had by the '90s greatly reduced, indeed threatened to wipe out, supplies of cognac, till then the main spirituous tipple of the English upper classes. This, and other reasons, such as the introduction of blended Scotch, caused them to turn to whisky.

Certain other aspects of the development of the industry will be found in the stories of some of the leading individual distillers, but one very important event must be mentioned, the formation of The DISTILLERS COMPANY LTD. in 1877, which was destined to revolutionize the production and sale of Scotch.

Production of Scotch (malt whisky) Despite the mystery of Scotch whisky to which I have previously referred, it is strange that the actual making of it is not basically a very complicated business. Since the peculiarity of Scotch lies in MALT whisky, not grains, this is the most important part of the whole thing. Most major malt distilleries are abolishing their malting floors in favour of central purchasing of malt. This arrives suitably flavoured by peat to the owner's requirements. But we may suppose for purposes of this section that we are taking the process through in a single place. The sequence would then be as follows. The barley (ideally from Scotland but the demand is such that some must come from England or be imported) is soaked in water for two or three days and spread at a depth of around two feet on the stone floor of the malting house. I am speaking of the long-established traditional method, although there are many totally satisfactory short cuts today, for the manpower involved in the traditional method would be formidable. The germinating barley generates a lot of heat and therefore it would be turned continually by men with wooden spades, working along the malting floor (See Saladin).

After this treatment the barley has sprouted a rootlet about a thumb-nail long. The germination is decelerated by a gradual thinning out of the depth of the barley on the floor. The barley seeds have now concentrated a lot of DIASTASE: I hate being too technical but this is essential to the process.

The next stage, and I emphasize that I am not necessarily describing what you will see in a particular distillery, for practice varies, is to dry the malt. If you have ever seen a Scotch whisky distillery you will have noted the tall ventilators, for "sassenachs" not wholly dissimilar to Kentish oast-houses. These are drying kilns, and what is taking place in them according to the traditional method is the vital drying of the malt which is spread on perforated floors and dried by fires from furnaces that would formerly have had no fuel but peat. The dried malt has a delicious aroma. The fully malted barley is now "dressed", to remove unwanted material and is not too finely ground. Appropriate quantities are then fed into the mash tun together with large amounts of hot water. The object of this is to let the diastase complete its job of converting remaining starch in the malt to sugar. This takes place quickly, and the resultant liquid, the WORT, is drained off and cooled. The process is repeated several times. The remaining solids are a valuable livestock feed.

In due course the wort goes into fermenting vessels (technically "wash backs") and yeast is added which sets up a violent fermentation. The result is an alcoholic liquid much akin to beer, the wash.

Scotch Whisky

The DISTILLING takes place in POT STILLS, two being required at a minimum. The first distillation produces "low wines" with a great deal of flavour and many impurities. In the second distillation the "foreshots" at the beginning of the run and the "feints" at the conclusion, are rejected, though not wasted, as being respectively too strong and too uninteresting, a system analogous to the rejection of "heads" and "tails" during gin rectification. It is on the expertize of the distiller that must depend the quality of the final whisky; using a SPIRIT SAFE he must decide when the whisky is in the precisely right condition. This is *not* a RECTIFICATION process as generally understood. The object is not entirely to "clean" the spirit, for it would then be virtually flavourless, but to retain those congenerics which give it character while eliminating most of those that are displeasing.

Maturing of Scotch When it became widely customary to mature Scotch in casks cannot be dated with any precision. Writing of George IV's visit to Scotland in 1822, Elizabeth Grant, of Glenlivet, spoke of procuring for her father, at the king's expressed command for pure malt (she was in charge of the cellars) "whisky long in wood, long in uncorked bottles, mild as milk, and with the true contraband *goût* in it." This indicates that reputable Scottish distillers were accustomed to maturing—it is also an interesting sidelight on what I have said on the history of Scotch that at Holyrood House the king drank illicitly distilled whisky! The reference to "uncorked bottles" is intriguing. The consensus of opinion is that wood-maturing was adopted from the cognac process, but there is no evidence that it was a particularly old-established practice in general commerce, and it is just as possible that the Scots were ahead. To transport whisky, if only for smuggling into England, they would have used casks; that spirit improves in wood was probably an accidental discovery, though the benefits to wine of such treatment were much earlier appreciated.

Indubitably part of the mystery of Scotch lies in what happens to malt whisky while it is lying in casks under lock and key in a hundred and more distilleries scattered across the country. Something does happen. The whisky is, to the palate, pleasing enough when the second distillation is completed and there are old hands who take their evening free dram not in an aged whisky but in a new one. Not long ago at Dalwhinnie Distillery, I had a dram of malt one morning not more than a day old. I thought it splendid, but I was warned not to have too much of it, and not just because it was in excess of 100° proof, but because it might produce the worst E.P.L. I had ever known! No one quite knows what happens when Scotch rests for five, ten, fifteen, twenty years in cask in the Highlands, or the Lowlands for that matter. But something does, and, allied to the other special factors, this makes Scotch unique. Certainly maturing renders innocuous certain displeasing fusel oils and the like which, however, are a part of the original and essential make up of the product. Maturing smooths, soothes, makes what was harsh bland, finally achieves that nectar which is Scotch.

Fifteen years is possibly the ideal ageing period for a malt whisky, though some authorities would go as far as 20, but after that it is generally conceded it may go downhill. Contrary to the widely accepted opinion, which has some scientific basis, that Scotch does not improve in bottle, Prof. R. J. S. McDowell, an authority for whom I have absolute respect, believes that a fine malt does just that and he suggests that his experience with whiskies that have been in bottle 35 years supports the theory that whisky could be "laid down" like wine. I am sorry I cannot wait.

The best casks for maturing whisky are sherry casks, but these must be reserved for the finest as there simply are not enough to go round. New casks, charred and "wine treated" with PAXARETE may be employed, or reconditioned Scottish-made casks, or, importantly, American whiskey casks brought in broken down into staves, and recoopered in Scotland and "wine-treated". If American LIGHT WHISKEY is successful, it could cause some embarrassment regarding casks. An advantage of using American casks is that they have already absorbed some four gallons each of whiskey and thus take up less from the Scotch for which they are used. As it is, through absorption and evaporation an estimated 4 million gallons of Scotch vanish each year to help perfume the already deliciously fragrant Scottish air.

At a time when maturing was not universally appreciated, the blenders realized its importance, one of the first being William SANDERSON (*Vat 69*). There was no law on the subject until 1915, and some extremely immature and toxic whiskies must have been around. The Act of Parliament making three years maturing the legal minimum was not a measure for consumer protection but part of the British government's campaign to reduce drinking during World War I. The law still stands, but, in fact, no reputable brand will be under an average of five years old. Though it is not customary to announce the age of blended whiskies, where a blended brand of Scotch does give an age it will be that of the youngest whisky in it.

Sweden is the first overseas country in the world to obtain an agreement with the Scotch Whisky Association to mature and blend whisky from Scotland. The first £8 million cargo of whisky was only 10 days old, but in Sweden it will be matured in cask for at least three years, bringing it into line with Scottish practice.

Scotch grain whisky Grain whisky is made by the PATENT STILL process and production greatly exceeds that of malt pot-still whisky. There are only rather over a dozen grain whisky distilleries in Scotland against well over 100 malt ones. Not all the production of grain distilleries is whisky; by their enormous production they can also supply the wants of some gin rectifiers. Grain whisky is now rarely drunk on its own; its function is to be blended with more or less malt to produce individual blends. But there was a period at the beginning of this century when it was strongly promoted, against malts. There was a considerable period of litigation and for a time it looked as though grain whisky might lose its title to be called whisky at all. However, a royal commission injected sanity into the battle of grain versus malt, and we have since seen the two types wedded into what the world recognizes as Scotch.

Blends, straights and vatted Another of the mysteries of Scotch lies in the amazing skill of the blenders. These uncanny experts have the vital job of maintaining the consistency of the blend or blends of the brand-owners for whom they work, an extremely difficult task. This may involve them in tasting a new malt whisky and assessing what its quality is likely to be, and how much they may require of it, in ten or more years time when they may not even be there to use it in the blend. They have to gauge what requirements will be, in thousands of gallons, of up to 60 different whiskies that may be needed in a single day's blending. (After this blending has taken place, casks of blended whisky will, for the top blends, be further stored for six months or so to marry the blends).

Scotch Whisky

At every step they are tasting and testing. Blending secrets are amongst the most jealously guarded in the trade. I understand that between 25-30 different malts, and no more than two or three grains, would be average in quantity, the proportion of malts to grains varying very much. I believe that of popular brands Buchanan's *Black & White* has the greatest number of individual whiskies. Obviously, the greater the number the greater the consistency of flavour is likely to be.

Single malts need little description. They are of a single distillation from a single distillery. Vatted straight malts are a blend of several different malts, but contain only malt whisky, no grain. Distribution of distilleries in Scotland is very widespread but the special concentration is on Speyside where conditions are considered ideal.

Digression In 1967 in Edinburgh a most unusual case was heard concerning Scotch. Dustman Benjamin Duffield found a new use for his wife's spin dryer. He had looked on dozens of times while the machinery on his council dustcart squeezed whisky out of filter pads discarded from a bonded warehouse. According to the prosecution this gave him an idea. He collected the filter pads from the warehouse of the *Vat 69* Company at Leith and used his own extraction unit, his wife's spin dryer. The dryer brought out the whisky from the pads and Duffield, who later became a garage-owner, bottled the results. He pleaded not guilty to attempting to avoid duty on the whisky, which consisted of four bottles and three jars at his garage and 11 bottles at his home. He was found not guilty.

Note There are some 100 brands of Scotch whisky fairly widely marketed in Britain and a much greater number exported. The Scotch Whisky Association says it is impossible to count the actual number of brands; I have heard it put at 2,000. I have selected those I consider best-known to the public: there are several other famous distilleries whose products are much sought within the trade but which are exclusively, or in effect exclusively, reserved for blending purposes.

Well-known Scotch whisky mixed drinks are ATHOLL BROSE, BLOOD AND SAND, BOBBY BURNS, ROB ROY, WHISKY MAC. See also Sours; Toddy.

SCOTCH WHISKY ASSOCIATION

Though its origins go back to an organization established in 1917, this body was consolidated in its present form in 1960 as a limited liability company, though by special licence it is not required to use "Ltd." in its title. It looks after the broad interests of the Scotch whisky industry; statistical information, publicity, legal matters, parliamentary and fiscal subjects, foreign legislation affecting exports, and is zealous in protecting the reputation of Scotch. Abuse of the word *Scotch*, adulteration, false description, forging labels continue; such things are common when a product is as prestigious as is Scotch, and the association unhesitatingly initiates action anywhere in the world to protect its members' interests. Anyone with a commercial interest in Scotch is eligible to apply to the council for election to membership (77 George Street, Edinburgh 2).

SCOTLAND

Whisky (popularly drunk with fizzy lemonade of all things) remains the main tipple, though the young of this hard-drinking land quickly joined the vogue for vodka; and rum, port, sherry (particularly cream sherry) have excellent sales. Gin has made inroads since the war, lager is a growth product in a big way, and beer has always been in demand. Brand loyalties to various whiskies are very pronounced; one street may demand so-and-so's, though in the next one it is not to be found in the bar. The variety of brands on general sale is greater than in England.

City pubs tend to dreariness, and this type of drinking is more happily done in the countryside: provided that is you do not strike an area where as the result of a local "veto poll" the district has become a dry one. This form of parochial prohibition has proved a curse, with "bothans" (illicit drinking dens) proliferating almost with impunity and bringing inevitably in their wake, because of lack of the control practised under a licensing system, drunkenness and alcoholism. The juvenile alcoholism rate is much higher in the Highlands than in the rest of the British Isles, and this is mainly due to the results of local vetos, i.e., prohibition. The Free Church of Scotland is violently T.T., and the Presbytery of the Isle of Lewis went on record as actually preferring bothans to legality as being "far less offensive than licensed premises would be!" I have seen a picture of one of these well-known bothan "clubs" within a hundred yards of the village kirk. They are places of a sordidness to make a back-street Glasgow bar seem like the Ritz. Really, the Scots deserve better social justice than this.

Scottish licensing laws, where they apply, are on the general English pattern as to hours. At one time only *bona fide* travellers could drink on a Sunday, a restriction inevitably abused; so permission for Sunday opening was granted for many areas. In the event, only some of the places entitled to took advantage of the relaxation following the first Sunday, when they were besieged by eager topers. The state has a small hand in the licensed trade, controlling 15 pubs in Gretna and 18 in Cromarty and Firth. As with CARLISLE, there are indications these local state monopolies will be ended.

With all her assets Scotland can perhaps afford the idiocy of the "veto poll". She has Scotch whisky, and since that receives a great deal of general and particularized attention in these pages, I will say no more about the great country that produces it.

SCOTTISH & NEWCASTLE BREWERIES LTD.

This is one of the six largest brewery companies in the United Kingdom, and the only one of them with its head office in Scotland,—at Abbey Brewery, Holyrood Road, Edinburgh. The group owns and controls three breweries; 2,000 licensed premises, including more than 120 hotels; as well as restaurants and off-licences spread throughout the country, the majority being in Scotland and the north-east of England.

Edinburgh is traditionally one of the most important brewing centres in Britain and one of the first people to go into the business of brewing professionally was a young man from West Lothian, named William Younger. In 1749 he established a brewery in Leith, and on his death his sons moved the brewery to Holyrood Abbey to tap the water from wells, which still exist to this day. In 1856, another brewer to gain repute set up his company in the village of Fountainbridge on the outskirts of Edinburgh. His name was William McEwan, and as well as being a master brewer he was a great public figure and benefactor.

In 1931, these two successful businesses, which in the interim had acquired company status, merged to form Scottish Brewers Ltd., although they continued to trade in competition with each other until 1959 when their trading identities were merged completely. In 1960 Scottish Brewers Ltd., and the Newcastle Breweries Ltd., merged to form Scottish & Newcastle Breweries Ltd.

The group produces a wide range of beers, the best known of which are McEwan's *Export, Younger's Special* (known in England

Scottish & Newcastle

as William Younger's *Tartan Bitter*); and *Newcastle Strong Brown Ale*.

Newcastle-upon-Tyne has always been famed for its ale and was said to be the first town in England to brew it. With the Industrial Revolution and the creation of new industries in the north-east of England, larger breweries came into being. One of these, founded in 1770 was John Barras & Company of Gateshead. When their Gateshead Brewery was bought by the North Eastern Railway they acquired the Tyne Brewery, and in 1890 several small breweries in North Shields, Gateshead and Sunderland linked with them to form The Newcastle Breweries Ltd.

The company made steady progress, acquiring two further small breweries and a large maltings which is still in use. In 1913 the first of many extensions to the Tyne Brewery was carried out and following the First World War the *blue star* was adopted as the company's trade mark. The famous bottled beer, *Newcastle Brown Ale*, was introduced in 1927. In the 1950s Robert Deuchar Limited of Newcastle and Duddingston; James Deucher Limited of Newcastle and Montrose; and John Rowell & Son Limited of Gateshead became part of The Newcastle Breweries.

Mackinlay-McPherson Limited is the wholly owned subsidiary company of Scottish & Newcastle Breweries which looks after the wine and spirit interests of the group. Started in 1961, this company is the result of the amalgamation of two long-established family firms: Charles Mackinlay & Company of Leith founded in 1815 and John E. McPherson & Sons of Newcastle, founded in 1857. The present, and fifth generation of the Mackinlay family is still engaged in blending Mackinlay's Scotch whisky.

Of the three breweries, two are in Edinburgh (Holyrood, home of William Younger's; and Fountain, home of McEwan's) and the Tyne Brewery in Newcastle (home of *Newcastle Strong Brown Ale*). All McEwan's and Younger's beers sold anywhere in the world are brewed in Edinburgh; and all Newcastle beers are brewed in Newcastle. The Holyrood Brewery, in addition to brewing *Younger's* and *McEwan's* ales, also brews *Harp* lager.

Scottish & Newcastle have considerable wine and spirit interests through their subsidiary company Mackinlay-McPherson Limited. At their premises in Leith the group's whiskies are blended and bottled for world distribution. At the company's premises in Newcastle all the other lines of wines and spirits which the company sells under its own name, are bottled prior to distribution.

The principal distilling interests of the group are at present carried on by two subsidiary companies, The Isle of Jura Distillery which was completely reconstructed and started to operate in 1963 and by Glenallachie Distillery Company Limited at Aberlour, which commenced production some five years later. In addition the company has a stake in Mackinlay & Birnie Limited which operates the Glen Mhor and Glen Albyn Distilleries in Inverness.

Scottish & Newcastle export beer and Scotch whisky to over 40 countries, using the ports of Leith, Grangemouth, Glasgow, Liverpool and London. Every Friday or Saturday, the company's *Scotch Ale* is shipped to Belgium (Antwerp) from Leith. This trade has gone on for more than a century and the market continues to flourish. Major markets include Canada, Jamaica, Gibraltar, and the Falkland Islands. Other markets are the United States of America, Chile, Spain, South Africa, Pakistan and British embassies round the world. A large amount of N.A.A.F.I. business is done in providing the armed services with liquor,

Seagram's

particularly in Germany, and there is a substantial turnover for ships' stores.

SCREWDRIVER
One of the drinks that launched VODKA in the U.S.A. in the '40s. A glass of iced fresh orange juice, spiked with vodka.

SEAGER EVANS & CO.
Old-established British distillers, controlled by SCHENLEY'S. *Seager's Gin* is fairly well-known in Britain and is also made in Chile, New Zealand, Canada and Mexico. One of its most important lines is *Long John* whisky, and in 1971 the firm was appropriately renamed Long John (International). In 1958 they acquired Coate's PLYMOUTH GIN.

Background note It is thought that Mr. Seager and Mr. Evans started in business in Maidstone and worked there between 1805 and 1813. Their principal business was gin at 12s. 6d. per gallon and 88 proof. They also sold "other delectable drinks". They moved to Pimlico, the area of London now surrounding Victoria Station, but shortly afterwards moved to Millbank, hard by the Houses of Parliament, where they built a distillery; and in short order they acquired others as well.

In 1832 the partners joined the exclusive Rectifiers' Club, established "to regulate conduct in the trade, protect its interests and make representation on its behalf to His Majesty's Government." Fellow members queray, Nicholson and Burnett, all names covered in this volume. Seager & Evans dealt mainly with the trade, but also had private customers, including the novelist Charles Dickens. There is extant an order dated 1867 from him for "another cask of best *Old Tom* gin." The next year, writing on the notepaper of *All The Year Round*, a journal he edited, he enclosed a bottle drawn from a cask, with a complaint as to its strength and flavour and the suggestion it may have been tampered with at Gad's Hill Station.

Evans died in 1856 and Seager in 1873. Seager Evans & Co. Ltd. was formed in 1898. There were various ups and downs, reflecting conditions in the trade, but in the late '20s and early '30s, the firm expanded greatly, establishing overseas subsidiaries and moving into Scotch whisky. They had long been, and are still, substantial wine merchants. In London they acquired 20 Queen Anne's Gate, a lovely Eighteenth-century mansion. One room was decorated as a replica of Nelson's cabin on the *H.M.S. Victory* and valuable relics were garnered for it (the connection between the British Navy and gin has long been close) though when they established this Nelsonian association, Seager's could not have known they were to acquire *Plymouth*.

SEAGRAM'S
This is the simple title by which readers will readily recognize what I should correctly call Distillers Corporation, Seagrams Ltd., of Montreal, Canada. In fact, that name covers some 60 subsidiary companies, a very high proportion of the business being accounted for by Joseph E. Seagram & Sons Inc., in the U.S.A.

This gigantic combine was built up since the end of Prohibition by a quiet sort of genius, Canadian-born Samuel Bronfman, who, with his sons, retains a dominant position. It is one of the largest corporations of its type in the world but according to the (1970) *Life* magazine listing of major companies outside the U.S.A. comes 116th in sales volume while The DISTILLERS COMPANY Ltd. is 112th. It has the world's largest-selling single brand of spirit *7 Crown* whiskey, doing around 8 million cases a year in the U.S.A. More likely to be familiar to Britons is *Seagram's V.O.* Canadian whisky, which sells about half that quantity in the

U.S.A. but is still the second biggest-selling whisky there. They own important champagne, bordeaux and burgundy interests.

Frankly, the 100-country operations of Seagram's are too vast to be sensibly condensed in a form suitable for this volume. They own, handle, or are otherwise concerned with, locally or globally, a great many of the products and firms of which I write. I cannot say how many: the ultimate "who owns what" of today's wine and spirit trade is of immense complexity.

SEC
The extremely misleading French word which, meaning DRY, in effect indicates that a wine so called is sweet.

SEKT
German sparkling wine made by the champagne method or by CUVE CLOSE. See also Henkell and Vin Mousseux.

SELTZER ("Alka-Seltzer"; "Bromo-Seltzer")
Excellent if one remembers to take them the "night before", which one rarely does. Taken before lapsing into slumber these preparations have infinitely more value than, as normally, taken the "morning after" by which time the damage has been done.

Eno's and *Andrew's* liver salts also have some curative or preventative powers in respect of potential or actual HANGOVERS. (One trouble is that the noise all these make fizzing in a glass can be distinctly upsetting in extreme cases of alcoholic remorse).

SEPPELT & SONS PTY. LTD., B.
The oldest and biggest producers of Australian wine, who commenced business in 1851, exported to England in 1870, and broke new ground in 1966 by sending red wine to Italy in competition with (or to supplement?) the native product.

SERPENT'S TOOTH
One measure of Irish whiskey, 2 measures of sweet vermouth, 1 measure of lemon juice, half-measure of kummel, dash of Angostura. Stir well with ice and strain into small wine glass.

7-UP
This American soft drink has gained international acceptance as a mixer with light rum, vodka, etc., or on its own, and is widely produced under licence (British distributors, HUNT's). Its slogan is "You like it—it likes you". Its ingredients are listed as "carbonated water, sugar, citric acid, sodium citrate, flavour derived from lemon and lime oils."

SEX
"Candy is dandy, but licker is quicker", wrote Ogden Nash, during Prohibition, I believe. See Aphrodisiac.

SHAMROCK
One measure of Irish whiskey, 1 measure of dry vermouth, 3 dashes each of green Chartreuse and green crème de menthe. Stir well with ice, and strain into cocktail-glass. Serve with green olive.

SHANDY
Once called *Shandy Gaff*. Fizzy lemonade or ginger beer with bitter. A pleasant, very mildly alcoholic drink for warm weather or when lingering in hot pubs without the desire to drink too much. The proportions should be about half and half, but the law does not lay this down. The city analyst at Leeds found shandies in his area concocted to the proportions 1 beer to 8 lemonade! There is a proprietary bottled shandy called *Chandy*.

SHEBEEN
Illegal Irish drinking den.

SHEPHERD NEAME
Only independent family brewery left in

Kent, in Faversham, which has a history of brewing going back to the Fourteenth Century: in fact, in 1327 it is recorded that of 252 traders in the ancient town, 84 were brewers. However, the concern whence the present company stemmed was founded much later, in 1698, still fairly old, even by English standards!

The Neames entered the scene in the early Nineteenth Century, assumed control in 1877, and are still very much there. Lately this most interesting company, owning 200 pubs, caused a mild trade sensation when, in opposition to the giants (see Brewers) they started exporting their *Abbey Ale* to Switzerland, with the likelihood of expanding into Germany.

SHERRY

Sherry was once called "sherris-sack" to differentiate it from other SACK, which term covered a great many heavy sweetened Mediterranean wines. But as sack gave way to port, marsala and malaga, the favoured Spanish product became known as sherry. The word is an obvious anglicization of Jerez, the Spanish town that is the sherry capital, itself derived from the Moorish *scheriz*. In Britain the simple description sherry may be applied only to wine from the designated part of Spain. "Sherry" from other sources, South Africa, Cyprus, Australia or British sherry (from imported concentrates), may bear the word only with the same prominence given to its provenance. This protection is not universal.

Jerez de la Frontera, some 80 miles south of Seville, is said to be the richest town *per capita* in Spain. The British element in the sherry trade has long been very strong, much of it stemming from the Peninsular War against Napoleon's armies. However, Spanish influence has overcome British prejudices and the town is entirely Iberian. It is not for visiting in the height of the torrid Andalusian summer: May is a good month, or September when the festival connected with the grape harvest is held. You will have accommodation difficulties if you do not make arrangements way ahead. It is easy to arrange to visit one of the great sherry firms, and well worth while.

Another town associated with sherry is Sanlucar de Barrameda, a sleepy old place perched on the water where the muddy Guadalquivir debouches into the Atlantic, where you can eat marvellous fish repasts, preceded by wonderful local sherry, on a shaded platform above the beach, looking across to a sun-drenched island where roam Europe's only wild camels. Ancient Puerto de Santa Maria on the Bay of Cadiz is also linked with the sherry trade. The industry is very closely controlled by an official body.

The production of sherry is special. It is made wholly from white grapes (Palomino) grown in a soil of such chalky whiteness that a view of a vineyard can be blinding even with the verdant vines, which grow close to the ground, and the lush bunches supported on stakes. When the ripe grapes have been picked they are laid on esparto grass mats in the sun for a period ranging from hours to many days, protected from the dew at night by matting or awnings. This further concentrates the sugar in order that the wine may be strong. There is still some pressing by traditional methods. This involves treading by men in heavy spiked boots: the spikes prevent excessive crushing of the pips which would unduly taint the wine with tannin. The residue is built up round a tall, threaded column and bound with esparto grass rope. Pressure is applied by turning a screw down the column which forces out any remaining juice. However, more modern ways of pressing are superseding the traditional methods.

Owing to the high temperatures, fermentation begins almost at once; this is

Sherry

called "tumultuous fermentation", by no means an exaggeration. After this subsides, the fermentation eases until it ceases around January the following year, all the sugar having been turned into alcohol and the wine consequently being entirely dry and distinctly strong. This takes place in the bodega, those vast above-ground "cellars" that are beautifully dim and cool, however tropical it may be outside.

Some of the wine (and no one can say which) will develop *flor*—a natural yeast in the air that is unique to the sherry district. This *flor* spreads its cells across the wine, both protecting it from any other contamination and giving it the character that will cause it to be classified as fino, if it be a wine of high quality. If not, the *flor* can be killed (it can never be grown artificially) and the wine classified differently, in which case it will receive an initial fortification of grape brandy rather higher than that given the fino.

The other main classifications of sherry are amontillado, named for its similarity to MONTILLA; sweeter oloroso (amoroso is virtually the same), and manzanilla. Amontillado has come to mean in general commerce a sherry rather heavier and less dry than a fino; an oloroso, at its aged best, is a magnificent dessert wine; and manzanilla is something quite on its own. This is an extremely dry wine with a very special character that appears to come from its making and storing at Sanlucar, for it does contain a hint of sea saltiness.

To my mind a fine manzanilla is the best of all aperitif wines. But there is a great deal of blending of different types in order to satisfy commercial demand for, say, an amontillado at a reasonable price, so the demarcation of the types has become distinctly blurred except at the upper end of the trade. There is also raya which is useful for blending into cheaper wines. It is a fact about sherry that a minute proportion of really good wine can work wonders on an indifferent one, much more so than with any other blended wine. All sherry is basically dry, other than the specially made *Pedro Ximenez* (normally contracted to *P.X.*), which is an excessively sweet wine, made from sun dried grapes, and reserved for sweetening sherry. For further colouring a *vino de color* may be used; this is a reduction of grape juice to concentrate the colour. This is used for brown sherry. *P.X.* is expensive and ordinary sweet sherries may be sweetened by simpler methods. A mixture of *P.X.* and *vino de color* is PAXARETE.

The pillar on which the production of sherry rests is the "solera" system. This, put very simply, is a series of casks within a bodega, the number depending on the quality of wine ultimately envisaged. As the finished sherry is drawn out of the last cask of the solera, that cask is topped up from the next senior one and so on back to the youngest wine. Thus old wine is constantly receiving an injection of younger ones, and the younger gain the authority of the more ancient. But all sherry on the market in normal commerce will be a blend of various finished wines.

Most sherry is exported for local bottling, but some of the very best will be Spanish bottled. The bottle life of sherry depends on its body, that of a normal fino is not very long. On the other hand some exceptional sweet sherries are made for improving in bottle: only a few merchants stock these. Decanted, or opened but kept in a well-corked bottle, a sweet sherry will keep for a week or more, a fino only half that time in good condition. The lighter sherries benefit from mild refrigeration. It is no longer considered beyond the pale to serve cream sherries "on the rocks". An amontillado may be run through ice in a Martini-mixing glass to produce a chilled aperitif. Cream sherries are commercially descriptive of the oloroso type; there are many of them, of varying quality.

The wrong glass for sherry is that in which it is often served, a small, stemmed glass filled to the brim. The best is a *copita*, the tall Spanish tulip-shaped, short-stemmed glass that is similar to a tasting-glass of the English wine trade, and only three-quarters filled.

Sherry lends itself to several drinks requiring fortified wine, notably GLOGG; or in a NOG; also SYLLABUB.

SHIPPER
Who shipped your wine is a matter of vital importance. I cannot stress too strongly how much more important it is that your wine was shipped by a firm whose name you have learned to respect.

SHLOER
Non-alcoholic apple-juice, much favoured in parts of Europe. In Britain, it is the brand-name for a well-known make of unfermented pure English apple-juice. Excellent for fruit cups, etc. A Beecham group product.

SHOWERINGS LTD.
On the great success of *Babycham*, the Showering family built up a cider business second only to BULMER, H. P., LTD., and comprising most of the rest of Britain's huge cider trade. They acquired BRITVIC, and, with Vine Products, a very large stake in British wines. After a much publicized battle, they won HARVEYS of Bristol. They are now amalgamated with the mighty ALLIED BREWERIES group.

SHRUB
A very popular drink in the Eighteenth Century in British grog-houses, consisting of spirit (gin, rum, brandy) with sugar and spices. The origin of the word is from the Arabic for syrup. Oscar Mendelsohn says in his superb *Dictionary of Drinks and Drinking* that there has been a revival of interest in this drink—he mentions fruit juice as an ingredient—in the Isles of Scilly.

SICHEL
Another of those names which give a guarantee of solid excellence. From H. Sichel Söhne comes the celebrated *Blue Nun Liebfraumilch*, and the name Sichel on French wines carries a similar cachet. The late Allan Sichel was an authority on claret and wrote the *Penguin Book of Wines*.

SIDECAR
Probably the most popular brandy cocktail: 1 measure of cognac, half-measure each of lemon juice and Cointreau. Shake with ice and strain.

SIKES See Hydrometer; Proof.

SILLERY
A term once virtually synonymous with champagne; the area produces still as well as sparkling champagne wine.

SILVER STREAK
Frappé of equal measures gin and kummel, or make with lemon juice as a shaken cocktail.

SIMON, ANDRE (1877–1970)
The best-known and best-loved name in the wine trade in Britain; merchant, *savant*, writer ... his name now lends authority to a widely distributed range of French *appellation contrôlée* wines, imported by Idle, Courteney & Co., who were one of the first to bring a branded table wine to the public with *appellation contrôlée guaranteed*.

SINGAPORE See Malaysia; Toddy.

SINGAPORE GIN SLING
Two measures of dry gin, juice of a lemon, heaped teaspoon of powdered sugar. Pour over ice in large glass, nearly top with soda-water. Add half-measure each Cointreau and cherry brandy. Stir. Decorate with slice of lemon, and serve with straws.

Single

SINGLE
A measure used in bars in England; usually so small that it does little but wet the glass.

SKOL INTERNATIONAL
A major British LAGER, owned by IND COOPE. It is becoming truly international by acquisition of overseas breweries for its production.

SLANG
Drinking, like sex, gambling, crime and service life, is one of the great subjects of slang terms. People seem to be at their most inventive when thinking of ways of talking about things which mean more to them than perhaps they would care to admit. Gleams of enjoyment and humour weave in and out of the tapestry of slang words used to describe drinks and drinking. Only the prosaic mind thinks in terms of "going for a drink": such a delicate and pleasing prospect might be broached by any of the following: "a modest quencher", or a "wet", or "a jolly-up". There are scores of expressions, such as "tippling", "to wattle" (from "What'll you have?"), "potting", "jarring", "laying the dust", "wetting your whistle" and, for the motoring fraternity, "tanking up".

Naval expressions abound, partly perhaps because of the natural associations induced by the sea and "drink". See elsewhere in this work for the meaning and the origin of "pushing out the BOAT", but perhaps the most famous phrase for drinking is "splicing the main-brace", which is nautical parlance dating from the early 1800s for giving out "grog". It well suggests the strengthening qualities of RUM. GROG derives from the grogram cloak worn by "Old Grog" himself, Admiral Vernon, who in 1740 ordered naval rum rations to be watered down. Thence also comes "seven-water grog", which refers to extremely weak rum, and to "have grog on board" and "groggy" meaning to be drunk.

There are so many expressions for this state, each suggesting varying degrees of inebriation, that it is a wonder the word itself is ever used. An amusing Scots colloquial expression, "to have been talking to Jamie Moore", suggests a mild state of *tipsiness*, like "tip merry" or having "a sheet in the wind" or "to have been to Jericho". "One over the eight" (eight being the permissible number of beers) probably did not suggest more than a tipsy state. But "three sheets in the wind", "jug-bitten", "whipped the cat", "had a skinful", "tight", "skew-whiff" (crooked), "blotto", "screwed", "scammered", "shot" and "sozzled" all suggest more extreme situations, which will result in a hang-over and a "fragile" feeling the next day.

Drinks themselves often get called by other names: gin was once called "sky-blue", "blue-ribbon", "blue tape" and "fuller's earth". See also Gin (History). "Sir John Barleycorn is the strongest knight" is a tribute to malt whisky. Whisky is "the hard stuff" in Glasgow, an expression which may be applied to other drinks in other places. "A line of the old author" is a delightful if old-fashioned expression for a drink of brandy, and a "Sir Cloudesley" for a beer and brandy maybe spiced and sweetened, after the famous Seventeenth-century naval commander. Brandy is also "red tape" (civil service types take note).

Rhyming slang has its share of drinking terms, some of the less well known being "apple fritter" (a drink of *bitter* beer), "Jumbo's trunk" (drunk) and "pick and choose" (on the booze). See also Salmon and trout. Let us not forget "Sir Walter Scott" (a *pot* of beer).

We shall not mention terms used by the perpetually sober, about drinks and drinkers, which tend to err on the grim side; however, we may as well include those two categories beloved of the trade: "the beerocracy" (brewers and publicans) and "the Beerage" (those brewers elevated to the Peerage).

Perhaps one of the most comprehensive and humorous publications about drinking slang was *The English Liberal Science: or a new-found Art and Order of Drinking*, a 1650 pamphlet. Drinkers included: "One that will drink though it be a mile to the bottom", and "one that will wind up his bottoms", and everyone knows: "one whose nose is dirty."

Some idea of the drinking habits of the time can be had from the descriptions in the pamphlet of the orders of drinkers at Oxford and Cambridge universities. Each is comically typified by a form of study, thus "he that disgoreth his stomach" studies physic. "He that going homewards falls in a ditch," is a "navigator," etc.

Soldiers' expressions included: "He that drinks in his boots, and jingling spurs," who is called colonel of a regiment; and "He that drinks three days together without respite,"—an old soldier. Sailors: "He that having over-drunk himself utters his stomach, in his next fellow's Boots or Shoes," who is dubbed "Admiral of the Narrow-Seas". The rest of these rich characterizations are to be found in Eric Partridge's excellent *A Dictionary of Slang and Unconventional English* (Volume two) under Tavern terms.

SLING
The origin of the word is probably from *schlingen* (to swallow). Applied to cocktails it appears in GIN SLING; SINGAPORE GIN SLING.

SLIVOVITZ
Plum brandy coming in various types and qualities; widely used in central Europe and the Balkans, but particularly associated with YUGOSLAVIA.

SLOE GIN
The most popular of cordials based on dry gin. There are one or two proprietary brands, notably *Pedlar*, but it is widely made at home when the sloe crop is good.

Half fill a bottle with fresh sloes that have been individually pricked. Add 2 inches of granulated sugar. Top with good quality dry gin. Leave a minimum of three months; shake once a week. Strain into fresh bottle, adjusting sweetness if necessary by adding sugar or gin.

I have made quite a lot of sloe gin: the trouble is that one feels one ought to taste it during the infusion period to see everything is going right. As a result I have never brought a complete bottle of this cordial to final fruition!

SMIRNOFF
This is the vodka which touched off the vodka-drinking craze in the U.S.A. that spread over much of the world, and having got a head start it enjoyed for some time a virtual monopoly. It is still a brand-leader, but in the United States its lead has been eroded by such brands as GORDON'S vodka and in Britain (where the rights were acquired by GILBEY'S) by the highly successful and ever-growing COSSACK vodka brand owned by D.C.L.

One should bear in mind that we are dealing with a brand name rather than a flavour, for certainly the flavourless vodkas which are the vogue today bear little resemblance to those produced by the original Smirnoff distillery. This was started by Peter Smirnoff in 1818 by the Cast Iron Bridge that, the Kremlin apart, was the only landmark remaining from the fire which baulked Napoleon of effectual occupation of the capital of Russia and forced his disastrous retreat. Eventually a vast distillery and warehouse grew up, known as the House of Smirnovka by the Iron Bridge, that was one of the great sights of Moscow.

By 1914 Smirnoff sold a million bottles a day and the family was reputed to own the world's richest industry. Exiled and impoverished by the revolution of 1917, after

Smith's Tadcaster Brewery

the First World War a fourth generation descendant of Peter, Vladimir Smirnoff, set up a distillery in Paris. The story then switches to the U.S.A. and is rightly continued under the HEUBLEIN banner.

SMITH'S (John) TADCASTER BREWERY CO. LTD.

It was in 1847 that John Smith took over the brewery of Backhouse and Hartley, founded in Tadcaster, Yorkshire, in 1758, and found that the water from the local springs was ideal for the brewing of beers of the highest quality and excellent character, on which has been built a reputation second to none in the country.

During the following 32 years John Smith built up such a thriving business that, when he died in 1879 and the business passed to his brother William and nephews Henry and Frank Riley, they decided that a new brewery would have to be built to meet the increasing demand for their beers and so, from the local limestone quarries that gave up their stone for the building of York Minster long years before, came the material for the new brewery, described by the *York Herald* at the time as "gigantic" and "entitled to rank as the largest and most complete brewery in Yorkshire", and which still stands as a landmark of mellow beauty today.

This growth brought more employment, for by this time the employees had increased from a dozen to a hundred, and already 16 branches had been opened in different towns throughout the firm's trading area.

Rapid growth continued, and within ten years output had increased from 500 to 3,000 barrels a week, but William Smith had died in the meantime and, at his wish, his nephews assumed the name of Riley-Smith.

In 1892 the business was registered as a limited liability company and has since gone from strength to strength, making alliances with care, including in recent years such companies as Whitworth Son & Nephew Ltd., the Barnsley Brewery Company Ltd., Yates's Castle Brewery Ltd., and Warwicks & Richardsons Ltd., to form a group controlling almost 2,000 licensed premises. The company was recently absorbed into the COURAGE group.

SMITH (Samuel) OLD BREWERY (Tadcaster) LTD.

There is justifiable confusion between this company and the other SMITH of Tadcaster, Yorkshire. Tadcaster was an important point for changing horses on stage-coaches plying the great south-north routes, and which the Smiths foresaw would not decline with the coming of the railways.

When John Smith died in 1879 he left the business to his brothers William and Samuel, who enjoyed a less than happy fraternal relationship. Samuel died one year later leaving a son, also Samuel, whom William Smith would not take into the business. William built a new brewery in 1884 (see previous entry) leaving the Old Brewery derelict in the hands of his nephew Samuel.

It is not known when activity recommenced at the Old Brewery, but it did. It was carried on by Samuel's son, who bore the same name. Samuel Smith III died in 1927, and his son Geoffrey developed the business, which now flourishes under continuing family control.

SMOKING

The habit of smoking during meals is so prevalent that to condemn it completely is unrealistic. It is by no means unknown for people of otherwise total refinement to pause during a course in a restaurant, smoke a cigarette, and continue eating after it is consumed. The most elegant of private table settings frequently include individual ashtrays and cigarette holders, clearly implying that guests are expected to smoke during the meal, if they so wish. However, by the non-provision of the necessary equipment, a host may show that he does not wish his guests to smoke.

It was once fashionable at long dinners to have a break halfway through for a water ice and a single cigarette, often the Russian variety. Gourmandizing was then resumed. This elegant habit might well be restored on formal occasions: it would stop untidy smoking at other times.

As for smoking and alcohol, undoubtedly abstinence from tobacco at a heavy drinking session will mitigate the resultant hang-over. Unfortunately, the desire to smoke is increased as one relaxes into alcoholic euphoria, and it needs great will-power to overcome this.

Digression I am reminded of the anecdote told of the first Lord Birkenhead. Excessively bored at a dinner party, he produced and lit one of his enormous cigars. His hostess thought she had got the noted wit in a corner and with heavy sarcasm said, "I trust, Lord Birkenhead, you will not mind if we eat while you smoke." Her distinguished guest pondered as he blew out a mouthful of fragrant smoke. "Not at all, dear lady," he replied, "not at all, provided you do not make too much noise about it."

SNOBBERY
This is an affliction which is increasing in Britain as the use of wine grows. Unfortunately, it is endemic in some wine-writing circles—though by no means all writers suffer from it—and such authors as Hugh Johnson in the best paperback on the subject, rightly and simply titled *Wine*, manages to display great knowledge without a trace of snobbery.

I define wine snobbery as the ostentatious airing of a little knowledge or the unnecessary show of considerable vinous erudition, the former being the greater social sin. It is summed up in the famous James Thurber cartoon for which I make no apology for repeating yet again. The host is explaining his wine: "It's only a naive domestic burgundy without any breeding but I think you'll be amused at its presumption." Wine waiters, unless they be greatly experienced, tend to perpetuate wine snobbery by superfluous use of cradles and a perhaps understandable inclination to treat carafe wines as if they were rare vintages.

There is also snobbery with other drinks, such as the ordering of "Napoleon" brandy to impress guests, when in fact such a cognac does not exist, or requests for unusual liqueurs, based not on their palatability but their cost. There is considerable cocktail snobbery, particularly in the matter of the Dry Martini, and here I plead guilty myself. But if one admits to a snobbery, is one being a snob?

SNOWBALL
Mixture of ADVOCAAT and fizzy lemonade much appreciated by young people in Britain. There is a proprietary bottled *Snowball*.

SOAVE
The delicious, dry, light white wine of the Verona district of Italy. Should be drunk chilled, but not excessively so. For my money, *Bolla* is the best brand.

SODA-WATER
Invented at the end of the Eighteenth Century. Known as *seltzer* in some countries. See Schweppes.

SOFT DRINKS See Non-alcoholic.

SOLERA See Sherry.

SOMMELIERS
Wine butler or waiter. There is an excellent organization known as the Guild of Sommeliers, divided into regional sections, which embraces many people professionally associated with wine, by no means only its serving.

SOPHISTICATED
In vinous terms this applies in its original pejorative sense, not the modern colloquial opposite—a sophisticated wine is an adulterated one.

SOURS
A fairly broad spectrum of spirit-based mixed drinks, without precise definition except that they contain, beside spirit, fruit juice, sugar and mineral water. Despite the name they are on the sweet side. The best known is probably the *Whisky Sour*: measure of whisky, teaspoon of powdered sugar, juice of half a lemon, (optional) teaspoon of egg white. Shake with ice, strain into tumbler and top with soda-water.

SOUTH AFRICA and SOUTH WEST AFRICA
For three centuries WINE has been a notable product of the country, the industry being highly developed and the products of first-rate quality. Brandy is distilled on a big scale, so are gin and straight cane spirit. Table wines, brandy and fortified wines are exported to more than 30 countries, particularly to Europe, Canada, the Far East, and to Britain which alone takes over 2 million gallons of South African SHERRY a year. The principal import is Scotch whisky. The usual additives for spirits pertain. There is a big demand for fruit-flavoured and other soft drinks, also grape and apple juice, of which there are naturally abundant supplies.

There are certain peculiarities of licensing laws. Women are not allowed into bars where liquor is poured (i.e., they are confined to lounges with waiter service) except in luxury hotels. Only residents of hotels and their *bona-fide* guests can get alcohol on Sundays or religious holidays.

It is illegal to exchange liquor for other goods: this odd law is an unrescinded one from World War II. There were then serious consumer shortages, such as in golf balls and whisky. Thus the happy possessor of golf balls would advertise he was prepared to exchange them for Scotch. I do not know why this form of barter was considered harmful, but it was outlawed.

During elections no liquor is sold except in clubs. The republic has happily so far (though I hear disquieting rumours as I write) escaped the scourge of T.V. On radio liquor advertising is limited to late evening. Duty-free wine may be given to non-European farmworkers. Purchase of liquor by the Bantu population was liberalized in 1963. In principle, off-licence sale permits for alcohol are granted on the basis of one per 2,000 inhabitants. Licensed establishments with classification as an hotel automatically get the right to open a liquor store, within the same municipal area; those not classified as hotels only sell wines. Taxation is considered high by producers, and, to instance brandy, is over 50 per cent of the average consumer price by the bottle (which would seem miraculously low in Britain!). The customary strength for spirits is 75° proof (British).

Wine In 1655, Jan van Riebeeck, commander of the first Dutch settlement in what is now Cape Province, planted the first vines to be grown in southern Africa, and four years later he recorded the first vintage. In 1679, Governor van der Stel established his farm at *Groot Constantia*, intent on improving local wines. In this he was aided by the arrival of French Huguenots who, settling in areas today famous for their products, such as the areas of Paarl and Stellenbosch, brought French viticultural knowledge with them. By the first decade of the Eighteenth Century South African dessert wines, sometimes referred to as "Constantia" or simply "Cape", enjoyed a good reputation in Europe. The annexation of the Cape by the British encouraged wine production, since

Plate 32. The end of American Prohibition was marked by great excitement. An attentive crowd listens to Ed Hull, the general manager of Hiram Walker and Sons Inc., at a ceremony to mark the dedication of a new bourbon distillery at Peoria, Illinois, in 1933.

Plate 33. Harvest sunshine beams on a grapepicker in the Barossa Valley, South Australia.

Britain was engaged in the Napoleonic wars, which hardly improved the export of French wines across the Channel, and Cape wines were very welcome.

All went well until anti-imperialist Gladstone abolished preferential tariffs, causing the collapse of South African wine export trade to Britain, where it could not compete with the French because of transport costs. A generation later the scourge of PHYLLOXERA decimated the vines, until the French antidote of grafting local vines on to resistant American roots was successfully adopted, so successfully, in fact, that a new menace was created, over-production. By the end of World War I, over-production had led to uneconomically low prices and the industry was rationalized by the Co-operative Wine Growers' Association of South Africa Ltd. (K.W.V.)

In 1924 legislation brought non-K.W.V. members into line with regulations governing the association. The buying public and import trade are more accustomed to thinking of S.A.W.F.A. (South African Wine Farmers' Association) as being the main body representing South African wine interests. In fact, this is a marketing organization established in London in 1931 and is now a wholly-owned subsidiary of K.W.V.

Thus South Africa has a long tradition as a wine-producing country, which is now allied to excellent quantitive and qualitative control, and modern marketing methods.

South Africa produces excellent wines in virtually every category, though undoubtedly the best known overseas are her fortified wines, notably South African sherries. It would not appear that the ruling that sherries other than from Spain may not enjoy in Britain the simple title sherry and must also be descriptive as to origin, has affected the popularity of South African products. Prior to this ruling people were quite content to ask for South African sherry, which meant a sound product at an attractive price. Indeed, the legal battle may well benefit South Africa since it now clearly separates her wines from lesser non-Spanish ones. South African port-style wines can be excellent value; in table wines the white wines with some similarity to Rhine wines are probably the best known as far as overseas markets are concerned, but there are good quality red wines also available. S.A.W.F.A. is trying to popularize South African table wine. Charles Kinlock and Gilbeys ship first class table wines from the Cape. See also Paarl.

SOUTHERN COMFORT
A fine 100° proof (U.S.) American liqueur originating in New Orleans and now distilled in St. Louis, Missouri. Lately available in Britain. Whiskey-based, it has a pleasing "peach" flavour. May be substituted as an interesting variation on whiskey in MANHATTAN and OLD-FASHIONED cocktails, or may be served as a HIGHBALL, SOUR or COLLINS.

SPAIN
Most people will immediately associate Spain with its greatest product, sherry. Inexpensive Spanish table wines, particularly the red, are the equal in quality to those of any other country's and Spanish brandy (*coñac*) may be very fine if you are lucky enough to find some long aged in wood. The Spanish brandy of normal commerce usually seems much better when drunk in Spain than in one's own land. Spanish brandy is usually "sweeter" and blander than cognac.

Import licences are required for spirits; there is an insatiable demand for Scotch whisky, and local "whisky" is produced. Gin, of the London dry type, is increasingly popular through the influence of tourists and because of its suitability for mixing warm-weather drinks. At least two quality brands are distilled in Spain. It is highly

Spain

advisable for visitors to buy gin bearing a well-known English name, as some Spanish gin is not only excessively potent but poorly refined, as you may discover to your cost the morning after.

Licensing laws are relaxed, and advertising restrictions non-existent. The Spaniards are big, indeed, sometimes exuberant, drinkers, but drunkenness is considered unseemly and is little encountered: it goes against innate Iberian good manners, and is deemed an offence against that human dignity by which the Spanish set such store. Aniseed-flavoured liqueurs (*anis*) are popular, and excellent "Bénédictine" and "Chartreuse" are made, but the most favoured digestive is *coñac*.

Wine The great wine of Spain is, of course, SHERRY. Though only producing half the total quantity of wine of the world's largest wine-producer, Italy, Spain is the world's third greatest total producer. Yet consumption of wine *per capita* in Spain is only half that of France, the biggest consumer. Obviously, there is a considerable excess of wine in the country and this has led to an active export trade in which Britain is an important customer quite apart from her huge sherry interests . . . and interest in sherry.

Spanish table wines, perhaps because of their cheapness, enjoy a reputation undeservedly below that of some other countries. They are, of course, much sought abroad (except in France) for blending. However, many of them are splendid in their own right for general use. I think the VINO CORRIENTE wines of Spain are better than the "ordinary" wines of either France or Italy, particularly the robust reds.

The best old rioja red wines, from northern Spain, have been noted by experts as superior to any but the higher quality bordeaux and burgundies. (Let us recall that of the world's total wine production, 3,500 million gallons give or take a few million, André Simon gave no more than 2 per cent as rating as fine wine). And I think the less-known rioja dry whites are remarkable value, and not as aciduous as some other cheap "dry" white wines. But it is certainly her reds for which Spain deserves consideration. I am glad to see that rioja is being put out more under its own title in Britain and not rechristened: it deserves to stand on its own feet, as vinous knowledge spreads.

Spanish sparkling wines (notably *Perelada* and others from the Costa Brava) can be excellent. Spanish burgundy and Spanish chablis, though still better than most *vin ordinaires*, are not in the rioja class; they are heavily blended wines, and may come from anywhere in the country, though the burgundy styles are likely to have originated mainly in Tarragona. Valdepenas is about the only other named Spanish table wine one is likely to encounter abroad; it is thinner than rioja but can be quite good. Most of it goes for *vino corriente*, young and served by the porrón.

Oh, some are fond of Spanish wine
And some are fond of French
And some'll swallow tay and stuff
Fit only for a wench.
John Masefield (*Capt. Sutton's Fancy*)

SPECIFIC GRAVITY

This term indicates the weight of a fluid as against the weight of the same volume of water. It applies particularly to British BEER taxation. In this connection water (liquor) is 1000. A "standard barrel" of beer (a hypothetical unit) is 36 gallons at a specific gravity of 1055. The whole procedure is typically complicated, like PROOF.

SPIRIT SAFE

A glass-fronted box through which spirit flows from the still. In the instance of Scotch whisky, the keys to the safe are held by the

SOME MAIN
WINE DISTRICTS
OF SPAIN AND
PORTUGAL

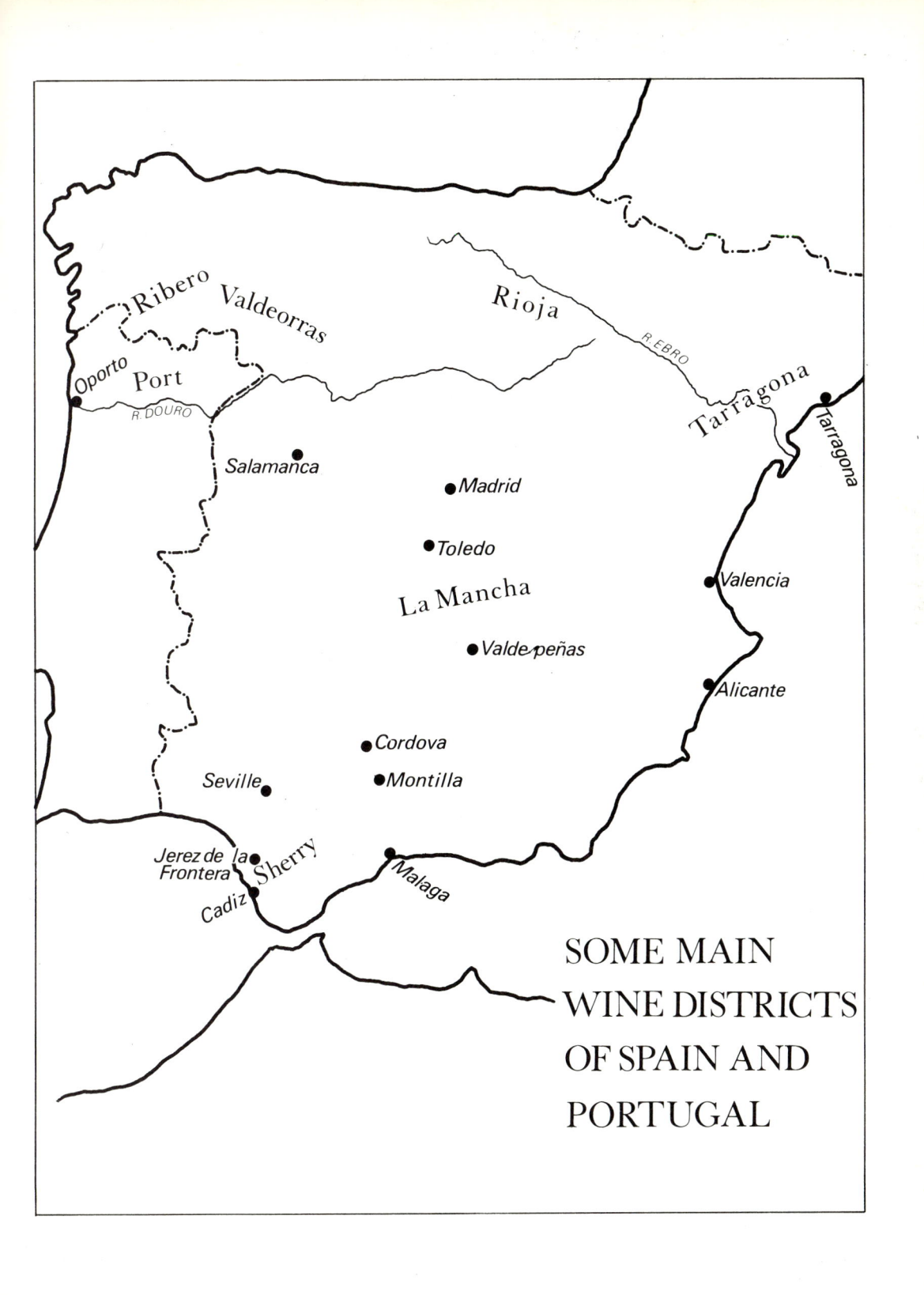

Spumante

customs officer; tests for proof strength can be made by reading instruments inside the container.

SPUMANTE
Italian for "sparkling"; qualitively the same applies as to VIN MOUSSEUX.

SPATLESE
German wines from late-picked grapes individually selected; indicative of high quality, sweetish wines.

SQUIRE'S GIN
A dry gin introduced a few years ago by a consortium of leading British brewers and sold principally through their "tied" outlets. A coloured version is known as *Cornhill*.

STANDFAST SCOTCH WHISKY
See Grant, Wm.

STARS
Since not only well-known brands but brandies of any provenance employ sundry constellations of "stars" on their labels, this system has become discredited, and increasingly it is the custom to give brand names rather than employ it. Where still used, a reputable brand's *three star* label should mean one with an average cask age of around five years. In France in 1940, I bought near Rouen an anonymous brandy with seven large stars on the label: it was awful. See V.S.O.

STELLENBOSCH
Lovely old town in the centre of South Africa's third largest wine district, producing notable red wines. Commercially, "Stellenbosch" is the title of a very important group of wine companies, producing, distributing and importing a wide range of liquors.

STEWART, J. & G.
Founded in 1779, this firm eventually took over Andrew USHER & Co., one of the great pioneers of blending.

STILL See Patent still; Pot still.

STOCK
The principal Italian brandy sold in Britain.

STOLICHNAYA
The principal Russian VODKA imported into the U.K., a finely-flavoured, matured grain spirit. *Krepkaya* (which appears to have been named after Lenin's wife, Krupskaya) is similar, but more powerful (CAPITAL WINES). Another equivalent brand is *Moscovskaya*.

STONE FENCE See Highball.

STOUT See Beer; Guinness.

STRATHCONON Scotch Whisky
A notable brand of straight (vatted) MALT whisky; blended from four of the greatest Highland malts produced in Scotland, each matured for 12 years or much longer. The name comes from the beautiful Glen Strathconon in the Scottish county of Ross and Cromarty, long associated with a family whose singularly illustrious member was James BUCHANAN.

STRAWS
It is not true that drinking alcohol through a straw increases the speed of your intoxication.

STREGA
Italian for "witch". Very popular sweet citrus liqueur.

STRENGTH
Wines and spirits come in a great variety of alcoholic strengths, and the following percentages of alcohol for normal commerce will be a guide. Spirits (in Britain) 40 per cent, other than vodka which is usually, for those made in the U.K., 37 per cent; fortified wines, 18 per cent; table wines, 10 per cent; vermouth, 18 per cent; champagne, 12 per cent. Cider, liqueurs, beer, vary considerably.

On the whole, Britons drink spirits at

slightly lower strengths than other countries, though stronger ones are obtainable in the premium field. There are also low-strength gins and some whiskies in the U.K. (65° proof instead of the usual 70°, or even lower): if a spirit seems quite remarkably inexpensive, check the proof printed on the label—it is not necessarily a bargain; you may simply be getting less alcohol for your money.

STRONG'S BREWERY

This important Hampshire Brewery, noted for the quality of its beer, which has lately associated itself with WHITBREAD's.

SUBSTITUTION

Fraudulent sale of one product under pretence it is another. See Refilling.

SUDAN

Camel lager-type beer and Scotch whisky are popular, a third of the latter being sold in miniature bottles. Cyprus sherry is also fancied and there are local sherries produced from grain or dates, opinion on the flavour of which I leave to those who have experienced them. Gin is also imported, as is brandy, and gin-and-tonic and whisky-and-soda have a hold on those who can afford them, which is an obvious British colonial influence.

I am informed that the more affluent but less sophisticated native population like imported sherry or brandy mixed with beer. Licensing laws have an approximate affinity to British ones. Imports are by restricted licence. No outdoor or cinema advertising is permitted for alcoholic drinks.

SUGAR

The basis of all ALCOHOL production. The sugar may be inherent in the material as in molasses or grapes or it may be coaxed from other vegetable matter by chemically changing the starch into sugar, as in MALTING of grain. A MASH of hot water and sugar-bearing vegetable matter produces a WORT, a sweetish liquid. The action of YEAST on this liquid in turn makes a fermented (alcoholic) WASH.

SUGAR SYRUP

Granulated sugar is not suitable for mixed drinks unless they are to be cooked, which is why I specify powdered sugar which dissolves quickly. Sugar syrup is an even better sweetening agent, and you can prepare a bottle of it and store it in the 'fridge. Boil one pound of sugar slowly in one pint of water. The same quantities as for dry sugar apply for recipes.

SULPHUR DIOXIDE (SO_2)

This gas is widely used in wine production, and one may discover references to sulphurization when straying into the field of oenology. For the purposes of this volume one may say that sulphur (do not think of the pungent aroma you may associate with the word) has long been used as an agent for arresting and slowing fermentation of wine.

SUZE

Famous gentian-flavoured French aperitif made by the firm of Pernod.

SWEDEN

As is to be expected in a country of sophisticated tastes, a high standard of living, which at the same time has highly restrictive laws concerning alcohol, there is what amounts to an obsession with the subject. On whether this is in any way related to the notorious incidence of suicides in Sweden is not for me to comment. There has been a temperance movement in the country for as long as anywhere; as early as 1840 the government started making grants to temperance societies. In 1892 school teachers were ordered to teach their pupils about the harmful effects of alcohol, which, though good-intentioned, surely raised curiosity about alcohol in young minds which would otherwise not have given it a thought?

Sweden

For some time the question of introducing total prohibition was much debated, but so disastrous a measure was not adopted, the views of Dr. Ivan Bratt prevailing, and a system of individual rationing and penalties, named after him, became law. Rationing was abolished in 1955, the Bratt system having (it is difficult to see how this surprised anyone) been "found lacking in efficiency if its cost was taken into consideration as well as the drawbacks inseparable from any rationing system, which tends to spread the habits it is designed to check." I quote Ragnar Lund, Board of Education, writing in *The Alcohol Problem in Sweden*, published by the Swedish temperance education board.

To summarize the present position. Anyone over 21 may buy drink in state retail company shops without restriction, if sober at the time. For each area, the state retail company has a "black list" of persons who, as a result of sundry offences, may not purchase alcohol: retail managers may request proof of identity. In restaurants, it is no longer obligatory that spirituous drinks be served only in connection with a meal, though local authorities may make this mandatory. Schnapps (*brannvin*) may, however, not be served other than in connection with food. The legal minimum age for consumption is 18. The profit on retail of alcohol is severely controlled. Under these very basic conditions, there exists a host of ancillary regulations. The severity of Swedish laws on drinking and driving are well known.

As is to be expected, the Association of Swedish Wine Merchants, who may act only through the two state monopolies, does not see eye to eye with the temperance organization. They assert that a concerted effort is being made to show that their role as agents is over and that their activities "run counter to one of the basic principles of Swedish alcohol policy, namely that all dealing in spirituous liquors should be carried on without private profit motives being involved," to quote an association hand-out. This association has since 1962 been affiliated to the Federation of Swedish Wholesale Merchants and Importers, a highly influential body comprising some 60 trade associations whose members have an annual turnover of around £2,000 million per annum.

A battle is being waged in the advertising field, and a reduction in advertising is officially favoured. However, it is held that further restrictions in this side of the trade would constitute the thin of the wedge leading to complete state take-over of all aspects of the liquor business.

Such statistics as I have show that the Swedes get through a fair amount of drink yearly per capita; around 6 litres of straight spirits (mostly schnapps, but they certainly like Scotch), some 33 litres of assorted beer, and a modest 3 litres of wine. Drunkenness is increasing.

To end on a temperance note; the Swedish Embassy in London tell me the most popular beverage in the country is coffee, the consumption being first or second highest in the world. All drunk black?

SWEDISH PUNSCH
A rum-based spirit.

SWEET
This is obviously the opposite to DRY. It is also a word meaning in our connotation precisely what it says. It is either obtained by the addition of some form of sugar, maybe honey, or, in sweet wines, is produced naturally by stopping complete fermentation of sugar into alcohol by the use of sulphur dioxide or grape alcohol. In the instance of fine sweet wines, by making them from very ripe grapes, practically raisins on the vine in some instances, the sugar content is so high that it kills the yeasts during fermentation, leaving in the wine much natural sugar.

SWITZERLAND

The most popular beverages are locally produced white wine, beer, mineral waters, cider, vermouth bitters and brandy, and the last named is exported. Swiss wines also go abroad but in no great quantity; they are delicate and light as a rule, and while some relish them, they tend to be expensive. The same categories of drinks are also imported, plus considerable quantities of Scotch and a certain amount of gin, the latter probably less for the citizens of the country than for the 700,000 alien residents who, forming an unusually high proportion of under 6 million inhabitants, obviously affect the overall drinking pattern. Taxes on drinks are high. For taverns there is strict licensing and operators must pass an examination to prove their competence. According to cantonal regulations there are limited (wine) or unlimited (all alcoholic drinks) licences for shops.

In French Switzerland *anis* drinks are popular and there is a firm tradition of drinking white wine with the famous "fondue". German Switzerland leans towards beer-drinking and takes much coffee. The Swiss take drinking-and-driving very seriously—as they do most things. There are different regulations in the 25 cantons concerning advertizing alcoholic drinks, but it is everywhere barred on radio and TV. The trend is towards reducing the number of taverns, and young people show an unusual penchant for soft drinks. The absinthe drunk in the West of Switzerland is known as the "Green Fairy", and is made by many farmers at home—which is forbidden by law!

Wine Swiss wines have not greatly caught on overseas; in London one may try them in the restaurants of the Swiss Centre, and I have found them expensive in relation to quality. Not that they are bad wines, but although produced fairly close to areas whence come first-class German, French and Italian wines, they lack distinction. Dôle is a sound and substantial red wine, and possibly the best known overseas. I think Swiss wines are for drinking in the country of origin, where one may find a curiosity known as *Glacier Wine*, very long stored in larchwood casks at a high altitude.

SWIZZLE STICK

A revolting instrument, sometimes expensively made in gold or silver, for the removal of the natural effervescence it has taken years to put into champagne. The tehnical name for this horror (though why should it need one?) is "mosser".

SYLLABUB

It is open to question whether this is a drink, but it is sometimes thus listed. Per serving use 2 measures of sweet sherry; 1 measure each of double cream and milk; teaspoon of powdered sugar. Beat together, adjusting sweetness to taste, and serve in shallow glasses with spoons. May be mildly chilled before serving.

SYLVANER

The second most important Rhineland (German or French) grape, also giving its name to wines made from it.

T

TAITTINGER
This champagne, long appreciated by connoisseurs, is nowadays enjoying a wider celebrity in the U.K. market, where the thirst for champagne, despite costs, is remarkable. A feature of *Taittinger* is the exceptionally large number of fine wines that make up a particular blend, and for the *1959 Brut*, a great year by all standards, no less than 38 wines contributed to this noble *cuvée*. Taittinger also cellar-store their champagnes in bottle above average length of time. *Taittinger Comtes de Champagne, Blanc de Blancs 1961*, made entirely from white grapes, and bottled in the beautiful Eighteenth Century style bottle, is extremely good value amongst premium de-luxe champagnes. This de-luxe champagne is one of the few made from Chardonnay grapes picked on the EPLUCHAGE system.

TALISKER
Much esteemed malt whisky from the distillery of that name; the only one on the famous Island of Skye (D.C.L.).

TANQUERAY DRY GIN
Exported from London (in association with Gordon's) by Chas. Tanqueray & Co., and available in some British bars, this gin has been successful in the U.S.A.

This extremely dry gin is marketed at 83° proof British (very strong by domestic standards), or 94.6° proof U.S. This makes it decidedly more expensive in Britain than most gins. Maintaining a Tanqueray/Gordon connection, a Tanqueray is on the board of his ancestors' modern company. Much more will be heard of this famous D.C.L. brand.

TANQUERAY, GORDON & CO. LTD.
Founded in 1769 in Southwark Street, London, on the south bank of the Thames, an area once famed for its distilleries and tanneries—an interesting combination from an olifactory viewpoint. The firm later moved to CLERKENWELL. John Alexander Gordon had only been in business for 11 years when the Gordon rioters cut a swathe through the metropolis, sacking many a liquor manufactory, though his escaped: the coincidence of names must have given the Scot some wry amusement.

Gordon's amalgamated with Charles Tanqueray & Co. in 1898. Shortly before World War II (the company having earlier joined D.C.L.) it was decided greatly to enlarge the distillery in Goswell Road, London. The distillery sustained heavy damage during the blitz of London during World War II and rebuilding continued on an adjacent site in Goswell Road. Reconstruction was not completed until 1957.

Gordon's gin, in its dark-green bottle, is the largest-selling gin in Britain. It is also the largest-seller in the U.S.A. where it is distilled (as in numerous other countries), and is the world's largest selling gin. Outside Britain it is recognized by its much-imitated clear bottle and distinctive labelling.

TASTEVIN
The little silver saucer for wine tasting, particularly associated with burgundy, of which antique examples are things of beauty. A tastevin is sometimes used as a badge of rank for a SOMMELIER, hanging round his neck by a cord or chain. Replicas or, regrettably, fine ones, are sometimes used as individual ashtrays. A true tastevin should be faceted, so that the silver may show up the colour and clarity of the wine. The object is more ceremonial than operative in our day

of clear glass, though its use is adhered to in some vinous circles.

TAVEL
Celebrated French Rhône *vin rosé* rather stronger than most.

TAWNY See Port.

TAYLOR'S
Famed vintage port house; they were pioneers of the "vintage style" PORT with their excellent *Taylor's Vintage Reserve*. This is now bottled in Portugal, and in accordance with the latest regulations on late bottling it cannot be bottled less than three years or more than six years after the vintage. It is shipped by Deinhard & Co.

TEACHER & SONS LTD., WM.
This Scotch whisky company has in recent years come up very strongly in the home market, so that in England it is only led by Haig. The founder, William Teacher, started his business at the early age of 19, in 1830, and by mid-century he had 19 licences in Glasgow. (The company disposed of the last of its retail outlets in 1960). He ran his "dram shops" on draconian lines, insisting on sobriety and closing his places at 10.30 p.m. instead of the permitted 11 p.m. (they opened at 8 a.m.), except on Saturdays. A generous tot of whisky cost threepence, a bottle two shillings or half-a-crown according to quality. He discouraged the sale of beer, permitted no smoking on the premises, and no additives whatever were supplied to go with a "dram". You did not linger in Mr. Teacher's establishments, but you obviously got value, for he prospered.

William Teacher had 11 children, including two sons who succeeded him, and achieved the respected nickname of *Old Thorough*. His sons had equal commercial application and showed great ability in the art of blending whisky, it then being the general practice for each wholesaler to blend his own. Teacher's moved into England to Manchester, in 1886, and a decade later, when the founder died, opened a London office. *Teacher's Highland Cream*—the company's sole product—was registered in 1884.

The firm is still strongly a family one, and the tradition of "family tasting" that goes back way into the last century is maintained, the whole board attending this important quality control ritual four times a week. Until 1891 Teacher's were entirely reliant on buying single whiskies, but in that year they built the Ardmore Distillery in Aberdeenshire. In 1913 they were the first whisky company to use stopper-corks in place of corks that required a corkscrew. In 1962 Teacher's opened a major blending and bottling warehouse at Craigpark, Glasgow, not all that far from where William Teacher first opened shop.

TEA PUNCH
Half-bottle each of Jamaica rum and brandy, half-pound of powdered sugar, 2 pints of very strong strained hot tea, one lemon. Heat metal punch bowl and pour in the rum and brandy. Add juice of the lemon, and also some lumps of sugar which have been rubbed on the lemon's rind. Ignite the contents of the bowl and slowly pour in the hot tea. See Non-alcoholic drinks for a non-alcoholic *Tea Punch*.

TEETOTAL
The word probably arose in the U.S.A. from Total Temperance, to separate complete abstainers from those who only eschewed spirits. See Prohibition.

Habitual teetotallers—there should be asylums for such people. But they would probably relapse into teetotalism as soon as they came out. Samuel Butler.

TELTSCHER BROTHERS LTD.
Major London importers of the Slovenian

Temperance

wines, notably *Lutomer Riesling*, the best-known brand of wine from YUGOSLAVIA.

TEMPERANCE

I am certainly in favour of temperance in its correct meaning, which is moderation; nor am I against it in its more common contemporary meaning of total abstinence. People are obviously entitled to abstain and even to put out propaganda in favour of their belief. But I am entirely opposed to the pussyfoots and prodnoses who wish by force of law to curtail reasonable social drinking by other people. Where they have succeeded they have left a legacy of deprivation, alcoholism, and evasion, and struck a further nail in the coffin of human liberty. *Digression* A friend of mine gave me a good tale from Hollywood. Robert Mitchum, as famous perhaps as a supporter of the licensed trade as he is as a film star, was addressing a large mixed audience. "There are, I believe," he said, "some of you who never touch alcohol in any shape or form. I respect your convictions wholeheartedly—but I am sincerely sorry for you at the same time. For when you wake up in the morning—that's as good as you're ever gonna feel."

TEMPERATURE

This is a matter for commonsense, which is not always in evidence. It is a simple fact that red wines show to best advantage if not too cold and white wines are more pleasant on the chilled side. But matters are too often carried to extremes. I know people who warm their reds excessively, and extravagantly cool their whites. Such practices are to the detriment of the wine. As to other drinks, we are so conscious of ICE that there must be some whisky-drinkers who hardly know what whisky tastes like for they chill and dilute it with chunks of ice until all flavour is masked and their taste buds numbed. On the other hand, a Dry Martini needs intense chilling. It is, of course, a matter of personal choice, but those who always use ice to excess are denying themselves part of the true pleasure of imbibing. See also Room Temperature.

TEQUILA

This is the traditional spirit of Mexico; an AGUARDIENTE of legendary ferocity. It is distilled from *pulque*, a popular intoxicant, the fermented sap of the maguey, member of the agave family, a vegetable that grows as slowly and closely resembles some cacti. This is distilled as *mezcal*, an ardent spirit with hallucinatory side-kicks, and tequila may be likened to a (sometimes) refined form of this.

Despite a flavour few people can actively enjoy, tequila has started to "take off" in the U.S.A. and there are those who are backing it to repeat the spectacular success of vodka. No one who has studied the vagaries of fashion in drinking would say this cannot happen, and tequila has a certain romantic virility in its image, of hirsute, bold Mexican bandits swigging it in gay abandon with jet-haired beauties perched on their knees, to the accompaniment of trilling guitar music! Yet I think it will require considerably more refinement before it conforms to current taste; a reduction in flavour. Tequila sales in the U.S.A. are now running at around 330,000 cases a year, and there is little doubt that it has growth potential, particularly if a fine flavour eventuates. In the U.K. the main importers claim a sale of some 800 cases.

Tequila is by custom drunk neat; first a lick of salt, then a tot of tequila (or straight from the bottle) and a direct squeeze of lime or lemon. The salt is politely taken from the back of the hand. To my mind this renders the spirit no more than just drinkable which, neat, I find it not. The MARGARITA cocktail is enjoying a vogue, but conventional additives are being taken with it, and I have even heard of tequila being used to desecrate a "Dry Martini".

THAILAND
Soft drinks dominate the beverage market, those with world-famous names being manufactured locally under licence. The principal imported spirit is Scotch. Beer is very expensive, about the equivalent of 1.25 dollars (U.S.) per litre, as it is highly taxed, but Thai rice spirit, which has some affinity to whisky, sells at the same price, so it is pretty obvious which gets chosen.

TIA MARIA
Jamaican coffee-flavoured liqueur with a fine rectified spirit base that is extremely popular in Britain.

TIED HOUSE
A PUBLIC HOUSE in Britain owned by a brewery.

TIO PEPE
Biggest selling of very dry Spanish SHERRY, owned by Gonzalez Byass. It was named after a relative of the firm's founder, "Uncle Joe", who asked his nephew to make him an ultra-dry fino sherry. A small solera was established for this purpose, no one supposing it would eventually dominate the bodega.

TIZER
Big-selling fizzy soft drink, in association with which an up-and-coming U.S.A. equivalent, *Crown Cola*, is being marketed in Britain.

TOAST
The drinking of "toasts", to someone's "health" or in their honour, stems from the distant past. Libations of wine were poured to the gods, or at the base of their statues, in ancient times. Long ago, the Jews, in whose rituals wine plays an honoured role, lifted a jar with the incantation, *Lekhayyim*, (freely translated: "Good Health").

The Greeks had a *sympiosarch* at banquets, to control drinking, who became the *arbiter bibendi* of the Romans, the authority whom we would now call the "toastmaster" or "master of ceremonies". In Rome, in the First Century, there was a custom of "drinking a name", a cupful of wine for each letter in the name of the person being saluted.

Legend has it that in the Fifth Century, a Saxon princess, Rowene, went to a British king with a golden chalice, raising it to him and saying: *"Waes hale"* ("be of good health"); hence wassail. The toast skol (skal, skoal) comes from *skalle*, Norse for skull: warriors would drink from the skull of a fallen enemy. That in the past drinking a toast could be dangerous is witnessed by old drinking vessels having glass or translucent bases so that the drinker might notice whether the friend or host to whom he was drinking had treacherous designs on him. At "loving cup" ceremonies, regularly practised at banquets in the City of London, a neighbour stands guard on each man drinking in turn as the cup passes. (This does not, of course, prevent him being "stabbed in the back" in the course of business!)

The social uses and abuses of drinking have ranged from the gross to the highly mannered. The flowery vinous graces of yesterday have in the daily round become debased in Britain into the casual "cheers" muttered over a pint of "wallop", of whatever is the locally drunk brew. This depressing word (frequently pronounced something like "chairs"—a reference to some Britons' rather sedentary attitude to life?) has long displaced in popular esteem "bung-ho!", "mud in yer eye", "bottoms up" and similarly obnoxious affectations and will, happily, itself be replaced.

The formal toast lingers on, notably the loyal toast to the sovereign. This has itself become somewhat perfunctory at many events. For no particularly good reason, it is not "done" to smoke at functions until after the loyal toast. This causes a state of acute anxiety among modern nicotine addicts as to

Toast

whether the toast will be announced before the fish or after the precooked frozen plastic chicken. It also engenders embarrassment when overseas visitors to Britain, justifiably ignorant of the finer points of British eccentricity, are present.

At one dinner of an Anglo-American complexion which I attended, in the House of Lords at that, the problem was easily solved. We heard grace pronounced, sat down, got up again to drink the loyal toast, sat down again—and lit up. Total abstainers may correctly drink the loyal toast in water. As to water, the once-outlawed Jacobites would drink to their exiled Stuart monarch in public by passing their glass over one containing water; thus, while ostensibly toasting a Hanoverian, they were in their minds drinking to "the king across the water". The British Royal Navy drink the loyal toast sitting down. It is said that the tall King William IV, the "Sailor King", as heir presumptive to the throne bumped his head when rising aboard a man-of-war to drink to George IV. As monarch, he decreed no naval officer need fear a similar accident.

A pretty conceit, especially favoured by the Tsarist aristocracy, was to crash the glass into the fireplace after drinking a toast, thus indicating the glass should not be used for drinking to another person. Intended as an honour, this tended to become simply a noisy exhibition of bibulous extravagance. A legendary refinement of Victorian "mashers" was to drink a chorus girl's health in champagne from her shoe. I have tried this; it does nothing to the shoe, ruins the wine, and reduces the girl in question to helpless mirth.

Toast is indeed just what it says. At one time in England it was customary to place toasted bread in wine, probably spiced bread. It is said that at Bath, where the ladies bathed in the spa waters in public without excessive benefit of attire, a *beau* (some versions say Charles II) dipped a glass in the cistern to drink to the charms of a beauty disporting herself therein, afterwards remarking that he liked not the drink but vastly admired the "toast". At all events, the word toast became attached to a person (*vide* "toast of the town") and thus to the act of drinking the health of, or toasting, an individual.

TODDY

1 Originally a hot spirituous drink now often taken cold. Whisky or brandy are particularly suitable bases. *Hot* Heaped teaspoon of sugar in warm glass; dissolve with a little boiling water. Add 2 measures of preferred spirit. Stir (traditionally with a sterling silver spoon in the case of Scotch). Pour in more boiling water. Top with more spirit. *Cold* Heaped teaspoon of powdered sugar (or sugar syrup to equal); 2 measures of preferred spirit; 2 measures of lemon juice. Mix these. Top with soda-water; top with more spirit. There is really no difference between this and a *Sling*, so this version may be made with gin or vodka. 2 Fermented palm sap (said to make superior ARRACK). Toddy is also much drunk in some tropical lands, under several names. It ferments speedily, becoming quickly very potent, and thus must be fresh. In Singapore, for instance, toddy parlours must sell their toddy the day it is made or destroy it. However, Alan Yeo, of Singapore, has found a way to settle the brew at around 6 per cent alcohol so that it may be canned without further fermentation. He has clarified and otherwise stabilized toddy and, apart from a large local market, he hopes to make considerable overseas sales.

TOKAY

Much romance attends this wine, the ancient drink of HUNGARY, recalling the great days of Budapest under the Austro-Hungarian Empire. The name may cover quite ordinary sweetish wines, but the best are truly noble and as dessert wines rival the richest

BEERENAUSLESE of Germany or the finest SAUTERNES. They are too costly for normal commerce. *Imperial Tokay* was said to be made in the old days by not pressing the over-ripe grapes at all but simply from such juice as the weight of the grapes in the vat extruded.

Digression The last time I tasted a fine tokay was during the war in a leaking nissen hut in a remote part of Norfolk. A friend of mine had carefully preserved a bottle. We were so depressed, both by our surroundings and an impending departure for North Africa (whither my fellow officer proceeded, but not I), that he decided to open it. We only had one chipped enamel mug to hand: this did slightly detract from the romance to which I have referred, but it was still a memorable occasion.

TOLLEMACHE & COBBOLD BREWERIES LTD.
The leading private family-controlled company of brewers covering East Anglia from Ipswich, their headquarters. They have houses as far afield as Walthamstow in East London. *Tolly* beers are highly esteemed.

TOMATIN DISTILLERS CO. LTD.
Established in 1897, high in the mountains to the south of Inverness, this Highland distillery was extended in 1909. Keeping to the forefront of modern techniques (without sacrificing any of the traditional skills) it developed into the largest Scottish malt distillery, with a production in excess of a million proof gallons of quality whisky a year, much in demand by blenders. It also has the distinction of being the only single malt distillery to be quoted as a public company on the Stock Exchange in London. *Tomatin* single 10-year-old straight malt combines lightness with a strong peat flavour which I personally find very attractive. It is something of a market rarity.

TOM & JERRY
A mighty American punch of some antiquity. There are many recipes. Try beating separately yolks and whites of 12 eggs. Into the yolks beat half-pound of powdered sugar with a tablespoon each of powdered cinnamon, cloves and allspice. Stir in 6 measures Jamaica rum. Fold in egg whites. Put a generous portion in a half-pint mug, adding 2 measures of whisky (of your preferred type); fill with mixture half-and-half water and milk, stirring briskly, and top with grated nutmeg.

TONIC WATER
The increasingly universal additive for gin. Its full title of *Indian Quinine Tonic Water* indicates its semi-medicinal origins in the full flowering of the British Raj in the last century. The word "tonic" may not be used in describing it in the U.S.A. SCHWEPPES is the leading brand and the one which put tonic water on the map.

TONNEAU
A theoretical cask of Bordeaux, holding four *barriques*: See Casks.

TRAMINER
One of the main grape varieties of the Rhineland, producing wine of decided flavour; normally dry, though it can be sweetish. *Gewürztraminer* is an alternative name: virtually the same, it is sometimes considered more prestigious and may be more spicy.

TRAPPISTINE
An attractive "Bénédictine-style" liqueur based not on cognac but armagnac.

TRES PALMAS
A superb dry sherry by La Riva (founded 1776).

TRESTER
German grape residue spirit, similar to MARC.

TRIPLE SEC
CURACAO liqueurs of which there are many. Because of this multiplication, COINTREAU dropped the term in favour of the family name.

TROCKEN
German for dry.

TROCKENBEERENAUSLESE
The ultimate in sweet German wines, made from individually selected grapes that have shrivelled on the vine and concentrated their sugar. Extremely expensive. See Eiswein.

TROPICAL LEMON
An attractive and fairly new British additive for gin or vodka, somewhere between bitter lemon and tonic water; a HUNT'S product. Schweppes have a similar drink called *Caribbean Lemon*.

TRUMAN HANBURY BUXTON & CO. LTD.
This celebrated London brewery company, although a large group has a substantial shareholding in it, has at the time of writing preserved its independence, and it is a prime example of a large, but not excessively large, brewing firm, where the individual touch can still be maintained and the family element has not been overshadowed, or killed, by absorption into a conglomerate.

The first mention of a Truman as a brewer was in 1381, when a William Truman attacked the Lord Mayor of London during Wat Tyler's revolt: his fate is not recorded. Not for nearly three centuries did the name reappear, another William Truman being recorded in 1613 as having a brewhouse in Old Street. This Truman had a son, John, who also went into brewing, but, to be truthful, there is no strict evidence of a connection between these early Trumans and the Joseph Truman who appears to have set up as a brewer in Brick Lane, Spitalfields (a noted London silk-spinning centre), in 1666. Truman's Brewery is still there.

Joseph left two sons, Joseph, who succeeded to the business, and Benjamin. This latter took over on his brother's death and he it was who put Truman's on the map. In particular he was a brewer of porter, said to have been first made in *The Old Blue Last*, a pub now owned by Truman's. Ben Truman (his name is commemorated in the firm's best-known beer) was knighted by George III, and commercial titles were not frequent then. He built the house whose drawing-room is now the company's boardroom: it contains his portrait by Gainsborough.

In 1766 it looked as if the firm would end; Sir Benjamin's only son died. At that time family continuity was almost vital. Shrewdly, Sir Benjamin willed his head clerk, James Grant, should head the company on his death. Grant held the post for 23 years, and was succeeded by one Sampson Hanbury. He was in control for 46 years. He brought in a nephew, a Buxton, in 1808. Shortly afterwards, another family, the Pryors, came on the scene through an amalgamation. Although their name was not incorporated in the company's title, the Pryors became as much involved as the Buxtons, and at the time of Truman's tercentenary, there were three Pryors and four Buxtons on the Board.

Postscript. Since I wrote the above, Truman's have been taken over—but since it was not a brewery merger they have retained their individuality.

TUBORG
An important Danish LAGER.

TULIP (Tulipe)
The best GLASS for any wine, other than fine champagne, which deserves a FLUTE.

TUN
From the French *tonne* (TONNEAU), a theoretical container used as a standard of

measurement; see Casks. The word is used widely in brewing, but nowadays not much in the wine trade. The "tonnage" of a ship was once determined by what quantity of *tonnes* of claret it could take, which gave rise to the measuring the tonnage of merchant ships by their cubic capacity, as opposed to their displacement as is the case with naval vessels.

TUNISIA

The most popular local drink is *boukha*, an *eau-de-vie* of no great strength, taken both before and after meals. Wine is inexpensive and similar to the better-known Algerian varieties. It is principally exported to France. Scotch whisky has taken its hold with those who can afford it. Leading French aperitifs are produced under licence, and so is Booth's *High & Dry* gin. Local production of potables is encouraged to save foreign exchange. After Scotch whisky, the leading imports are champagne, cognac and beers.

Governmental policy is to discourage the drinking of alcohol through heavy taxation, but at the same time there are no restrictive laws on promotion of drinks. Sale of alcohol is only through officially licensed outlets. Spirit consumption is low among the indigenous population, but, as a market, Tunisia should develop through the extension of her tourist industry, and visitors should find no cause to miss their favourite refreshment.

TURKEY

Raki (ARRACK) is the most popular and best known of Turkish alcoholic drinks, distilled from wine and flavoured with aniseed, and the Turkish variety is better than some. Latterly both wine and beer have eroded raki's traditional popularity. Wine, beer and raki and a variety of liqueurs are exported, and Scotch whisky is virtually the sole imported drink, mainly for the big city hotel trade and the tourist industry. A local whisky-style spirit is distilled, as are brandy, gin and vodka. Vermouth is produced. Raki is either drunk neat or with water, for other spirits soda-water is the general additive, though increased tourism may mean the introduction of other mixers.

All spirits are manufactured by a state monopoly, and there are few licensing restrictions on their sale.

Turkey is a very important grape-growing country, the annual production being over 3 million tons. Large quantities are exported as fruit, and table grapes are much appreciated locally. Over 100,000 tons of sultanas are made each year. Wine production is around 40 million litres. The monopoly has five distilleries producing 14 million litres of raki per annum, and seven wineries producing 14 million litres, the rest of the annual production being shared between 230 private firms. The monopoly's liqueur distillery makes 600,000 litres of sundry liqueurs. Production of vodka is $1\frac{1}{2}$ million litres, of brandy 400,000 litres and of gin 50,000, though I am informed these figures may be greater since no particularly recent statistics are available. They do, however, indicate an active potable industry and a fair national thirst.

TURKISH BLOOD

An abominable mixture of strong ale and red burgundy.

U

U.K.B.G.
United Kingdom Bartenders' Guild; see Bartender.

ULLAGE
1 Waste or spoilt beer. 2 Unwanted air space in wine cask or bottle which will probably cause OXIDATION.

ULSTER See Northern Ireland.

UNDERBERG
The splendid German cure for upset stomachs and HANG-OVERS. Pour the contents of the little bottle (it is highly alcoholic) down your throat and I think the most stubborn matutinal malaise will be lightened within 15 minutes.

UNITED KINGDOM See Great Britain

UNITED RUM MERCHANTS
The principal products of this company (owned by Booker Merchants Ltd.) include LAMB'S *Navy Rum* and the big-selling *Lemon Hart*. They distribute TIA MARIA in the U.K.

UNITED STATES OF AMERICA
Seventeen states are known as "control states". They are Maine, New Hampshire, Vermont, Pennsylvania, Ohio, Michigan, Virginia, West Virginia, North Carolina, Mississippi, Iowa, Washington, Oregon, Montana, Utah, Wyoming and Idaho. Within these political boundaries the state governments control the regulation and sale of alcoholic beverages. This control includes setting standards for prices, brands, advertising and display. Some of the state agencies control wholesaling and retailing, others control only wholesaling while the retail stores are independent.

The other 33 non-control (licence states), plus the District of Columbia, are still answerable to state boards, but these boards act as overseers rather than laying down rules for prices, brands, etc. Basically the difference is one of state enterprise (control states) versus individual enterprise (licence states).

One of the problems in the United States is that state laws are not uniform. For instance, a gallon is legal in New Jersey but not in neighbouring New York. So, theoretically, if you bring a gallon bottle of gin through the two-minute tunnel ride from New Jersey to New York, you are guilty of smuggling. "Nowhere in human experience are there more inexplicable laws than those which exist in regulations of alcohol sales and service," says The Bourbon Institute, New York. (Compare this with a similar quotation towards the beginning of the Great Britain entry.)

Here are a few exotic examples of American laws and bye-laws. You may not drink from a bottle in Coolidge, Arkansas. In Maine, the first state to go "dry", customers in bars must be seated and the same goes for the State of Washington. Once served, you must not move to join your friends unless a waiter carries your glass. Maine also prohibits the traditional saloon swing-doors. In Boston, "men-only" bars are closed on Sundays, but lounges admitting women may remain open.

In Natchez, Mississippi, it is illegal to serve beer to an elephant, and in Chicago you must not give it to your dog. In San Francisco you may not ride a horse to a bar. In Cushing, Oklahoma, do not drink in public in your underwear: it is illegal. In Kentucky it is unlawful to drink in your home! St. Louis, Missouri, specifically forbids the amusing habit of sitting on the sidewalk and quaffing beer from a bucket. In Alabama, drinks "on the house" are not permitted.

United States

Beer may not be sold in Nebraska unless soup be ready to serve as an accompaniment.

Bartenders in Current, Nebraska, can be fined for one spot on their apron. In the State of New York bars cannot obtain permits for all-night extensions on Christmas Eve nor on the night of a big football game. It appears that only Nevada is completely wide open, having no closing times, no bye-laws, no restrictions.

As to inebriation, apart from normal penalties, in Council Bluff, Iowa, you court extra risk if you climb trees or play baseball while intoxicated. In Sausalito, California, you may get drunk only if you have obtained permission from the "Board of Supervisors". An intoxicated person in Dupont, Pennsylvania, must down a dose of castor oil. Obviously, most of these regulations are unrepealed local frontier legislation, a source of neglect or amusement, but they also reflect the truth of The Bourbon Institute's statement.

Advertising is also controlled. Until lately it was forbidden to depict women in liquor ads, and though this is now legal, the practice is frowned on. In many states, the depiction of Santa Claus in advertisements is not allowed, and nowhere may biblical or religious figures (bourbon whiskey owes its origins to a clergyman) or presidents or high members of the government by mentioned.

In Iowa, advertisements must not contain the words "saloon", "bar" or "nightclub". The phrase "contains no headaches" is everywhere prohibited on bottles. In Kansas, liquor advertisements must not be tied to that mighty commercial institution, Father's Day. A total of 13 states forbid prices to be shown in liquor advertisements, and one insists they be shown. Some states have regulations about use of colour in advertising and size of advertisements.

Of course, there are laws that are strictly enforced. A macabre item was sent me by my U.S. correspondents. It is a report, circularized to all licensees, from the New York State Liquor Authority, and my friends called it "an example of American-style unadulterated bureaucratic nomenclature." Here it is complete:

"Fay and Tow Gan Tong, 67-11, Fresh Pond Road, Ridgewood, L.I., restaurant liquor license, *Cancelled*, effective February 7, 1966. Violation: that the licensee Fay Tong, violated Rule 36 of the Rules of the State Liquor Authority by his conduct in killing his wife and co-licensee Tow Gan Tong".

Some General Comments The United States' single greatest contribution to the world of drinks has been BOURBON whiskey. American whiskey (bourbon, RYE, BLENDED) is the nation's favourite spirituous drink. Vodka is number two. CANADIAN WHISKY is extremely popular in many states, and while Scotch has recently made inroads into domestic whiskey sales, it has not affected those of imported Canadian whisky, which outsells Scotch in about half the states. Both imported whiskies retail in most states at around the same price, though of course transport costs for Canadian are minimized for states near the 49th Parallel and must everywhere be lower than for Scotch.

An interesting statistic in connection with whisky consumption in the U.S.A., and a prime example of how misleading statistics may be, is that tables show the citizens of the District of Columbia as drinking each year 4.7 (U.S.) gallons of whisky (40 per cent of it Scotch). Statistically every man, woman and child in the District consumes this amount: say four times the national average. Palpably this is not so; it is simply that as the federal capital, Washington, D.C., attracts multitudes of visitors, has throngs of official guests and caters for many administrators, legislators and officials, who in aggregate vastly

United States

outnumber the residents. For similar reasons, sparsely populated Nevada shows the next highest consumption of all types of whisky.

The United States is much too vast, too diverse in cultures, to be dealt with in the comparatively tidy way one can cope with compact countries. Only the broadest of generalities can be mentioned concerning its drinking patterns, which vary regionally to a huge extent, ranging as they do from the totally permissive to the strictest of abstentionist societies. Tens of millions regularly drink alcohol; on the other hand, millions eschew even tea and coffee as sinful.

The nationwide temperance movements have not recovered from the abject failure of PROHIBITION. That "great experiment" left in its wake the inheritance of an actual alcoholism problem much worse than the one it sought to cure. It is a problem Americans are tackling with their accustomed energy: yet the resultant publicity may have made it loom larger as a menace than it really is. Lethal drug addiction is, surely, a much greater evil than resource to the bottle.

As the French invented the sensible habit of the quiet aperitif at the end of the day's work, the Americans invented the "cocktail hour" for the same purpose—a *detente*, a pause between work and play, between office and home, and a moment of domiciliary relaxation before tackling the latest domestic crisis. Perhaps the temperament of the metropolitan American sometimes makes him "work" even at his pleasure a little too hard. Where the Parisian lingers over a vermouth-cassis in a tranquil café, and the Londoner stolidly contemplates his pint or gin-and-tonic, the New Yorker smartly dashes down three large cocktails in his favourite bar. There is quite a widely held theory in Europe that Americans cannot "hold their liquor". I believe this is quite erroneous. It is simply that they like to do everything fast, including drinking. It might be a better world if the Briton speeded up, the American slowed down.

Americans may be said to have invented the COCKTAIL. Their influence on the drinking patterns of the sophisticated world has long been very strong: it might almost be said that what the U.S.A. drinks today, the world will drink tomorrow. I speak only in a rather narrow sense of fashion in drinking. The VODKA craze started in the U.S.A. The Dry Martini cult is entirely of American origin. The universal use of ice in liquor or mixed drinks is largely due to American insistence on it. The vogue for "light" rum (and light drinks in general) started in the States. American influence played a major role in the global march of Scotch.

Americans take their habits with them round the world. They are world leaders; so even people who *profess* not to like them, adopt their customs. Thus it was when Britain led; even those who objected to her took on her ways. I wonder what will happen to the newest American vogue, drinking TEQUILA. It is as yet marginal, but then so was vodka 15 years ago. We will know in 1972 whether American LIGHT WHISKEY (a potentially very important development) is likely to be a success.

But while they have so greatly influenced cosmopolitan drinking habits, Americans have exported little of their profusion of potable products (always excepting *Coke*). Bourbon is indeed available in smart bars throughout the world, and has a growth potential, but Scotch reigns supreme in whisky. American beer—vastly popular in the U.S.A.—is not to the palate of most other nations, accustomed to their own brews. American gin makes no headway overseas against London's. American wines, excellent and more and more appreciated in the U.S., cannot easily compete commercially with other countries', but fresh export efforts are being made for them.

United States

So the United States exports habits, and imports liquor. It imports in enormous quantities, to satisfy the catholic tastes of a nation of growing discrimination. It has the means of satisfying its demand for the finest potables, whether from its own rich store or from the vineyards and distilleries of the entire world. Surely the U.S.A. could be the discerning drinker's paradise.

Wines It is generally deemed unfortunate that cost virtually prohibits the exchange of wine between Europe and the United States. The traffic is almost wholly one way, although interested persons may obtain a little Californian wine in London.

Legend has it that when the Vikings reached the eastern coast of North America they found vines and named the land "Vinland", and wild grapes certainly existed there when the first English settlers arrived, but these made only the poorest of wine. Not until hybridization with European and other indigenous grapes occurred was tolerable wine produced in the east.

But it is to the west that one must look for the major history of American wine-making, and I am indebted for it to the Wine Institute of California.

In 1969 the California wine industry celebrated its 200th anniversary. California is the U.S.A.'s largest agricultural state. Grapes are its main fruit crop, and half of the grapes are made into wine (ranging from the sweetest of the sweet to the driest of the dry) which currently satisfies nearly 75 per cent of America's total consumption of wine. Virtually all of these wine grapes are of the classic European wine grape varieties first introduced into California by Jean Louis Vignes, a Frenchman from the Bordeaux wine district; and later imported in large numbers by the Hungarian Count Agoston Haraszthy.

The California wine story began in the year 1769 when the Franciscan missionary, Father Junipero Serra, planted the first vines at Mission San Diego. Early wine production in California was primarily designed to meet the needs of the church. The so-called "Mission Grape", a Spanish variety which the missionaries planted, has never been clearly identified. An English sea captain described it as "bluish-black and the size of a musket ball". An essential part of mission life, wine was used for religious ceremonies, for the table, for the sick, and for the refreshment of weary travellers.

Settlers in New England had long attempted to grow wine-grape vines imported from Europe, but the soil and climate in the east had proved inhospitable. However, in establishing their 21 missions throughout California the Spanish Franciscan friars discovered that this was a land perfectly suited for wine growing. The wine made here was better than any previously known in the New World.

Later on, the sale of wine became economically important to the Spanish missions. The English sea captain, Vancouver, commented that the Californian mission gardens surpassed anything he had seen. "Vines, figs and fruit trees of various sorts flourished in great perfection." Accounts left by visitors indicated that the friars lived well. For example, Harrison Rogers, a member of the Jedediah Smith expedition, spent several months at San Gabriel in 1826–27. There was "plenty of wine" at supper and "sigars" afterwards. When the U.S. fleet dropped anchor in 1843, Commodore Jones and a number of his officers were guests at a mission where they were presented with several casks of wine in the hope that enough would be left for the President of the United States "so he might know the excellence of California wine."

However, the flourishing infant industry shortly shrivelled on the vine. Between 1834–46 the Mexican government introduced

United States

legislation which confiscated the friars' vast properties and turned their wine production over to secular management, a move which was to prove unproductive, to say the least.

Sir Edward Belcher, who spent time in California on his around-the-world voyage, wrote of the general decay of the missions. "These were the only places of resort for travellers throughout California, but now a meal cannot be procured without difficulty."

From the time that the Franciscan missionaries introduced the "Mission Grape" in 1769, there was practically no other cultivated variety grown in California until the commercial growers arrived on the scene. About 1824 Joseph Chapman, one of the first Americans to settle in California, planted some 4,000 vines at the Lueblo of Los Angeles. In 1831 he was followed by Jean Louis Vignes, the son of a Bordeaux wine family. Vignes started a commercial vineyard. Soon he was producing the best wine and brandy in California. Others followed, and within a generation, wine was a main industry of the Los Angeles district.

Vignes was apparently the first to realize that to produce finer wines, choicer varieties must be brought from Europe to replace the mission grapes. The "Mission Grape", after all, had not originally been selected for its fine wine characteristics, but for its durability in the arid climate of North Mexico. In the 1830s Vignes sent to France for cuttings of choice grape vines. Chosen and packed with the utmost care, they were shipped to Boston and then around Cape Horn to California. Vignes reported the cuttings were received in good condition and, upon planting, flourished in his vineyard.

How many friends Vignes induced to leave France and start vineyards in California cannot now be estimated, but at least eight of his relatives emigrated.

In 1851, when he was 80 years of age, Vignes offered his property for sale. The advertisement read: "The vineyard, with 40,000 vines, 32,000 now bearing grapes, will yield 1,000 barrels of wine per annum, the quality of which is well-known to be superior." But it took four years to find a buyer, namely his nephew, Jean Louis Sansevain. The sale price was $42,000.

Despite the efforts of the early pioneers, the foundation for the modern wine industry was the great Californian "gold rush". The men pouring into California at this time were bent on making quick money from gold. However, it soon became apparent that there were surer ways of getting rich. Within the period of a few years the American population of California increased from under 500 to several hundred thousand. The hordes of "forty-niners" had to be fed, and, eventually many men turned to the land and the business of producing food, and wine. James Marshall, for example, the man who first discovered gold and started the "gold rush", benefited little from his discovery. He existed by the proceeds of his vineyard at Coloma.

Vignes started it, but the great change from the mission grape to finer varieties in California was brought about by another aristocrat, who arrived in the state in the "gold rush" year of '49, 19 years after Vignes' first wine vine importations from France. This newcomer was Agoston Haraszthy, a Hungarian nobleman, now called "the father of modern California viticulture."

"Colonel" Haraszthy had fled from his homeland for patriotically political reasons. He founded Sauk City, Wisconsin. Then ailing, he decided to settle in sunny California "for his health". He made his home first in San Diego in 1849, where he experimented with European grape varieties. He was successful, decided to push northward and started a series of test vine plantings with the view of discovering precisely which imported vine was the best suited to each of California's astonishing number of sub-climates.

United States

Like Vignes, Haraszthy was convinced that wines equal to Europe's best could never be made without an assortment of fine grape varieties.

In July 1861, the "Colonel" left on a five-month trip to Europe that was to take him through France, the Netherlands, Rhenish Prussia, Bavaria, Baden, Spain, Switzerland, Italy and England. He purchased 100,000 vine cuttings of about 300 varieties, paying for the vines and freight charges out of his own pocket. He had, however, been assured by Governor John G. Downey, and the state legislature, that his travelling expenses and money laid out for the vines would be refunded by the next legislature.

All but 5 per cent of the Haraszthy vines reached California in good condition. When the Colonel himself arrived back, he urged that the State of California take charge of the cuttings immediately. At the same time he submitted his report and a bill for $12,000. At this point California's first scientific experiment in viticulture struck an unexpected snag.

The California legislature refused to reimburse Haraszthy. Many guesses have been hazarded as to why the administration's promised financial support was withdrawn so suddenly. One theory that has prevailed is that the Colonel harboured secessionist sympathies, while the state supported the Union cause. However, records show that during the year 1861 California's commercial affairs were subject to the depression which existed in most other areas of the nation. The state was burdened with an enormous debt. And to add to these fiscal problems, the end of the year brought disastrous floods to the San Joaquin and Sacramento valleys. It is therefore a possibility that this state of affairs influenced the governor's change of heart concerning Haraszthy's expenses. In any case, the "Colonel" did not get a cent from the state. For one year Haraszthy's thousands of vines overran his state, while he struggled for governmental reimbursement of the money he had laid out. Finally, in desperation, he had to start peddling the vines to individual farmers and grape growers in lots of tens, twenties and occasionally a "large order" of a hundred.

Identification tags were lost or smudged so the names could not be determined, adding to the general confusion regarding the true nomenclature of many of the vines now growing in the state. Nevertheless, 100,000 choice foreign vines had been introduced into California and the wine growers of the state knew that while the mission grapes produced an acceptable wine, it was the later-imported grapes which were going to produce finer wines.

Though their names were often lost, the "foreign" grapes were widely planted and eventually the varieties of the various grapes were rediscovered. Later, a massive viticultural effort was directed towards matching each variety of classic grape with California's wide range of local climate-and-soil combinations, until the grower could judge in which location each type of vine could be expected to be most successful.

In the middle of the Nineteenth Century a scourge in the shape of a root louse, PHYLLOXERA, devastated the ancient vineyards of France, Italy, Spain and Germany. With classic European-type grapes growing in abundance in the uniquely suitable Californian climate, however, it looked as if the prospects for California's 100-year-old industry were excellent. But in 1874 a vineyard in Sonoma County, close to the old Haraszthy home, was found dying from the pest. Nothing was known that could stop it. And within five years the root louse, *Phylloxera*, was ravaging vineyards, duplicating its trail of devastation in Europe.

At this point, it looked as if the classic and great wines of the world, which had been

United States

passed from one civilization to another from the time of the Phoenicians, would finally vanish from the face of the earth. Deliverance came, however, from an unexpected quarter: it was discovered that the hardy roots of the indigenous American vines which grew in the eastern and central parts of this country and which had failed to provide worthwhile wine, nevertheless flourished undamaged by *Phylloxera* because the insect was virtually endemic in certain of these areas.

Although grafting of the *Vitis vinifera* had never been successful in the Eastern and Central States because of the inhospitable soil and climate, it was found that when the eastern *Phylloxera*-resistant rootstock was transplanted to California and Europe, grafting of the famous *V. vinifera* could succeed.

The tremendous task of replanting the vineyards of the world followed. Today the vast majority of the *V. vinifera* wines of California and Europe alike grow on the once despised but fortunately *Phylloxera*-resistant all-American roots.

California missed the main impact of the world-wide *Phylloxera* attack, but was hit heavily by PROHIBITION.

When the wineries reopened in 1934, it meant starting from scratch for most winemakers. It was not only a matter of 13 years of legislated neglect; but a generation of Americans had been deprived of exposure to the pleasures of wine.

During Prohibition, however, the authorities had conceded the continuation of a limited volume of wine-making for sacramental and medicinal purposes. Furthermore, individual citizens were permitted to make homemade wine if they were the heads of families and the wine was used only in the family and not sold. Thus Prohibition, while breaking many of the great vintners, brought into being thousands of little wine-making operations in basements throughout the country. The quality of the wine was generally poor, but the phenomenon at least served to keep some of California's vineyards in production. After repeal, the California wine industry itself encouraged the state to establish quality standards for California wines.

Today, the wines of California are at a level of excellence never previously achieved. There are almost 200 wineries and wine cellars producing all types of wines from a variety of grapes grown commercially in the state's nine wine districts. Because of rigidly enforced quality standards, the advanced state of science in the U.S., and the perennially good grape harvest, the wines of California are consistently excellent.

And the wines are earning increasing consumer loyalty among the most sophisticated wine connoisseurs. "The best standard wines of California can hold their own with the best standard wines of the world," writes wine expert John Hutchinson in *Wines of the World* (McGraw Hill).

What of the state's very best? Hugh Johnson in *Wine* pulls out all the stops: "The finest of their local wines," he proclaims, "are now comparable with the classic wines of Europe."

Quite apart from the historical aspects of the story of the 200 years of California wine, wine today is of rapidly increasing interest to large numbers of Americans. Since 1955, consumption of California table wines has more than doubled, to 71 million gallons a year.

The other major wine-making area of the U.S.A., though way behind California, is New York State, which is principally noted for its sparkling "champagne" wines, which enjoy a prestige over those of California that disinterested experts seem to think unjustified. The best are properly fermented in bottle.

Ohio comes next quantitively, and though a number of other states have wineries (Oregon is thought to have excellent though unrealized potential) they are of little importance in this context.

Broadly, American wines are often named after the grape variety from which they are made, allied to a brand-owner's name and possibly a proprietary trade name, with or without a more general description such as "sauterne", "burgundy". Almost any variation on those descriptive themes will be found, and all types of table and fortified wines, including blends similar to France's *vins ordinaires*.

Note Three Californian wines (PAUL MASSON) are now being marketed in Britain by Stowells of Chelsea, at prices roughly comparable to those of equivalent French wines. See also Christian Brothers.

URUGUAY

Soft drinks, *Coca-Colas* and the like, are widely drunk, with an annual consumption of around 120 million litres for a population of well under 3 millions. In addition, *mate*, the infusion from the *Yerba mate* plant, is extremely popular. It is known as "Paraguyan tea", but, in fact, is imported from Brazil. Consumption is 24,000 kilos a year. Beer is tending to increase in sales, the three local brands averaging 55 million litres a year. Wines of all types, including sparkling ones made on the *champenoise* method, are produced at around 30 per cent (Gay Lussac), sweetened and flavoured with gentian and local consumption of manufactured drinks runs at a very high level. Sundry cane and grape spirits (brandy style) are distilled, the single most popular one being *amarga*, produced at around 30 per cent (GAY-LUSSAC), sweetened and flavoured with gentian and other ingredients. The production of this is about 1 million litres. The liquor industry is divided between state and private enterprise.

The principal imported drink is whisky, and a few fine wines and liqueurs, but these carry the very heavy tax of 225 per cent of their c.i.f. value. Bars and restaurants are licensed by the government, and the same applies to liquor stores for bottle sales. There is complete liberty in the promotion of alcoholic drinks, though the state does not advertise its principal products in this field. A thirsty, happy land.

USHER'S SCOTCH WHISKIES

Usher's Extra and *Usher's Green Stripe* are the best known of the whiskies of Andrew Usher and Co. (now incorporated in the D.C.L. subsidiary J. & G. Stewart). Andrew Usher, with big grain whisky interests, was a pioneer of blending. At a time when malt and grain distillers tended to be at loggerheads, he established a liaison with the Smiths of GLENLIVET, and this may be said largely to have fathered Scotch as we understand it today. See Scotch whisky.

U.S.S.R.

A considerable producer of a variety of wine, Russia's distinctive contribution to the world's drinks has, of course, been VODKA. A very wide number of varieties are produced, regional tastes showing marked differences. Leningrad, Kiev and Moscow are major distilling centres but naturally there are others in the different republics. Vodka may be obtained with flavourings ranging from the most delicate to that of red pepper. Excellent liqueurs are produced, and much brandy, and vermouth is very popular. Some wine is exported. I have drunk smooth but robust Russian table wines that I consider superior to French wines in the same (inexpensive) price range. The Russians drink vast quantities of their own sparkling wine: the best from the Crimea has earned good marks even from French experts. Beer is good and visitors report "soft drinks" as outstanding.

Most of the vodka exported, to many countries in the world, is of slightly less

U.S.S.R.

strength than that on the domestic market. The best known is *Stolichnaya*, a refined spirit, wood-mellowed, with the subtle aroma imparted by numerous herbal ingredients. This is quite different to the neutral Anglo-American vodkas which require additives. Russian vodka should be chilled and drunk neat in small tots. Always eat something between each tot: if you cannot afford Russian caviar to go with it, try slivers of smoked salmon or soused herring or that type of tit-bit. Old "Moscow hands" have been known to opine that only vodka renders supportable the fantastic time normally elapsing in restaurants between ordering food and receiving it.

Wines and spirits are sold through state shops, restaurants and hotels; also through co-operative shops and at collective farm markets. Imported liquors in a wide range are sold through special "foreign-currency-only" bars and stores. Spirits may not be sold before 10.00 hours, but there are no restrictions on quantities sold by the bottle. No alcohol is allowed to persons under 16. Recently there has been official propaganda against inebriation, considerable promotion of Russian wines, and some reduction in the once amazing number of places where vodka could be bought in cities; but liquor laws are liberal. There is, however, growing evidence of increased Soviet anti-alcoholism. A senior member of the government has forecast legislation against excessive addiction to vodka (which may by now have been passed), and an army medical officer has written a newspaper feature which says that some soldiers in the Red Army have been found to drink anti-freeze mixture from trucks. It is suggested that alcoholics should have enforced cures at their own expense.

Legislation is fairly uniform throughout the country. Drunks are not harshly treated; intoxication is considered rather a social misdemeanour, or sickness, than a crime.

The Russians tried eradicating vodka once. It was made a state monopoly in 1895, and it was outlawed by the Czar in 1914, a ban maintained by the Soviet government until 1925. The lesson of this form of prohibition, with its resultant evils, has not been forgotten.

The Russians historically rivalled the English as topers; they are a convivial people who perhaps will one day enjoy on a bigger scale, apart from their national products, the virtues of Scotch whisky and London gin. Token shipments of both these have been made. It was a pleasing sight for me, and an augury of happy Anglo-Soviet relations, to see cases bearing famous names, brands carrying the royal warrant, being loaded into a Russian freighter at the London docks.

Digression The Russian trades union journal *Trud* reported that two explosions in one month in the same Siberian town had been caused by people trying to distil their own vodka at home.

Wine The highly developed Russian wine industry is expanding rapidly not only because it is a valuable export but because it is considered desirable to try to switch at least part of the deep national thirst for stimulants from vodka to wine. In the event, it is indeed probable that wine consumption will grow, but as a supplement to vodka-imbibing rather than as a replacement for it. Russian viticulture was enriched after the war by the annexation of Bessarabia which produced some of the best Romanian wine. The range of wines is very wide, most of it coming from the area bordering the Caspian and Black Seas. My only personal experience has been with the "burgundy" styles, full-bodied and smooth, and inexpensive. Russian sparkling wines are rated excellent, but the internal taste is for ones much sweeter than normally appreciated in Britain; rich, sweet dessert wines are the most popular in Russia. A large quantity of red vermouth is made.

V

VALDEPENAS
Powerful dry white and red Spanish wines.

VALDESPINO
A fine brand of sherries, notably *Fino*, one of the London Rubber Co.'s numerous brand subsidiaries.

VALPOLICELLA
The red Italian wine almost as well known overseas as CHIANTI, though it is normally smoother and generally lighter. As a type it has been compared with BEAUJOLAIS, and, like that wine, should be drunk on the cool side and not at ROOM TEMPERATURE.

VAN DE HUM
Distinctive and popular South African sweet liqueur based on tangerines. The name roughly translated from Afrikaans as "what's-his-name". *Brandy Hum*, the liqueur broken down with local brandy, is also much drunk.

VAT
Any large container for wine, beer or spirit, which may be in wood, glass or steel.

VAT 69
Famous Scotch whisky produced by William SANDERSON.

VAUX LTD.
Important northern England brewing concern, established in 1830 in Sunderland. Cuthbert Vaux who had previously been a partner in a brewery in Matlock Street, from 1806, started up with two of his sons in Union Street, Sunderland in 1837 as C. Vaux & Sons. The brewery had to move to its present site in Castle Street because of the coming of the railway in 1875.

Associated Breweries Ltd., was registered in 1927 to acquire The North Eastern Breweries Ltd. (also of Sunderland) and C. Vaux & Sons Ltd., and changed its name to Vaux & Associated Breweries Ltd., in 1941. All these companies have followed the usual pattern of the trade and absorbed smaller breweries from time to time.

The sales area covered in England now extends from the Scots' Borders down into Yorkshire and across to Cumberland and Westmorland. The company also has considerable interests north of the Border, mainly through Thos. Usher & Sons Ltd., whose sales area covers the whole of Scotland. In addition to being maltsters and brewers the company are wine and spirit merchants and manufacture mineral waters. They own about 900 licensed premises and some 25 high class hotels which go under the sign of the *Swallow*.

Over the last few years their main advertising theme has been the encouragement of sport in the North of England and to this end they sponsor many events, including horse and pigeon racing, so that the Vaux Gold Tankard is recognized as the premier award in the north in many fields. To encourage individual participation, the Vaux School of Sport in Durham is also financed.

V.D.S.Q.
Vins delimités de qualité supérieure, a form of APPELATION CONTROLEE, or indication of origin, for wines better than the run of the mill commercial blends but not meriting *appellation contrôlée* status. It is all pretty arbitrary, for experts will tell you there are V.D.S.Q. wines that are superior to some *appellation contrôlée* ones.

Vendange

VENDANGE
French term used by wine snobs when referring to the grape harvest.

VENENCIA
A small elongated cup, the fancier ones in silver, on the end of a whippy cane about three feet long, used to take samples from Spanish wine butts and particularly associated with JEREZ. A master of the use of a *venencia* can fill a fistful of glasses, pouring the wine from about 4 feet away, without spilling a drop. Use by amateur visitors is strictly for laughs and beneficial to the local dry cleaners.

VENEZUELA
This rich country is an important market for Scotch whisky, particularly de-luxe brands, and BUCHANAN'S is the leader. With the less affluent, rum and beer are the main stimulants. I feel there is also a demand for exotic liqueurs; I have a bottle of Venezuelan *Ponche Crema*, a strange drink the like of which I have not found elsewhere.

VERMOUTH
This is made all over the world. But the two great countries concerned with it are ITALY, where it was commercially invented, and to a lesser extent FRANCE. France produces one distinctive type of vermouth, CHAMBERY, dry and delicate, an excellent aperitif on its own rather than used in a mix.

There are really only three other types of vermouth, *bianco*, light coloured and the sweetest, which is principally an Italian product; "dry", and "sweet" (red), the most used vermouth internationally. Carpano's PUNT E MES is a vermouth but so distinctive that it is dealt with separately.

Dry (the English word is always used) vermouth is also known as "French", and sweet vermouth as "Italian", but this is misleading for both countries make both types. It is more than likely that the dry vermouth in your DRY MARTINI (which was invented by an Italian) was made in Italy, and your gin-and-Italian may easily have been made with vermouth from France.

We can now go on to trace the origins of this very important drink, which Alexis Lichine declines to dignify with the word "wine". I hate quarrelling with authorities, but he must be wrong. *Absinthianum vinum* was drunk by the Ancient Romans, and this had connections with *vinum Hippocraticum*, the legendary cure-all invented in the Fifth Century B.C. by Hippocrates, who, it is quite possible, knew the virtues of *Artemisia absinthium*, the wormwood plant. *Vermutwein* was used long ago in Bavaria, probably as a vermifuge. Wormwood, for all its bad reputation in ABSINTHE, has medicinal values. These were the forerunners of vermouth.

Towards the end of the Sixteenth Century, a Signor Alessio, from Piedmont (and the region is important for that is the vermouth centre today) discovered the secret of preparing *vermutwein* and took it with him to France. It was appreciated as a medicine in court circles, and not only in France, though Alessio does not seem to have found any chance of commercializing his secret, and presumably returned to Italy.

Meanwhile the French had gallicized the name to *vermout*. We then hear no more about it until 1678 when one Leonardo Fioravanti claimed high salubrious virtues for wormwood-flavoured wine. Vermouth does not seem to have left the doctor's consulting room but written references make it clear that around this time vermouth of a sort was well known in northern Italy. The powerful distillers' guild of Turin appears to have established an early lead in production in Piedmont, of which Turin is the capital. This lead remains unaltered.

The House of CINZANO was established in 1757. However, Carpano (PUNT E MES) is thought to have first launched a "brand" of vermouth in 1786. Others followed and *Turin* vermouth, made solely with Piedmontese wines and herbs from the locality, set a standard of excellence that received official recognition in 1840 when King Carlo Alberto issued licences requiring those who wished to sell *Turin* vermouth to establish the quality and origin of their products. Licence No. 1 went to MARTINI & ROSSI. Incidentally, the English added the quite unnecessary "h" in the word.

In outline modern vermouth is made by an infusion of herbs prepared according to the brand's formula. There will probably be between 30 and 50 brands, many coming from the ends of the earth. There are formulas from the past listing 200. Highly clarified white wine (and it is good sound matured wine, contrary to popular belief) is introduced to the infusion, together with grape spirit, and the whole fully "married". Sugar is added for "sweet" and *bianco* types, and flavourless caramel for the "sweet" (red). After resting, the vermouth goes under refrigeration at about 10 degrees below freezing. This stops any tendency to throw a deposit if long stored. The final stage is pasteurization and very complete filtration, prior to bottling.

A great deal of vermouth is exported from Italy and France in bulk. The industry thrives on an enormous scale in Italy, where there are about 80 producers, but the vast proportion of manufacture is in the hands of no more than half a dozen firms, if as many.

Vermouth has the merit of keeping almost indefinitely; it will neither improve nor deteriorate in bottle. When opened, it also has a very long store life, but I recommend putting it into a smaller container when the bottle is more than half-empty unless it is shortly to be used.

Vermouth is again being much drunk on its own, with ice, or as a long drink with soda-water. It mixes wonderfully well with spirits or other wines, and is, of course, an ingredient of many celebrated mixed drinks. There are one or two that are dominated by vermouth: AMERICANO; PERFECT.

(Some leading vermouth firms are listed under their own names).

VEUVE CLICQUOT-PONSARDIN
To the estimable Widow Clicquot is attributed the system of *remuage* in the making of CHAMPAGNE, thus perfecting the wine in recognizable modern form, and her name is a legend in the trade, rating little behind that of Dom Perignon and with the added attraction that we know positive facts about her. Married to a small vineyard proprietor and wine-maker of Rheims, and an ardent student of viticulture, on her husband's death she took over and vastly expanded the business.

When the Russian army was quartered at Rheims during the occupation of France after Waterloo, the officers acquired a taste for champagne. The Widow Clicquot, in collaboration with far-seeing partners, pursued this market and Russians became her most important clients. To please the Russian taste for sweet wines, the adding of a *dosage* of sugar after the *dégorgement* became the practice. *Clicquot* is among the leaders of quality non-vintage champagnes; the vintages are also notable.

VEUVE DU VERNAY
A leading brand of VIN MOUSSEUX, selling over half-a-million bottles a year in the U.K. (Edouard Robinson Ltd., London). In the early years of the century, M. Charmat, whose family still own *Veuve du Vernay*, perfected the CUVE CLOSE principle which made it possible to produce excellent sparkling wine without the expensive REMUAGE that is a feature of CHAMPAGNE production. The brand is the biggest-selling French sparkling wine other than champagne.

VIEILLE CURE
A splendid French liqueur, insufficiently

appreciated outside France, of which the name literally means "old rectory", a reference to the origins of this nectar in an abbey near Bordeaux.

VIN DE PAYS
Local French wines; applying not to great burgundies in, say Beaune, but to unimportant but often very pleasing little wines that have neither the character nor incentive to travel more than a few miles from their point of origin.

VIN D'HONNEUR
"Wine of honour", referring to the ancient French habit of using wine ceremonially on many occasions. The only occasion on which I have experience was at a civic reception. It was a speudo-champagne of exceptional sickliness which I dubbed *"vin d' horreur"* on the spot.

The above, however, does not apply to the range of good quality table wines marketed under the name of *Vin d'Honneur* by Imported Wines Ltd.

VINEGAR
Presumably the first *vin aigre* (sour wine) was in fact just that, though it is now made from cider, malt or other bases. OXIDATION of wine produces the acetic acid which is vinegar's prime flavour. The process is, of course, artificially accelerated in commercial production.

VIN FOU
A wine from the Jura region, basically made by the champagne method but exceptionally effervescent; hence its name, *Crazy Wine*.

VINHO VERDE
Literally "green", but more accurately, "young", wine from the north-western extreme of Portugal. An ancient wine-growing district whence wines have been exported since the Eighteenth Century. Characteristics are pallidity, natural mild effervescence and light fresh taste, which suits them well for the current British mass market.

VIN MOUSSEUX
French sparkling wine of the same basic family as German SEKT, Italian ASTI, and a host of other effervescent bottlings of greatly varying quality. There are some ghastly *vin mousseux*, mercifully retained for the French market, that are little more than vaguely alcoholic, artificially carbonated, diluted second-rate grape juice. But there are *vin mousseux* that are superior to some wines qualifying as champagne. The normal run of *vin mousseux* is made on the CUVE CLOSE principle, a perfectly acceptable method which is used for lesser champagnes. An outstanding exception is KRITER which has successfully evolved a method of its own. In France, avoid extremely sweet wines bearing little more on their labels than the words *vin mousseux*.

VINO CORRIENTE
The Spanish equivalent of the French *vin ordinaire*, and often sounder.

VINO DE PASTO
A slightly inferior sherry (an undistinguished but pleasant amontillado) or, in Spain, a local beverage wine. One does not see it about much these days.

VIN ORDINAIRE
The common, blended wines used daily in French households and humbler restaurants; sometimes totally unlabelled, sometimes with proprietary names. They can be very *ordinaire* indeed.

VINO TINTO
Any Spanish red wine.

VIN ROSE
This can be made by mixing red and white wines, though properly it is produced by leaving red grape skins in contact with the juice for a shorter time during fermentation

Vodka

than for the production of red wine. It is fashionable today, and some pleasing *vin rosé* is produced in several countries; the best probably comes from ANJOU. Essentially, it is a hot day al fresco lunch wine or for drinking as a cooler, and its employment as a beverage wine with serious meals is, in my opinion, to do it, and your guests, a disservice.

VINTAGE

Actually the gathering of the grape harvest. In practice, since climatic conditions vary greatly from year to year, in the principal countries producing fine wines, France and Germany, there may be no declared "vintage" for several years; on the other hand one winemaker may be much luckier than his fairly close neighbour. In a "bad" year some excellent wine will be produced; in a "great" year, there will be some poor wines, even in the best areas. It is up to individuals to declare they are making a vintage wine. In the case of PORT we see particularly how one producer will declare a vintage in a year when few others do: collective declaration of a vintage is rare. To a lesser degree this pertains to CHAMPAGNE. There is much more agreement on "big" years in Bordeaux and Burgundy.

Since they can be extremely misleading, there are in this book no vintage charts.

VINTNERS' LIVERY COMPANY

As long ago as 1363, Edward III granted the Vintners of the City of London certain trading privileges, though they did not get their charter until 1437. The Vintners controlled and broadly policed much of the trade in wine in the City and its environs, and it is a live organization to this day when some livery companies, such as the Pewterers' (once actively connected with the liquor trade), have little practical purpose left.

Free Vintners still have the right to trade in wine without a normal licence—but a Free Vintner, if he does not obey minutely the normal licensing regulations will not be a Free Vintner for long! The Vintners share with the Crown and the Dyers' Company the ownership of the swans on the upper River Thames.

VIRGIN ISLANDS (British)

Rum, without brand names or labels, sold in bulk from small local distilleries, is the main production. Some of this is exported to the neighbouring U.S. Virgin Islands. Traditional spirits are imported. Beer, *Coke* and fruit-flavoured sodas, as well as the local rum, are specially popular beverages. Sweet mineral waters are favoured with spirits.

Gin and coconut water is a particular favourite for festive occasions. It is a simple enough drink—if you have a fresh green nut handy. Open it and spike liberally with gin. Well-known composer of calypsos, Rubena Connor of Tortola, wrote one for the 1966 August festival, the big local holiday. This calypso is still constantly played on the radio. The principal refrain goes:

> *T'will be gin and coconut water*
> *Gin and coconut water*
> *Gin and coconut water*
> *That's the best drink of all.*

PLANTER'S PUNCH is much demanded by tourists, and under that title I append some notes received from Tortola.

VIRGIN ISLANDS, U.S.

The situation is similar to the British Virgin Islands, except that a considerable amount of rum (of the *Bacardi* "type") is exported to the U.S.A. It would be fair to say it is not highly esteemed by connoisseurs. American whiskeys and other spirits, particularly Scotch, are imported, and gin and coconut-water is a local favourite drink.

VODKA

The legendary origin of vodka dates from the Twelfth Century in the Russian monastery-

Vodka

fort of Viatka. Its invention was certainly for medicinal purposes, as were all important distillations, for the art of distilling was in early times a rare one, and it was originally called *zhiznennia voda* (water of life), the Russian equivalent of the universal *aqua vitae*. Two centuries later it had passed into more general use and was also known as *vodnyi vinnyi* (aqueous wine) spirit, which seems to indicate a vinous base. The name vodka (little water) came in in the Sixteenth Century. For some time the spirit was distilled from a rye base, and after the Eighteenth Century from maize, barley and, popularly, from potatoes. It is also claimed vodka was a Polish invention.

The use, and misuse, of vodka spread all over Russian dominated lands, and into adjacent ones, so that in some form it was a common drink of all classes from Lapland north of the arctic circle to the Persian Gulf. But it stopped short at the Rhine and the North Sea.

Modern Russian vodka is said to be of the *Petrovskaya* type, originating from a formula invented by that curious half-genius, half-madman, Peter the Great, who spent some time on his mysterious trips abroad incognito near SCHIEDAM where, with his insatiable curiosity, he doubtless interested himself in the activities of pioneer Dutch commercial distillers: in fact, the Russians might have turned to gin!

The original Russian vodkas were certainly pretty crude efforts and various berries and herbal ingredients were infused into them. Today Russian vodka is made in a great many flavourings, which separates it firmly from British and American vodkas, which are essentially flavourless neutral spirits designed to add power to other flavours and not to be drunk straight. Russian, and Polish, export vodkas are of high quality and enjoy a mild popularity. I like them drunk traditionally, chilled and neat—accompanied by a rich friend's caviare! Vodka has for so long been made in so many varieties in so many countries (there are a dozen different spellings of the name, at least) that it has lost its identity. The word has come to mean a flavoured or unflavoured spirit of whatever type the inhabitants of a given country think of as vodka. Few drinks could be more disparate than a strong cayenne-infused Russian spirit and a delicate flavourless English one: yet both are accepted in their own worlds as vodka.

During World War I, the Czar banned vodka, and the Soviets maintained this restriction until the normal excesses associated with PROHIBITION (illicit distilling and increased inebriation) made themselves obvious. Distilling under a state monopoly was instituted in 1925, but there is thought to be considerable illegal manufacture in the U.S.S.R., and alcoholism is an admitted social problem.

The principal Russian export vodka brand is STOLICHNAYA and the Polish leader VYBOROVA. From Poland comes ZUBROWKA (*Bison* brand), a rather pleasing spirit flavoured with a grass of that name (the bottle contains a blade of it) that grows in a remote part of the country, where Europe's remaining wild buffalo graze. *Zubrowka* is also produced in Russia.

The brand-leader in the U.S.A. and Britain is SMIRNOFF, which in the U.K. is increasingly closely followed by COSSACK. There are also an increasing number of minority brands, some imported from the Continent.

A number of excellent COCKTAILS are closely associated with vodka: BLACK RUSSIAN, BLOODY MARY, BULL SHOT, MOSCOW MULE and SCREWDRIVER being the best-known. Dry Martini is quite often made with vodka in place of gin. (A vodka recipe book is available free from Publicity Department, Buchanan

Booth's Agencies Ltd., 1 Oxendon Street, London, S.W.1.)

VOLEUR
French slang for indentation found in base of wine BOTTLES.

VOSNE-ROMANEE
BURGUNDY *commune* embracing some of the greatest names of the whole area.

VOUGEOT, CLOS DE
Celebrated BURGUNDY vineyards and *commune*.

VOUVRAY
The most important district of the LOIRE, producing delicious light white wines.

V.S.O.: V.S.O.P., V.V.S.O.P.
For COGNAC, *Very Special Old, Very Special Old Pale; Very, Very Special Old Pale*. Only the second variation is much used, for de-luxe product makers tend to invent special brand names. Until the advent of Scotch whisky, brandy was the most popular spirit in England. A great deal of it was poor stuff heavily disguised with caramel which darkened the spirit. The reputable cognac and brandy producers began marketing *V.S.O.P.* as a guarantee that this product was good and had no caramel added. The use of English not only indicates the British origins of many famous cognac concerns, but the supreme importance of the British market. "Pale" denotes a change to lighter-coloured brandies from the much darker ones once fashionable, at a date which I cannot pinpoint but would say it was about the middle of the last century.

V.S.O. should be about 15 years in wood; *V.S.O.P.* about 20 years, and *V.V.S.O.P.* 30 years or more. There is no rule. *V.O.* (very old) is hardly used in cognac, nor the obsolete *V.V.O.* (very very old) and they were always more or less meaningless. The only well-known current use of *V.O.* I can think of is in whisky, *Seagram's V.O.*

VULGARITY
This is really a do-it-yourself section, but I will start you off with things which, in a drinking context, I find inexpressibly vulgar: exaggerated balloon brandy snifters, excessively heavy cut-glass wine glasses, enormous plain wine glasses, peculiarly-shaped cocktail-glasses, lamps and holders for warming brandy snifters, silver-plated claret cradles, gold-plated cocktail accessories, ostentatious modern decanter labels and . . . swizzle sticks . . . Why not compile your own list?

W

WALES
Every seven years, where there is organized opposition to Sunday opening of public houses, a poll is held. As a result of the last one, Breconshire, Denbighshire, Flintshire, Glamorgan, Montgomery, Pembrokeshire and Radnorshire and the County Boroughs of Cardiff, Merthyr, Newport and Swansea have Sunday opening. Anglesey, Caernarvon, Cardigan, Carmarthen and Merioneth do not have Sunday opening. Licensing laws, including those applying in Monmouthshire, are similar to those pertaining in England, with the same anomalies.

WALKER & SONS, LTD., JOHN
Put quite simply, *Johnnie Walker* Old Scotch whisky is by far the largest-selling Scotch in the world. The famous square bottle, with

Walker & Sons

either the infinitely popular *Red*, or the prestigious (de-luxe) *Black*, diagonal label, is universally a synonym for great Scotch.

Recalling the celebrated slogan of Walker's: "Born 1820..." we will go back to that date and see whence sprang this immense success. In that year, John Walker set up a small grocery and wine and spirit business in Kilmarnock, still the hub of the company's activities. The whisky trade was in a state of chaos (see the Scotch story) but enlightenment was just around the corner. Kilmarnock was a growing town, its lace, carpets and knitwear attracted buyers, including many from the south of Britain, and these took back a taste for Scotch. The canny carpet manufacturers sometimes included a cask of Scotch in a consignment to their English customers: John Walker was the supplier of much of this.

Things were going well for him until 1852, when a cloudburst hit Kilmarnock and washed his business literally down the drain. But, like Robert the Bruce, he tried again, and, helped by a devoted wife, not only restored his trade but greatly increased it. He became an important wholesaler and supplier of ships through the prosperous port of Glasgow, which may have caused his son, Alexander, to think in terms of export, for it was Alexander Walker who set the firm on its path to global triumph. In 1880, Walker's established a London office. The firm's main product was then Walker's *Kilmarnock*. Alexander Walker was responsible for creating the *Johnnie Walker* image. In 1908 he commissioned the celebrated commercial artist, Tom Browne, to paint the peripatetic neo-regency dandy, and no trademark is better known. Though he has been redrawn, it is essentially Tom Browne's "Johnnie Walker" who dominates Scotch today.

Alexander Walker died in 1919. The company assumed its present title in 1923, and is now a star in the D.C.L. galaxy.

In 1937, a 7-acre site was acquired in Hill Street, Kilmarnock, and a major development was planned—to integrate blending, storage and despatch in a single unit. The war inevitably delayed this project and the complex was not completed until 1956. However, even the optimism of the company's planners was overtaken by the tremendous expansion in sales of *Johnnie Walker* and within a decade the Hill Street establishment was strained to its limits. So another 32 acres were acquired in the vicinity, at Barleith, linked by rail to Hill Street, and the two sites were designed to operate as one enormous entity. The Barleith section was officially opened by Princess Alexandra in 1968, and on the same day Her Royal Highness inaugurated a second bottling hall at Hill Street.

Johnnie Walker is "... still going strong." And how!

WARAGI

A potent beverage sometimes called "African gin". It is certainly not a true gin. It is made from maize, millet, barley and sometimes bananas, so is often referred to as "Banana gin". Very popular in Uganda, although it is by now also being distilled in Tanzania and Kenya, it is similar to the spirit called *Moshi*.

WARRE & CO. LTD.

Founded in 1670, during the reign of Charles II and his Portuguese queen, Catherine of Braganza, Warre & Company is not only the oldest British port house but the largest independent and privately owned port shipping business in Oporto today. Its history indeed reflects that of the British community in Oporto, for the names Warre, Noble, Steart, Murat and Lawson are common to the fortunes of both. A little more than 200 years later a young Scotsman, James Symington, left Paisley to settle in Portugal. Today his descendants (no less than 32 in Oporto alone) wholly own the Warre business, a

Water

dynasty which saw its beginnings in 1905 when he took a partnership in Warre & Co.

Warres have always enjoyed a fine reputation for their vintage ports, the demand for which has increased very greatly in recent years. So much so that during the last decade more Warre's vintage port has been shipped to the U.K. than any other vintage port. The 1960 vintage in fact attracted so much attention that the demand could not be satisfied.

A feature of Warre's lodges in Oporto are the rows of enormous vats, the largest holding approximately 30,000 gallons. It is in these vats and in casks that a wine like *Warrior*, reserve vintage, upon which Warre's have founded much of their fine reputation, is aged and matured. *Warrior* has been shipped by the house of Warre for nearly three centuries and is thus the oldest brand shipped by the oldest British shippers.

WASH
The alcoholic liquid formed by the fermentation of WORT, from which whisky is distilled. It is a sort of beer with an alcoholic strength around 10 per cent.

WASSAIL
The "wassail bowl", a kind of primitive punch, was a feature of old-English yuletide feasts. See Toasts.

WATER
Water plays a vital part in the production, and often in the enjoyment, of high-quality spirits and beer. Suitable water has, in Britain, led to the establishment of whole industries. The fine water of the burns of Scotland still contributes much to world-conquering Scotch whisky. Burton's water from the River Trent may no longer be vital to its beer, but because of its former purity that town became a mighty brewing centre. London is synonymous with gin, and its two greatest distilleries are where they are because of CLERKENWELL's once copious pure water. In Ireland, Guinness chose Dublin not only because it was the capital but because of the *then* clear-running Liffey.

In many instances, technology has taken over from nature, but geographical manufacturing traditions were established for perfectly practical reasons largely connected with water. Distilled or demineralized water is now widely used and this has made it practicable to duplicate some products away from their traditional habitat, Scotch being the outstanding exception (for reasons not wholly, but certainly partly, aqueous).

Today we *mostly* enjoy metropolitan water supplies of a salubrity none doubts, but they vary greatly from one source to another, and the attainment of this wholesomeness may mean treatment which not only renders them totally unsuitable for manufacture of potables but even unpleasant for drinking. Hence the industrial use of distilled water (which is self-explanatory), an entirely inert "dead" fluid, or demineralized water (favoured by some gin distillers), which, when wholly purified, has a little "life" left in it. By these means, large-scale manufacturers may employ urban main water supplies. Some, of course, have their own Artesian wells.

As for using water to dilute spirits for drinking, the Scots (if admitting Scotch may be diluted at all!) swear by their own swift streams. Such water has been bottled for sale and I have beside me as I write a plastic container holding a single fluid ounce of water from the distilling centre of Dumbarton: labelled *Scotch Rocks*, its export destination is self-evident. Those who care for spirits diluted, simply with water, have (in Britain) the exceptionally good *Malvern Water* and (not always available) the naturally-sparkling *Appolinaris*, should their locality not be blessed with palatable public water.

The French have long suspected their tap-water, an attitude no longer generally justified on health grounds, and many a thrifty Parisian

Water

household spends seemingly disproportionate sums weekly on mineral waters for imbibing or for diluting the children's wine. Traditionally obsessed with their digestion and their livers (see France for the alcohol problem), the French place much faith in the salutiferous virtues of a wide range of bottled spring waters, of which *Vichy*, *Evian*, *Vittel* and *Perrier* are perhaps the best known overseas. Myself, I find *Vichy* possibly beneficial for P.A.G. (*q.v.*).

From Italy, *Pellegrino* is exported. Americans customarily use water of such arctic temperature as must kill any character good or bad it may possess. Their term "branch water" means plain as opposed to "charged" or soda-water.

One might mention that those concerned with purity of water, and who use ICE, frequently insist on a special bottled water and then pour it over any commercial ice chipped from a block that may not (but indeed *may*) have been standing at the corner outside after delivery.

Old H_2O enjoys a mixed reputation as a potable; some despise it, some fear it, some laud it, according to geography, faith and the state of local viticulture... but its importance is undeniable.

Water (mineral) In the third quarter of the Eighteenth Century, European chemists experimented with reproducing the "spa" waters, then fashionable, the first being seltzer-water. Hence originated an international industry. The types and brands of mineral waters throughout the world are now legion. Particulars of the best known will be found under separate headings (e.g. Soda; Tonic-water) and in sections dealing with a few outstanding firms in this trade.

No longer drink only water but use a little wine for the sake of your stomach and your frequent ailments.   St. Paul

WATNEY MANN LTD.

This is currently the fourth largest brewery group in Britain. It was formed in 1958 by the amalgamation of Watney Combe Reid & Co. Limited (formed in 1898 by the amalgamation of three famous London breweries, Watney & Co., Combe & Co., and Reids Brewery Co.) and Mann, Crossman & Paulin Limited.

Watney & Co. owned two breweries: the Stag Brewery, Pimlico, where brewing had been begun by the Greene family as long ago as 1660, and Mortlake Brewery, reputed to have been founded in 1487 by John Morgan, which supplied the king's household at the nearby Palace of Sheen.

Combe & Co. owned the Castle Street Brewery in Long Acre, in which business Harvey Christian Combe, later Lord Mayor of London, became a partner in 1787. The brewery buildings still stand, although now used for other purposes. Reids Brewery Co. owned the Griffin Brewery in Liquorpond Street, CLERKENWELL, founded in 1763, which originally belonged to the Meux family, the first Reid becoming a partner in 1793.

The Albion Brewery of Mann, Crossman and Paulin Limited was built as a speculation in the year 1808, replacing a small brewhouse adjoining the *Blind Beggar* public house in Whitechapel Road, London, E.1. The first tenant was John Hoffman, who occupied it until 1819 when it was sold to Blake & Mann, Brewers, of Lambeth. James Mann was joined in 1847 by Robert Crossman and William Paulin and in 1863 the alms houses which fronted the road were replaced by the present offices and the whole brewery was modernized and extended.

In 1872 a brewery was built in Burton-on-Trent but was sold some 20 years later and the bottling store in Raven Row, opposite the Albion Brewery, was completed in 1888. In 1929 Brandon's Putney brewery was acquired and brewing continued here until 1950, the premises afterwards being used as a bottling store.

Since 1958 a number of other companies have joined the group, which now has national coverage, with over 21,000 staff and employees.

There is also an Irish company, Watney Mann (Ireland) Limited, with a brewery at Cork, and a Belgian company (Watneys S.A.), with breweries in Brussels, Chatelet and Waarloos, making it the second largest brewing group in Belgium. The latter company also has a substantial holding in Supermarché de Vins, Brussels, which has a chain of over 40 wine and spirit supermarkets and a wholesaling organization. Apart from these interests in Belgium, Watney Mann beers are sold in many other export markets including France, Germany, Italy, Austria, Spain, Malta and Gibraltar, as well as extensively in the U.S.A. In all these countries, the company has pioneered the "British pub", either on its own or in association with local interests.

In the United Kingdom the Group brews some 60 different beers, the most celebrated being *Red Barrel*, the first keg beer and the current brand leader. The name *Red Barrel* has now been superseded, and the firm has introduced its new keg, *Watney's Red*.

The story of *Red Barrel* begins in 1929, when the head brewer at Watneys Mortlake Brewery, on one of his regular trips to see what was new in brewing on the Continent, discovered something that was to revolutionize the brewing and racking of beer throughout the world. This was a new machine, developed by an Austrian firm, which pasteurized beer in bulk and filled metal containers under sterile conditions. This machine, the only one of its kind, was purchased and installed at Mortlake. Exhaustive tests confirmed that this new technique afforded a means of providing draught beer in prime condition for the lucrative markets of India and the Far and Middle East. The first *Red Barrel* installation in the British Isles was at the East Sheen Lawn Tennis Club in 1933.

In all, the group has, in the United Kingdom, some 6,500 on-licences (pubs) and 1,250 off-licences. In addition, Watney Mann Hotels Limited operates 30 hotels and Watney Lyon Motels Limited has 9 motels.

The group has considerable interests in the soft drinks market through a subsidiary, COCA-COLA Southern Bottlers Limited, through which it holds the bottling concession for the whole of the South of England, with seven plants operating in East Anglia, London and the West Country. In addition, it has a one-third share (with Schweppes and Courage Barclay & Simonds) in Cantrell & Cochrane (Gt. Britain) Limited, a soft drinks company with almost national coverage.

Until recently Watney Mann had a large direct stake in the wine and spirit market, but these interests it disposed of in 1968 to INTERNATIONAL DISTILLERS AND VINTNERS LTD., in which company it now has a $37\frac{1}{2}$ per cent holding. This had strengthened the group's position in the wine and spirit trade and made possible substantial economies in purchasing, stock holding, rationalization of production and distribution. Watney Mann now have a substantial interest in a highly successful company owning or holding agencies for many international brands including HENNESSY cognac, BOLS liqueurs, SMIRNOFF vodka, GILBEY'S gin, J. & B. RARE whisky, HEIDSIECK *Dry Monopole* champagne, Bouchard Père et Fils, burgundies, and *Carafino* and *Justina* table wines. By an agreement with the famous Danish brewery, Carlsberg, the group has the exclusive marketing rights for draught *Carlsberg* lager in the U.K. It also bottles the product and distributes it widely.

In the field of leisure, there are two subsidiary companies, Schooner Inns Limited and Watney Mann (Entertainments) Limited.

Weeper

The former specializes in good quality, reasonably priced food and drink served in unorthodox and colourful surroundings, and the latter is developing a chain of *Birds Nests* (pubs with disc-jockeys, dancing, food and drink), primarily for the young, and *Rainbow Rooms*, nightclub-style pubs which offer live music, dancing and cabaret.

WEEPER
A bottle of wine, the cork of which leaks when lying in the bin. If you spot one, use at once, taking care it is not so far gone as to have oxidized.

WHAT WITH WHAT
I was somewhat at a loss as to how to head this subject, with which I will deal with as much brevity as possible. There are two aspects: first, what wine should one take with which food. Fortunately the largely, but not entirely, snobbish rules have been replaced by a more commonsense attitude (I deal partially with this under the general subject of Wine). I would add that the easiest and most sensible rules to follow are, in the case of fine wines, that the food should not obliterate them: thus, a delicate Rhine wine is not the ideal accompaniment to well-hung grouse, but a Rhône wine is; a burgundy is hardly suitable with oysters, but a chablis is. Other than that, personal preferences should be followed.

The other aspect is what additives it is correct to take with spirits. I did once hear a man call for "Napoleon" brandy and, when the bartender had served him with his nearest approximation to this mythical nectar, he demanded "Where's the soda?" I was shocked. But, in fact, one's "mixer" is purely a matter for personal preference. A Scotch-drinking friend of mine always has it with bitter-lemon, which I find detestable, but if he likes it that way, I admire him for insisting on so drinking it. After all, the most popular additive to Scotch in Scotland itself is fizzy lemonade (but do not ask for it if you are fortunate enough to visit a Highland malt distillery!).

Incidentally, there is nothing wrong with drinking spirits with a meal.

WHISK(E)Y
Whisky of sorts is made all over the world, and the title can embrace the roughest "moonshine" or the rarest product of the Highlands of Scotland. Good whisky was once made in Wales. Queen Victoria, a whisky-drinker in later years, accepted a cask of it. Production ceased around the turn of the century. Whisky, mainly illicit, was also distilled in Northumberland. The word itself is simply a derivative from *aqua vitae*. There are traditionally four countries producing whiskies. For general descriptions, see American whiskey; Canadian whisky; Irish whiskey; Scotch whisky. Certain individual companies are listed separately where I deemed their history of interest.

Spanish whisky is quite well established and so is Australian. On Japanese whisky I give a special note under JAPAN.

Some whisky-based drinks are listed in relation to the type of whisky normally associated with them, but there is a high degree of interchangability according to personal preference.

Whisk(e)y cocktails and mixed drinks are listed after the type with which they are principally associated and appear as individual entries.

Digression "A quart of whisky swallowed in five minutes shortly before a nuclear explosion reduces the dangers of radiation damage to the body by half. Unfortunately, the alcoholic cure would probably be as fatal as the disease." Prof. Robert Haynes, University of California.

Note The modern insertion of an "e" in American and Irish spelling and its omission for Scotch and Canadian whisky is of modern origin; most dictionaries will give them as alternatives. Formerly either was used at the writer's discretion, and as late as 1909, in the very important report by the Royal Commission on *Whiskey and other Potable Spirits*, the "e" is used throughout regardless of whether the reference is to Scotland or Ireland.

WHISKY MAC
Half and half of Scotch whisky and ginger wine. (I prefer *Crabbie's Green*). This is an excellent "warmer" and I do not think it should be iced.

WHITBREAD & CO. LTD.
This very famous London brewery is now a large group with far-ranging interests at home and abroad (see Breweries). It has had its headquarters in Chiswell Street, CLERKENWELL, since 1750. It was in 1734 that young Samuel Whitbread came to London to learn the mysteries of the brewers' craft, which he did so successfully that in 1742 he was able, in partnership, to establish a business in Moorfields, moving to Clerkenwell only eight years later. The present chairman is Col. W. H. Whitbread, seventh member of the family to head this giant concern, a remarkable record even by British traditions of continuity.

Samuel Whitbread was a man not only dedicated to his trade but to philanthropy and religion: no work at all was permitted on his behalf on Sundays. He was a pioneer in the use of steam, commissioning James Watt himself to design a "stupendous steam engine" to raise water and grind barley. This accomplished work "equal to fourteen horses" in the estimation of one of Whitbread's assistants, writing to a friend. Later the engine was improved, and 24 horses were laid off at a saving of £40 a head a year. The machine cost a mere £1,000 and was surprisingly easy on fuel.

A few years later King George III and Queen Charlotte came to see this marvel of contemporary engineering.

In 1802, Whitbread's Brewery was one of the great sights of London and was described at the time as having capital equipment worth the then huge sum of £500,000, and as producing London's best beer.

Whitbread's were early exporters of beer. I do not know if they were the first with *India Pale Ale* (*I.P.A.*) but they were well represented on the scene. They also moved quickly into the bottled beer market when about a century ago the glass tax was substantially reduced. Much more recently they were pioneers in sending London brews by road-tanker to the Continent. Their *Britannia* tavern at the Brussels international exhibition in 1958 probably sparked off the craze for English pubs across the Channel. When such improvements became feasible after the war, they were among the first to start refurbishing public houses in keeping with modern tastes, specializing in using a "theme", the decorative motif being based on a character or the special interests of the locality. Perhaps *The Sherlock Holmes* in Northumberland Avenue is the most remarkable. *The Printer's Devil* in Fetter Lane, off Fleet Street, hub of London's newspaper world, has aptly fascinating relics and pictures. Whitbread's brew *Mackeson's* stout and other famous beers. The wine and spirit section of their business comes under the well-known "flag" of Stowell's of Chelsea.

WHITE HORSE DISTILLERS LTD.
The company was formerly known as Mackie & Company (Distillers) Ltd., and the last surviving member of the family, Sir Peter Jeffrey Mackie, Bt., died in 1924.

The Mackies came from a Stirlingshire family with a history going back at least as far as the year 1632. The last direct male

White Horse Distillers

descendant of the Mackies, James Logan Mackie, son of Sir Peter Jeffrey Mackie, and named after his uncle, was killed in action in 1917. On the day of his death he still retained the house in the Canongate in Edinburgh conveyed by his ancestors in the year 1650. It was from this family association with old Edinburgh that ultimately the well-known trade mark of the *White Horse* arose.

The associations of a white horse are many. It appears carved in chalk on many of the chalk downs of western England. Alfred the Great, King of England, adopted it as his symbol of power and victory: a roughly hewn figure of the white horse in Berkshire was carved to celebrate his victory over the Danes over 1,000 years ago. Napoleon rode on a white horse. Many people remember Lord Roberts' milk-white "Voronel". Lady Godiva is traditionally supposed to have ridden naked on a white horse through the streets of Coventry.

The leaders of Prince Charlie's bid for the throne in 1745 foregathered at the *White Horse* inn at Edinburgh. It was considerations of this kind that led Sir Peter Jeffrey Mackie's forbears to adopt the sign of the *White Horse* inn at Edinburgh for their whisky.

The business activities of the company cannot be traced farther back than the year 1801, but this date is confirmed by a mahogany writing desk now at the Mackie Street Warehouse, Glasgow. Attached to this desk is a silver plate bearing the following inscription: "This desk was occupied by partners in turn, William Grahame 1801, Alexander Grahame 1830, J. Logan Mackie 1845, Peter Jeffrey Mackie 1878, Andrew H. Holm 1888, G. H. Johnson 1896, J. Logan Mackie 1914, G. O. L. Campbell 1921."

Prior to the year 1883 full records are not available, but in May of that year, we find established at 5 Dixon Street, Glasgow, the firm of James Logan Mackie, the partners of which were James Logan Mackie, who was the uncle of Sir Peter Jeffrey Mackie and a Captain Grahame. The firm carried on business as distillers at Lagavulin Distillery in the Island of Islay and also handled brandies and clarets. Even in those days the fame of 10-year-old *Lagavulin* ranked high and business grew rapidly. The Lagavulin distillery is still flourishing today, although the whisky produced is mostly used for blending.

In the year 1890 the name of the firm was altered to Mackie & Company, the partners being James Logan Mackie and Peter Jeffrey Mackie. Shortly after this, James Logan Mackie retired from business and a private limited liability company was floated.

This was a boom time in the trade and business continued to increase both at home and overseas. At this time, in order to cope with the ever increasing volume of business, the company purchased considerable property at Port Dundas, Glasgow, which is now known as the Mackie Street Warehouse.

In addition to the business with the 10-year-old *Lagavulin* whisky, the demand for *White Horse* was rapidly increasing. Not only did Mackie & Company handle these two lines but they were also agents for the production of Laphroaig distillery, and on completion, therefore, of the new Craigellachie distillery on Speyside.

During the four or five years prior to the outbreak of war in 1914, the progress of Mackie & Company (Distillers) Limited was outstanding both at home and in overseas markets. With the outbreak of the war, however, came the cessation of distilling. As soon as the war was over steps were taken to build up once again that part of the trade which had been lost and to consolidate the position still further.

The absorption of other business and stock of mature whisky was of paramount importance. Chief among the concerns acquired then were the Craigellachie-Glenlivet Distillery Company Ltd., G. R. Mackenzie, Glasgow and Greenless & Colville Ltd. Through the latter was acquired the Hazelburn distillery which has since ceased to function as a distillery.

Sir Peter Mackie died in 1924 at the age of 69, and on his death the company was re-formed under the title of White Horse Distillers Limited, his son-in-law, G. O. L. Mackie Campbell, assuming the chairmanship.

It is interesting to recall that about that time, so vast had the firm's traffic between Glasgow, Islay and Campbelltown become, that a small tramp steamer was built expressly for the purpose of carrying casks of whisky. This vessel was called the *Pibroch*, and plied regularly between these three places. The vessel became quite famous and a successor, bearing the same name, is still owned by The Distillers Company Ltd. for the same purpose and can often be seen on the Clyde.

In 1926 White Horse Distillers Ltd. made their grand coup, by launching the famous *White Horse* screwcap bottle. Hitherto all bottles were sealed with the original cork and manufactured caps of any kind were unknown on whisky bottles. The screw-cap met with instant success and sales doubled within the course of a few months.

Expansion continued and ultimately in 1928 warehouses at Provanmill, Glasgow, were purchased, reorganized and re-equipped. It was in this same year that White Horse Distillers Ltd. joined The Distillers Company Limited.

The Mackie Street warehouses were rebuilt in 1937 so that all activities in the blending and bottling of *White Horse* could be undertaken under one roof. At that time the company discontinued the use of Provanmill.

Business continued to expand rapidly, particularly in overseas markets and with expansion came the acquisition of further warehouse accommodation at Tayport Street and Canal Bank Street, Glasgow.

Mackie Street warehouse has since been extended to accommodate, in addition to the bottling and despatch facilities, the warehousing of some 16,000 casks for maturing.

WHITE LADY
Invented in Harry's *New York Bar* (5 Rue Daunou, Paris), founded 1911, in the "roaring 'twenties". Here the International Bar Flies club was established in 1924.

One measure of dry gin, half-measure each of lemon juice and Cointreau. Shake with ice and strain into cocktail glass.

I have held considerable disputation with my many professional bartender friends as to whether this drink should have white of egg added to it. Opinion is much divided; so are recipe books. I plump for egg white.

WHITE PORT See Port.

WHITE SATIN GIN See Burnett's.

WHITE WINE PUNCH
Third of a pint of SUGAR SYRUP, three-quarters of a pint fresh LEMON JUICE, half bottle of brandy, bottle of dry sherry, 3 bottles of dry inexpensive white wine, two large cups of strong tea. Mix in large bowl or jugs and refrigerate. Before serving add siphon soda-water and decorate with rounds of cucumber.

WHYTE & MACKAY LTD.
This firm, established in 1844, put out a brand of Scotch whisky under their own name which, while extensively advertized in England, is much better known in Scotland, where it is among the four largest-selling blends, and overseas. In 1960 the company amalgamated with Mackenzie Brothers of Dalmore, Ross-shire, one of the largest independent distilleries in Scotland.

WIDOW, THE
Affectionate English name sometimes used by devotees of VEUVE CLICQUOT champagne.

WILLIAM LAWSON'S SCOTCH WHISKY
A brand generally better known overseas than in Britain; owned by MARTINI & ROSSI.

WILLIAMS & HUMBERT LTD.
Most stories end with a marriage. The story of Williams & Humbert begins with a marriage, when Alexander Williams, living in Jerez de la Frontera and working there for an English firm of sherry shippers, married Amy Humbert. Two years later in 1877 he started his own sherry business in Spain and London and was joined in partnership by his youngest brother-in-law, Arthur Humbert. With one exception, all the present directors are members of the two families or related to them.

In the intervening years the business has greatly expanded and, in 1959, the company sold the equivalent of over $4\frac{1}{4}$ million bottles of their sherry.

Williams & Humbert have always had establishments in Jerez and London, and, for about 20 years before PROHIBITION, they had an office in New York.

The company's new London office, named Sherry House, in Crutched Friars, has been built on the site of the old offices, which were destroyed during the blitz. In 1958 Williams & Humbert bought a property, which straddles the main Southampton-Salisbury road (A36), about 6 miles north-west of Southampton, comprising an old house, some outbuildings and about 15 acres of parkland. The house, formerly called Little Testwood House, but now rechristened Testwood House, has been carefully restored and is now used as the offices of the Southampton branch. Discreet but efficient new buildings have been erected immediately behind the old house, to hold a large bonded stock of various sherries, the new bottling plant, and other necessary adjuncts. Parts of the house probably date from the Fifteenth Century and others from the Sixteenth, Eighteenth and Nineteenth Centuries, the façade being substantially of the Eighteenth Century.

The company's most notable of many fine products is *Dry Sack* sherry, the biggest-selling medium dry sherry in Britain. DRY is an excellent selling word, and is found in the title of two other important medium dry (or, if you prefer it, medium sweet) sherries, as well as in the names or descriptions of other drinks no connoisseur would rate as dry.

Note People visiting southern Spain are invited by Williams & Humbert to call on the firm in JEREZ, if a few days notice be given, for a visit to the bodegas, which I can heartily recommend. The phone number is Jerez 41910; the postal address: Apartado de Correos No. 23 Jerez de la Frontera. For prior arrangements, write to Sherry House, 39 Crutched Friars, London, E.C.3.

I should in fairness add that other important sherry houses offer similar facilities, but it is Williams & Humbert who provided me with precise information. (The same firm can give you information on visits to Bénédictine; and to major wine companies in Bordeaux, Beaune and Epernay.)

WINE
This article is mainly concerned with the process of making wine (not in too much detail) and drinking, buying, keeping and serving wines. Each particular type of wine that deserves special mention will be found under its own name, not under the country of origin (e.g., champagne will be found under "C"). Wine districts (e.g., Loire) and other topics (e.g., Riesling) are listed separately. Each major wine-producing country is dealt with under the title of the country, the section on wine invariably following the main part of the article on the country and headed *Wine*.

Wine

The following countries are dealt with in this way: Algeria, Australia, Austria, Bulgaria, Canada, Chile, Cyprus, France, Germany, Greece, Italy, New Zealand, Portugal, South Africa, Spain, Switzerland, United States, U.S.S.R. and Yugoslavia. Great Britain also has a special section referring to wine. See also Egypt, Hungary, Israel and Luxembourg.

Basis of wine-making Although wine has been made since the dawn of civilization, it still retains many mysteries. That it exists at all is due to the yeast that appears on grapes as they ripen: none can explain precisely whence or why it comes. It is this natural yeast, attacking the sugar in the juice when the grapes are pressed, that converts the sugar into alcohol. This is FERMENTATION, common to all production of potable alcohol, that turns juice into wine.

Pressing is done in various ways. It may be extremely primitive, a casual bruising of the grapes and leaving nature to take its course. It may be in traditional style with "picturesque peasants" jumping on the grapes, barefoot or in special boots. It can be done with presses ranging from ancient wooden hand-operated ones to mechanical monsters. Some large-scale producers employ rotating drums. In the most modern method the grapes go into a huge container in which there is a giant rubber balloon. When this is inflated it gently pushes the grapes against the porous sides of the tank, forcing out the juice but not breaking the pips: excessive crushing of pips gives the wine an unpleasant tang.

There were wines like the almost legendary *Imperial* TOKAY that were made without pressing at all: only such juice as the weight of grapes in the vat exuded went to make the wine. Sometimes only light pressure is used for the best wines, subsequent pressings being used for lesser grades. I shall go into no technical details as it is not my desire, nor capability, to blind with science.

White wine can be made from white or black grapes or a mixture of them: only the juice is fermented. For red wine black grapes only are used and the skins are left in during fermentation. *Rosé*, which is seldom a serious wine, is either made with a proportion of skins of red grapes left in the juice or by the later addition of some red wine to a white one.

Fermentation produces large quantities of CARBON DIOXIDE (which is sometimes considered worth trapping commercially). For still wines this all escapes from the wine. For sparkling wines the carbon dioxide made during secondary fermentation is retained. For PETILLANT wines some of the gas may be retained.

Wine is ready for drinking the moment fermentation has ceased: anyone who has enjoyed BEAUJOLAIS *de l'année* knows this. But normally some MATURING occurs.

The variations in wine of colour, sweetness, flavour, additives, age, preparation, strength and quality are stupendous. No one has ever listed, nor could, the entire wines of the world. Some 3,500 million gallons of wine are produced globally each year. The great André Simon once opined that only 2 per cent of this could by any definition be called fine wine.

In order that wine shall not dominate this volume which is intended to have broad scope, while by no means ignoring wine's immense importance, I shall be as brief as the subject permits. I have no intention to add to the gigantic bibliography of wine, wherein large volumes have been devoted, not just to a single type but even to a single château. For those embarking on a vinous culture course, I think they could not do better than to start with Hugh Johnson's *Wine*. This combines comprehensiveness with entire readability and is well larded with personal opinion.

Drinking wine Most wine is simply for drinking: only great ones are for sipping and dis-

Wine

cussing. That is a truism, but in an age where wine snobbery is prevalent it needs repeating.

The habit of drinking wine as a beverage, largely unaccompanied by food, has much grown up in Britain and has been fostered by the trade through promotion of "wine & cheese" parties, which I personally find the dullest social events imaginable. Wine and cheese by all means, at the conclusion of a good dinner, but not as an end in themselves.

Sound wine is certainly a healthy drink, but large quantities on an empty stomach induce a certain liverishness, and we may note that the French are perpetually concerned with the condition of their livers.

With food, wine is certainly very pleasant and appreciation of it has grown in such places as Britain and the U.S.A. In the latter, though American wine production is great, use of wine at table has been very regionalized, vast areas remaining vinous "deserts".

A great deal of nonsense has been talked about which wine goes with what. For those neither obsessed with a misplaced sense of "correctness" nor slaves to the whims of would-be social arbiters, there is only one rule: drink what you best like. For instance, against "the rules" I believe a claret to be the perfect accompaniment of grilled sole.

Certainly the temperature of wine is important, but again there is a tendency to arbitrary rules. The British usually believe all red wines should be served at ROOM TEMPERATURE. In fact a true beaujolais is pleasanter on the cool side. While it is true that white wines are customarily chilled, as are sparkling ones, virtually to freeze (as restaurants often do) a fine chablis is to destroy the flavour. If one must have rules, I would say the cheaper the white wine, and the sweeter, the colder it should be. Except, of course, for a rare old sauterne—its exquisite bouquet will not rise at its best if it be more than cellar cool. Once more, drink your wine the way you prefer it, and do not snub the American who prefers his burgundy iced. If he likes it thus it is only his business (see also Glasses).

Buying wine If you are wealthy this provides no problem. If you are poor the question hardly arises. But if you are just comfortably placed you do have a problem, if only whether to splash out on a few bottles of great wine or to spread your means. A modest home cellar should have one or two bottles of really good wine, but I think you will be happier if most of your stock is sound wine that you feel you can drink fairly regularly without feeling guilty about the budget. If you have a few pounds capital, a most pleasant investment, not speculation, is a well-rounded wine stock. Do not be frightened of going into one of the famous remaining independent old wine merchants, for example, Christopher's of Jermyn Street, or Norton & Langridge in the City of London; say what you have to spend and ask their advice.

If you have a little more capital, invest it in wines for "laying down". If you have not room yourself, you will usually have to pay a small rental for space, but it is well worth it. By the time your wine is ready for drinking, it is quite possible you will have to make the choice between imbibing it and selling it at a handsome profit.

As to more casual buying, I see no reason to repeat what I say towards the end of the cautionary entry on Appellation contrôlée.

Keeping wine To keep wine in good condition for any length of time a proper cellar is required, but failing that try to arrange home storage somewhere where the temperature varies as little as possible, certainly not in a centrally-heated room nor one where arctic conditions prevail in winter.

Should you use only half a bottle of wine at one go, do not fall for the snobbery that you cannot keep it till the next meal. If it is a fine wine, you probably will finish it anyway.

Wine Lists

Otherwise, cork it up and it will be perfectly satisfactory for 24 hours, particularly if it is red. You can buy a special device for resealing the bottle, it is vital that you do close it, and it will keep a half-used bottle of champagne in excellent condition for several days (in the least cold part of the 'fridge). For a table wine, if you have difficulty reinserting the cork, cut a "V" out of the base and it will return readily.

Serving wine Inexpensive table wines are now being sold with tear-off foil tops that conveniently require no corkscrew, but you must seal the top if reusing (see above). However, an efficient CORKSCREW is an essential bit of domestic equipment. There is no particular merit in risking a cardiac by gripping the bottle between your feet and tugging on a traditional corkscrew, of which some are abominably designed.

Even if your wine is an old one with some sediment, provided you have handled it with care and let it rest well, decanting is not essential. Careful pouring is all that is needed. And remember Somerset Maugham's dictum that you hold a woman by the waist and a bottle by the neck (though one has an impression the master might have preferred to have reversed the process!).

If you do decant, do it most carefully over a light so that you can stop pouring the moment the sediment approaches the neck. To decant newish, blended wines is an affectation, as is the use of claret cradles except for very old wines. I do not recommend ever having wines decanted in restaurants: one risks the expense of providing the waiter with an extra glass with *his* dinner.

At home, the host should have satisfied himself in advance that his wine is in good condition, not CORKED, and so for him to pour a little into his glass first and sip it before serving his guests can only mean that he is indicating it is not poisoned. This should normally be a superfluous gesture. In restaurants, after the bottle has been opened, the host should taste the wine for flavour and temperature. But carafe wines, being recommended as the "house" wine and presumably tested by the management, should not be so treated. When this pantomime is performed, it is my wont to say, "If you have no confidence in your wine, do not expect me to have any."

Wine-based drinks Under their own entries I give the following drinks with wine bases: Bishop, Champagne (Drinks), Claret Cup, Kir, Mulled wine, Red Wine Punch, White Wine Punch, Sangaree. Principally these are ideas on which to experiment with your own vinous whimsies.

I rather like bad wine, said Lord Mountchesney, One gets so bored with good wine.
Disraeli (*Sybil*)

WINE GALLON
Sometimes "bulk gallon", a technical term occasionally encountered in trade statistical tables, meaning a gallon by volume regardless of strength, as opposed to the PROOF gallon.

WINE LISTS
Whether these be a merchant's retail list or a restaurant list, the first essential is that they should be informative, which restaurant lists very frequently are not, even in places which should know better. A château-bottled wine with a year is information enough, but simply *Beaune 196?* is not. Who has handled it? Often I have found that the wine waiter has no idea and I have had to send for the bottle in order to read the label.

The mark-up on wines in restaurants is excessive enough, a hang-over from the days when (in Britain) the price of meals was strictly controlled and the only real profit was from drinks. Meal prices have rocketed but wine mark-ups have not come down. While he is being stung, the customer is entitled to know what he is ordering, but the Briton, always afraid of "making a fuss", usually humbly selects from a list that gives him

Wolfschmidt

minimal information. Customers should demand their rights.
Note Do not get the notion wine lists are something fairly modern. Thousands of years ago the Assyrian Emperor Assurbanurpal had one in his palace.

WOLFSCHMIDT
A name celebrated for KUMMEL; also a brand of VODKA.

WORT
The liquid drawn from a MASH.

WORTHINGTON
See Bass Charrington.

WYBOROVA
An excellent Polish vodka, available in the U.K.

XYZ

X.O.
Extra Old COGNAC; the term is specially associated with HENNESSY.

YANKEE INVIGORATOR
Beat an egg in a cocktail shaker. Add three-quarters pint of strong cold coffee, measure of brandy, half-measure of port; sugar to taste, plenty of ice. Shake well and strain into large goblet.

YEAST
This is a highly technical matter, there being many types of yeast. In the instance of wine, natural yeast forms on the ripening grapes. For the production of beer and making a wash from which spirits will be distilled, yeast is introduced to produce FERMENTATION.

YOUNG & CO.'S BREWERY LTD.
While this splendid independent, small, respected family-controlled company can trace its origins with some certainty to a brewery in existence in 1675, it was not until the purchase of the business descended from that brewery by Charles Allen Young and a partner in 1831 that the family connection began. It has remained unbroken ever since, making Young's one of the rare remaining concerns of its type in London.

Their Ram Brewery, Wandsworth, London, presents an almost unique combination, in these days, of modern techniques allied to such fascinating relics as a farrier's workshop and a harness room to look after the famous Young's stable of prize-winning shire horses. They have diversified into wine and spirits, and in 1961 started exporting light ale to Belgium. *Young's* beers are highly esteemed by connoisseurs, and have won many awards.

YOUNGER, WILLIAM
Celebrated Scottish brewers, now incorporated in SCOTTISH & NEWCASTLE BREWERIES.

YQUEM
Château d'Yquem is the most renowned of SAUTERNES and there has unfortunately evolved round it an element of patentation and snobbery; it is alarmingly a sign of plutocracy to order it. It is just a superb and expensive dessert wine.

YUGOSLAVIA
I am informed from Belgrade that the basic laws governing the manufacture and marketing of wines, brandies and other alcoholic drinks are the following: "*The Law on Wine/Official Gazettes No. 31/57* and *27/65* regu-

lating the production and marketing of wines. *The Statute/Official Gazettes No. 31/57* and ..." so I am afraid we will have to leave those questions alone.

The country's favourite drinks are brandy, not dissimilar to cognac; slivovitz; a double-distilled plum brandy coming as high as 50 per cent alcohol *bardaklija*; both red and white wines, *pétillant* wines and cherry brandy.

A German cognac-style brandy is produced under licence, and under Scotch and German licences (I have not heard before of the Scots granting a licence) *Racke* whisky is made. It has a "slight taste of smoke" to quote my informants. Scotch whisky is imported, also Italian vermouths, Czech and German beers and Russian sparkling wine.

If you are drinking with a Yugoslav, it would be correct to clink glasses with him and say *Ziveli* (be sure to say it civilly!). This corresponds to "Cheers!", "Skol", "Santé", etc.

Births, marriages and happy events are marked by serving the best slivovitz. "This selected brandy is carried along in a jar by a pretty lad having the duty to invite the inhabitants of the locality to the celebration..." The jar is called *bardak*, a Turkish word, and this form of slivovitz has thus become known as *Bardaklija* and is marketed under that name.

On solemn occasions, while glasses are still clinked, one does not say "Ziveli"; instead ritual kisses on the cheeks are exchanged. On deaths and at burials "commemorative wines and brandies are served in abundant quantities to the memory of the defunct". "Navip", the state monopoly, is the only major producer, and is a substantial exporter.

Wine Before World War II, Yugoslavian wines were hardly known outside Central Europe. Today, Yugoslav *Lutomer Riesling* (imported by Teltscher Brothers) is claimed to be the largest selling single brand of dry white wine in the U.K., running at around 3 million bottles a year. ("Dry" is used here comparatively as against definitely sweet: I think medium dry would be a better description). This wine appeals to British tastes for a "hock" at an extremely interesting price. Many other wines are produced for internal consumption or export, but it is the Riesling types that predominate.

ZOMBIE

The "Z" section of an alphabetical book is always a bit short of material. This drink is rather a joke. I take this recipe from *Shaking in the Sixties* (and 'seventies?) by Eddie Clarke, one-time famous bartender and now proprietor of the splendid Albemarle Club in London's West End. Three-quarters measure each of unsweetened pineapple juice, canned papaya juice; apricot brandy and powdered sugar; juice of a large lime; measure of heavy dark rum (90° proof); 2 measures of dark rum. Shake well with cracked ice and pour entire contents into tall frosted "Zombie" glass (you will have one, of course). Fill with ice. Decorate with mint, cube of pineapple and cherry on a stick. Float on top dash of 150° proof tropical rum (I do not know where you find that); sprinkle powdered sugar on top and serve with straws.

ZUBROWKA See Vodka.

And when Thyself with shining Foot shall pass
  Among the Guests Star-scatter'd on the Grass,
And in thy joyous Errand reach the Spot
  Where I made one—turn down an empty Glass!

Fitzgerald, *The Rubaiyat of Omar Khayyam*

ACKNOWLEDGEMENTS

Apart from recourse to established authorities, in reinforcement of my own knowledge, it is obvious that I have had call on the valued services of many firms and specialist consultants in compiling this book. In most instances due acknowledgement is inherent in the relevant entry or is separately emphasized. However, some sources have, perhaps inadvertently, supplied me with more general information than that exclusively pertinent to their brand or product, and as such merit due credit.

In the instance of newspapers and journals, acknowledgement may cover a specific item discovered in one of their pages or may relate to a more complete indebtedness for keeping me up to date (so far as such a volume can be) with vital information. In the instance of individuals and organizations (often one and the same) I name those not manifestly covered in the text in one way or another, and I hope that the following lists contain not too many glaring omissions; for an author can be no better than his references, and should not pretend otherwise, or may be subject to criticism as an ingrate.

BIBLIOGRAPHY
(books, annuals and directories)

The Bartender's Golden Book, O. Blunier (Mortgarten-Verlag Ag., Zurich, 1935).
The Book of Unusual Quotations, (Cassell & Co., London).
The Complete Imbiber, 1969; ed. Cyril Ray (published for F.S. Matta, by Hutchinson of London).
The Dictionary of Drinks & Drinking, Oscar A. Mendelsohn, (Macmillan, London, 1965).
Dictionary of Wines, Spirits & Liqueurs, André Simon, (Herbert Jenkins, London, 1961).
Directory, Wine & Spirit Trade Review, 1970, William Reed Ltd., London.
Drinks of the World, James New and John Ashton, (Leadenhall Press, London, 1892).
Encyclopaedia of Wines & Spirits, Alexis Lichine (Cassell, London).
English Social History, George Macaulay Trevelyan, O.M. (Longmans, Green & Co., London).
The Fine Art of Mixing Drinks, David A. Embury (Faber & Faber, London).
The Grapes are Growing, Kenneth Slessor (Oswald Zeigler Publications, Sydney, N.S.W.).
Grossman's Guide to Wines, Spirits & Beers, Harold J. Grossman (Scribner's, New York City; Frederick Muller, London).

A History of the English Public House, H.M. Monckton (Bodley Head, London).
Innkeeping, J. G. Miles (Barrie & Rockliff, London, for National Trade Development Council).
International Guide to Drinks, United Kingdom Bartenders Guild.
The Kindred Spirit, Lord Kinross, with H.K. Humphreys, (Newman Neame, London, 1959).
Liquor Handbook, 1969, Gavin-Jobson Associates Inc., New York City.
Liquor, The Servant of Man, Maurice E. Chafetz (Phoenix, London).
The London Distiller, London, printed for Tho. Huntington and Wil. Nealand, and to be sold at their shop in Duck Lane; 1652.
Off the Shelf, Brown & Pank Ltd., London.
The Penguin Book of Wines, Allan Sichel.
Prohibition, Andrew Sinclair (Four Square Books, London).
Raise Your Glasses, Douglas Sutherland (MacDonald, London).
Ridley's Wine & Spirit Handbook (Ridley's, London).
Scotch Whisky—its Past and Present, David Daiches (Andre Deutsch, London).
Scotch Whisky, Questions and Answers, Scotch Whisky Association.
Society, Culture & Drinking Patterns, ed. David J. Pittman and Charles R. Snyder (John Wiley & Sons Inc., New York City).
The Whiskies of Scotland, R.J.S. McDowall (John Murray, London).
Wine, Hugh Johnson (Sphere Books, London).
Wine & Spirits, L.W. Marrison (Pengin Books, 1965).
Wines & Spirits, Alec Waugh, & others (Time-Life Books).
Wines and Spirits of the World, ed. Alec Gold (Virtue, London, 1968).

NEWSPAPERS and JOURNALS

Bar, Toronto; *Bartender*, London; *Daily Mail*, London; *Daily Express*, London; *Daily Telegraph Magazine*, London; *Chief Steward*, London (now *Marine & Air Catering*); *Envoy*, Magazine, London (defunct); *Financial Times*, London; *Harper's*, Wine & Spirit Trade Gazette, London; *International Beverage News*, London; *Irish Medical Association, Journal of the*, Dublin; *Journée Vinicole*, Montpellier, France; *Maclean's Magazine*, Toronto; *Morning Advertiser*, London; *National Guardian*, Glasgow; *Newsweek Magazine*; *Off-Licence Journal*, London; *Off-Licence News*, London; *Paris Match*; *Ridley's Wine & Spirit Trade Circular*, London; *Server*, New York City; *Sunday Telegraph*, London; *Sunday Times*, London; *Sunday Times Magazine*, London; *Time Magazine*; *Wine & Food*, London (now with *House & Garden*); *Wine Magazine*, London; *Winemine*, Peter Dominic Ltd.

COMPANIES, ORGANIZATIONS and INDIVIDUALS

Monty ACKROYD, Esq., England; ALLEN & ELLIOTT Ltd., Lagos, Nigeria; Gunnar AMUNDSEN A/S, Oslo; ASSOCIATED ENTERPRISES Ltd., Jamaica; H.P. BAGAT, Esq., Phipson & Co., Calcutta; BAHAMAS BLENDERS Ltd., Nassau; Etablissements R.B-BEAUMAINE, Brussels; Geo. W. BENNETT, BRYSON & Co. Ltd., St. John's, Antigua; Roy BLUNT, Esq., Booth's Distilleries Ltd., London; H.L. BOULTON & CO. S.A., Caracas; The BOURBON Institute, New York City; BRITISH AMERICAN ASSOCIATES S.A., Lima, Peru; BROWN, GORE & WELCH Ltd., London; H.P. BULMER Ltd., Hereford; Carl BYOIR Associates, New York City; CALDBECK MAC-GREGOR & Co., Thailand, Hong Kong, Malaysia; CHATILLON S.A., Montevideo; COMPAGNIA D'IMPORTAZIONE di Prodotti Alimentari Dolciari Vini Liquori, Bologna; The CROWN CORK CO. Ltd., Middlesex, England; John G. CUTSURIDIS Ltd., Khartoum; The DISTILLERS Company Ltd., Edinburgh and London; Daniel J. EDELMAN Inc., San Francisco and London; John EWINGS, Esq., N. Ireland; S.I. FAWEHINMI Esq., Yaba, Nigeria; The FRIENDS OF WINE, London; G.A. GABRUELIDES, Nicosia; Edouard GALULA, Tunis; Dennis GRAHAME Esq., Martini & Rossi, London; GREEK DISTILLERS, Athens; C.R. HAMMERSLEY, Esq., Tortola, British Virgin Islands; C.F. HARRISON & Co., Barbados, W.I.; DEPARTMENT OF HEALTH, Dublin; Maurice HEWETT, Esq., England; J.H. JAFFE & Co., Jersey; The K.M.V., South Africa; Lesley LAKE (Public Relations) Ltd., London; John LEWIS, Esq., Wales; LI WAN PO & Co., Mauritius; LICOR, C por A, Dominica; LONSDALE Information, London; EL LOUVRE S.A., Curacao, N.A.; Hugh MACKAY, Esq., London; George MARSHALL, Esq., London; MARTINI & ROSSI, Netherlands, Spain, Morocco, W. Germany, Argentina, Portugal, Chile, Switzerland; MILLER y Cia, Las Palmas de Gran Canaria; Alec NICHOLAS, Teheran; Gerry PALMER Ltd., St. Vincent, W.I.; James PORTER, Esq., London; M. & E. RUEFF, Vienna; RUSSELL-COBB Ltd., London; The SCOTCH WHISKY Association, Edinburgh; B. SEPPELT & Sons (Pty.) Ltd., Australia; Dr. J.G.B. SIEGART & SONS, Port of Spain, Trinidad; SILVESTRE & BROSTELLA S.A., Panama; SIMONDS-FARSONS-CISK Ltd., Malta, G.C.; SORIAMOUNT TRADING, Manila; SOUTHERN COMFORT Corporation, St. Louis, Mo.; John STARR, Esq., Paris; The STELLENBOSCH Farmers' Winery Ltd., South Africa; George SANDEMAN & Sons, Lisbon and Oporto; C. SFANKIANOS, Addis Ababa; TOYO JOZO Co., Tokyo; Mrs. Pamela VANDYKE PRICE, London; VESTAPANE-CONGO, Kinhasa; Mr. John WATLEY, Centennial Wine Society, Toronto; Louis WOLF, Copenhagen; Ted WORNER Associates, New York City.

If you copy from a single source it's plagiarism, but if you copy from multiple sources it's research. Words In Sheep's Clothing, Prof. Mario Pei, (Allen & Unwin, London).

THE WORLD OF DRINKS AND DRINKING

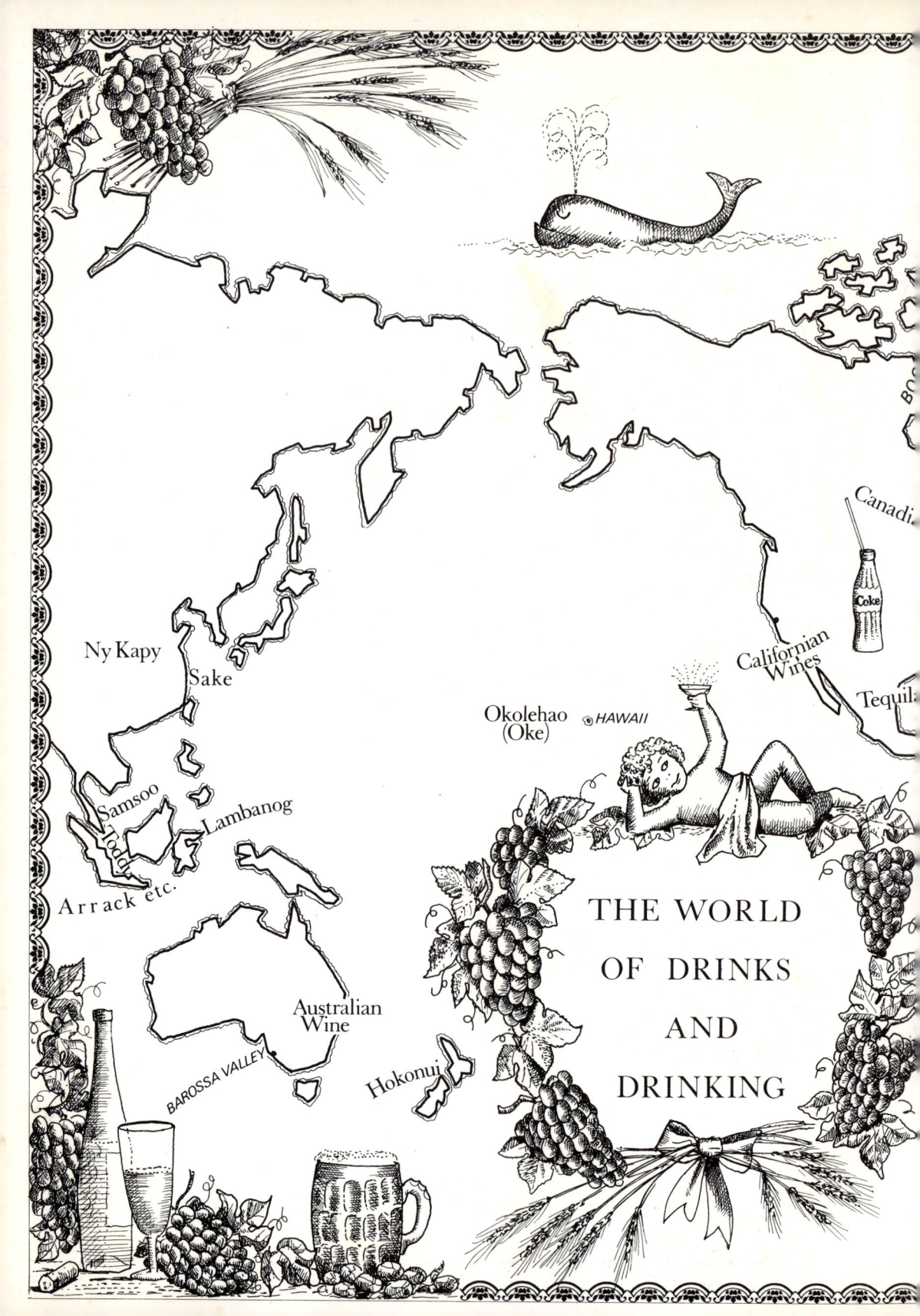